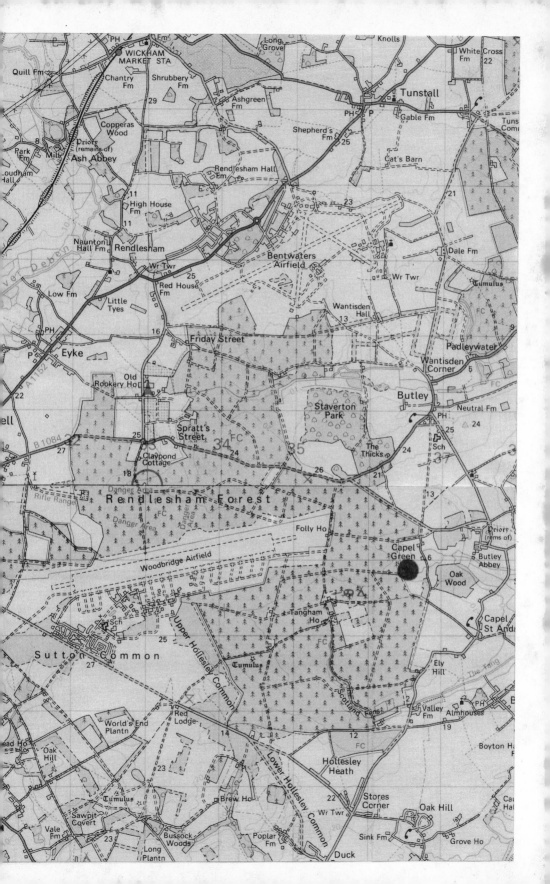

LEFT AT EAST GATE

A First-hand Account of

the Bentwaters-

Woodbridge UFO

Incident, Its Cover-up,

and Investigation

By Larry Warren and Peter Robbins

Michael O'Mara Books Limited

First published in Great Britain in 1997 by
Michael O'Mara Books Limited
9 Lion Yard
Tremadoc Road
London SW4 7NQ

A CIP catalogue record for this book is available from the British Library

ISBN 1-85479-231-8

1 3 5 7 9 10 8 6 4 2

Designed by Pauline Neuwirth, Neuwirth & Associates, Inc.

Manufactured in the United States of America

This book is dedicated to Joann Warren, the first American civilian to learn about the Bentwaters incident. It is also dedicated to the memory of Detective Sergeant Pete Mazzola, New York Police Department.

CONTENTS

FOREWORD
by Anthony Grey

Something very extraordinary indeed happened at Rendlesham Forest in Suffolk, eastern England in late December 1980. Whatever the explanation turns out to be, when we understand fully, our perceptions of science, technology, and much more besides are bound to undergo a historic sea-change. It seems almost certain, too, that we will by then have a new and clearer comprehension of our place in the universe. At that time the authors of this book will, I feel sure, have the satisfaction of knowing they played a significant role in helping bring this about.

For sadly, the military and civilian authorities in Britain and the United States have so far resisted revealing what they know about those extraordinary happenings at two neighboring air bases, RAF Bentwaters and RAF Woodbridge, situated on the edge of Rendlesham Forest. At the time the bases were manned largely by American forces, and an important arsenal of nuclear weapons for use by NATO was stored there. This I believe gives the UFO sightings reported in the region of the bases greater significance than other such sightings in modern times.

Roswell, New Mexico, has become a famous location in UFO history because of the alleged crash of an extra-terrestrial "flying saucer" space-craft there in the late 1940's. In my view, Rendlesham Forest will eventually be seen to eclipse Roswell in importance, not least because a considerable number of highly-trained military ground troops and their officers were mobilised in an effort to observe and confront the moving UFOs when they descended to ground level in the forest. Among the personnel was one of this book's authors, then Airman First Class Larry Warren, aged 19, who had recently joined the units assigned to guard the nuclear weapons, particularly against terrorist ground attack.

The UFOs appeared on three successive nights immediately following Christmas 1980. Nothing substantial about the sightings appeared in news media for nearly three years. In those days Cold War tension was high and the base was on alert because the Soviet Union had massed troops on Poland's borders. Moscow was threatening to invade Poland because of the activities of the dissident trade union Solidarity, and President Reagan and NATO had warned the Warsaw pact that any Soviet incursion could trigger East-West hostilities. But now this book reveals that witnesses, who included at least one high-ranking American officer, saw the UFOs fly low over the bases, directing laser-like beams of light down into the bunkers where the nuclear weapons were stored.

Nor are such incidents unique, since one of the most respected international writers on the subject, Timothy Good, assures me that similar UFO overflights of nuclear weapons bases have occured in other countries including Russia and Canada. Afterwards, he claims, some nuclear warheads were found disabled. Yet the British Ministry of Defence maintains stolidly to this day that "nothing of defence interest" occurred at the twin Suffolk air bases in late December 1980, which is patently untrue.

All these factors place the Rendlesham Forest UFO incidents in a class of their own and give this first comprehensive account by a military participant its true significance. This became clear to me when I first met Larry Warren and Peter Robbins during a UFO conference at Sheffield University in the summer of 1995. With my producer, Angela Hind, I was researching an investigatory radio documentary series entitled "UFOs—Fact, Fiction or Fantasy?" which was broadcast internationally on the BBC World Service in the spring of 1996. Some weeks after the Sheffield conference, Larry Warren and his co-author took us over the route from the East Gate of RAF Woodbridge to the very spot where Larry said he had advanced under orders to within a few feet of a landed UFO. We recorded an interview as we went. The UFO shimmered strangely, beings of some kind made an appearance, and a senior American officer approached them, he said. Even fifteen years after the original experience, re-visiting the scene, not for the first time, produced an unmistakable tension in the former security guard.

During this meeting and others that followed, the earnest intent of both authors became very evident. Preparing this book had already occupied nine difficult years of their lives but their determination to see it through and make known the truth of their different experiences and investigations was paramount. They have overcome many alarming instances of official obstruction and their investigations appear to have been scrupulously thorough. They have often needed to call on considerable reserves of courage and nerve to persist in their enquiries, and they have more than once felt endangered. For this reason alone they are to be congratulated on their dogged persistence.

The most disturbing aspects of the story by far are the apparent attempts by the US military authorities and others to confuse and undermine Larry Warren's perceptions of what he is sure he experienced and felt on that night of 28 December 1980. On both sides of the Atlantic a miasma of official deceit and misinformation unfortunately surrounds the whole topic of UFOs and the question of extra-terrestrial intrusion on our planet. Larry Warren says he was told in a matter of fact tone by a an officer at a debriefing soon after his experience that numerous civilizations visit this planet from time to time and some are a permanent presence here. If that statement was made in good faith, it is surely high time somebody more authoritative announced it openly to the world.

· Clearly all reports of UFO sightings and the now worldwide rash of claimed alien abduction experiences must be investigated with a rigoruous degree of scepticism. It is a commonplace truth that 90 per cent of all UFO reports can usually be attributed in the end to some conventional explanation. It would also be rash for us to dismiss completely those scientific theories which suggest that some UFO experiences might somehow be self-generated by the human mind—or even more ominously that some secret terrestrial techniques may have been developed that would make it possible to induce realistic hallucinatory or holographic experiences into the minds of individuals or groups of individuals against their will. Whether anything of this kind was even partially connected with the events in Rendlesham Forest or its aftermath, it is impossible to say for sure—but hints of at least the existence

of experiments in this field surface frequently enough here and else-
where to cloud the picture further. At the forest site, significant radiation readings were taken, strange physical injuries were sustained by
some of the troops involved, and psychological turmoil and worse followed for others. One man is believed to have gone missing, at least
temporarily. These simple facts alone urgently require official explanation.

A momentum to force discussion of such things into the open, whatever their nature, is now growing worldwide. But the final truth about
such questions which are so vital to our future will only become known
if we keep pressing questions to governments through our elected representatives and the media. We need encouragement to sustain these
efforts and *LEFT AT EAST GATE* is a splendid new inspiration in this
direction. Larry Warren and Peter Robbins in their different comple-
mentary roles are both to be greatly commended for their courage and
tenacity in producing this extraordinarily revealing account.

Anthony Grey
2 September 1996

(Anthony Grey, a former foreign correspondent with Reuters in Eastern Europe and China, is the author of the international best-selling
historical novels, *Saigon, Peking* and *Tokyo Bay*.)

INTRODUCTION

Concerning government, it is . . . in both these respects in which things are deemed secret; for some things are secret because they are hard to know, and some because they are not fit to utter.

Francis Bacon

*S*uffolk, East Anglia, southeast England. One night late in December, 1980, a nineteen-year-old air-force security policeman, armed with an M16 rifle, stood guard at a remote point on the perimeter of a large American air base. There, he monitored an unusual sequence of radio transmissions describing unidentified lights above the forest several miles to the southeast. Soon, Airman First Class Lawrence Warren and other air-force personnel brought to that area witnessed a series of events that no one had prepared them for. Had either British or American officials disclosed the true nature of what occurred there that night, the special relationship then existing between the two governments might have been so compromised as to be unsalvagable. Some of humanity's most profound beliefs would have been swept away as well.

No information was ever released. Instead, the nature and reality of the occurrences were suppressed and confounded under the American National Security Act of 1947 and Her Majesty's Official Secrets Act. The matter was soon relegated to the colorful realm of East Anglian folklore; to all appearances, things returned to normal. They remained so until 2 October 1983 when the story literally exploded in the English press with Larry Warren's firsthand account, under a pseudonym. By month's end, both houses of Parliament had held highly vocal debates on the subject; behind closed doors, a potential diplomatic crisis had been set in motion.

Officially, the cause of this air-force close encounter has never been deemed worthy of investigation by any branch or office of the British Ministry of Defence or the U.S. Department of Defense. Both acknowledge that it happened, but maintain that, whatever it was, it was not a threat to the security of Great Britain or the military bases dotting that nation.

The heart of this book is Larry Warren's story: the first and loudest of the Bentwaters whistle-blowers, in his own words. It marks the first time a bona fide military witness has come forward to give such a fully detailed account of a service-related UFO incident, as well as its devastating personal aftermath. His account makes clear why he has continued to pursue the matter so doggedly, and what that effort has cost him.

I first met Larry in 1984, but it was not until after I'd interviewed him in 1987 that he asked me to consider writing a book with him. The proposal was straightforward enough: as long as he got to tell his side of the story, I would be free to pursue and publish any findings I could substantiate—no matter how they might reflect on him. Not the kind of offer you would expect from someone with something to hide. As it turned out, there were things he was keeping from me, and with good reason. They all came out in due time. Our initial interview progressed into an intensive, nine-year investigation of the events in question and Larry's place in them as witness. With the publication of Left at East Gate, *Larry Warren has quite literally chosen to put himself, as well as the reality of those incidents, on trial. So be it. He has a case. But don't take my word alone. Witnesses have been questioned, depositions taken, sites revisited, and exhibits placed into evidence for you to consider. The chain of evidence led us from America, to England, to a non-human intelligence, and to America's super-seret National Security Agency.*

It is the nature of governments to keep certain things from their people, either for the "public good" or to maintain official control. But the process of enforcing secrecy results in the gradual erosion of democratic institutions in the name of national security. In the Bentwaters case, truth and reason have been the casualties for the citizens of the United States and Great Britain.

How much longer will habitual government secrecy continue to confound the UFO issue? Our hope is that readers will give us a fair hearing, then begin to pursue answers to that question for themselves.

Peter Robbins
New York City, 1996

LEFT AT EAST GATE

PART 1

LARRY WARREN

*Fate does not practice the art of gradations.
Her wheel turns sometimes so fast that we can
scarcely distinguish between one revolution and
another, or the link between yesterday and today.*

Victor Hugo[1]

1. EARLY YEARS

My name is Larry Warren. I was born in August 1961 in New York City. I never knew my natural mother. Only seventeen and unwed at the time of my birth, she had little choice but to surrender me to the Catholic Charities for adoption. She had named me William Patrick Kane, but at four months old, I got a new name and a chance at a better life.

My new mother and father, Joann and Larry, brought me home to Cornwall on Hudson, New York. They had met in 1953 at an insurance-industry Christmas party in Boston. Married in 1954, they settled in the lower Hudson River valley after my father's assignment at West Point ended. My father had completed his degree at Boston College before entering the army and was an accomplished golfer, ranking with Arnold Palmer in national collegiate statistics. He volunteered for the army, as he says, "to get it out of the way." Otherwise the draft would have gotten him.

My mother was an artist and a bit of a rebel. I would assume many of her traits over the years, especially her outspoken way of letting people know when something wasn't right. I can remember a lot of laughter in our house.

During that time, the cold war was in full swing. JFK was president, and Neil Sedaka was at the top of the pop charts. The Cuban missile crisis in 1962 was nearly the end of all of us, my parents later told me. I remember JFK's face on our black-and-white RCA TV; even at my early age, it conveyed a friendly image to me. Now that was charisma!

In the South, blacks still rode in the back of the bus; segregation in all areas of everyday life was reality. Our family drove down to Georgia in 1963. During a stop at a segregated diner, I saw a boy about my age at the other end of the counter. I had a toy race car, and he pointed to it with excitement. We jumped off our stools and ran toward each other. I was proud of the car and wanted to show it off, and he wanted to see it. We were both too young to notice the difference in our skin color and too young to read the White Only sign that divided our dining areas.

We met halfway. A white waitress yelled at the boy for approaching us. My mother was off her stool in an instant, telling the woman to back off. My mother recalls the waitress mumbling something about goddamned Yankees under her breath as she retreated. I was lucky to witness ignorance firsthand and to grow up in a nonracist home.

We were then living in a large white house in Vailsgate, New York. Just before Thanksgiving, my mother was wrapping Christmas presents and I was eating my lunch, when the bulletin came blasting through our kitchen radio: "The president of the United States is dead. President Kennedy had just been assassinated in Dallas, Texas." My mother was shocked and accidentally stepped on some already wrapped presents on the floor. My dad came home early from work that day; I guess most dads in America did.

Early in 1964, the Beatles arrived in New York. My parents' friends had older children, and I became a first-wave fan through them. They gave me some photographs of the group, and we plastered the walls of my bedroom with them. The Beatles' music had me hooked at two and a half years old. And I remain so.

Later that year, we adopted my sister, Nancy, or Sam, as she is still known to us because of her childhood fascination with Toucan Sam, the colorful bird on the Fruit Loops cereal box. We picked her up at Catholic Charities in New York City, though I thought we had bought her at Macy's department store. Different as night and day, we celebrated our birthdays every year and our special days, the days on which we were adopted. As soon as my sister and I could comprehend the spoken word, our parents sensitively explained adoption to us, and it's a fact of which we are both proud.

Around 1965, I encountered what most adults would call imaginary friends. To me they looked a lot like Casper the ghost, except they had arms, legs, and big black eyes. They would come out of my closet at night and talk to me. I wasn't frightened, and soon they would go away.

Still living in Vailsgate, I spent much of my time playing on a nearby railroad track. Strange kids approached me one hot summer day and told me I'd get hurt if I didn't get off the tracks. I say "strange," because they didn't seem to be standing on the ground. They showed me some dolls representing a traditional nuclear family; suddenly the dolls disappeared. When I asked them where they lived, one pointed to a silver house trailer all by itself in a marshy area near the tracks. We'd play again, one told me. I walked home, avoiding the old lady who yelled at me when I cut through her yard to get to the tracks. My dad would walk with me at night when he got home from work. We went to the tracks that evening, and I remember feeling strange because the silver trailer was gone from the swampland.

I told my mother often about the magic dolls that could disappear. I was shown them one more time, while sitting on the curb in front of our house, by a person who seemed to appear out of thin air. This was again in broad daylight; I ran to tell my mother, but when she got to the door the person and the dolls were gone.

Casper and friends continued to visit me at night. But I told no one because they warned me they would go down a giant drain if I did. I remember Casper and his friends took me outside and pointed out the drain they would go down if I told anyone about them—it was in the middle of our sidewalk. In reality, we had no drain in our yard.

As the sixties progressed, we moved back to Cornwall on Hudson. I played ice hockey at West Point and wanted to grow up to be just like my heroes, Phil Esposito and Bobby Orr of the Boston Bruins. In my house, you had to like the Boston teams. Ice hockey was also a great way for a kid to expend energy; for me, it kept a growing aggression in check.

I spent my days in Catholic school and got into mischief every now and then. At the same time, I was fascinated with religion and the mysticism that surrounded it. We had been told that Jesus lived in the holy tabernacle by one of the sisters at the school, so I sneaked into Saint Thomas Church with a friend to find out the truth. Believing we would see a three-inch-tall Jesus inside, we opened it cautiously. I can remember feeling crushed to find the container empty, but a little relieved as well.

The body count from Vietnam was announced nightly by Walter Cronkite. Our neighbor's son, Art, had been home from Vietnam just a few days when he accidentally rolled his parents' car through the side of our garage. I remember Art from before he went into the army, when he gave me a wooden tower he had built and used as a kid.

We watched the race riots in the late sixties—I should say, the glowing red horizon to the north over strife-ridden Newburgh, New York—from a hill on our property. During a dinner party for business associates of my dad's, I heard a lady express concern that the riots would spill over into our peaceful community. How protected we seemed as the distant sky grew brighter and the Chinese lanterns suspended in the yard maintained a constant soft glow.

Soon Dr. King and Bobby Kennedy were assassinated. The conflict in Vietnam intensified. And in my world, my parents' marriage disintegrated. This is a tough time for any kid, and my sister and I moved through the process the best we could, still in Catholic school. The same nun who had told me Jesus lived in the tabernacle, now informed me and everyone in my third-grade class that, not only would my parents go to hell because they were getting divorced, but my sister and I would join them there too. In those days, children my age did not challenge authority in school. Had my parents known, I'm sure they would have removed us from that paranoiac and damaging educational system. But they were wrapped in their own pain, and I don't know that I could have conveyed my own.

My friends would still visit me on occasion. In 1971, I went to live with my dad in Pittsfield, Massachusetts, with his new wife, Sandy, and her son, Scott. I now had to get used to the public school system, where even the surface differences seemed radical. I could wear sneakers to school instead of shoes—liberation indeed. In 1972, I joined the school book club. I wrote my first book report about a UFO sighting over Brooklyn, New York. The story was one of many in a book of strange events by Frank Edwards—my first exposure in print to the subject of UFOs. My father even drew a flying saucer on the book report's cover for me. By then, I had no memory of the small people who had entered my room, or if I did, their impact was buried; I certainly made no connection between them and UFOs.

During the summer of 1972, Scott and I would sit on top of a storage shed in our backyard looking for anything strange in the skies, often mistaking aircraft for the beginning of an invasion and driving my father and Sandy crazy.

That summer, we staged our own backyard Olympics, complete with tinfoil medals and some bizarre events for the neighborhood kids to participate in. I got into a fight with Michael Martin, who lived across the street, so he boycotted our Olympics and put on his own games, complete with gold-colored foil awards. It was during these '72 games that the Israeli team fell victim to Arab terrorists. At eleven years old, it was impossible not to feel shocked. That tragic event ended our games, but somehow the Olympics in Munich continued.

My father was transferred to Hartford, Connecticut, in mid-1973. There I continued to play hockey, but school was a struggle. In the fall, TV news reported on a large-scale UFO wave and the story of two men, Charles Hickson and Calvin Parker, who were abducted by aliens in Pascagoula, Mississippi. My interest in UFOs reemerged. I watched the news often to hear anything about the subject, but most of the broadcasts focused on the latest Watergate news.

I discovered the roots of rock and roll that year with the help of *Dick Clark's Twenty Years of Rock and Roll* album. After listening to the classics, I wanted to get a guitar and create some of my own.

My mother and sister now lived in Glens Falls, a small city forty minutes north of Albany, New York. After visiting them, returning to Connecticut grew more difficult. I felt my father demanded too much. I know he only wanted me to be the best at whatever I did, but my mother encouraged my artistic side.

On the humid and overcast night of 19 August 1974, during a month-long visit to Glens Falls, a strange thing happened. I had gone to bed in my sister's room; she was sharing my mother's bed in the rear of the apartment. I was not given to nightmares, but at some point I bolted upright from a sound sleep with a fear of something in the room, something I could not see. I grabbed a blanket and went into my mother's room. She and my sister were sleeping soundly. I lay down on the floor and fell back asleep. Sometime later I woke again, to the sound of my name being called twice. As I struggled to stand, a giant weight seemed to push me back to the floor.

I could see my mother looking at something outside the window. We spoke, but I can't recall what we said. I tried to see what was at the window but couldn't. Everything occurred in slow motion, and when I finally succeeded in focusing on the window, my vision went black. My last recollection was of moving slowly back to the floor. My sister never woke up.

The next day, my mother and I were pretty quiet. That afternoon, she drew a picture of what she had seen and told me what she remembered. It was a very strange object, like two diamonds connected by a bar. I felt confused by what she said. Writing book reports about UFOs was one thing, but this? Why didn't I get to see the craft? The event really shook us up. My sister didn't remember a thing about it.

That evening, Sam walked in from a trip to Lake George and told us to turn on the radio. UFOs were flying over the Glens Falls region. Local radio station WWSC turned its full attention to the objects in the sky, and hundreds of cars blocked Dix Avenue to get a look at them. State police from Saratoga watched a giant blimplike object actually draw water from Saratoga Lake and then move off to the south at tremendous speed. The Albany County Airport and Federal Aviation Authority (FAA) tracked its speed at three thousand miles per hour.[2] I was listening with half interest to the reports, when a kid called in to say he had given milk and cookies to the Martians in his backyard. I turned off the radio in disgust.

During this period, I had decided I could no longer live with my father and returned to Connecticut to tell him so. Two days later, I returned to my mother's to stay. It was a stress-filled time for all involved, but particularly rough on me. In Glens Falls, I began seventh grade and gave up hockey; few people in the area had an interest in it, and there were no leagues at the time, so I learned to play guitar and formed my first band.

I visited my father during school holidays. On my return from a 1975 New Year's visit, my mother met me at the bus terminal in Albany. It is a forty-minute drive to Glens Falls on the Adirondack Northway. As we approached an overpass in the vicinity of Saratoga Springs, something flew south at eye level on my side of our '73 Plymouth Duster. We both saw it. A ball of dull colors, it made a whooshing sound and rocked the car as it passed. My mother pulled over to the side of I-87's northbound lane and stopped the car. In front of us was the overpass; above it, a brilliantly lit and well-defined object. We could see windows and what appeared to be silhouettes behind them. The object moved slowly to the right, and I felt a buzzing sensation in my head and an electrical charge in the air. Everything was in slow motion, very dreamlike, as though we were in a vacuum.

The whole event seemed to last five minutes at most, but arriving home, we found my sister very concerned. It had taken us three hours to make a forty-minute trip. We also realized that we had seen no traffic on the highway during our UFO sighting. So disturbing was the experience that we rarely spoke of it for years.

I moved on to high school with great expectations for my future, though I had no idea what direction my life would take. New York State's educational system labeled high school kids early on, then placed them academically. I was one of the kids disadvantaged by that system. Without decent salaries, many of my teachers seemed unhappy and frustrated. Unfortunately, many had a limited worldview as well, so we were often at odds.

I found sanctuary from scholastic boredom in the high school library, looking through old copies of *Time* or *Life*. Music was also a lifesaver. My friend Pat Cifone and I watched the Beatles play themselves in *A Hard Day's Night* and decided: "That's a good job!" The screaming girls probably had a lot to do with our decision.

My lack of interest in school caught up with me in tenth grade, when all of my teachers were called into a roundtable "confrontation" with my mother and me. After twenty minutes, I spoke my mind and announced that I wanted to quit school and join the army. My social studies teacher, John Strough, spoke next, saying that I was the best student in his class. It was true, because he made learning interesting and I respected him. He even seemed to like his job.

John had turned the attack around on the other teachers; now they wondered what they were doing wrong regarding my education. His support kept me in high school, and his friendship made a difference at a critical point in my life. Soon my grades improved, and classes became a bit more interesting.

My interest in UFOs had all but vanished by 1978. Not many articles were being published on the topic, and every book seemed just like the one before. As far as I was concerned, I'd outgrown UFOs. The events I'd experienced with my mother were distant memories.

No matter what was going on, no matter how good the party was, at 11:30 every Saturday night, my friends and I tuned in to *Saturday Night Live*. It was our mission from God to keep up with the latest antics of John Belushi and Dan Ackroyd. Walking home from a friend's house after watching *SNL* in the dead of winter 1978, I saw a gigantic UFO in the distance, or at least it seemed distant, but the details of the thing were so well defined that the sighting scared the hell out of me. I ran home and told my mother and our neighbor Sue Hickerson. The UFO had been too close for comfort.

During my junior year of high school, I was an exchange student in Great Britain. Our high school had an ongoing relationship with the Mayflower School in Billericay, Essex, and twenty of us were lucky enough to go. I'd be attending classes there and living with a host family. My mother worked hard to raise the money.

Once in England, my life changed considerably. The English girls chased me around the school yard, and I loved every minute of it. I lived with a family named Harrison in a cottage set far away from the clonelike council houses, and traveled to Stratford-upon-Avon, Brighton, and London. In England, I met my first serious girlfriend; her name was Joann, and I was crazy about her. I loved England. Finally, a place where I seemed to fit in.

When it was time to return to the States, I didn't want to go. As the bus pulled up to our high school, my mother knew that I was the one holding up the oversized Union Jack to the window.

My time in England had given me newfound confidence and the overwhelming desire to go back to England as soon as I could. In the meantime, I would make 1979 my best year in high school for sure.

In my senior year, my mother and father began to ask that unavoidable question: "Larry, what are you going to do with yourself after you graduate?" I still hadn't given it much thought. Most of my friends were set on becoming rock stars, but I knew it was an unlikely goal for any of us.

In November 1979, a mob of Iranian students stormed the American embassy in Teheran and took fifty-two Americans hostage. That night we saw them on *Nightline*. Those blindfolded and humiliated Americans were an awful sight, and most Americans wanted blood as a result. After tossing the idea around over the summer, I decided to enlist in the service—but which branch? When I found out the army couldn't send me to England and the air force could, my choice was made. The post-Vietnam distrust of the military had begun to fade as the nation's feelings toward Iran brought out a nationalism Americans hadn't seen in years.

I enlisted in the U.S. Air Force at the end of November. I had the distinction of being the last person to get a guaranteed country of choice: England, of course. I chose AFSC 81130, the security-specialist field. Having always been a slave to fashion, I was attracted to the blue berets worn by security police, but didn't give much thought to the details of the job itself. My family was happy with my decision, and I was glad that I wouldn't end up bagging groceries in some supermarket after graduation.

By 1 January 1980, I had managed to convince my friends Jeff Lindsey and Steve Maden to sign up, too; we'd go through basic training together! My friend Pete Jones was going into the navy, and we'd insult each other's respective service branch during band rehearsals, but it was all in fun. I graduated from high school that June, skipping the graduation parties. Instead, Jeff Lindsey and I sat on the picnic table in his backyard and drank beer with his older brother, who told us about the sixties. We just hoped we had made the right decision. But if worse came to worse, we'd be there for each other, no matter what.

I'd been a member of a rather successful local rock band over the preceding year, and part of me wondered if the band might hit it big. It seemed we could have. Everyone loved the music we played; the local paper even called us the region's answer to the Eagles. The other guys in the group tried to get Pete and me to reconsider our decisions, but in vain: we were committed, and nothing would change our minds. We played our last concert to over three thousand people in Lake George's Shepard Park on 14 July 1980. That night we were approached by a booking agent. He wanted to sign us to play a bar tour, but Pete and I said thanks, but no thanks. That night was the Sweet River Band's last waltz and my childhood's end.

Later, I just went home; it was time to hang up the ax and grow up. In less than a week, I'd be making the biggest change in my life to date. The world was wide open to me now. I'd be back in the U.K. by fall. In the air force, I planned to experience everything I could.

22 August 1974
From the *Post-Star*, Glens Falls, New York:

> A crowd of several hundred persons gathered on Dix Avenue late Tuesday and early Wednesday to watch several objects in the sky. The unidentified flying objects were seen over a large portion of the Northeast on the brilliantly clear night. Casting off color changes, the objects were seen to hover in the air as well as move in various directions at high rates of speed.
>
> First reports came from persons in the Malta and Round Lake areas of Saratoga county. State Police reported "innumerable sightings of flying objects in the air over Saratoga County."
>
> The Civil Air Patrol at Albany sent units into the air to investigate. The pilot of

one airplane said he was flying over Albany at 8,000 feet when a silent object flew over his craft at a tremendous rate of speed.

When the objects were first seen in the Glens Falls area, over West Mountain, radio station WWSC began getting telephone calls from listeners asking about the strange colored objects in the night sky. . . .

By midnight the crowd had grown to more than 100 persons. . . . The crowd continued to grow in size, and as the cars and spectators filled the street, Glens Falls police, who had now been joined by units of the State Police, asked the crowd to move to East Field on Dix Avenue. Within an hour hundreds of persons had gathered . . . to watch the movements of the unknown objects. . . .

State Police were involved at Loudonville, Saratoga and Glens Falls in answering calls and trying to check on the objects. Warren, Washington and Saratoga county sheriff departments and other law enforcement agencies, all said they had no information on what the object might be.

The office of public information at Plattsburgh Air Force Base said they had no information on what the objects might be and had no sightings in the area of the large airbase.

Excerpt from a 1979 letter to Joann Warren from Shirley Harrison of Billericay, Essex:

Dear Mrs. Warren,

I wanted to write and tell you just how much we enjoyed having Larry to stay with us over the last 10 days—he was a delight to have around the house, well mannered and a great ambassador for the USA!! We enjoyed his tales of American life and feel we know you all a little bit better now. . . . It seems very quiet since Wednesday when they left and I am sure the Billericay girls will never be the same!![3]

2. 22 June 1980— ENTERING THE USAF

At 8:00 P.M., Tuesday, 21 July 1980, I had just returned home from a party and some last-minute good-byes to friends. Walking into our apartment, I noticed a flurry of activity to my right: my sister. Earlier in the day, I'd given her the OK to start moving into my room. When she got the word, she transformed herself into a human tornado. I couldn't blame her; Sam had shared a room with my mother for the last five years. Gone now were the rock posters that had covered my walls—the Beatles, Wings, Yes, Led Zeppelin, and others. In their place: John Travolta, the Bee Gees, and Charlie's Angels. With all the activity, she didn't notice as I began to pack a small suitcase with the only clothing I'd be allowed to bring to Lackland Air Force Base.

My mother was tense that night, and I was unsure I'd made the right choice. We had what I called the Last Supper. I'd requested meatloaf. I made and received phone calls from relatives, my father, and a girl-friend I could not wait to escape from. My mother gave me a pep talk, telling me I was doing the right thing. She and I stayed up talking till midnight. She would be taking a half day off work, so she could drive me to Albany to be sworn into the air force and then on to Albany Airport.

Because my sister was sleeping in her new room, I was on the living room couch that night. I tried to sleep but couldn't. My life was going to change literally overnight, and I couldn't wait. On TV, HBO had a movie I'd not yet seen, starring Peter Sellers and Shirley MacLaine. The film was called *Being There*, and it was brilliant. It depicted the false power we project onto politicians and corporate elitists in this country. Chauncey Gardner (Sellers), through fate, gets caught up in a system he was never part of to begin with and is given ridiculous wealth, power, and influence because the phonies already in power see his simplicity as genius. His entire vocabulary is derived from watching TV. At the end of the film, a group of corporate CEOs gather at a funeral for Chauncey's mentor in a wealthy Chicago suburb and begin discussing Chauncey's chances for presidency in the next election. Chauncey wanders away from the group, walks to a small lake, tests the depth with his umbrella, then begins to walk across the lake on top of the water as the credits roll. The film said many things to me. It was almost 4:00 A.M. before I drifted off to sleep.

I rose with the sun. *Today is the day*, I thought. My mother and I had breakfast. I double-checked all the supplies I was required to take to basic and all the paperwork. I called Jeff and Steve because I was afraid they would back out and I'd have to face basic training alone. They assured me they'd show up. My fears put to rest, I said good-bye to my sister and my cat, Mikey.

Heading south on I-87, my mother was already making plans for my return in late October. At that point, I thought basic training would kill me, and I'd never see home again!

A song ended on the radio and the news came on: Peter Sellers had died of a heart attack at age fifty-four the previous night. *Being There* would be his last film—just hours before, I'd watched it and now he was dead. I felt a strange sense of life's lack of permanency.

At the Albany Armed Forces Induction Center, my mother waited with other proud parents for us to pass our last-minute spot check and, finally, for the official swearing-in ceremony. Jeff's mother and stepfather were there, but Steve's parents were not. It was sad. Steve had a Bill Murray–like sense of humor; he was a natural comedian, but I know he felt alone that day. The swearing-in ceremony was brief and painless. In photos taken that day, I look terrified and very young, with sideburns Elvis would have been proud of.

We were given our travel orders and plane tickets and read the riot act: No drinking on the plane, and behave ourselves because we now represent the U.S. Air Force! About seven of us were leaving from

Albany that day, all from the northern Hudson valley. It was great that we would be assigned to the same basic military training school (BMTS) squadron in Texas. At Albany County Airport, my mother waited with me until I boarded the plane. I was relieved to discover it was a U.S. Air flight. A sergeant had told us we would be flying to Texas on a cargo plane, and it would be the ride from hell.

Walking up the steps to the aircraft, I turned and waved to my mother. She was crying a little and waved back to me. That was the hard part. I waved and smiled, but inside I was scared to death. In moments, it seemed, we were airborne; we were really on our way to the Lone Star State. Needless to say, I had one or two beers, and some of the other guys got hammered on mixed drinks and harassed the flight attendants. So much for the riot act!

We changed planes in Pittsburgh and had some time to walk around the airport. At a newsstand, I picked up the current copy of *Rolling Stone*; the Grateful Dead were on the cover, promoting their new album, *Go to Heaven*. Pittsburgh Airport was expanding at the time, and the terminal was a mass of confusion. A big argument ensued between some passengers and U.S. Air staff. Diana Ross and her entourage were on our flight, and some luggage got bumped to make room for her suitcases. I spent the rest of the day worried that my suitcase wouldn't be on the plane when we arrived in Texas and drove Jeff crazy wondering where my bags were. Later that afternoon, we stopped briefly in Houston. Texas was in the middle of its worst heat wave in a hundred years, and the aircraft cabin heated up fast. On the approach to the airport, I saw numerous dead cattle in an area near the badly depleted Rio Grande.

San Antonio International Airport was the last stop for us. We left the jet and looked around. Out of nowhere, an army sergeant appeared to round us up like sheep. I was confused, since I was in the air force; but the two service branches work together in San Antonio, as I soon found out. We were allowed to get our bags, then had to wait in a lounge area for our names to be called. I phoned home and complained about the way the army sergeant had yelled at us and about how I thought I had made a mistake. My mother said, "What do you expect, Larry? The fun and games are over." How right she was. Just then, it sank in that there was no turning back: my name was called.

The heat was stifling outside the terminal; it was ten at night and dark. I couldn't believe the size of the cockroaches on the ground and jumped on the bus quickly to avoid being eaten by one. With a full bus, we turned onto the Loop 410 and headed for Lackland AFB, or "Happy Valley," as the bus driver called it. He gave us a pep talk and promised that if we were good boys and girls, we'd survive basic training and escape with few scars.

Minutes later, our bus rolled under an overpass on which a huge sign read "Welcome to Lackland AFB." We stopped in front of a large building. Over the door another sign read "Gateway to the Air Force." Briefly my mind envisioned a cave and the sign above the opening: Gateway to Hell.

Every one of my fellow travelers lit cigarettes as soon as their feet touched the ground. I stood alone, wondering what to do. I didn't smoke at that time and was singled out by a staff sergeant to be first to in-process because of it!

I entered the building cautiously and approached a desk. I handed over our group orders and in return was given a manila ID tag stamped 3702 BMTS. This would be my training squadron.

All males were required to sit in yellow chairs, while females were directed to blue ones. That was the first of many head games. I felt males should take the blue, and women the yellow—conditioning from childhood, I imagine. A tech sergeant welcomed us to the air force and assured us his would be the last kind words we would hear for a while. He ordered us to form lines and walk to the buses that would take us to our respective squadron buildings. I was happy as hell that Jeff and Steve were in my squadron. I wanted company during this nightmare and knew we'd help each other through it.

The bus was so overcrowded I found myself in the back and on the floor with two or three people on top of me. It felt as if we were riding on the Greater Calcutta Transit System. The bus seemed to drive aimlessly around the base for about forty-five minutes; I sensed the place was gigantic. Finally, we stopped and were ordered off. I was in front of the giant fortress-like building that I'd call home for the next six weeks.

All fifty of us were now ordered by a trained assistant to stand at attention under the building's massive overhang. We stood in silence. Suddenly I heard the sound of metal on concrete, like tapping. A door swung open and out walked our new training instructors, with taps on their shoes. It was Sergeant Harvey and Staff Sergeant Garza and, boy, did they look happy to see us.

3. | THE MAKING OF AIRMAN WARREN

My first night in basic proved a lot worse than I had expected. Sergeant Harvey told us the rules in his own special way, and my ears rang for the next six hours. Jeff was very tense, and I reassured him.

It was tough adjusting to the regimentation. Sergeant Garza had left before we entered the building, but he'd be back in the morning without a doubt. I feared him the most. He stood perhaps five feet four inches, tops, and was a former marine and Vietnam vet of Mexican-American descent. He had a look that could freeze a glass of water.

I hadn't brought shower shoes because I felt they looked ridiculous. That first night was the last time I attempted to negotiate my point of view with a training instructor (TI); I ended up in the shower with my Adidas sneakers on. The next morning, as we marched to get our hair cut off, my every step squirted water during the five-mile march. All I could think of was Liberace's "Dancing Waters."

As basic training progressed, everyone from New York underwent unending harassment from some of the Southern guys. They thought we were all pickpockets or car thieves. The biases were amazing. I remember the day Jeff was forced to defend the Empire State from someone under the misconception that New York was a concrete jungle from Long Island Sound to the Canadian border. Some folks should travel a little more.

Basic training did some good things for me: it built endurance and respect and instilled a sense of responsibility. I was the chow runner, a job that helped me avoid some backbreaking calisthenics every day. We studied a great deal, but bad study habits from high school hung on and I was bored silly. We studied military bearing, rank structure, and, of course, how to fold our underwear in six-inch squares, a skill I'll carry to the grave.

I called my mom every chance I got, and she really kept my spirits up those first weeks. Every morning at 4:00 A.M., we were blasted out of bed by reveille played over the scratchy PA system. We were called pickles, because at the time we didn't have rank or any other ID on our drab green uniforms. By the third week, my hair began to return, and I was getting into pretty good shape. We ran 1.4 miles every morning, but the majority of our time was spent in the classroom.

Tensions did surface occasionally, not unusual when fifty people are confined to a relatively small area. It's a law of nature, I guess. But most problems were worked out without involving our TIs. That was the whole idea: to learn self-control and problem-solving skills.

Every Wednesday was mail call. Sergeant Garza would throw the letters at us like a knife thrower at the circus. Letters from home were a great boost to our morale. We were not allowed to watch TV. I think the only news we heard was the death of the shah of Iran, who had been living at Lackland AFB that spring.

The Texas heat remained dangerously high, and most days were black-flag days, which meant no outside training for anyone. Our training was carried out in the BMTS building's open bays. We also had to drink at least eight glasses of water every day to avoid dehydration. Stories about saltpeter in the water were rampant, but I didn't notice anything. On Sundays, I would go to church. It was a break from the insane pace of training and, I must admit, gave me some peace of mind.

The high point of basic was the day my father, who was in San Antonio on business, paid me a visit. I was the only one I knew of who was allowed a visit with a parent during that time. I had a half hour with my dad, and he said he'd return to Texas when I was in the Air Force Security Police Academy. It was a great boost to see him. He reflected on his army days and seemed to know just what I was going through.

Our sense of pride grew daily as our knowledge of the military increased. Inside, I fought to maintain my own identity; I was afraid they
were trying to brainwash us. We were told that negotiations to free our
hostages in Iran had once again broken down. It made all of us mad
as hell, but increased our resolve to complete training fast.

Before I knew it, we were in our last week. Many of us would remain
at Lackland to attend the security police academy. I had made some
great friends in those six weeks, and now we were about to be dispersed
to various tech schools around the country; it was an exciting day.

On the last day of training, Sergeant Garza woke us up at 3:00 A.M.
to look at his new low rider. It somehow made him seem more human,
and we all had a great laugh. Later that day, I called our flight for chow
for the last time, then jumped in the air like Pete Townsend of The
Who, windmill and all! If I had been caught doing that, I'd have been
set back three weeks or, most likely, sent to the rubber room. But the
worst was now over!

We were graduated by Lackland's base commander at our final pa-
rade. In the late afternoon, we said good-bye to the guys who would
be leaving the base. Before I moved out of the dorm, I left a note of
encouragement under my pillow. I thought it might help the kid who
got my bed next.

Steve was off to Keesler AFB. Jeff and I carried our things over to
the security police academy, where we were assigned our room and
training squadron. Then we took off for a bar called Way Out West
and had our first beers in six weeks.

That night, Jeff, our friend from Detroit, Richie Mizel, and I sat on
a wall across the street from the 3702 squadron building and watched
Sergeant Garza introduce himself to a new group of recruits. We felt a
little bad for the guys, but laughed our asses off when Sergeant Garza
called them "damn ass dumb asses!"

The next morning, we began phase one of training at the security
police academy. Our training went from 6:00 A.M. to 4:00 P.M., Monday
through Friday. Once again, the emphasis was on classroom instruction. We studied military law, nuclear security, SWAT tactics, and riot
control. We looked forward to phase two of training most of all, when
we would get our duty assignments and berets.

It was a great feeling to pass my phase-one test. We'd been given a
good foundation and extensive knowledge of the security police field.
Now, we would experience hands-on training in all phases necessary to

perform our job. Much of phase two would take place on Fort Sam Houston Army Reserve at an air-force encampment called Camp Bullis, or Bullshit, depending on whom you spoke to.

At this point in our training, air base ground defense (ABGD) was assigned. If chosen, you were in for another six weeks of training. If you were lucky, you would be passed over and do that training on your first base. If all went well, I'd be on my way home 28 October.

I now had my beret and felt proud to wear it. Our instructors often were frustrated because a lot of cops wore theirs improperly, causing the berets to resemble Jiffy-Pop popcorn packages on their heads. We all had different flashes on our berets: I wore USAFE, for United States Air Force, Europe; Jeff, SAC (Strategic Air Command); others, PACAF, for Pacific Air Command Air Force, and TAC, for Tactical. Richie Mizel never made it to phase two. He wanted a stateside assignment and feared he'd be stationed in Turkey. He got Turkey. At the firing range the next day, he put five rounds into the tin roof above him. Jeff wanted an East Coast base, but was assigned to Guam. I knew I was going to the U.K., and my assignment was RAF Alconbury.

Weeks later, as we left Lackland for Camp Bullis, I saw Mizel in civilian clothes, suitcase in hand, at a bus stop. From the bus, I yelled to him: "Hey, Mizel, where ya going?" He just smiled and said, "Detroit." I wished him luck with a wave as he faded away into the south Texas haze.

At Bullis we got hands-on training in self-defense, nuclear security in a simulated weapons-storage area (WSA), building-clearing techniques, and simulated combat situations. We also practiced further riot-control drills. I felt as if we were on the set of *M*A*S*H*, because we lived in tents. We had to shake out our clothing all the time for spiders and other nasty things. One night, the guys in the tent next door gave our tent trouble, and a minor fight broke out. Later that night, I heard a loud bang on our wooden door. Thinking it was our neighbors again, I kicked the door open and pulled an on-duty, armed security police sergeant into our tent. He almost rapped me over the head with his flashlight, but some quick talking on my part saved my face, literally.

On weekends, we would all head over to the makeshift nightclub across the road. The big attraction for us, besides the cheap beer, was an overinflated stripper who wore tech-sergeant stripes on her boobs. We'd all compete with each other to see who would score with her. No one ever did!

After a drill one day, we sat in bleachers while our instructor told us tales about the real world of security police. He'd been stationed at Wright-Paterson AFB in Dayton, Ohio. Someone asked what his duties had been at that base. The instructor, with a grin on his face, answered: "I guarded UFOs!" No one, including me, pursued that one.

In my last week before going home on leave, a friend asked if I'd be interested in swapping assignments in England because his girlfriend was based at Alconbury. He was scheduled for RAF Bentwaters. Bentwaters was closer to London, so I jumped at the chance. The change was effected in a matter of hours through administration.

I began making plans for my month-long leave: Jeff and I would look up high school friends. After all, we were doing something with our lives, and in Glens Falls everyone our age was lucky to find a job at minimum wage.

The end was now here. On our last training day, we were issued plane tickets home. After words of praise from our instructors, my flight got into formation and began double-timing down a hill past the makeshift nightclub, yelling our cadence at the top of our lungs: "S.S. the Best, Element One, Second to None." As we passed the club's outside patio, I noticed some Green Berets having some beers. The guys in the front of our line saw them and got nervous; one tripped and fell. Moments later the rest of us followed suit. Picture almost fifty guys in a pile. The Green Berets didn't look impressed at all; but I was laughing so hard I couldn't get off the ground. It was like a Three Stooges movie.

The next morning was overcast, but my spirits were up. I packed my uniforms and clothes. We all boarded buses heading back to Lackland AFB for graduation ceremonies. Once back at the security police academy, we met the SP training commander. In alphabetical order, we each received a badge and certification of training. My badge number was W0806, and I was proud to receive it. Airman, First Class Lawrence P. Warren was now a security police officer in the USAF, but still had so much to learn.

At San Antonio International, I boarded American Airlines flight 2307 to Albany. Jeff and I had a few drinks, and when the aircraft left the ground, we didn't look back once. We were going home.

1980 Developments |

August 1980

Joann Warren receives a letter from the military training school at Lackland Air Force Base:

> Dear Parent:
>
> We are proud to have your son in Basic Training and on the Air Force Team. The exciting and challenging jobs in today's Air Force will add immensely to his personal growth and development. We feel we have the very best training program available anywhere in the world. . . .
>
> I take great personal pride in accepting your son as one of the newest members of the Air Force Team and share your pride in knowing he has answered his country's call in joining the United States Air Force—A Great Way of Life.
>
> Sincerely
> (signed)
> Richard D. Paul, Colonel, USAF
> Commander[4]

30 September 1980

From the affidavit of Eugene F. Yeates, Chief, Office of Policy, the National Security Agency, in response to the Freedom of Information action filed by Citizens Against UFO Secrecy (CAUS):

> The Status and Mission of NSA
> 16. . . . The COMINT reports being withheld from the plaintiff are all based on intercepted foreign communications. . . . No meaningful portion of any of the records could be segregated and released without identifying the communications underlying the communications intelligence report. . . .
> 17. . . . The COMINT reports being withheld from the plaintiff are classified in their entirety to protect intelligence sources and methods. . . . [The records in question] were properly Classified Top Secret pursuant to Executive Order 11652, Section 1 9AO . . . the disclosure of which could result in exceptionally grave damage to the national security. . . .
> 18. Release of the COMINT records being withheld from the plaintiff or any portion of them would disclose information about the nature of the NSA's activities including its functions and thereby jeopardize the intelligence collection mission of the Agency.[5]

28 October 1980

The U.S. Air Force certifies that Airman Lawrence P. Warren has successfully completed its security-specialist course at Lackland AFB. The creed of an air force security policeman is repeated by all course graduates:

I am a security policeman.

I hold allegiance to my country, devotion to duty, and personal integrity above all.

I wear my badge of authority with dignity and restraint, and promote by example high standards of conduct, appearance, courtesy, and performance.

I seek no favor because of my position.

I perform my duties in a firm, courteous, and impartial manner, regardless of anyone's color, race, religion, national origin, or sex.

I strive to merit the respect of my fellow airmen and all with whom I come in contact.[6]

14 November 1980

Federal judge Gerhard Gesell reads Eugene Yeates's top-secret NSA affidavit. Though the judge won't be seeing any of the 239 UFO-related documents the agency now admits to having in its possession, the Washington District Court decides against CAUS and grants NSA's motion for summary judgment four days later.[7] Their finding:

. . . that release of this material could seriously jeopardize the work of the Agency and the security of the United States.

. . . that in camera affidavit presents factual considerations which aided the court in determining that the public interest in disclosure is far outweighed by the sensitive nature of the materials and the obvious effect on national security their release may well entail.

CAUS appeals the verdict.

4. HOME OF THE BRAVE

A conspiracy of silence speaks louder than words.
John Lennon[8]

Department of the Air Force
81ST Security Police Squadron (USAFE)
APO New York 09755

AB Lawrence P. Warren
3280 Technical Training Gp
Lackland AFB TX 78236

Dear Lawrence,

Welcome to RAF Bentwaters/Woodbridge and the 81st Security Police Squadron. We are looking forward to your arrival and your help in maintaining the 81st's reputation as the best security police squadron in USAFE.

I have asked Amn James C. Gouge to be your sponsor. He knows the squadron and can answer your questions about England. . . .

Most of our single airmen live in modern dorms on Bentwaters where they are close to the services and conveniences of the base. If you want to live off base, you must process through the base housing referral office. . . . Off-base housing is limited, hard to find, expensive, and not built to the standards most Americans would expect.

. . . Again, welcome. Have a pleasant trip and I'll meet you when you arrive.
Your tour in the United Kingdom will be rewarding I'm sure.

Sincerely,
Malcolm S. Zickler, Major, USAF[9]
Commander

At 6:30 A.M., 1 December 1980, I was looking out the window of the
stretch DC-Eight. From that altitude, I could see the curve in the
earth and the sun beginning to rise. The cloud cover was heavy, but
hiding beneath was Great Britain. People began to wake up. Slowly,
drowsy air force personnel made their way to the rear of the aircraft.
Many people on this flight were returning to Europe from leave or
were en route to a new duty assignment like mine. I had not slept all
night. I'd drawn some strange works of art on my orders and talked
with another SP I'd met, Rick Bertalino. I hoped Bentwaters wasn't as
bad as he was painting it.

I began to doze, thinking back on my trip to Essex, England, in 1979.
Joann, my first English girlfriend, had kept in touch, and I planned to
phone her as soon as I could. To me, she was perfect: very attractive
and English!

Suddenly my daydream was shattered by the pilot's announcement
that our flight had been diverted to Stanstead Airfield, an inactive airport north of London. Conditions at RAF Mildenhall, Norfolk, were
hazardous—fog, ice, and God knows what else. We would be landing
in five minutes, and, much to my relief, we would be allowed to deplane
and get some air.

This had been a quick transatlantic crossing for me. I already missed
my family, but was excited to be back in England. It was a place I felt
right at home, yet it was half a world away from where I grew up. The
No Smoking signs lit up, followed by the announcement to buckle our
seat belts. As beams of early morning sunlight entered the cabin from
the left side of the aircraft, the flight attendants took their seats. We were
about to touch down. The English countryside sped by, then range
lights, and finally black tarmac. But something was wrong—upon touch
down, the aircraft was very unstable. We were sliding on ice and coming
close to the side of the runway. I gripped the arms of my chair and really
felt we were not going to make it, and I was not alone. Children were
crying in fear and adults closed their eyes, but soon it was over: the jet
had stopped. By the looks of the flight crew's faces, I knew we had had

a close call, unspoken but very obvious. Descending the tall steps to the tarmac, I felt the air brisk and sharp. I walked forward stretching my legs and was just happy to be on the ground again.

Once inside Stanstead's almost empty terminal, we were greeted by a friendly old gent dressed smartly in his British Airways valet uniform. I remember his name was Charles. He had many questions for me, like "What were the Yanks doing at Stanstead? How did we find England?" I told him we had turned right at Greenland. I could tell that Charles didn't encounter many people at this airport. He spoke proudly of the place and of plans to reopen the airport and expand it, to bring it back to its once glorious prime, to compete with Heathrow and Gatwick.

I felt poor Charles had been put aside, like most older people are when big corporations have little use for them anymore. But Charles in his terrific British way made me feel great. I was back!

Now it was time to board the jet again. Conditions in Norfolk had improved, we were told. Once in the air, it seemed we were over RAF Mildenhall in seconds. It was snowing in Norfolk, and I was happy to land there without further incident.

The terminal at Mildenhall was bustling with activity. Signs pointed to buses going to air bases throughout Great Britain: Lakenheath, Greenham Common, Upper Hayford. I passed through customs without a problem, and Rick led me to the English charter coach for Bentwaters.

It was now late afternoon. The drive from Norfolk to Suffolk lasted about an hour, passing through many small villages along the way. Soon we approached the main gate to the base. The sign read: RAF Bentwaters—Home of the 81st Tactical Fighter Wing—U.S. Air Force—Col. Gordon E. Williams, Commander. The bus turned right, stopped at a guard post, and moved on.

I'd arrived at RAF Bentwaters and didn't know what to feel or expect. But there was something about the place I still can't pinpoint, something just not right about the area. I felt it that first day in 1980, but brushed away the thought as fast as I could.

The bus stopped at the All Ranks Club, and we were greeted by our sponsors. Mine was a staff sergeant. He greeted me warmly, helped me unload my bags from the bus storage hold, and we walked to his car, making small talk. He was a law-enforcement officer and had been in the air force for about eight years. I asked as much as I could about the base. Driving to my new dorm, he showed me the points of interest:

the bowling alley and movie theater, then featuring a film called *Exterminator.*

At this point, I wanted to catch the next bus out of Dodge. Bentwaters just wasn't like the bases in the States at all. I feared I would become a bowler and start wearing funny shirts and shoes. My saving thought was that I was planning to go to London the first chance I got.

I moved into my dorm and found out my roommate was a guy I had flown over with. Later that evening, I walked around the base and made two phone calls, one to my mother and the other to Joann. Jo curtly told me that since I was now in the U.S. Air Force, she would not have anything to do with me, then hung up the phone! Obviously, things had changed for her because I was now in the military.

On the phone with my mother, I told her how bleak the base seemed and how unhappy I was. Of course, she told me all would be well. I made the calls from a secured phone located in a little room at the AFFRES Center. The public phone system in England was poor at best, so I was advised to use this system, even though conversations on these lines were usually monitored for security reasons, a practice known as COMSEC—Communications Security—a feature on every NATO installation.

That night I tried to organize my room and talked with my roommate. Our dorm rooms had two beds, a closet, and brown curtains on the windows, if you were lucky. The rest was up to you.

My building's occupants consisted of security police, who were rarely quiet. At one end of the hall, you could hear "Burn Rubber" by the Gap Band, in the middle of the hall, "Shook Me All Night Long," by AC-DC, and at the other end of the building, "Looking for Love in All the Wrong Places," by Mickey Gilley, at full blast. Most American music was represented at all times of the day and night—rock, country, and disco.

This was because everyone worked different shifts and sleep was rare; many cops moved off base for these reasons.

2 December 1980

Welcome: You are assigned to "D" Flight. Your Shift Commander is Major Zickler and your Flight Chief is SMSgt Farias. . . . We would like for this period of processing to go as smoothly as possible. In order to accomplish this you will be required to report to the First Sergeant each duty day at 0730, hours. . . .

If you have any problems during your inprocessing, please contact one of the following individuals:[five individuals are listed, sergeant through senior master sergeants]. . . . After duty hours contact the LE desk.

Signed/ Senior Master Sergeant Lee Swain

"I understand that I am to report to the First Sergeant as stated above."

Countersigned/ Airman Warren

SMSGT Swain notes in the lower right "Amn-Warren will be posted to Duty Roster-D-Flight 10/December/80—Intro Training will commence 5-12-80."[10]

That first night, I slept fitfully, disoriented. The next morning, I had a lot to do. The day began with our introduction to the chief of security police, Major Malcolm Zickler. I found him very pleasant. He welcomed us and asked each of us where we came from in the States. He was from West Hartford, Connecticut, and I told him I had lived in Southington, so we had some common ground. We were then shown the law-enforcement offices, and their function was explained to us. At 11:00 A.M., my group of new arrivals attended an incoming briefing given by Wing Commander Gordon Williams. Civilian dependents also were there, plus officers and their families. Williams welcomed us to the base and wished us luck. He went on to explain the mission of the 81st Tactical Fighter Wing and offered suggestions on how we could contribute to the mission's success. It was basically a pep talk, but the sun was bright and I felt better about the base already.

Later in the briefing, Police Constable Eric Bermen was introduced. Eric was the British police liaison stationed on Bentwaters. He oversaw U.K. law as it applied to our installation and informed us about British driving laws—laws I found very strict.

The meeting over, I walked to the mess hall for lunch. There I ran into many airmen I'd trained with in Texas: Steve Longaro, Mark Tompson, Steve LaPlume, and Greg Battram. We had a reunion, and as I was about to take a seat, I ran into someone I'd gone to high school with. I remembered his face from the class of '77. After the shock wore off—*What a small world*, I thought—I'd found another friend, Larry Walls. In the air force several years already, Larry was a mechanic with hopes of joining Air Rescue and Recovery—no small goal.

Now I felt a lot more grounded. I made some great friends, and they would later help me when all hell broke loose.

On Wednesday morning at 6:00 A.M., I began my first base-security-procedure class. The classes continued over the next two weeks and included extensive ABGD training. Each base in NATO had its own security system, so new SPs had to be well versed in all aspects before joining their flight.

The classes continued until three in the afternoon, Monday through Friday. Communications security was covered along with requalification on firearms, arrest procedures, nuclear security, riot control, and British law. The classes took place on Woodbridge base, six miles away. Both bases were under the same command, but Woodbridge was a bit larger. The U.S. high school was there, some base housing, and two squadrons of A-10s. RAF Woodbridge was also home to the Sixty-seventh Air Rescue and Recovery Squadron, consisting of five C-130 transports plus ten CH-53 helicopters, known as Jolly Green Giants. Also nearby, one could find the Woody Bar; its fireplace appears briefly in the film *Twelve O'Clock High.*

Classes were hard and tests frequent. But it wasn't all work. During breaks, we exchanged stories we had heard about the base, some very strange indeed. "East End Charlie" was one. Rumor had it he was a German Luftwaffe pilot who had had the misfortune of being shot down near Woodbridge during the Battle of Britain. When irate townspeople caught him, they burned him alive. Now his ghost walks the flight line of Woodbridge and is said to be quite playful. I never saw him but was told he sat on the hood of the base fire department's patrol vehicle and burned his handprints into the metal. The driver ran away when Charlie laughed at him; who wouldn't? The hood was said to be hanging up for all to see at the Woodbridge motor pool, but I don't know anyone who ever checked it out.

"The Lady Without a Face" was another famous ghost story. She rode a bike along the lonely stretches of road between Bentwaters and Woodbridge bases, frightening GIs. How she came to have no face I was never told. And how she got hold of a bike, I didn't want to know.

Most of the guys in my classes I'd gone to tech school with; for the most part, we all got along well. We were all a bit nervous about joining our flight because this was the real deal at last.

We were warned about the druids, who held ceremonies very close to the Bentwaters flight line; we were officially told they were harmless and not to bother them. That was a bit unnerving for me. It was just great to find out Suffolk was the hub of witchcraft for the world! We laughed at the little town names, such as Eyke or Butley Village. It was said Butley was inhabited by witches and our presence was not the least welcome. *No problem,* I thought.

At the end of our first week's training, I was anxious to get off base and head for London. On Friday, I hooked up with a girl I'd met in Texas. She had sent me letters, and we had made plans to go to London back in July. Another couple joined us for the weekend.

J. J. Cabs—without which we all would have been stranded—was a taxi service based on Bentwaters. It was run by an Arab family, and, though its service was invaluable to air force personnel, some people called them towel heads. Much of the hostility stemmed from the on-going hostage situation in Iran. I didn't think it was fair, but at this point in time, there was a lot of anti-Arab sentiment on the base.

We pulled up in front of Ipswich train station at about eight o'clock, halfway into the two-hour trip to London. The girl I was with chose that time to tell me she was out of money and hadn't brought her paycheck. Even so, it felt great arriving at Liverpool Street Station. That weekend was a lot of fun, and we hit most of the nightspots in Soho. My lady friend cost me a week's pay, but what the hell—if this was freedom, I liked it.

That was a three-day weekend, so classes would resume on Tuesday. On Monday, I explored the countryside near the base and found numerous ruins from the Middle Ages, as well as many relics from World War II. Monday night, I felt uneasy as I went to bed. At around four the next morning, I bolted up wide awake, thinking I'd heard a loud noise; but my roommate was asleep and all was quiet. I wrote it off as a bad dream and went back to sleep.

Later that morning, in class on Woodbridge base, some of the guys who had just returned from Liverpool, real Beatle fans like me, were full of stories about the landmarks they had visited. The Cavern Club was gone, but in its place was a museum dedicated to the band. One of the guys had even bought Beatle boots. Jay, one of the kids who'd made the trip, said out of the blue, "Wouldn't it be weird if one of the Beatles died?" We wondered if there would be a big funeral. All of us planned to see John Lennon in London that spring; we made plans to get a busload of us together. "Would John and Paul play again?" we wondered aloud.

Our instructor entered the room. He overheard us talking about the Beatles and told us that one of the Beatles had been shot a few hours before in New York City. He'd just heard it on the radio. There were no further details.

I felt as if I was in a vacuum. I couldn't believe it. Who was it, I wondered. Then it clicked. John Lennon lived in New York. That morning, I proceeded to fail my first written test. All the other guys were in shock as well. That afternoon, I wandered around base in a fog. Back in my dorm, Lennon's last album played on most stereos. I went to the All Ranks Club to escape it; however, the tributes were already airing on the BBC and ITV. Seeing the stock footage of a youthful Lennon singing with the Beatles, I couldn't help but smile. A few days later, I and others went up to Liverpool to observe ten minutes of silence for him.

19 December 1980
Joann Warren writes to her son:

> We have put up the Christmas tree and it really looks nice. Again I said I would have a small tree but Sammy got her way again and we have a pretty good size one. . . .
>
> You said on the telephone you went to services in Liverpool for John Lennon, please let me know what that was like. The United States did observe 10 minutes of silence on Sunday at 2:00 PM. The Boston Pops Orchestra did "Hey Jude" in his memory. It was a terrible thing that happened. . . .
>
> Larry, I wish I knew what you were doing for Christmas. Please call as I am looking forward to that. . . .

Over the next week, I completed the remaining courses, requalified at the range with the M16 rifle and even the dreaded M-203 grenade launcher, and rode with law-enforcement patrols. I withdrew a bit during the weeks leading up to Christmas; I don't think I got in touch with my family, though my mother sent letters every week. I was now assigned to D Flight and worked my first week in the weapons-storage area, mainly checking access badges—not very exciting work.

One incident that week I won't forget. One night, just before our first three-day break, which extended over the Christmas holiday, a few other SPs and I were assigned to an active aircraft area on the Bentwaters flight line. About halfway into the shift, we realized someone was shooting at us. They were firing from the woods just beyond the perimeter fence. The bullets seemed to be from a small-caliber weapon. We knew this because the report wasn't very loud. However, bullets are bullets. I hit the ground when a few rounds struck an A-10 not far from my position. The aircraft were loaded with active bombs because they were due to go on training runs in Norfolk the next morning, making the situation even graver.

I called central security control and reported a Helping Hand—a procedure aptly titled! Out on the tarmac, a fellow SP named Russ was low-crawling and calling out on his handheld Motorola that the Vietcong were on the wire! He had to be restrained, because we were not allowed to return fire off base, due to a treaty with Britain. After about fifteen minutes, whoever had done the shooting was gone. The weapon turned out to be a 22-caliber rifle. Damage assessment showed that only two rounds had hit the A-10, no more than scratching its titanium surface. Russ was eventually snapped out and put under observation; I never worked with him again.

There was so much hostility toward U.S. service personnel in England at the time I believe that shooting incident was a symptom of it. Whoever shot at us was never found. At this point, I started to dislike being in England. I felt that we were here defending their country, and the British were shooting at us in return, meanwhile partying on our base because the booze and cigarettes were cheap. Sadly, the anti-Americanism had a reverse effect on us; it's why many American servicemen disliked their host country.

The day before Christmas, I left for Germany with my friend Mark. We had met two German girls in London the previous week at Le Beat Route, a club on Greek Street. We had gotten along well at the time, and the girls had invited us to spend the holiday with them and their families near Frankfurt. We had a great time, despite a severe language barrier. However, I think the girls lost interest in Mark and me on the second night. We just sat around and stared at their parents and they at us, while the girls went out with their German boyfriends. On or about 27 December, we flew back to RAF Mildenhall to begin our shift the next night.

1980 Developments |

11 December 1980

PERSONAL DATA

PREPARED 80 DEC 11 21:16   REPORT ON INDIVIDUAL

...TO: 81 SECURITY POLICE SQ
BENTWATERS RAF UNKIN

1. A1C WARREN LAWRENCE P (SS#), HAS HAD HIS CAFSC-SEI UPDATED TO 327 (AB GRND DEFENSE). MEMBER IS CURRENTLY FILLING POSITION NUMBER 0103463 AND SEI 327 WAS DESIGNATED TO THAT POSITION. MEMBER'S SPEC-EXP-RQMT-DT IS 01DEC80.

2. THE FOLLOWING ADDITIONAL DATA IS PROVIDED FOR YOUR INFORMA-TION: . . .

C. DUTY TITLE IS: SECURITY SPECIALIST

D. DT-EFF-DATE IS: 01DEC80

3. MEMBER'S MASTER PERSONNEL FILE HAS ALREADY BEEN UPDATED. IF YOU DO NOT CONCUR NOTIFY CBPO/DPMPC OF ACTION YOU WANT TAKEN NO LATER THAN (written) 19DEC80.

(signed)
THOMAS A. MOSELEY, TSGT, USAF
NCOIC, CLASSIFICATION AND TRAINING

Warren also receives his personal reliability pledge (PRP) on 11 December. Personnel cannot be cleared to work on a nuclear base without it.[11]

15 December 1980
Airman Warren completes the last area of security-police training necessary to qualify for immediate posting to Bentwaters' D Flight. His instructors have been senior NCOs Huntzinger and Slack.[12]

25 December 1980
Christmas night. Unidentifieds are first observed above northern Portugal heading toward Germany, then over southern England. There, residents of Kent and Sussex watch the cometlike objects break up into smaller lights. Radar operators at RAF Watton track and record an unidentified over Suffolk until it is lost in the vicinity of Rendlesham Forest.[13]

25–26 December 1980
From a statement by Airman, First Class John Burroughs, Law Enforcement, RAF Bentwaters:

On the night of December 25–26 at around 03:00 while on patrol down at East Gate, myself and my partner saw lights coming from the woods due east of the gate. The lights were red and blue, the red one above the blue one and they were flashing on and off. . . . There was radio traffic back and forth and the decision was made by the shift commander that I should accompany two security guys into the woods. . . .

We crossed a small open field that led into the trees where the lights were coming from and as we were coming into the trees, there were strange noises, like a woman was screaming, also the woods lit up and you could hear the farm animals making a lot of noise and there was a lot of movement in the woods. All three of us hit the ground and whatever it was started moving back. . . . After a minute or two, we got up and moved into the trees and the lights moved out into the open field. . . .

Everything seemed like it was different when we were in that clearing, the sky didn't seem the same . . . it was like a weird feeling, like everything seemed slower than you were actually doing; and all of a sudden when the object was gone, everything was like normal again. . . .

[The UFO:] a bank of lights, differently colored lights that threw off an image of like a craft. I never saw anything metallic or anything hard.[14]

Sergeant Jim Penniston also witnesses the encounter:

The air was filled with electricity and we saw an object about the size of a tank. It was triangular, moulded of black glass and had symbols on it. Suddenly it shot off faster than any aircraft I have ever observed.[15]

27 December 1980
Today's *Times* (London) carries the brief article, ''Meteor as Cause of Bright Lights'':

An unidentified flying object spotted on Thursday night by hundreds of people all over England was almost certainly a meteor breaking up, officers at the Royal Air Force observer base at West Drayton, London, said yesterday.

After many calls were made to the base and Heathrow airport, London, a search was started for any aircraft in the area. Flight Lieutenant Duncan Swift, in charge of the emergency desk at West Drayton, received reports from as far away as Cornwall and Yorkshire.

The base said: ''All reports indicate a large meteor breaking up, or a satellite. The reports were all the same, a large, bright light followed by a mass of smaller ones.

"As soon as the reports began to come in we looked for any aircraft that might have been in trouble, but there were none around." The object was on a north-easterly course and high in the sky.

The film "Airport 1975" was shown on television on Thursday night, raising the public awareness to the possibility of aircraft in trouble.

East Anglia. That evening, Derek Kersey drives from Orford to Eyke. As he approaches a turnoff for Woodbridge, he hears a shrieking sound. It is not coming from his car, an Austin 1100, but from *above* the car. The Austin immediately begins to slow, and the driver observes a huge red glow off to his left. Unable to control the speed or sluggish wheel, he pulls to the side and stops. Kersey has no problem restarting the engine after the glow passes. The only other car he remembers seeing on that drive is a police car with its lights flashing.[16]

Roy Wilkinson is at home in Essex that evening when his phone rings. It is the wife of one of his mates at work. The couple live near Wood-bridge and know of Roy's interest in UFOs; she is calling to say that unidentified lights have been spotted over the area. Wilkinson gets what specifics he can, thanks her, and ends the call. The amateur photographer goes for his camera first, then grabs some film and a jacket. He is out the door in record time and tears up to Suffolk, arriving in the area close to midnight.

Somewhere near the eastern perimeter of RAF Woodbridge, Wilkinson sees a lighted area in the woods and pulls up on a forestry trail. After turning off the ignition he loads his camera, then heads toward the glow. The Rendlesham Forest is "black as hell" but the light through the trees draws him on, until he feels a hand on his shoulder. The Essex resident turns to face two armed air force law-enforcement police, who ask him to accompany them back the way he came: more an order than a request. The cops escort the intruder from the site and place him in a vehicle.

Wilkinson is driven to a guard shack, where the film is removed from his camera before it is returned. After being made to wait alone for a time, he is taken to Woodbridge and turned over to local police without comment or charges. Woodbridge police have no reason to detain the man and release him within minutes. Wilkinson is returned to his car and reaches home before dawn, without a photograph or an idea of what he had nearly stumbled upon.[17]

PART 1
Notes

1. Elbert Hubbard, *Scrap Book*, unpaginated.
2. *The Post-Star* (Glens Falls, NY) 20 August 1974 incident.
3. Letter on file.
4. Letter on file.
5. *CAUS vs. NSA*, Civil Action No. 80–1562, 30 September 1980. Credit: P. Gersten.
6. *Air Force Manual: Basic Security Specialists Course*, L3ABR 81130–002, 6 February 1979, p. 137.
7. From a note on Stanton T. Friedman's copy of the Yeates NSA affidavit.
8. Dedication from the album jacket for John Lennon's *Walls and Bridges* (1974). Lennon signed the quote by his rock and roll pseudonym, Dr. Winston O. Boogie.
9. Date of letter obscured, but probably written on or about 1 December 1980.
10. From Larry Warren's Eighty-first Security Police in-processing sheet; on file.
11. Document on file; AF form 2095 on file.
12. AF form 1098 on file.
13. Jenny Randles, "Bentwaters, Part I: Did a UFO Land Beside a NATO Base in England?" *Fate* 46, no. 9 (September 1993), pp. 46–47.
14. Antonio Huneeus, "Bentwaters, Part III: The Testimony of John Burroughs," *Fate* 46, no. 9 (September 1993), pp. 70–71.
15. John Sweeney, "The A–Z of Conspiracy," *The Observer*, 12 February 1995, p. 12.
16. Derek Kersey, interview by Peter Robbins and Larry Warren, Tunstall, Suffolk, 19 November 1993.
17. Roy Wilkinson, interview by Peter Robbins and Larry Warren, Eyke, Suffolk, 2 September 1995. Tape on file.

PART 2

BENTWATERS

1. THE BENTWATERS INCIDENT

There are moments that go beyond each of our poor little lives.
Charles de Gaulle[1]

From 26 to 29 December 1980, RAF Bentwaters and Woodbridge air bases had nightly visits of unusual flying objects. On or about Christmas Eve, three airmen encountered a triangular object in Rendlesham Forest.

At first the lights were thought to be from an aircraft that had gone down in the vast expanse of pine, and the men received permission to investigate. Because of the strangeness of what they witnessed and the treatment they received afterward, these men still have not adjusted to what they experienced. I know all three of them, and, like me, they still carry the fear of what happened those nights with them.

Early on 28 December, I got away from the base for the day with my roommate, Alabama. We took the base taxi to Ipswich and did some sight-seeing. One of the points of interest was the Corn Exchange, an open market area located in a picturesque section of the city. I wanted to find a music store; I was in the market for a Marshall amplifier and thought I'd get a great deal since they are manufactured in England.

We happened into Axe Music on Christchurch Road. After unsuccessfully bargaining with the owner of the store for a few hours, I left. We walked past the infamous off-limits clubs, like the Running Buck and the Railway Bar, past the football stadium where the Ipswich Town

Super Blues play soccer. My security-police flight was returning to work that night after a three-day break. My shift was from 11:30 P.M. to 6:30 A.M. the next day. D Flight worked swing and midshifts, so every other week we would work those ungodly hours.

Alabama and I caught the last bus back to Bentwaters at around 6:00 P.M. It was important for us to get back on time and be ready for work: iron our uniforms, shine our boots, and, most important, get something decent to eat. On the flight line, the food was terrible at best. The menu consisted of either green eggs or "bag nasties," pre-packed bag lunches with potato chips as their only edible component.

To our surprise, the bus dropped us and three other airmen off in the town of Woodbridge. This meant we faced a four-mile walk back to Bentwaters, and it was getting late. We stopped at the Cherry Tree Pub for a Coke, then went on. We noticed a small car parked along the road, a man maybe thirty years old was standing next to it. He said he had just seen something strange fly overhead, so he had pulled the car over to investigate. We saw nothing. I told him it was most likely an A-10; the man shrugged it off and drove away. Later, we felt stupid that we hadn't asked him for a ride to the base.

I was back in my dorm around eight, got my uniform ready, and grabbed my alert bag, containing a flak vest, chemical suit, gas mask, and other equipment. The base was on alert at that time because the Soviet Union was on the brink of moving armored units into Poland to stop the new solidarity movement and the general unrest it had sparked. NATO forces were ready to respond if the Red Army crossed the line. Most of our A-10 tank busters had already left for forward operating locations in West Germany the previous week; very few air-craft remained at Bentwaters. This was a tense time in Europe, although we didn't feel war was imminent.

At 10:00 P.M., I made my way to the base movie theater and joined the rest of D Flight. We would be driven to the flight line by bus and dropped off at Central Security Control. Before we got our posting for the night, we had to be inspected to determine if we were fit for duty. This proce-dure is called guard mount and enables the flight chief to check out the general condition of the security police. They look for signs of a cop be-ing intoxicated (we were not allowed to drink alcohol twenty-four hours before our shift), on narcotics (legal or illegal), or otherwise impaired. Afterward, we would be assigned to posts on Bentwaters or Woodbridge bases, depending on their respective need for manpower.

As usual, guard mount was uneventful that night. I was assigned to

Bentwaters Perimeter Post 18. It is not a very important position in comparison to active aircraft areas or the weapons-storage area. I checked out my M16 rifle from the armory at 11:15 and was dropped off at my post. Manned only during alerts, it was at the end of the Bentwaters flight line at the very end of the runway. I was alone but did have a Motorola radio for communications.

The weather was mild for late December; the temperature was in the forties. It was a very dark night with no moon visible and a few wisps of clouds. A radio check from Central Security Control would be made to my post every fifteen minutes. I recall having responded to two of them when I overheard a glut of radio transmissions originating from the Bentwaters weapons-storage area's observation tower and the Woodbridge flight tower. The transmissions took place between cops who were observing "some funny-looking lights bobbing up and down" over the forest near Woodbridge base some five miles away. Whatever they saw, they had a great vantage point since the WSA tower is eighty feet high. Cops began making jokes about what was being reported. Our flight chief came on the open channel and warned everyone to stop. I strained to see anything unusual and was frustrated to see nothing. I was not aware that very strange things had been taking place in the base's vicinity on previous nights.

Soon I began to feel uneasy. Strange things were being reported, and I was far away from other posts. Suddenly, out of the pitch black to my right, the sound of hooves beating the ground shot past my ears. Five panic-stricken deer were running to the fence line from a nearby field. Three deer turned left when they reached the fence and continued in a panic. The other two jumped the fence with ease, bounded across the runway past me, and disappeared into the night. It was a beautiful but unnerving sight. I wondered what could have frightened them. No aircraft were up, so that was not the cause. I started to feel anxious, as if I were being watched.

Five minutes later, a security-police pickup truck arrived at my post. Sergeant Adrian Bustinza was driving with Second Lieutenant Englund next to him; two other SPs were in the bed of the truck. The lieutenant told me to announce over the Motorola that I was being relieved from my post. I waited for clearance from Central Security Control; they acknowledged my request, and the post was deactivated. I could see tension in the other guys' faces. Bustinza told me to get in the back— he said we were heading to the Bentwaters motor pool to get light-alls, bright spotlights with powerful generators mounted on trailers.

As soon as we arrived at the motor pool, a security-police captain ran to our truck. He told us to hurry and gas up the equipment. We mounted a unit to the rear of the pickup. Bustinza filled it with gas; its gauge read full, but the captain said it was not full, and an argument ensued. Such tension between officers and enlisted people was unusual.

Anticipation was in the air. I hadn't the slightest idea what was happening. I asked someone in the motor pool what all this was for and was told we were replacing malfunctioning equipment. Another truck pulled up and did the same.

We left the motor pool area quickly; I could hear radio communications from Woodbridge base. Much of it was hard to translate, but I do recall a dispatch to the law-enforcement desk on Bentwaters requesting that someone contact the base's commanding officer, Gordon Williams. Then, radio transmissions bled together again.

In a matter of minutes, we were at the main gate on Bentwaters. All of us in the back of the truck were still armed, but we had removed the ammo clips from our M16 rifles, standard procedure when on public roads surrounding the base. At the gate, I could see two law-enforcement cars and three other pickup trucks; other SPs were in those vehicles as well.

Our truck and the one that followed were the only ones with light-alls in tow. The vehicles in front started moving and we followed. I leaned forward and asked Bustinza, through the cab's rear window, where we were going. The answer was Woodbridge base.

We made small talk in the back of the truck concerning what this was all about. I thought we were on a readiness exercise; the other cops agreed. Still, I couldn't help wondering why we had not been issued blanks for our weapons.

The road to Woodbridge base is narrow. The village of Eyke and a farm or two are the only points of civilization on the route. Driving through Eyke with the convoy's blue lights flashing, I thought: *How rude of us, we'll wake everyone up.*

We got through the little village fast and wound our way through the countryside. The tall Corsican pines of the local forest were dense around us, creating a cathedral-like effect because of the light from our trucks.

As the convoy rounded a sharp curve on the East Gate Road, out of the dark flashed the outer range lights of RAF Woodbridge. A law-enforcement car was half blocking the road, where some SPs were placing red flares. As our vehicles were motioned forward through the makeshift roadblock, I noticed a civilian car—a Ford Cortina, stark white and looking out of place among the military activity. In the car was a young woman and, next to her, a small girl who appeared to be sleeping. A law-enforcement cop leaned on her car door; I heard him clearly tell the driver there might be some unexploded ordnance in the area. They were checking it out and would not delay her long.

We moved on. I felt excited, cautious, and curious all at once. For some reason, the bomb story just didn't sound sincere. What was really going on? Certainly not war games with the Royal Army: that much was now obvious.

Facing me were the rapidly fading lights of Woodbridge field. To my left was a pine forest I later learned was called Rendlesham. We passed another law-enforcement car. One of the cops in the cab of the truck ahead of us yelled, "Where the hell are we supposed to go?" A law-enforcement cop, standing on the side of the road, responded, "Turn left at East Gate."

After a few more feet, we did. I could see our flashing blue lights cast shadows through the trees. and the occasional group of rabbits scatter as we moved on

We continued slowly down the narrow dirt logging road. After approximately one-half mile, the trucks and cars entered a large clearing. Other trucks were already parked in the area; we stopped. I got off the pickup and waited for orders. I saw that about fifteen men in uniform and several others in civilian clothes were heading down a narrow trail on foot. I watched as their flashlights faded into the darkness.

Just then, the chief of security police arrived at the site and stepped from his car into a rather large mud puddle. We broke up over his mishap. It was the last time I would laugh that night.

A truck from the armory arrived, and we were ordered to turn in our weapons by a senior NCO. Our M16s and GAUs were stored in the racks at the back of the truck and locked up. I was asked to turn in my Motorola radio, as were other lower-ranking people. The time was now about 12:30 A.M. I found myself checking my thirty-dollar Timex often over the next hour.

A flight commander joined Bustinza, two other airmen, and me. He was a captain I had not encountered before. Second Lieutenant Englund had left the parking area with a group of men almost as soon as we arrived. Lieutenant Colonel Halt may have been with him. We were ordered not to talk unnecessarily. The captain told the two men with radios in our group to maintain radio silence as well. Now, conversation was very cryptic, spoken in low and ominous tones over our radio's open channels. We were suddenly motioned to follow the captain down the footpath and into the woods. Without hesitation, I followed.

After roughly one hundred yards, we turned right and continued deeper into the forest. The pines were very dense at this point. Off to my left, I could see an area illuminated by large flashlights and a ground flare or two. I could see silhouettes of people moving around that area. I also noticed what looked like orange or red plastic surveyor's tape wrapped around some trees. The lighting effect was eerie. My mind was still processing information, unimpaired.

Then I heard a radio transmission: "You people have to avoid those hot spots. Remember they're marked, October Number One. Over." I knew the code "October One" meant first officer on site. What "hot spot" meant, I didn't know. Maybe we were going to fight a forest fire, but why us? We were cops, not firemen.

I could see other small groups of SPs in the distance, their flashlights slashing the dark. The forest was deathly calm. Then, things became almost dreamlike, and I began to feel uneasy. The tightness in my solar plexus was overpowering. Something was wrong. Radio transmissions were loud now and coming from coded responses to unclear questions.

We moved on for another quarter mile through Rendlesham Forest, then stopped again. I could see, maybe a hundred feet in front of me, a large field with a broken wire fence at its perimeter. Just beyond were numerous military personnel. They seemed to be walking around something on the ground, something illuminated. It would grow bright enough to light up the forest, then dim.

As we approached the field, Bustinza said to me in a half whisper, "This is just like what happened to me in Alaska." Near the fence line, leaning against a tree, an airman crouched down, head in hands, crying. A master sergeant was trying to console him. *What the hell is going on?* I thought.

We moved closer, up a slight incline, thornbushes tearing at my pants. Now, I could see what was in the field: it looked like a ground fog, but was somehow lit up from within. It glowed very brightly, with the definition of a roughly shaped circle approximately one foot in height.

It was yellow-green and at times appeared almost transparent. Two disaster-preparedness officers walked very close to it in a counterclockwise direction with yellow Geiger counters in hand. Someone was snapping pictures. Off to my right, I saw personnel operating motion-picture cameras—one was handheld, the other mounted on a tripod—filming this amazing sight.

We joined the forty-odd other men already in the field, just looking at the bizarre object on the ground in front of us. Two cows walked out of the dark to my left. They looked dazed, but none of the human activity seemed to faze them. I asked: "Where did they come from?" Bustinza pointed to a farmhouse about two hundred yards away. I could see a light on in an upper-floor window. I briefly wondered if the home's occupants could see what I was seeing.

The radios were active. I could hear what sounded like pilot communications. Someone repeated over the air: "Here it comes. Here it comes. Here it comes." Over the far end of the field, from the direction of the North Sea, I noticed a small red light. The light came closer each second. At first I thought it was an aircraft, but it came at us too fast and silently. I noticed at this time that my movements had become very slow, as if I were in a vacuum. This was the last time I checked my watch. It was almost 1:30 A.M. My arm felt like lead as I lifted and dropped it.

The red light cleared the pines bordering the field and quickly made a downward arc until it was directly over the illuminated fog. Only about twenty feet above the ground, the object was now stationary and roughly the size of a basketball. I had never seen its color before, but red comes closest.

As my mind tried to register what I was looking at, the ball of light exploded in a blinding flash. Shards of light and particles fell onto the fog. Several cops ran into the woods. I couldn't move; I tried to cover my eyes, but was too late. I was numb and very likely in shock. Why I didn't run, I don't know. I wanted to, but I was cemented in place.

The explosion produced no noticeable heat. But now, right in front of me was a machine occupying the spot where the fog had been. It was big and almost the shape of a pyramid. At the top of the object was that same off-red glow. The main body was pearl white, with a rainbow-color effect. Its image was constantly distorting; its shape was best seen by peripheral vision. At the base was a bank of extremely bright cobalt-blue lights. Below that, I thought I could make out what looked like dark landing gear. Covering the entire surface were what looked like boxes, pipes, and strange extensions.

The thing looked solid and very heavy. I'll never understand why, but it seemed old and advanced at the same time. With no identifying markings, flags, windows, or doors, it was unlike anything I'd ever seen.

The men who had held their ground after the explosion watched trans-fixed, the cameras filming all the while.

The object had three deltalike appendages protruding from the main body, giving it an almost threatening appearance. I was twenty to twenty-five feet from it. We were told not to move. A senior officer ordered us to keep a tight cordon on the area. This was considered a Covered Wagon, or Security Option Three, a procedure to ensure the security of a nuclear device. I felt nauseated, and the hairs on my arms stood on end. The air was supercharged.

An officer approached Bustinza and me. He asked us to walk with him, very close to the object. A disaster-preparedness man led the way with a Geiger counter in hand. I did not want any of this. We got to within ten or fifteen feet of the thing. Our four shadows touched the object, but there were no lights in the field to cast them. It seemed to be pulling our shadows onto itself.

We walked ten paces to the left and then to the right. By now my eyes were watering profusely, so that every time I would get a fix on the object, its image would blur. Each time we stopped walking, our shadows would move as if taking one more step.

We then were ordered back to our original positions, about twenty-five feet away. I looked behind me, saw the field's barbed-wire fence, and marked an old knotted oak tree for future reference—in case I ever returned to the spot.

Some of the people who had run off into the woods were called back. I could see their faces in the distance, but they held their ground. To my right were two English policemen from the town of Woodbridge. One had a camera and was snapping pictures. An airman was ordered to take it away; he did so forcefully and an argument ensued. By now, the level of tension had increased twofold. Things were out of control and the confusion continued. I noticed that some of the senior people seemed to know what they were doing: it was as if they were following some sort of procedure.

The cameras continued to roll. Suddenly, a staff car arrived at the end of a trail. Colonel Gordon Williams and other staff officers got out and spoke with officers already on site. Most of them were not in uni-form, and some, including Williams, appeared to have been pulled from some official function or party. Commander Williams seemed ner-vous as he and others grouped together in intense discussion.

Now a glowing ball of light, bluish gold in color, came slowly from behind the right delta on the object. It moved with deliberation and purpose, about one foot above the ground. It stopped about ten feet away from the machine, and I noticed something strange within its glow. I thought: *Why are there kids here?*

Bustinza asked under his breath, "Can you see them?" I saw their eyes and knew then that they definitely were not kids. All personnel seemed in a trance and just watched them. The glow had faded a bit, so their features were easier to see. The one light then broke into three separate glowing cylinders, each containing what appeared to be a living creature.

They were small, about three to four feet tall and somewhat ghostlike in appearance. They had large heads with catlike black eyes. I could not see other facial features. They were not human at all, but I was not frightened. Each wore very bright, almost silvery clothing. I could not see any life-support devices attached to the entities.

After a short duration, Colonel Williams approached them slowly. Standing about five feet apart, they seemed to stare at each other. Williams, well over six feet tall, looked down at them. The entities appeared to cock their heads back slowly so they could see his face. It was amazing. It was then I knew they were really alive. I could not hear any conversation. I don't think there was any communication in the traditional sense, but I believe they were communicating.

Suddenly, behind me, I heard a loud noise, as if a tree had fallen in the woods. The beings' arms immediately moved up close to their chests, as if in defense. They floated backward to a point almost under the craft. Now, I could see a white membrane cover their eyes.

After a tense moment, they slowly moved back toward Williams. He then turned to another officer, who handed him something I could not see. Williams turned and faced the beings again. Their eyes were black again, arms at their sides. They glided to within five feet of the commander. Just then a master sergeant walked over to some cops on my left. I noticed small groups of SPs beginning to leave the field.

Our group was told to return to the trucks and wait. The sergeant gave me a pat on the back as I turned to walk away. Once again looking to my right, I saw the old knotted oak and burned its image into my mind. I stepped over the wire fence, up the slight incline, and took a last look at the object and the entities. They were where I had last seen them; Commander Williams was conversing with other officers. I then turned away, the thorns once again tearing at my pants.

During the walk back to the trucks, we were quiet. There were many strange lights flying through the trees, and beams of blue light shooting from the night sky to the ground. I felt we were being watched.

Back at the parking area, we picked up our weapons from the armorer's vehicle and got into the trucks. Ours was the first to leave the area. Later, I heard that some amazing things had gone on in the parking area as well.

During the ride back to Bentwaters, I wondered if similar events were happening simultaneously all over the world. At that moment, it wouldn't have surprised me: I fully expected this to be on the front page of every newspaper the next day.

We got back to Central Security Control at about 4:30 A.M. I returned my weapon to the armory, then joined other groups from my flight in the lounge to drink coffee and stare at the walls. At 6:30, A Flight reported for the day shift. Some of the men began making jokes about little green men and flying saucers. We were too drained to react; we only shook our heads in disgust. I was relieved from duty, caught a police bus, then went straight to my room and collapsed on the floor.

My eyes hurt. I had a bad taste in my mouth and a ringing in my ears. I walked to the mirror over my dresser and saw that I had produced a shock of gray hair over the last four hours. I didn't sleep. I couldn't; the sun was now bright. I wanted to go outside and rejoin the real world and look, in the cold light of day, into the faces of others who had been there.

I thought doing that would make what I'd seen fall into some logical part of my mind. But it never has.

2. THE NEXT DAY

I emerged from the dorm building, not knowing what to expect and feeling like a survivor of a nuclear holocaust leaving his shelter for the first time. It was 7:30 A.M.; the sun had a calming effect on me. I still felt a bit sick and dizzy; I saw people around me beginning their day as usual, but felt strangely removed from the rest of the world. I paused for a moment and thought about the last twenty-four hours: *This can't be real, no way.* Countless emotions welled up inside. The base had now taken on an ominous look. People seemed out of touch, or perhaps I was out of touch; I just couldn't get it together. The daylight was like an old friend, helping me to maintain my sense of denial.

A car nearly hit me as I stepped off a curb. I informed the nervous driver that he'd be arrested next time if he ignored the zebra crossing. I turned away and made a beeline for the mess hall. I knew there I'd find other cops who saw the UFO, and I wouldn't feel so alone.

Inside the mess hall, it was business as usual; the morning breakfast club at RAF Bentwaters was in full swing. I scanned the room. At the SP table off to my left, almost segregated from the rest of the dining area, were ten or so cops. The gun rack was half full with M16s, and some guys from A Flight seemed uncomfortable. Most of the cops at the table were from D Flight. The haunted looks on their faces told everyone they didn't want to be bothered.

I slid my tray along the steel-and-glass counter, filled a plate with food I knew I wouldn't eat, then made my way to the SP table. I could hear the buzz; every table I passed seemed to be talking about the UFO incident. Versions of the story ranged from the ridiculous to the mundane. The rumors had begun.

I sat down quietly at the table. Staff Sergeant Jim Penniston and a few others were there. They knew what had happened. Some guys talked about anything else that came to mind, but I had an overwhelming need to talk about the UFO: *What happened to us in that forest?* I could sense other guys felt the same way. Out of the blue, Steve Longaro leaned over and asked me if the last twenty-four hours had been a dream. I smiled and shook my head, not really knowing for sure. Suddenly the few A Flight cops at the table let loose with the questions: Was it really a UFO? What did the aliens look like? I was responding as openly as I could when Penniston looked in my direction and said, "Hey, Warren, shut the fuck up!"

I stared back at him for a moment, repressing the urge to throw my tray at him. Pushing it away, I stood up to leave and headed for the door. I wondered what Penniston knew that I didn't. I resented him for silencing me—the cover-up was already beginning. I walked back to the SP dorm feeling an overwhelming need to talk about what I'd seen.

Back in my room, I put on an Eric Clapton album and played "Blues Power" over and over, trying to concentrate and learn the bass line on my guitar. It was a distraction I could lose myself in.

The door to my room opened and Art Henderson entered. Looking a little worried, he waved a handwritten phone message in my face. I took off my headphones, took the message, and read it. Art said he'd taken the call in the dayroom and it sounded important. The note said I was to be at the law-enforcement desk at 11:00 A.M. sharp, in uniform, to see Major Zickler. I knew what it was about: the UFO. Art asked if the stories were true. I told him that more had happened than he could imagine. The time was nearly 10:00 A.M.

I changed into uniform and made my way over to the Bentwaters flight line. Many scenarios ran through my mind concerning what lay in store. I knew now that the air force would try to cover up what we'd seen; didn't they always? But how could they keep *all* of us quiet? I ran across the soccer pitch, past the base clinic, and then along the edge of an old air-raid ditch, briefly picturing people diving into it as the Luftwaffe screamed in from above.

I moved fast. Generally late for everything, I couldn't be today: it was too important. Running faster, dodging cars, I crossed the roundabout and passed the Bentwaters main-gate sign, then the guard shack at a slight jog, and said, "Hi," to the cop manning the post. Directly ahead, at the top of a slight incline, was the law-enforcement desk. In front of the drab, green building at least twelve people were standing in a group, I recognized Major Zickler first. The majority were like myself, airmen below the rank of sergeant. All had seen the UFO.

I was late. As I joined the ranks, Major Zickler asked if I made a habit of being late for appointments. I said, "No, sir," and the chief let it go at that. Zickler told us that we were going to be debriefed concerning what we had experienced in Rendlesham Forest. First and foremost, we were to give our full cooperation to the debriefers.

After the major walked away, a tech sergeant from disaster preparedness walked around us holding a Geiger counter. I don't know if we made the device react, but one airman did seem to cause some interest. He took what looked like a small rock out of his jacket pocket and showed it to the tech sergeant. The sergeant placed it in a small plastic bag and dropped it into a metal box next to the building.

I noticed two nice cars with government plates parked across the street. The front door of the law-enforcement desk opened, and the assistant chief of security police, Major Dury, motioned us inside.

We were all very quiet. The office was strangely void of personnel, only an airman operating the law-enforcement communications console. We faced a long counter on which numerous documents were arranged in stacks, one for each of us. I tried to scan them, but they were too much to absorb. A staff sergeant named Jackson, whom I recognized from the Air Force Office of Special Investigation (AFOSI), told us to sign our names at the bottom of each document and not to forget to write our Social Security numbers under our names.

Someone asked if we could read the documents we were signing. Major Dury told him we could read them later, there wasn't any time now.

As I leafed through mine, I tried to remember all I could in the time I had. One was a Joint Army Navy Air Publication (JANAP) 146, a rather standard, all-encompassing security document. A few others seemed routine as well, not unlike the papers I had signed when I entered the air force, basically reaffirming our security oaths. But two stapled pages stood apart from the rest. As I read them, I got mad: the document was a typed statement as to what each of us had seen in the forest. Each statement was the same—a whitewash of what we had witnessed the night before. It stated that we had only seen some unusual lights in the trees, and nothing more. I couldn't believe it.

An airman named Russell protested the contents of the statement, saying it was not accurate. We were told to sign them and go into Major Zickler's office.

I signed the damned thing and walked into the chief's office. Two rows of metal folding chairs had been set up. At the front of the room was a movie screen. I noticed one of the guys in our group looked very distraught; I remembered him as having been noticeably upset out in the forest. Immediately, we were told to sit down and not to talk.

In the far left corner of the office stood three men. Two were dressed in suits and looked like civilian businessmen. The third wore a naval officer's uniform. Each had a laminated photo ID affixed to his lapel. I tried to read what the IDs said but wasn't close enough.

I felt safer taking a seat in the second row, feeling somewhat less exposed. Directly behind me stood a movie projector on a table with a reel of film ready to go. My first thought was that we might have to view training films, as we had in tech school. Again Major Zickler told us to give full cooperation to the debriefers, then left his office.

As soon as the door closed, the navy officer stepped forward and introduced himself as Commander Richardson of the Office of Naval Intelligence (ONI), based in London. Of average height and maybe thirty-eight years old, Richardson seemed pleasant. He then introduced the two men in suits as representing the Armed Forces Security Service (AFSS).[2] They were only introduced as members of that agency and given no military rank. They looked intimidating.

Commander Richardson told us that we were being brought together to understand our circumstances better and our government's policy on situations relating to the previous night's events.

He went on to tell us straightforwardly that what we had seen in the forest represented technology far advanced to our own. You could have heard a pin drop. He said that numerous civilizations visit this planet from time to time, and that some are a "permanent presence here." "Our government has known of this for longer than most of you in this room have been alive."

Amazing as it was, he seemed quite comfortable with what he was telling us. I had the impression he was giving us a lot of "information" and very little hard-core fact; nothing you could quote with much confidence or accuracy. Nevertheless, what we heard was amazing! The two AFSS agents remained quiet throughout Richardson's lecture, but their eyes scanned the room constantly.

Though Richardson made himself accessible, I never asked a question. Nobody else did either. Every airman in that room was scared. We were told that our security clearances had been upgraded (I had had a SECRET clearance up to that time). In the event we talked about the UFO, we'd face stiffer penalties for doing so.

Richardson continued: We were not to discuss any aspects of the incident with anyone on base. If pressed on what we saw, we were only to say that we had seen some lights in the trees, nothing more. The local press might already have gotten wind of what had gone on, and we were to have our guard up just in case. We were not to write about it in letters home or discuss the topic on the phone. It was implied that if we did, we could face a court-martial, or worse.

Then we were fed a lot of propaganda on how our country was counting on us to cooperate. It seemed the main concern was that we not stir up people on base. It would disrupt the mission, our job performance, and so on. I wanted to know who *they* were. The AFSS guys remained silent about that aspect.

Richardson then told us we were going to view a film that should help us understand how serious the matter was, and the need for so much security. One of the AFSS men switched off the lights. The other walked behind me and turned on the projector.

The first segment was World War II–era footage, shot through the canopy of an aircraft. Far below was a body of water. Though the film was a grainy black and white, it had obviously been shot on a bright, sunny day. Suddenly six or seven disklike objects passed under the plane in a perfect V formation. As soon as the disks flew out of sight, that segment ended.

The next part was Korean War era, again black and white. Shot from the ground, the film showed the jagged, mountainous terrain Korea is known for. A North Korean MIG appeared in the upper right of the frame and looked to be in the process of attacking a target on the ground just out of sight of the camera. Suddenly a bright ball of light passed the right wing of the MIG and vanished at tremendous speed. The MIG then spiraled toward the ground, out of control, and exploded into a hillside. Rather unsteadily, the camera panned back to the open sky, and the clip ended.

The next segment, in color, stood out from the previous footage. This was shot with a handheld camera, at what looked like a Special Forces firebase camp somewhere in the highlands of Vietnam. The sun was bright. It showed some soldiers, a few without shirts, goofing off and mugging for the camera. One was wearing a green beret with the red flash of the Seventh Special Forces Group.

Then, some men in the front started pointing down the hill. The camera followed. Beyond the bloodred dirt hill, past the concertina razor wire, was dense jungle of low scrub, vines, and brush, along with a few trees. Then you saw it: a dark green, almost black, boomerang-shaped object slowly rising out of the jungle. Vines fell from its surface back to the jungle floor as a few birds flew past. The object rose steadily with the camera following until it was a small, black dot. Finally, the sun whited out the image.

Next were rapid clips from space missions showing clearly defined objects next to Apollo spacecrafts. Then came spectacular footage from the surface of the moon—three disklike objects were perched on a crater rim. Also, brief shots of strange, boxlike structures on the moon. After about fifteen minutes, it was over.

There had been no narration, and no further explanation of what we had seen followed.

The lights came back on. The AFSS agents spoke. One of them said it should be clear to us now why there was a need for security. Then we heard more propaganda. I was getting angry about the head games being played. To my left, I heard a low, droning sound. I looked to see the guy next to me; he had his eyes closed and was praying under his breath. On his lap was a small Bible. I knew some of the guys were starting to crack; I think the debriefers knew, too. Was that their intention?

I refuse to crack, I told myself. These guys were being so subversive about what had happened to *us*. I felt more angry than scared. After more propaganda, I finally asked a question: What would happen if we talked about the UFO? One of the AFSS agents responded that we could have great careers in the air force or the civilian world, if we were smart enough to toe the line. "One or two of you won't," but he felt that would be no problem. "Bullets are cheap," he said with a smile. We all laughed; it was sick. We had just been threatened, and yet we laughed and smiled, like kidnap victims with their kidnappers.

The ONI officer ended the debriefing by telling us to forget about it and get on with our lives. Then the chief came back in to his office and dismissed us. I left the building quickly.

Outside, I saw another bunch of guys waiting for their debriefing. Most had the rank of sergeant and above; Bustinza was one of them. The day had turned cold and overcast; I walked toward Bentwaters housing. On the way, Steve Longaro joined me. Steve said he'd learned that a few men had been sent out to the forest to create a false landing site, Penniston among them. The brass, it seemed, expected the media in some form or another. I knew that many civilians must have seen *some* part of the incidents and wondered what the air force planned to do with them. The night before, we had all heard about the English guy law enforcement had caught at the forest perimeter with a camera. This thing was too big to be kept quiet.

In the afternoon, I went to the rec center for a hot dog and a Coke. A woman named Vicki worked there, and it was always good to see her.

Inside, I saw Greg Battram and we started to talk. After a minute or two, he paused, then said that he had been out there, too. He'd arrived before we had and witnessed earlier aspects of the landing. Among several airmen already heading back to Woodbridge base at the time, he'd actually seen my group arrive on site. I did remember the pickup truck passing four armed airmen walking toward us along the logging road.

I knew I was breaking the rules, but I just didn't care: I told him the whole story. I trusted Greg. We'd gotten to know each other back in Texas; I also respected him because he had been a marine in Vietnam.

I ran through recollections of the entire event. Greg had also seen the yellow mist on the ground, but then the men he was with got scared and moved out of the area. When I finished, he seemed shaken, but disappointed that he had missed the major event.

I wasn't thinking about the consequences now: I had to call my mother—I knew she would believe me. Greg said the best way to call her would be from a public telephone; that way the call would not be monitored. He even went with me to make the call.

We made our way over to a public phone box near the base commissary. I didn't have enough change for a lengthy conversation, so I reversed the charges. A New York Telephone operator took over from the international operator, and shortly a phone rang in Glens Falls. When my mother picked up, I let loose with a torrent of information.

"Mom, would you believe it, a UFO landed near the base last night."

I just kept talking. I was going so fast she had to stop me: "*What* happened?" So I started again. Suddenly the line went dead. I looked at Greg and told him I'd been cut off. He told me to call the operator and find out what had happened. I got a local operator in Suffolk and told her about the disconnection. She paused a moment, then asked if I was calling from the base. I said, "Yes." "I'm sorry, but you were cut off from the base. Do you want to try the call again?" I just hung up the phone, looked at Greg, and said, "Shit. I'm in trouble." I knew it, and so did he. I told Greg I'd see him later. As I ran back to the dorm, Greg yelled after me, "*Larry, be careful.*"

Back in my room, I wondered if my mother was worried because of the disconnection. I'd write her, some kind of cryptic letter, and let her know I was OK. But I wasn't. It was just before 3:00 P.M. when I got a phone message to report to a Captain Colman at the base communications center on the Bentwaters flight line. I *was* in trouble.

The communications center was a hardened concrete building, half covered with earth and very secure. I was scared to death as I approached the door. Once inside, I was amazed at the array of electronic equipment—lighted grid maps of Great Britain and Europe and what looked like radar systems and satellite tracking equipment.

A tech sergeant led me down a hall and into a small office. There I identified myself as Airman Warren, and Captain Colman, a black officer in his early thirties, told me to sit down. Just then an Office of Special Investigation (OSI) sergeant I recognized came into the room. Colman said he had a few questions for me: "Have you given out sensitive information over the phone?" "No," I said, but the TEAC reel-to-reel recorder on his desk made me feel uneasy.

Colman asked again. This time I didn't answer. He then switched on the tape player, and I listened to the conversation I had just had with my mother. It was brief but incriminating. I told the captain I hadn't meant to cause a problem, but I couldn't help it. The OSI sergeant said I could receive a letter of reprimand out of this, but felt he could talk Major Zickler out of it. Captain Colman then offered me a choice: the loss of my stripes or a three-hundred-dollar fine, to be deducted in monthly increments. I chose the fine; my stripes would take forever to get back.

I signed a payroll-deduction form, then Colman told me he didn't care what I'd been talking about, but he advised me to review some books on communications security. The OSI sergeant said I should keep my mouth shut. I agreed and was told I could leave. I stood, saluted, and left.

Outside, it was still cold and gray, but I felt a great sense of relief—it was over. At that moment, I decided I would put the whole thing out of my mind. I couldn't do anything about it anyway.

Walking down the hill toward the roundabout, I noticed a giant oak tree full of black birds, I mean *hundreds* of them, just sitting on its branches. The sight reminded me of Alfred Hitchcock's *The Birds*, but the sight also had a calming effect on me. Suddenly, an RAF Vulcan bomber flew overhead. The noise was deafening and the ground shook. The birds scattered in all directions, filling the sky in panicked flight. The old oak tree was now bare. My sense of dread returned.

3. | UNDERGROUND

It was now dark, five, maybe six o'clock. I reflected on my lenient treatment at the Office of Communications Security (COMSEC) squadron. Only a small fine and no letter of reprimand. Man, I was lucky.

I knew my mother would be concerned. Had she heard all I said on the phone? Probably not. I'd have to write her a letter and mail it from one of the towns off base. No one would know, and I'd be free to say more about what had happened.

I was drained of energy, but it was too late to get any sleep. I'd have to catch up in the morning, maybe after a six-pack—and boy, did that sound good. Eating was out of the question. I had no time. I walked downstairs to the dayroom and caught the news on ITV and a little bit of *Fawlty Towers*. The dorm phone rang, and my friend, Dave, answered it. I heard him say from the hall, "Yes, he's right here," as he pointed the receiver in my direction. I had a sinking feeling as I approached the phone. Every time the phone rang that day, I found myself in more hot water.

"Hello, Airman Warren?" "Yes, this is Warren." I didn't know the male voice on the other end. The call sounded as if it were a long-distance connection, as if the caller's voice were in a vacuum. "Airman

Warren, could you meet a car in the dorm parking lot in twenty minutes?" I asked, "Who are you?"

The voice responded that it wasn't important, "Please meet the car in *twenty* minutes." I asked how I would recognize the car. The voice said, "It will be a dark-blue sedan, upscale, you'll know it when you see it!" I asked if his request concerned the UFO incident. "Yes," the voice responded. "Am I in trouble? Will I be late for my shift? I have to work tonight."

The answer to both questions was "no." He continued: "You do not have to be in uniform. And Warren, remember, twenty minutes. OK? Another airman will be with you. You won't miss the car, will you?" "No, sir." The man hung up. While staring at some pro-IRA graffiti on the wall in front of me, I hesitantly did the same.

Upstairs in my room, I grabbed a heavy jacket and headed for the parking lot. The weather had turned colder and more winterlike, but the brisk air sharpened my senses. I wished I had been stationed in California or a warmer climate. Anywhere but England; it just wasn't fun anymore.

I could see the car now; it looked like a Lincoln town car. As I got closer, its orange and blue New York State plates made me strangely homesick. Across the lot, another airman walked toward the car. It was Adrian Bustinza. He had been in the field with me the night before.

As we neared the car, I turned to Adrian and said, "How are you doing?" He just waved back. The car was in the far end of the lot near the new housing construction site. Not a soul was in the lot with us. The front doors opened. Two men got out of the car; they were dressed in civilian clothes. I can't remember the details of their faces. They opened the doors to the backseat. Once I was next to the car, I looked at the interior before I climbed in. I knew something was wrong: the interior was just too bright, with a greenish glow, as if the dash lights were amplified five hundred times. It was eerie. The men said nothing, and as I bent forward to get in, everything went black. I was in a void. I knew I was seated in the car, and I knew Adrian was next to me, but I couldn't talk or move. However, I could hear. I felt like I'd been anesthetized.

I heard no conversation in the car, though I wanted to hear *anything* to take me out of my semiconscious state. But that's all I can remember until I heard the engine of an A-10 taking off. I was on the Bentwaters flight line. I knew it, but that was all I knew. Suddenly, I felt fresh air hit my face; I could smell it. I was now out of the car and walking or moving in some direction. I sensed people around me, but I was never touched or pushed.

Next I had a definite sensation of descent, as if I were in an elevator, causing pressure changes in my ears. Then I lost consciousness. Regaining my vision, I found myself in a small cafeteria-style dining area, complete with stainless steel and glass serving areas. The workers wore standard sanitary caps with white overalls. A few airmen were scattered around the room at different tables, looking very lost. I felt heavily sedated.

A hamburger was on a tray in front of me, but I cannot remember eating. The lighting was strange, the walls were covered in cream-colored tiles. Next, I was walking along a hallway. This image is very clear: rooms containing high-tech machines and computers of some sort and male and female technicians dressed in orange and blue uniforms lining each side of the narrow corridor.

I was in a small group of airmen; leading the way were two men dressed in black SWAT-type uniforms. They said little if anything to us as we stopped in front of a large, pressurized door. A small alarm sounded as the seal was electronically broken. The massive door quietly moved to the right, disappearing into the tiled wall. I remember our being motioned forward into a large, semidark, rectangular-shaped room. The lighting was, again, strange, with a dull, silvery tone to it. To my left was an opening in the wall. The floor continued about five feet into it and ended at an angled glass, or Plexiglas, full-length window with glass sides for peripheral vision. The opening was perhaps six feet tall by four feet wide. Only two or three people could fit into it at a time.

I stepped into the confined area and felt as if I was no longer on earth. I found myself looking into a *gigantic*, dark cavernous space. It reminded me of the interior of the Houston Astrodome in a strange way. Beads of humidity rolled down the other side of the seamless glass. Far below, I saw movement on a liquid black floor—perhaps people, perhaps not. Also, an object much like the one I'd seen the night before, but not so illuminated, was resting in a far corner of the facility. In the black void were other strange objects, all different in shape, slowly flying across my line of sight.

I looked to my right to see a large opening in a wall; it looked familiar to me. I'd seen something similar before—I just couldn't remember where. The curving tiled walls looked wet, and three large bands of light were visible from my vantage point. One of our escorts said it was a tunnel that led to the North Sea.

I turned away and was directed to the large door along with the other men. It opened. We were now motioned forward. Turning left, we walked down a longer hallway and entered a small room. There we were directed to large, red cushioned chairs; they looked a little like airplane seats. I sat in the first row, Adrian was to my right. Directly in front of us was a large translucent screen, about five feet tall and four feet wide. Suddenly, I could do nothing but look straight at it; my head could not turn left or right. I was frozen in place. The screen grew bright, yet the light was soft on my eyes. Through it, I saw a silhouette of somebody, but detail was impossible to make out.

I didn't feel any fear at this time. I had a heightened sense of curiosity, along with an intense need to talk to the small figure behind the screen. It never moved. But all around me I knew conversation was taking place. I couldn't hear it, I *sensed* it. I don't know how long it was before its voice pierced my brain, but when it did, I was amazed. A strange sensation indeed: somebody was talking to me without words, yet I was fully aware of the conversation. The voice was soft and reassuring, definitely male, with an accent I couldn't identify.

It would be impossible to try to repeat the interaction verbatim because I can't remember the order of the conversation. Some points stand out clearly, though. The voice communicated telepathically. It addressed me by my first name. The voice went on to demonstrate a great familiarity with events from my life: my being adopted, my parents' separation, my love of music and creativity, my disappointment with religion, my instinct for aggression, and my quest for inner and outer peace. It knew I had an open mind. The voice knew my strengths and weaknesses and ended every statement or description of my life by saying, "Do you remember?"

I wasn't offended by the intrusions; I never felt threatened. Each time it asked if I remembered, I did not answer; I knew it didn't mean for me to remember events of my life. It wanted me to remember something else, but I couldn't, or didn't want to.

I "thought back" at the figure during a lull in the conversation. I asked who it was and where I was. Its response was direct and to the point. The figure was a being from a place I would never understand. It was not from my reality. It never said another planet or anything like that. It only made the point that I could not comprehend what it was or where it came from.

It went on to say that I was in a facility far below the air bases. The installations contained many of its kind, along with human support personnel. The facility had been there since the 1940s and expanded in the late 1960s. The crafts they traveled in entered and exited via an extensive tunnel system. One exit was a mile off Lowestoft, Suffolk, another, near the Orford Key.

The silhouette went on to say there are many civilizations from off this earth existing here; they are intimate with the U.S., USSR, U.K., and Japanese governments at their highest levels and have been here since World War II. I was disturbed when it said religion was created for the human race, and still don't believe it. Maybe I just don't want to. It went on to say the cold war was nonexistent and that third-world countries are where our future battles would be fought.

Its race has blended into our society at all levels. This facility is one of many processing zones throughout the world. This facility and others like it are vital; contamination safeguards are in place to ensure this, one being the technical ability to make Bentwaters and Woodbridge bases vanish. I didn't know what that meant, but assumed it to be in the literal sense.

I was selected, along with others, because "they" knew us. I vaguely remember it telling me about politics and corporations and that I would not remember most of my experience, mainly for my own protection. The last part of the communication was like a farewell. The being said: "Larry, in your life, strive to remember." Once again, I fell into blackness.

I regained consciousness while walking through a door. The sunlight was brilliant. As the door slammed shut behind me, I noticed to my left a few airmen working on a light-all while a crew chief barked orders at them. To my right, two A-10s were taxiing for takeoff. Across the road, a lone security policeman was manning his post in a priority-aircraft area. A car passed, containing some pilots. They were laughing about something, maybe the mission that awaited them, or maybe at the "snaps" picking up garbage with pointed sticks. I was back, but from where? I turned around with a vengeance and opened the door I'd just passed through. I had taken two steps forward when a female administrative clerk behind a desk asked if she could help me. I stared at her, looking for any hint or expression on her face that would tell me she knew—there was nothing.

"No, thank you," I said, then turned and left the building, the Bentwaters photo-processing lab. I walked quickly to a transport bus and got aboard. During the ride back to the dorm area, I strove to remember all that had happened while simultaneously wanting to kill the memory. Everyone on the bus was excited because that night was New Year's Eve.

Back at my dorm, a note on my door informed me that I'd be changing shifts and would not have to report for work until the start of the next week on 2 January. It was signed by my shift supervisor.

I ran into Steve LaPlume in the hallway. He asked where I had been the last two days. He said, "Larry, I heard you were on emergency leave." I didn't know how to answer him. Two days—what the hell was going on?

I remember buying two bottles of champagne that day and hiding one near a garbage dumpster, should I need it. I was invited to a New Year's party at the women's barracks that night. I plied myself well with beer and champagne and recall how important it seemed at one point to try to fit inside a refrigerator; I got trashed.

A few brief hours into 1981, Rick Bertalino and Lieutenant Colonel Halt entered the room and ordered all males out of the building. It was past curfew. I remember Halt extracting me from the refrigerator and asking if I was OK to get home or would I need a ride. I turned and put my arm on his shoulder, wished him a happy new year, and offered him a drink of champagne. He declined and showed me to the door. Once outside, as I staggered across the lawn en route to my dorm, a girl I knew called me from her first-floor window. I walked back to the building and, with a short run, dived through her open window, taking out her stereo in the process. I think I passed out when I hit the floor. I never did make it to that second bottle of champagne.

As the first morning of 1981 dawned, I woke with one of the worst hangovers of my life, and, worse, a new insight I didn't want: I'd left part of my soul somewhere underground.

4. | *1981—*
WE HAVE TO TELL SOMEONE!

The year 1981 came in like a lion, and it seemed appropriate—I felt as if I'd been caged in a psychotic circus. Nobody was talking about the UFO, at least none of us who'd been directly involved. The debriefing's fear tactics and propaganda were working. I felt alone, horribly alone, and was desperate to find a way out of Bentwaters forever.

On 6 January, I wrote a letter to my mother. It was postmarked the seventh:

Dear Ma, Sam & Mike,

How's things at home—I hope good—I am o.k. Please don't be too upset that it has taken me so long to write. I think that was because I told you all I was doing on the phone and could not think of anything to say. . . .

Remember I was telling you about that U.F.O. that landed—well I'll tell you the whole story on it. Over Europe and England a bunch of lights were seen—Over London one of the lights broke into about twenty smaller lights—and flew in all directions. At about three in the morning, a guy I know in D-Flight of Security Police told me he responded to a falling star outside the Weapons Storage Area—I can't tell you what they keep in there but use your imagination! Anyway he reported it and then everyone started feeling strange—then a guy on the Backgate at Woodbridge reported a bright light moving through the pine forest. An officer and two sergeants responded but they could not take weapons because they were off base.

Over the radio they reported seeing a pie-shaped object—about 7 by 8 ft in size. But they said every time they would get near it, it would seem farther away all of a sudden. They also said that all of the animals in the forest were going nuts.

Then all of a sudden the light went out—and over the radio they said they didn't like the situation and wanted to go back to base—but they were told to keep on investigating.

Then they said the thing appeared behind them—it seemed like it was playing games. After 3 and a half miles of following the thing through the countryside and woods—the thing just disappeared in a field—it was only about 10 ft off the ground. This is what a friend of mine said he heard on the radio.

At that same time, me and five other guys were walking up a dark path about 2 miles from base . . . cause we couldn't get a ride and we felt like we were being watched and it was strange cause there were no street lights—Then we saw a bright light go right over us about 50 ft up and just fly over a field. It was silent. We first thought it was an A-10 Jet. But they scream. So we ran away, because witchcraft and black magic is big in this part of Suffolk and we thought that witches were in the woods. That light just seemed to jump over the trees—Then the next day it turned out that we were in the same place as the U.F.O. so I think we saw it too. Now the three people who saw it can't and won't talk about it at all. And supposedly no animals have gone back into the woods yet—They did find two landing sights—and supposedly some equipment left behind.

A big C-130 came in and took something in a crate away a few days later and the guards were flown in from somewhere else—it is strange, and now I hear that strange things have been going on in the forest for the past weeks—and remember we *did* get cut off on the phone. . . . Say hi to everyone and I'll call soon.

Love, Larry

P.S. The picture is of me in London about a month ago . . . tell Sam to write.

(P.S. Ma, When I get home I'll tell you the truth about the U.F.O.: I can't in the mail, they read it!)[3]

A few days later I found myself reassigned to the administrative section for security police. Here, I was always under the watchful eye of OSI personnel who shared the office. I'd identified myself as a security risk early on; obviously, the brass were taking no chances with me.

For the most part, my days were spent running errands and making coffee for the office. In one respect, my reassignment was great: I now worked nine to five and had my weekends off, just like real people. But I felt a lot of animosity about not being on the flight line with D Flight. Major Drury explained that my reassignment was just a matter of good sense; it was felt that my strong communications skills would be more valuable in the SP communications center. In no way should I interpret the reassignment as any sort of negative reflection on me. I didn't believe a word of it.

On 19 January, I was handed orders for Ramstein AFB in West Germany. I couldn't believe my eyes: I was to be included in a small group of security police, who, along with a few K-9 units, would be leaving base the next morning by C-130 transport plane. We were heading to Germany to provide security and crowd control for the American hostages who were about to return from Iran! As their release had not yet been announced to the press, we were advised not to discuss our assignment until after our return. I felt proud to be part of the event.

I will always remember the smiles on those men's faces as they stepped onto the tarmac. I shook hands with the ones who walked past my position, saying to each: "Welcome home." For these people, 444 days of hell were over, and readjustment was about to begin. It was perhaps the first time since the UFO incident I was able to forget about my own predicament for a while. We transferred to Wiesbaden with them and secured the hospital area for the next three days while most were given their first physical in over a year. Finally, it was time to return to RAF Bentwaters, and depression.

Back on base, it was business as usual. Nobody was talking about the incident, and nobody seemed to care that the hostages were free. They just worked and drank, which is what I started to do. In my mailbox, there was a letter from my mother waiting for me, a response to my letter of 6 January.

I had made numerous friends at Bentwaters, some who had gone through the strange events with me; however, we never talked about it. It seemed nobody was even thinking about it anymore—very strange. Some of the cops I'd trained with were now snapped out; they had gotten into some sort of trouble and lost their PRP. Most spent their days doing maintenance on the base, waiting for a discharge or a return-to-duty notice. Most were only guilty of hating the base and doing whatever they had to do to get out.

I remained in operations, looking through records to see if I could discover what was really going on. I asked all sorts of questions of people I thought I could trust: the age of the base, construction of certain facilities, and its real role in NATO.

The first week in February, I met a master sergeant who'd been on the base since 1968. He told me that, indeed, there were facilities on the two bases that most people were not aware of but that my digging for information would only get me in trouble. I decided to keep digging.

On a cold, rainy February afternoon, I finally struck gold. It was in the form of a file containing security plans for major subterranean construction under Bentwaters between the years 1966 and 1968. Most of the documents were dedicated to the security of the underground sites and contained instructions dealing with civil engineers and British contractors. They also contained references to construction data listed as restricted, most of which was not in the file.

There was something under Bentwaters that people were not supposed to know about; the file I held established that. Suddenly, it was taken out of my hands by Major Drury, who asked me what the hell I was doing in the file cabinet.

I thought fast and replied that I was only trying to familiarize myself with the complex filing system. Drury then asked what my interest in dated security plans was. I said I loved history and was just curious about the history of the base; also, that as the file was not marked restricted, I'd felt no harm would be done by looking at it.

Major Drury was skeptical, and why not? My nose was as long as Pinocchio's. Drury walked away with the file, but before shutting the cabinet, I glanced at another file titled "Continuing Sub-Facility Security and OPS." That's what I wanted. I'd wait until the next day, but that was not to be—the next morning I was reassigned to the security-police supply section. No reason was given, but it was clear that someone knew what I was up to.

On a Friday afternoon in early February, Steve LaPlume and I were making plans for a trip to London to see The Who in March at Wembley Arena. Steve brought up the UFO topic; I tried to skirt the issue, but it was useless. He told me about an event that had occurred two weeks before the incident. He and an airman Palmer were working a swing shift on Woodbridge base, just shooting the breeze near East Gate, when they caught sight of an unusual light formation moving slowly and silently over Rendlesham Forest. Steve placed a call to Central Security Control to report the sighting. The response of the shift commander at Bentwaters was far from usual. Steve was asked its location, distance, speed estimate, the color of the lights, and other questions. The on-duty shift commander told the two airmen to "remain in position and keep watching the sky for any further activity." Personnel were on their way to check out the object. In fifteen minutes or less, Deputy Base Commander Charles Halt, Wing Commander Gordon Williams, Colonel Sawyer, and other officers were surrounding the two airmen. Steve said the officers were in an unusual state of excitement, "like children at an Easter egg hunt."

Another bizarre element was that some of the officers' wives and children were in tow. Steve pointed out the last known location of the lights, then the officers and their families rushed out into the forest, flashlights and cameras in hand. It was the last Steve saw of them that night. He'd found the sighting most unspectacular, but felt the behavior of the officers had been weird.

It was then I told Steve about the December incident. I didn't tell him that life-forms had been sighted, as I was uncomfortable with the fact and didn't want to risk ridicule, especially from a friend.

That weekend, I traveled to Holland on a three-day break. For a nineteen-year-old, Amsterdam is the biggest amusement park on earth. The red-light district on Canal Street was unbelievable: anything could be had in the pre-AIDS days of 1981.

At 2:00 A.M. the morning after I returned, the door to my dorm room burst open. I made out the forms of two law-enforcement cops and smelled the drug-detection German shepherds sniffing around the room. The cops searched my dresser, closet, under my bed, even through my toiletries. They said they were looking for hash.

I was pissed off and terrified at the same time: I knew I was being set up. I'd half expected it, but drugs—no way. I told the cops, one of whom had had some involvement in the UFO incidents, that they had a lot of nerve trying to fuck over their own people. He replied that I wasn't their people. I told them that, if they found drugs, the drugs would have been planted by them, and I'd be saying so in a major London newspaper office the first thing next morning. Eventually they left, empty-handed.

I sat on the edge of the bed shaking; sooner or later, they would get me. That scare motivated me to start planning a departure from Ben-twaters. I knew I would have to discuss the UFO with other witnesses ASAP; I'd already heard that a few were getting hassled like me. If we could just get together, maybe we could hold the ace card.

Later that day, I caught sight of Bustinza, talking to someone on the day phone. Adrian seemed very angry; he slammed down the receiver and walked away cursing to himself. I would approach him first; I knew he was also disgusted with the way we'd been treated, but I'd have to wait until the time was right.

Many events followed in rapid succession. Some were tragic. One of the first odd things I noticed was that some of my fellow cops, ones who'd also seen the UFO, were suddenly no longer on base. The poor kid who'd read his Bible during the debriefing was so shook up about being told that religion had been invented to maintain order and control that soon after he went AWOL. He flew to Chicago, where he was met by the FBI, put on the next plane to England, and returned to duty. He'd told me he felt the place was evil and that, if he didn't get out, he'd die. Shortly thereafter, he blew his head off while on post. I saw the aftermath of his suicide, and it wasn't pleasant. People who didn't know the truth said he had been unstable to begin with; I knew otherwise.

For the base commanders, the tragedy was just one more thing to cover up. For me, it was one more thing to expose. I believe that in the opinion of some we witnesses might be better off dead. I was not going to end up a statistic. It was time to act.

From late February 1981 on, I worked at the supply section, bored to death. I felt confined and sensed I was being watched by at least one of the sergeants in the office. I got along with all of them just fine, but something was out of sync.

The office was manned by Master Sergeant Fred Smith, Technical Sergeant George Laws, and an airman named Dean Thompson, who had been injured in a motorcycle accident and was awaiting discharge. I found the assignment relaxing, without the usual pressures on the flight line or in operations. The subject of UFOs only came up once, when Thompson asked Sergeant Penniston if he'd seen any UFOs lately. Penniston went right through the roof; he'd been the one who told me to shut up the morning after the incident. I took great pleasure in torturing him, and I think Dean did, too.

After a few weeks, I felt comfortable enough to talk about the incident with the guys in the office. A few days later, Sergeant Laws was replaced by Staff Sergeant Mark Reese. This guy seemed too sharp to be a staff sergeant. He was well-spoken and drove a Datsun 280Z—far out of reach of the average NCO, especially in 1981. He'd arrived at Bentwaters after a long assignment in New Mexico. Reese lived off base and had a girlfriend who worked in crypto, no small feat for someone new to the U.K.; housing on and off base was in great demand, and finding a girlfriend was even more difficult.

Reese and I got along well at first and, as time went on, had a number of in-depth conversations about the air force, England, and life in general. Although he seemed to have it all together, his story stretched my credulity to the limit. Reese never wanted to hang out with me or the other airmen, but always asked what I did on weekends and whom I spent time with, along with other personal questions that I found quite intrusive.

Some weekends I'd attend elaborate parties at an estate called Loudham Hall, about ten miles south of Bentwaters. The estate's owner, a woman named Doby, befriended a number of the airmen and let us have the run of the house. It had seventeen or so bedrooms, and Doby's parents were well connected to the royal family. In the sixties, her mother used to phone the flight tower at Bentwaters and ask that the F-4 Phantoms not fly during her nap time! I've been told that aircraft changed their flight patterns to comply with her request. Doby was known to drive her black Porsche Targa into active aircraft areas just to say "hi" to her friends. She once blocked eight taxiing A-10s with the car so she could drop off lunch to her boyfriend, Jim, a fellow SP.

Doby had some high-profile friends who would drop over from time to time. They included English actor Nigel Davenport, Paul McCartney's brother Mike, the queen's dog groomers, and the CEO of British Petroleum: it was like *The Ed Sullivan Show*. We'd have rap sessions about all sorts of things, including UFOs, but I could never bring myself to give out details about the incident that had occurred only ten miles away.

It was felt by all that there was something strange about the air bases. If only they had known the truth. I felt that my friend from British Petroleum did. Drunk one Saturday, he began to remark about the vast tunnel systems around the base and the headaches they were causing him; he never explained what he meant by that complaint.

I arrived at supply the following Monday morning to find the mood in the office very tense. Sergeant Smith took me aside, pointed to a wheelbarrow, then ordered me to pick up the rocks around the build-ing that gave a "landscape from hell" look. I was to take them across the road, make a pile, dismantle the pile, and reverse the process. I'd confided my thoughts about the situation at Bentwaters to Sergeant Smith the week before. Was the rock incident my punishment? I pro-tested loudly, but without result. It felt as if Smith was carrying out somebody else's orders, and the task was clearly designed to humiliate me.

I saw Sergeant Reese on about my fourth wheelbarrow trip across the road. I was so frustrated, I looked him in the eye. "Mark, do you know what is under this base? Do you know they have a massive facility down there? I've been in it. I saw strange aircraft, and, you know, Mark, there's something else down there, too. Maybe aliens, I'm not sure." My face was red with anger.

The reaction from Reese: "Larry, there is nothing you can do about it, so why push it? That's why you are in trouble. You will never get anyplace pursuing it. Just forget about it."

I looked at the sergeant in complete disbelief. He seemed to have known all along. I felt as if I was in a remake of *Invasion of the Body Snatchers.* But this was true: some people at RAF Bentwaters were not what they seemed to be. I decided to concentrate on getting out of the air force and not making any more waves.

My eyesight had been impaired since that explosion of light just be-fore the UFO appeared. Sunlight hurt my eyes; what appeared to be sea horses floated in my line of sight. I had gone to the clinic on Bentwaters for an exam; a doctor told me I might have burns to my retinas. He sent me to RAF Lakenheath for a more in-depth eye exam in early February. It was later confirmed that I had been exposed to a source of high-intensity light that had caused a degree of damage to my vision. The ranking doctor explained it was as if I had looked di-rectly at a welder's torch for twenty minutes without blinking. He noted the beginnings of scar tissue forming at the inner corner of each eye, recommending a powerful antibiotic eyedrops prescription, and possi-bly glasses. I tried to tell the doctor what had happened, but he didn't want to know.

The base hosted numerous high-ranking U.S. government officials that February and March. They included the secretary of the air force, members of the Joint Chiefs of Staff, and several senators—reasons unknown. In mid-March a temporary duty (TDY) assignment came my way that took me to Egypt for the first Operation Bright Star desert war games. I spent two weeks at a place called Area A, got sunburned, ate bad food, and fell off a camel. I was sad to learn that King Tut was on a major U.S. museum tour, but at least I saw the pyramids.

I returned from the Middle East with a lot of energy and a great tan, the healthiest I'd been since late December. On 31 March 1981, I was unpacking souvenirs in my room when all hell broke out in the hallway: President Reagan had just been shot. First reports said the president was dead. Bentwaters entered a level-two alert status, and I was posted to ride shotgun with law-enforcement patrols. Later that day, the president's condition stabilized, the base's alert status returned to level one, and I returned to SP supply.

Spring was now evident in England and seemed to renew life. Even the air base looked a little better. I was notified that I would be an honor guard for Wing Commander Gordon Williams's testimonial. I would also secure general officers' parking for his change-of-command ceremony the following day on the Bentwaters flight line. Williams had scored his first star and was going to Germany after only a year and a half at Bentwaters.

The next day at the ceremony, I took my post in the general-officer parking area. It was an extravagant affair. High-ranking NATO officers from all over Europe drove past my post. Captain Mike Verrano swung by in his jeep to ask how I was doing. I told him I must have hit my head because I was seeing stars. Verrano laughed and drove off. I had never seen so many generals in one place in my life.

Williams's car stopped at my post, and he rolled down his window: I saluted and wished him success in his new assignment. We maintained eye contact for some time; he knew that I knew. "You look sharp, airman," he said, "and you're doing a good job." His car then proceeded on to hangar sixteen for the start of the ceremony.

I tried to imagine the weight of the UFO incident on the man's shoulders and how he'd dealt with what he knew. I respected him and, in a sense, felt sorry for him. It started to rain, and in time I heard applause. Williams was now a brigadier general; the man had earned it.

That night found me surrounded by our base commanders. I dipped into the martinis and enjoyed myself for the first time in a long while, but Williams looked older than he had when I first met him at the incoming briefing in early December. Other officers I'd seen out in that farmer's field were also present, and they all looked like haunted men.

The next day, Steve LaPlume told me to watch my back—OSI wanted him to set me up. Although he refused to help them, he warned that they were gonna get me on a false drug charge of some sort. "Bullshit," I said. I walked into the OSI office on the flight line and was greeted by two agents. "I heard you had a problem with me!" I announced.

The office door was closed, I was read my rights, and the game of good cop/bad cop began, with one trying to gain my trust while the other made ridiculous accusations. I told them they were full of it and would have to try harder to get anything on me. One of them pulled a file, supposedly about me, and read off a number of drug offenses I'd committed on Bentwaters between August and November 1980.

Hearing myself painted as a Colombian drug lord, I began to laugh. I think the agents thought I'd lost my mind. I told them that if it were true, they'd have had one hell of a case against me. "What do you mean by that, Warren, 'if it were true'?" I slammed the brakes on my laughter and the room fell silent. "If you assholes had done your home-work, you would have known I arrived here on *December* first. You lose, boys," I said with a smile. The "good cop" tossed the file on a desk and told me to get the fuck out of the office. I did.

Later that afternoon, I spoke with Colonel Persky, a base lawyer, about my predicament. Right away, he found a breach of contract on the air force's part: I wasn't doing the job I'd trained to do. Persky advised me to pursue that avenue. He said he felt that someone with considerable power wanted me out of the way. I thought about what I was doing, then signed the Request for Separation form. Persky would handle the rest. All I knew was that, if approved, I was going back to the world, and soon.

That evening I spoke with LaPlume in the All Ranks Club. He was getting out soon, too, and was sorry he'd fallen into OSI's trap. he was my friend and didn't want to get me into any more trouble. Forgiving him was easy. On the TV over the bar, the first shuttle, *Columbia,* was being launched in Florida. America was back in space.

I felt that, with my discharge in progress, it was time to tell some people what had happened in the forest. Throughout April, a number of us met in small groups in the dorms and discussed the implications of the incident. Most of the guys were scared to death, but at least we could vent our frustrations without getting hung out to dry. Some guys cried. The anxiety we all felt was overwhelming.

The last week of April, I received my approval for honorable discharge; the date, 18 May. One extremely foggy night, I found a note pushed under the door to my room. It was from Bustinza. He wanted to talk; a time and place would be decided later. Celebrating at a barbecue, Bustinza told me to meet him in his room that night. I got there about 10:00 P.M., and he threw his roommate out.

Adrian said he knew I was getting out sooner than he and wanted me to have some facts before I left. He and others wanted the story out and felt I could get the ball rolling, and I agreed. He told me that Airman Burroughs had pictures of the UFO and that a few others had other evidence. Adrian had been put through the wringer along with me and found his loyalty to the air force faltering. He had also had earlier UFO experiences and noted that some OSI agents on Bentwaters had been at his last base, a base with a high incidence of UFO activity.

We shared our thoughts about the underground base, and although I was unsure about what was real and what was imagined, he assured me the place existed and was an alien installation. My mind was blown.

Adrian went on to say that the air bases were just a front for such installations. But for what reason? "Go to the newspapers, TV. Do anything to get this out, Larry. The bastards have hurt too many of us to let them get away with it." I agreed. Afterward, he cried and so did I. Then we shook on it. I opened the door to leave, and five eavesdropping airmen fell into the room, just like in a Marx Brothers movie. How would I get the story out? I didn't know, but decided there and then I'd commit every resource I had to force the truth out into the open. I wouldn't turn back!

I shipped some boxes home in early May, but still had tons of stuff to carry. My paperwork had come in, with my orders cut for out-processing at McGuire AFB in New Jersey. But I had one last mission to accomplish before I left the base. At one point in the discharge process, I had to carry my service records from one location to another. On the way, I stopped off at the base print shop, and a friend who worked there ran off copies of every record I had.

I was driven to RAF Mildenhall on 18 May; with me were Greg Battram, Larry Walls, and two other friends. It was tough to say good-bye; we had all been through so much together. As the DC-8 left the ground, everyone on board let out a massive cheer, and I watched as England faded from view.

I spent the next two days out-processing at McGuire and wondering if I'd made the right decision. I knew my family was disappointed, but then they didn't know the truth. Another day passed before I stepped off the Greyhound in Albany, New York, on 21 May. Still in uniform, I wandered about the city and tried to acclimate myself to the U.S. of A. It was hot and very summerlike, and I watched state employees eat their lunches on the lawn of the Empire State Plaza. I looked at the American flag flying over the state capitol building, saluted a navy officer, and had lunch at McDonald's.

My mother met me at the bus terminal at one. During our drive down Capitol Avenue, I wondered if the past six months had been a dream. The incident in the forest and the underground base seemed so unreal to me now. Maybe I just wanted it to be. I wondered what the hell I was going to do with my life now.

5. 1981— BACK TO THE WORLD

My return was not triumphant. America seemed a little worse off than when I'd left it, and the economic recession grew steadily that summer of 1981. In some ways though, it was nice to be back home. I hooked up with some of my old friends, though not Pete Jones, who was sailing the seven seas with the navy; his absence left a gap.

I had little interest in dusting off my guitar or pursuing anything I liked. I had lost my muse. I worked days as a desk clerk in a local motel, drank at night, and, when I got home, fought with my family.

Reagan fired the air-traffic controllers that summer, the Rolling Stones toured the United States, and singer Harry Chapin was killed in a car crash. Meanwhile, I was wasting away. On one of the many nights I hung out with various people, drinking, and behaving as if I were three, I ran into Harold Sawn, an old school friend, and for some reason felt compelled to tell him about the UFO incident. Harold thought it was a pretty wild tale, but I assured him it had happened. Other than my mother, he was the first person I'd spoken with at any length about the incident after leaving the air force.

One night in September, I met my mother at a nearby restaurant for dinner. I'd spent the entire summer doing nothing and knew it. I wanted to tell her I'd decided to reenlist in the air force. After four months of feeling useless, it was an easy decision to make. Earlier that day, I'd gone to the recruiting office and spoken with Jack Gorman, the recruiter who had put me in the air force in 1979. Jack told me reenlisting would be as easy as sliced bread, but he needed my DD214 before we could begin the process. I actually missed the air force now. Just months earlier that thought would have seemed ridiculous to me, but maybe now I could recover the sense of pride I had developed as an air force cop—the pride I'd lost at Bentwaters.

My mother was very happy with my decision—her apartment was too small for the three of us, and my behavior had been erratic at best. I was just impossible to live with.

The decision to go back in made me feel good about myself. Over the next week, I rounded up all the paperwork I would need. Everything proceeded well. The only job openings were in the security-police field, and I decided law enforcement would be the better choice, as security was a rather boring job. I knew law enforcement would involve a lot of police work, so Gorman set me up for the law-enforcement school at Lackland. I didn't need basic training, so requalifying would be a snap.

I waited for Gorman's phone call and finally went down to Albany for another physical. I passed, and the way was now clear to in-process back into the USAF. Jack would call me when an opening became available in the law-enforcement tech school. In the meantime, I kept busy working at the motel and a local radio station at night.

Since coming home, I hadn't mentioned the incident to anyone but our neighbor and family friend, Sue Hickerson. She had been at my mother's apartment the day after the incident, when I called from Bentwaters. Sue remembered the call and my mother's concern when the phone disconnected.

One afternoon, I picked up the phone to call a friend, but didn't get a dial tone. On the other end of the line, I could hear someone moving around what sounded like paper. I said hello about twenty times, but there was no response. Was our phone tapped? I called my sister into the room so she could listen. I'd hang up the receiver, then pick it up, but the moving-paper sounds were still there. Then I could hear voices, distant and indistinct—so did my sister.

By now I was losing patience and began yelling into the receiver, "Is anyone there?" Finally a male voice asked, "Who is this?" and I responded, "This is Larry." "Oh, shit," he said. The connection was broken and the dial tone returned. Our phone service had been disrupted since my return, but I hadn't given much thought to what the problem might be. I did ask a friend who worked for New York Telephone to check out our phone lines. He told me afterward there had been a third, unknown party on the line from time to time. The phone company attempted a trace, but as soon as the process began, the tap would disengage.

Soon after, Jack Gorman called and asked if I had been born. I thought it was a joke at first and told him I was sure I had been but would check into it and get back to him. But his tone was serious: "Larry, this is really strange, the FBI claims they haven't got any record of you." Jack went on to say the FBI is always used for military background checks. I'd gone through the same process in 1979 and had had no problems getting my clearance then.

"What the hell is wrong now?" I wondered. Jack had never encountered a similar difficulty. He asked me to come to the office the next day so we could get to the bottom of the problem.

Gorman felt that an excessive amount of red tape surrounded me and my military records. For instance, he could not understand the reenlistment code on my DD214 service record: a 4-M. Jack said the number 4 meant no reentry into the military; the code letter M was not listed in any of the regulation books at the recruiting office. An ideal reentry code would be 1-A, and I should not have received anything less. I asked if the letter "M" might mean "medical." The medical discharge code was a different letter. Anyway, I had left the air force because of a breach of contract on the air force's part, not mine. That was noted on the DD214. How could I have wound up with a reenlistment code that didn't exist? Every time Jack entered my service number into the air-force central data bank, the return on his computer screen would read: "Do not process. Nothing follows."

Jack promised he'd get me into the air force again. He thought the delay was caused by some error and could be worked out soon. Something told me the UFO incident might be the reason for the problem, but how could I tell that to Jack? He'd laugh in my face. I decided to give him a few days to work out the bugs. If he failed, I'd tell him a little about the incident. If he didn't send me to the rubber room, maybe then we could attack the problem from a different angle.

The end of September was approaching. I *had* to go back to the air force soon: my motel job was seasonal and would end shortly, the job at the radio station didn't pay enough to live on, and I felt like a failure.

Most of the people I'd gone to high school with didn't seem changed at all. I'd been out of high school only a year and a half and knew I'd changed drastically. I sensed that the few people who were aware of my situation looked on it only as an interesting story. *I* was only accepting a small fraction of what had happened in England, and when dreams or memories of certain events came to me, I'd distract myself any way I could. I wasn't sleeping well, and my patience and temperament were severely affected. The problems with my military records only elevated my stress level.

Toward 1 October 1981, I met with Jack and his partner, Larry Schoff, at the recruiting office. Entering the room, the sergeants seemed uncomfortable with what they had to tell me; I knew I'd reached the end of the line. Jack asked me to have a seat. He said that my chances looked pretty bad for reenlistment at this point: "Larry, we just keep on running into stone walls. We can't get any information on you. The FBI won't respond with the clearance information, and the Department of the Air Force has told us not to proceed with any reenlistment concerning you."

Jack went on to say he thought I was being blacklisted and that he had never encountered this problem. "What the hell did you get yourself into over there?" I knew it was time to tell him about the incident. Just then the commander of the office, a senior master sergeant, came into the room, showing great interest in what I had to say.

After about an hour and a half, I finished telling the recruiters about the UFO incident, minus aliens and underground installation—anything that sounded *too* far out. I was somewhat relieved to hear the senior master sergeant say my story didn't surprise him; Gorman and Schoff didn't seem skeptical either. The senior master sergeant told me that because I had stirred up the dust at Bentwaters, the air force, or someone else, didn't want me back in. That was the first time I heard the word "whistle-blower" applied to me. The office commander said that I'd have constant problems if I pursued reenlistment, but suggested I get in contact with my local congressman, Gerald Solomon, to see if he could help. The sergeant said he had seen situations like this before in his almost twenty years of service, and he was powerless to help me.

I felt angry and depressed. The bastards had lied to me at Bentwaters, telling me I could come back in if I wanted to. Now it was quite clear they had just wanted to get rid of me, and my lawyer back at the base had been in on the scam. Christ, he should have told me about the code as he reviewed my application for discharge, but he never did. Now I felt like a fool.

Jack wished me luck, then showed me the door. I felt they were anxious to get rid of me, too. I felt betrayed beyond belief but just couldn't give up. Didn't I have a right to know what was going on?

A few days later, I decided to try enlisting in the army—at least they didn't have anything against me. The sergeant who worked in the office was great and really wanted me in officer's candidate school; he said my test scores reflected leadership ability. His first name was Chip, and he reminded me of myself, only older. He was somewhat rebellious and seemed to know right from wrong. After I explained my situation to him (UFO and all), he became all the more resolute about getting through the bureaucratic bullshit surrounding me. However, the exact same thing happened again: he got drowned in red tape. The last time I saw him, he was almost as mad as I was. He thought it was wrong, the way I was being officially erased. Chip promised he would dig for answers until someone in the Department of Defense told him what was going on with me. He also recommended I complain to my congressman.

The very next morning, I picked up the local paper and was shocked to read that Chip had been killed in a freak car accident. It seemed that a trailer hitch separated from a car and crashed head-on into his. He had been on his way home from work.

The army recruiter's death left me a bit unnerved, but prompted me to visit Congressman Solomon's local office in nearby Saratoga. I spoke in person to one of the congressman's assistants because Solomon was in Washington at the time. She assured me he would look into the matter as soon as possible. I didn't mention the UFO connection because my paperwork was strange enough; any intelligent person would notice that something was amiss.

I left the office feeling confident that Congressman Solomon would find out what was wrong with my records and all would be well. Deep down, though, I sensed I was in over my head. The phone taps, doctored service records, and the FBI's claiming no record of my birth were starting to make some sense. I remembered that AFSS agent who had actually said, ''Bullets are cheap,'' during our debriefing. I wondered how soon it would be until I had an accident.

My mother and sister could not stand my mood swings. One moment, I was confident, the next, lost with no way out. I was getting sick of feeling that reenlistment was like a quest for the Holy Grail. At night, I still drank to forget. My life in Glens Falls had become stagnant. With winter fast approaching, it would only get worse.

I eventually received a letter from Gerry Solomon acknowledging my request for help. In it, he assured me he was contacting the Department of the Air Force; as soon as he got an answer, he'd get back to me. Shortly after this, I received another letter from Headquarters, Air Force Accounting and Finance Center, in Denver, Colorado. It was a bill for $95.42. If I did not remit, the sum would be subtracted from my taxes at year's end. No reason was given for the debt, only that I'd incurred it at RAF Bentwaters.

I knew it was the remainder of my fine for calling home after the incident. I had left the service owing $95.42 of the original $300.00. After what I'd been through, I thought they had a lot of nerve trying to collect the pitiful sum, and I'd be damned if I paid them. I just couldn't believe they played with people in this way.

Soon after, I received another letter from Solomon; attached was a letter written by a Lieutenant Colonel Thomas Alison. It informed Solomon that five months *after* my discharge, the air force's surgeon general and the air training command had disqualified me from reentry because of a disability I didn't even know I had—not being able fully to extend my right arm bilaterally! This disqualification was in no way a negative reflection on my character or prior service record—how sweet!

I couldn't believe it. I hadn't received a medical discharge, and yet I'd been disqualified five months after I'd left for a false medical reason. If the air force maintained I could not fully extend my arm, why had they taken me in the first place? Fully extending my right arm, I picked up the letters, paused a second, and dropped them into the garbage can. The next morning I retrieved the letters; I really didn't know why, but felt that someday I might need them.

As fall turned to winter, I fell deeper into a void: doing menial work for minimum wage, not having a car, and losing my girlfriend. At home, things finally disintegrated.

One night, around the first anniversary of the UFO incident, I got into an argument with my mother. I ended up grabbing my framed basic-training photo from the desk and smashing it against the desk's edge. Shards of glass flew in all directions, and a small piece hit my sister near her eye. My mother pointed to the door, then turned her attention to Sam. I went to my room, packed a suitcase, and left. Nobody had a choice: I had really lost it. Thank God, Sam wasn't injured by the glass.

I closed out the year on a couch at my school friend Paul Perkett's house. Drinking was a constant in my life, and some moments I thought about ending it all. How could things have turned out so bad in just one year?

1981 Developments |

Early January 1981

Shortly after New Year's Day, an unusual observation is reported to RAF Woodbridge. Forestry workers say they have located a number of trees not far from the base perimeter, all of whose tops have been scorched. Their report is met with a simple request: that they make no further mention of the scene to anyone.

Also early in January 1981:

> One of Brenda Butler's trusted contacts at the Woodbridge base passed an astonishing piece of information to her. He said that a UFO had come down in the forest, about 2 miles (3 kilometers) from the base. It seems that this was probably on 30 December. The contact, a high-ranking officer, visited the scene along with the base commander and security personnel. They carried no weapons—these were expressly forbidden. The commander talked for some time with "small aliens" (1 metre) tall and wearing silver suits, who were suspended in "shafts of light" beside the landed craft.
>
> The officer refuses to give Brenda Butler details of the craft's shape which I [Jenny Randles] understood to be quite distinctive. The craft is photographed but without official permission; cameras are confiscated. She agrees to keep the officer's confidence and within four weeks rumors of the incident reach her from other, varied sources. . . . [4]

13 January 1981

> SUBJECT: Unexplained Lights
> TO: RAF/CC

> 1. Early in the morning of 27 Dec 80 (approximately 0300L), two USAF security police patrolmen saw unusual lights outside the back gate at RAF Woodbridge. Thinking an aircraft might have crashed or been forced down, they called for

permission to go outside the gate to investigate. The on-duty flight chief responded and allowed three patrolmen to proceed *on foot*. The individuals reported seeing a strange glowing object in the forest. The object was described as being metallic in appearance and triangular in shape, approximately two to three meters across the base and approximately two meters high. It illuminated the entire forest with a white light. The object itself had a pulsing red light on top and a bank(s) of blue lights underneath. The object was hovering or on legs. As the patrolmen approached the object, it maneuvered through the trees and disappeared. At this time the animals on a nearby farm went into a frenzy. The object was briefly sighted approximately an hour later near the back gate.

2. The next day, three depressions 1 ½" deep and 7" in diameter were found where the object had been sighted on the ground. The following night (29 Dec 80) the area was checked for radiation. Beta/gamma readings of 0.1 milliroentgens were recorded with peak readings in the three depressions and near the center of the triangle formed by the depressions. A nearby tree had moderate (.05–.07) readings on the side of the tree toward the depressions.

3. Later in the night a red sun-like light was seen through the trees. It moved about and pulsed. At one point it appeared to throw off glowing particles and then broke into five separate white objects and then disappeared. Immediately thereafter, three star-like objects were noticed in the sky, two objects to the north and one to the south, all of which were about 10° off the horizon. The objects moved rapidly in sharp angular movements and displayed red, green and blue lights. The objects to the north appeared to be elliptical through an 8–12 power lens. They then turned to full circles. The objects to the north remained in the sky for an hour or more. The object to the south was visible for two or three hours and beamed down a stream of light from time to time. Numerous individuals, including the undersigned, witnessed the activities in paragraphs 2 and 3.

(Signed)
CHARLES I. HALT, Lt Col, USAF
Deputy Base Commander[5]

19 January 1981
Airman Warren receives a memorandum, to the attention of "patient concerned," from the air force clinic at Bentwaters; its subject is Referral Medical/Surgical Appointment. "Sensitive Medical Data" is written on the lower right corner of the envelope.

21 January 1981

Two days later, Joann Warren writes Larry:

> Received your first letter today! I was so glad to receive it, all 7 pages. Thank you for the picture! You look very good.
>
> As you know Larry, the hostages were finally released yesterday. I listened to the radio all day at work and watched TV last night when they were flown into Algiers and then on to Frankfurt. Of course you know me, I cried with each family of the hostages as they talked with them and got their reactions on their release. . . .
>
> Well enough of that! You certainly explained your situation with the UFO and as you know Larry, what was seen by others and yourself was just that, a UFO! It must have been quite an experience! . . . [6]

2 February 1981

Warren keeps his 1:00 P.M. appointment at Lakenheath Hospital. Noted on the blue five-by-seven Medical/Dental Appointment Form is the name of the examining physician, Dr. Echols, and the clinic, Opti/Ret, or Optical/Retinal. "Burn/Exp" is written below; "Exp" stands for "Exposure."

March 1981

The farmer who had made the report to the base on 30 December 1980 is located by Jenny Randles and Brenda Butler but refuses to speak with them, as does the Woodbridge base commander. Jenny writes:

> It is very difficult to evaluate this complex and infuriating affair. Aside from Harry Harris and Dorothy (Dot) Street, no one except Brenda Butler had talked to the personnel from the base who had released this information. All other investigators had come up against a wall of denials . . . we do have the independently recorded testimony of the civilian radar operator and the serviceman who had returned to the USA.[7]

29 March 1981

Larry Warren has written nothing to his family since 6 January. In Glens Falls on a Sunday afternoon in March, a worried Joann Warren writes:

> Dear Larry:
>
> Honey we haven't heard from you in so long, I hope everything is alright? Please drop me a line soon.

I imagine you received my letter about my new job. . . .

Did you go to see the "Who"?

Are things better over there or the same?

Are you eating well?

We miss you honey, as usual I say a prayer for you every night. I will try & write more often, at least once a week. Learning my new job I am quite tired at night, I know you understand!

All our love honey & please write soon. Don't make me worry about you! Take care. . . .

Love, Mom

22 April 1981

Request for Separation

1. I approve the Honorable discharge of A1C Lawrence P. Warren from the United States Air Force to be effective on or about 15 May 1981.

2. I carefully reviewed his application and conclude that the intent of the AFR 39–10, Chapter 3, Section B . . . —(Nonfulfillment of Guaranteed Training Enlistee Program Agreement)—has not been met. Approval of A1C Warren's request to separate from the service is in the best interests of himself and the United States Air Force.

Stamped "Signed," Gordon E. Williams, Colonel, USAF, Commander[8]

16 May 1981

PERSONAL DATA

PREPARED 81 MAY 16:09

REPORT ON INDIVIDUAL

SEPARATION APPROVAL NOTIFICATION

A1C: WARREN LAWRENCE P (SS#)   OFFICE SYMBOL: SPOSD

UNIT: 81 SECURITY POLICE SQ
BENTWATERS RAF UNKIN 09755   DUTY PHONE: 2175

THIS IS AN IN-SYSTEM NOTIFICATION OR CONFIRMATION OF SEPARATION APPROVAL TO BE EFFECTIVE AT 810518. SEPARATION PROGRAM DESIGNATOR KDQ APPLIES. CHARACTERIZATION OF SERVICE CODE 1 APPLIES. AN EXPLANATION OF THE SEPARATION PROGRAM DESIGNATOR CODE AND

CHARACTERIZATION OF SERVICE CODE WILL BE PROVIDED BY YOUR CBPO REPRESENTATIVE AT THE TIME YOU ACKNOWLEDGE THIS NOTIFICATION.

SIGNATURE OF THE MEMBER: (signed) LAWRENCE P. WARREN
DATE NOTIFICATION ACKNOWLEDGED: (written) 15 MAY 81 . . .

CBPO NOTE: AUTOMATIC ACTION HAS BEEN SET FOR GENERATION OF PTI 992 (CONFIRMATION) ON THE SEPARATION
EFFECTIVE DATE. . . .

*NOTE: TERMINATION OCCUPATIONAL PHYSICAL
REQUIRED/CONTACT ENVIRONMENTAL MEDICINE.[9]

18 May 1981
Larry Warren is honorably discharged from the air force.

In Manchester, England, Harry Harris, an attorney, confirms the authenticity of Brenda Butler's military contact. Harris has also spoken with the officer, and details of the account given Brenda a year prior were reiterated. Norman Oliver, editor of the British UFO Research Association's journal, receives a similar account. Rumors of an "air crash" or "something queer" having happened at the air base are labeled gossip, springing from the account of a farmer who'd seen "a brightly lit object descend into the forest."[10]

6. 1982—
BLOWING THE WHISTLE

I couldn't have gotten much lower than I was in January 1982. I spent my days and nights with people lost in drugs and alcohol. My mother and I hadn't spoken for weeks. I found myself getting into some bizarre situations with women, but unable to communicate with any of them. While I was frustrated with people for accepting the norm and blinding themselves to what was really going on, I was doing a fine job of that myself.

Eventually, I did call my mother. She suggested I call my father and ask if I could live with him in Connecticut to get a fresh start. I rejected the idea at first; my dad and I hadn't had a real conversation since my leave from tech school more than a year earlier. I couldn't imagine he'd want to hear from me now. Then, during yet another night of boozing, someone decided to spike my drink with LSD. When the hallucinations wore off, I really felt like killing someone. I realized it was time to get away from Glens Falls.

I called my dad, and he told me the house rules. I agreed to follow them, and the next morning my mother dropped me off at the bus station. I was now on my way to Hartford, Connecticut. It was a relief to escape.

By March, I'd acclimated myself to my new situation. I was having fun again. At twenty-one, I felt life was just beginning. I got a job and a car and had some freedom.

I eventually told my brother, Scott, about Bentwaters, but I don't think he believed any of it. Though I was playing my guitar again and in search of a band, my heart was not in it. I wanted to meet a nice girl, but couldn't find my center of gravity in a real relationship. Not being able to escape my experience at Bentwaters, I thought that once a woman got to know me and my background, I'd get dumped.

By this time, I'd read enough about other people's UFO encounters to know they usually got ridiculed, and I wanted no part of it. I still wanted to get back into the air force. As far as I was concerned, the air force did not have a right to keep me from reenlisting, so I was determined to keep trying.

At the Meriden Recruiting Center in Connecticut, the computer gave the same old response: "Do not process. Nothing follows." Recruiters tried in vain to get any information on me. Once again I felt obliged to tell them an edited version of the UFO incident. When I'd finished, a staff sergeant there looked at me without a hint of surprise and said, "Son, with all the red tape that surrounds your name, you either committed a murder or some other major crime, or what you're telling us is true. I believe you, but I'm powerless to help you." He suggested I give up the quest for my sanity's sake. It felt good to be believed, and I appreciated that at least he'd been honest with me.

I was noticing that most of the senior military people I talked to about the UFO did not seem surprised. Some of them told me about other UFO accounts they had heard in the service—some sounded as wild as mine. It was obvious a number of these recruiters felt the air force and other branches of government had a hand in some sort of UFO cover-up. It had taken me almost two years to accept, but I was beginning to realize that I was a sacrifice to that cover-up.

I pressed on, trying the army again, and again was shot down. The Department of Defense even told one recruiter that they had no record of my ever having been in the air force! It amazed me: at the congressman's level, I'd been discharged on the basis of a nonexistent medical condition; at the recruiter's level of available information, I did not exist.

In Southington, Connecticut, an army recruiter advised me to try to gain access to my files via the National Military Records Center in Saint Louis. The center contains the records of every American ever to have served in the military, from the Revolutionary War to the present. I found the phone number through information, called, and made contact with a very helpful woman. She asked my Social Security number, branch of service, and date of discharge, then promised to call me back when she had my records in her hand.

That afternoon, I told my father about the latest steps I was taking to get back in. He still didn't know what had happened to me in England; I'd been afraid he wouldn't believe me and was holding off telling him until I had to. I was sure he was confused by the problems I was having with reenlistment. The time to tell him was fast approaching.

Later that day, the woman from the Military Records Center called back to say she had not been able to locate my service record. Somehow I wasn't surprised. Frustrated, she explained how highly unusual it was that records as recent as mine should be so difficult to access. My dad, who was in the room, gave me a sideways glance. He wanted to know what was happening on the phone.

I asked her if she could give me any advice, as I'd been having similar problems for months. She advised me to get in touch with Randolph AFB in Texas, where the USAF kept its central data bank. If my file could not be tracked down there, at least they could tell me where it had been sent. She gave me their phone number and asked me to call her the next day; she wanted to check a few more avenues before giving up. I thanked her and hung up the receiver. After updating my father, I called Randolph.

After speaking at length with a staff sergeant, I asked him if he thought I was being jerked around. He asked me to stay on the line while he brought up my service record on his screen. After about five minutes of silence, the sergeant said that he thought I *was* being jerked around. "Larry, I want you to talk to my boss. Let's see what he can find." He transferred me to a Captain Green, who asked for an overview of my problem. After hearing of my failed attempts to rejoin the air force, he found he was able to access only the most basic information on me. The rest was restricted, including the whereabouts of my military records.

I then told Captain Green the restriction might be due to an incident I was involved in at RAF Bentwaters in 1980. He paused, then responded: "I know what you're talking about. You're gonna have trouble." I had not mentioned anything about UFOs. He simply knew.

Green suggested I try my congressman. There was nothing he could do from Randolph. The decision to restrict my service record had been made in a high place. I *had* tried my congressman, I said, and he couldn't help; with that, our conversation ended. Pissed off, depressed, and a little scared, I wondered how much longer I could go on fighting.

Calling Saint Louis again, I spoke with the same woman. She told me that after putting several fruitless hours into the search, she'd met with the director of the records center. Did I have a pencil and paper handy? she asked. She had some instructions to relay to me. Early that morning, a directive concerning me had been faxed from the Department of Defense in Washington. It stated that, due to the sensitive nature of my service time, if I wanted to see my files, I must first secure legal representation and appear, with counsel, in Washington at a pre-arranged date. There we would meet with the Department of the Air Force board of eligibility advisers, including their own legal representation. A determination would be made concerning the requested access; there was no guarantee I would get it.

The woman told me she had seen this happen a few times before, and the process could end up costing a lot of money. My records, she said, were now stored with the National Security Agency (NSA) at Fort Meade in Maryland. The agency's name went in one ear and out the other. I thanked her and hung up; I felt I'd lost.

In early April, my father told me of a business associate who was also a colonel in the Connecticut National Guard. Dave was a good acquaintance; he and my father both worked in the insurance industry and were frequent golfing partners. Recently, my father had told Dave about the trouble I'd been having and asked if he could help in any way.

As my father talked, it occurred to me that if Dave could just get me past the bullshit, why shouldn't I join the National Guard? I was in school, studying for a career in media and broadcasting, and the guard could pay for it.

On a rainy Saturday, my father and I drove north of Hartford to the headquarters of the Connecticut National Guard at Bradley Field to meet with Dave. We had a productive talk, and without mentioning the UFO incident, I summed up the problems I'd been having with the air force. Dave laughed and with confidence said he would get through the red tape—I would be in the service again.

By June, I began to wonder what had happened to Colonel Dave. We hadn't heard a word from him since our meeting. My father said he'd be seeing him in a few weeks at an insurance-industry function and he'd find out what he could then. Around this time, I started having some strange experiences at my father's house.

Sometimes during the day, sometimes at night, I'd see helicopters passing over our neighborhood. They had camera-like equipment suspended from their undercarriages, and you couldn't make out any markings or numbers on them; they were painted a very dark green or black.

We were finally getting cable television in Southington, and utility trucks were a common sight in our neighborhood. One day, an unmarked van parked across the street from our house, and a man on the passenger's side got out. The guy aimed a camera with a telephoto lens on our property and began snapping away in broad daylight. Some of our neighbors were watching as well.

One night in late June, I woke up to see what looked like at least five small people in my bedroom. I sat up and cleared my head, but they were still standing there, staring at me. Then they just faded away. I was scared, but fell back to sleep.

The next night at dinner, my seven-year-old brother, Bill, announced that he hadn't slept very well the night before because an "airplane" had come to his window and "sang to him." I felt very uncomfortable about Bill's story, but kept my mouth shut: Dad, Sandy, and Scott attributed it to a dream.

A week later, my father told me he had run into Colonel Dave, but that Dave hadn't seemed very happy about their meeting. Dave basically ignored him at the insurance function, and when my father *did* ask if he had made any headway in my case, Dave just shook his head and walked away. I could tell that my father was concerned.

Feeling responsible for this latest event, I knew it was time to tell my father and Sandy what had happened at RAF Bentwaters. I felt my dad would be the last to believe it; he was so practical and well-grounded. For the next two hours, they sat and listened as I recounted my experiences at the base. When I'd finished, we just sat in the kitchen and stared at one another for what seemed an eternity. My father broke the silence. "I believe you," he said. "Now it all makes sense." Sandy was as open-minded and supportive as anyone could be. My father felt the colonel had found out something that had scared the hell out of him. Whatever it had been, they never spoke after that. I was relieved to get it off my chest.

Even so, disturbing, recurring dreams troubled my sleep. I didn't

rest any easier knowing our government routinely covered up the kind
of incident I'd been involved in, and I wondered how the other guys
were dealing with their memories. Were any of them going through
the kind of hell I was? I was progressing quite well at school and busy
with work. As time passed, UFOs were finally becoming the last thing
on my mind, and I liked it that way.

In September 1982, I met a wonderful girl named Cindy. She really
had a lot of soul and was intelligent and a few years older than I. Soon
we found ourselves in a steady relationship. I was damned if she was
going to find out about Bentwaters—that would end everything.

In late December, I was having a terrible time with a wisdom tooth,
and my father suggested I visit his dentist. I ended up having oral
surgery. Back home and on pain killers for the twelve stitches in my
jaw, I started thumbing through the *Hartford Courant* when a photo in
the living section stopped me cold: a woman with a model of an alien.

The woman's name was Betty Andreasson, and the copy went on to
recount her UFO experience and abduction by the type of alien depicted in the model. There was also an interview with her husband,
Bob Luca, a mechanic at Middletown Toyota. They lived in Cheshire,
Connecticut, only one town over from Southington.

I don't know why, but my first reaction toward these two people I'd
never even met was anger. Then, after briefly ridiculing them to myself,
I ran to the phone, dialed Middletown Toyota, and asked for Bob.
When he picked up the line, I said that I had been involved in a military
UFO incident and needed to talk to someone about it. Bob was easy-
going and suggested we meet the next night for coffee at his and Betty's
home. I got their address, thanked him, and said I'd see him tomorrow,
but hung up the phone wondering why I'd even called.

The next night, I arrived at their home feeling apprehensive. Betty
and Bob's warmth and openness soon put me at ease. A terrific artist,
Betty had numerous artworks around the house depicting various
phases of her experience. As we walked into their living room, I nearly
fainted at the sight of Betty's full-scale papier-mâché alien standing in
the corner.

We ended up talking for hours about our experiences. As best I
could, I drew them a sketch of the Bentwaters UFO and provided numerous details of the incident on paper: names, locations, approximate
date. Betty told me they had two friends who were writing a book on
the government cover-up of UFO incidents. Betty said the men, Larry
Fawcett, a Coventry, Connecticut, police lieutenant, and Barry Green-

wood, a Massachusetts UFO researcher, would probably be very interested in talking with me. They were, in fact, founders of an organization called Citizens Against UFO Secrecy, or CAUS. Bob promised to contact Larry Fawcett for me. Perhaps we could all have dinner together the following week. That was fine by me.

Bob asked if I'd considered going public with my experience. I said I hadn't really thought about it. Betty then told me about the ups and downs of being in the public eye on the subject. From the way she described it, it did not sound easy or enjoyable, and there was little to gain. She said that because no former military person had ever come forward with such a claim, I'd likely be attacked from both sides—first by the skeptics, then by the UFO research community itself. The prospects were not appealing, but it was an idea to think about carefully.

Before I left, Betty inscribed a copy of *The Andreasson Affair* to me; the book had been written by Raymond Fowler, a respected writer in the field, documenting many of her experiences. I was glad I'd taken the chance and called Bob; they were terrific people and had helped me to put my experiences in some perspective.

During the drive home, I shrugged off the thought of becoming a public figure in the UFO field. I'd only be laughed at and attacked. Who needed that? Besides, this Larry Fawcett guy wouldn't find anything on Bentwaters, at least not in government records.

1982 Developments |

February 1982
Airman Terry Bastian flies to England for duty at RAF Bentwaters:

> We got there in February of '82 just after all this had happened, and you heard stories just like everyone else did around the base about the UFO landing. . . .

While stationed at Bentwaters, the airman explores much of the surrounding area on his own time. Despite his interest in the UFO incident and an awareness of the landing site's location, at no time during this two-year period does Terry walk the expanse of Capel Green or any of its immediate surroundings: "It was an off-limits location."[11]

May–June 1982

The American magazine *Frontiers of Science* reports this variation of the third night's incidents:

> An utterly fantastic UFO case is under intense investigation in England. If true, it could be the breakthrough ufologists have been waiting for.
>
> As reported in the January 1982 issue of *Case Histories*, published by the Northern UFO Network (c/o Jenny Randles . . . , England), the story is this:
>
> On December 30, 1980, a farmer in the vicinity of Rendlesham forest . . . called Woodbridge Air Force Base to report a plane crash. The base police investigated and reported the "plane" was a UFO. Someone from the base newspaper went to the scene with both still and movie cameras and filmed the object on the ground.
>
> The base commander took a high-level security team to view the damaged object. According to a member of the team, three entities (about three feet tall and dressed in silvery suits) were suspended in mid-air beside the craft, repairing the damage. The commander is said to have spoken with the entities while they worked. Four hours later the craft took off at great speed.
>
> The commander confiscated all cameras and imposed a total news blackout on the incident. According to one source, the U.S. Air Force arrived several days later and took tapes of radar trackings of the UFO. The story could be dismissed if it weren't for the fact that various aspects of the account have come from independent witnesses—several of them firsthand, all so far unidentified. More on this astonishing case as details become available.[12]

In his book *Clearing the Air*, newsman Daniel Schorr refers to the NSA as "one of the deepest secrets." Former CIA official Victor Marchetti calls it "the most secretive member of the intelligence community," and Harrison E. Salisbury, Pulitzer Prize–winning former editor and correspondent for the *New York Times*, writes, "Not one American in 10,000 has even heard its name." In addition, Moscow's *Literary Gazette* has noted, "Even the mouths of those in the 'intelligence community' . . . shut automatically at the mention of NSA's secret operations, and their faces acquire a vacant look." Author James Bamford notes in *The Puzzle Palace*:

> Despite its size and power, however, no law has been enacted prohibiting the NSA from engaging in any activity. There are only laws to prohibit the release of any information about the Agency. "No statute establishes the NSA," Senate In-

telligence Committee chairman Frank Church reported, "or defines the permissible scope of its responsibilities. . . ."

In addition to being free of legal restrictions, the NSA has technological capacities for eavesdropping beyond imagination. . . . [13]

7. 1983— FRONT PAGE NEWS

January 1983 found most of us in southern New England freezing our tails off—it was a rough winter. I spent the holidays in Glens Falls with my mother and sister and found the town much nicer to visit than to live in. I was seeing Cindy often and continued to work while attending night school.

Bob Luca followed up on his promise and arranged for me to meet with Larry Fawcett in mid-February. Just before our meeting, I spoke with Fawcett on the phone, and he asked me questions about the Bentwaters incidents. To my surprise, Larry said he'd already heard rumors; they were coming from researchers in England. He asked that I bring any service-related documents and photos in my possession to our meeting.

On a Saturday night, I joined Bob, Betty, Larry, and his wife, Lois, for dinner at an Italian restaurant near New Britain, Connecticut. There, I let loose with a flood of information, but did not mention anything about the life-forms we had seen. I also told him that after the UFO had appeared in the field, I'd blacked out and remembered nothing until I woke up in my room.

Fawcett seemed to know I wasn't telling the whole story. After all, he was a cop. But until other witnesses testified to that part of the incident, I wasn't going to mention it. I told him about the underground complex, but said that Adrian Bustinza had told me about the facility. Talking about it was easier for me that way; that was the part of my experience that still gave me the most trouble.

Fawcett tried playing good cop/bad cop, but I was evasive—he'd have to establish some trust with me first. Before we left the restaurant, I provided him with many facts about the incident, including the names of the senior officers, NCOs, and enlisted men I knew who had been directly involved. I drew rough maps of the area and located the field as best I could from memory. Fawcett needed everything I had because he planned to file a request through the freedom of Information Act (FOIA), with the hope of unearthing some actual documentation. He needed an exact date. The best approximate date I could give was after Christmas but before New Year's Eve 1980. He said he'd run with that.

I said good night, with Larry telling me he would be in touch. I was nervous that I might have started something I would not want to finish, but still doubted that CAUS would be able to find anything of value.

My family was worried about my going public on the Bentwaters incident, as Fawcett was now calling it, and I couldn't blame them. Cindy still had no idea. Our relationship was growing stronger, and I was still afraid to tell her about it.

One night about a month after meeting with Fawcett, as I was sitting at the kitchen table reading the paper and worrying about what he was doing with my military records, I suddenly had an urge to drive to a convenience store about a mile down the road. Sandy was on the phone. I asked her if she needed anything; she didn't. I had no reason to go, but drove to the store just the same.

Once there, I walked over to the magazine rack and began flipping through the March 1983 issue of *Omni* magazine. Though *Omni* was not a favorite of mine, I continued scanning the pages. A column called "Anti-Matter" caught my eye. There was a picture of three aliens in silver suits standing next to a UFO; the background resembled the English countryside. The article began: "On the night of December 30, 1980, a spaceship crashed into Rendlesham Forest near RAF Woodbridge, England."

I stopped reading, closed the magazine, and almost walked out of the store without paying for it. The cashier caught up with me at the door, where I apologized and paid her. She said, "You look like you've just seen a ghost." "I think I just did," I said.

Back at the house, Sandy was still on the phone. Excited, I jumped around the kitchen, shouting, "My God, other guys are talking." Sandy must have thought I'd gone nuts. "What do you want?" she asked. I showed her the article, and after a few seconds she hung up the phone. I think it was at that moment the reality of what I'd said ten months earlier at the kitchen table hit home for her. *Others were talking!* Though the sources were unnamed, the account was fairly accurate, with the exception of the crash.

Two officers were named in the article: Colonel Ted Conrad, our base commander, and a Colonel Cochran, whom I'd never heard of. Gordon Williams was not mentioned, and I found the omission curious. But, for the first time, an account of the Bentwaters incident had been published in a major American magazine.

My elation soon turned to caution: Would Larry Fawcett think I'd gotten my information from this article? No, I'd told Betty and Bob my story two months before the piece came out. I called them all with the news, though. Larry was home and in the middle of preparing our FOIA request with Barry Greenwood and Robert Todd of Maryland, CAUS's chief researcher at the time. Larry knew this wasn't just another wild flying-saucer tale; he reiterated, "This case has a lot of potential."

In April, I drove up to Coventry, Connecticut, and met the rest of Larry's family. He had an office set up in his basement, and we spent hours going over details of my account. That day, he tape-recorded my account for the first time. He also explained the objectives he and Barry had laid out for their projected book, *Clear Intent.* The idea was to use authentic UFO-related government documents to prove that official investigations of the phenomenon had continued after 1969, the year the air force claimed such investigations had ceased. It sounded like a great idea, and I wished him luck. Larry told me they wanted to include my story in *Clear Intent,* but needed more than just my word.

Robert Todd filed CAUS's FOIA request about Bentwaters on 7 May 1983. Nearly five weeks of denials followed—all authored by the base's public affairs officer, Captain Kathleen McCollom. They ran from the absurd to the insulting, each concluding with the statement that the U.S. Air Force had stopped investigating UFOs in 1969. Fawcett kept me apprised of the official responses. I figured we were heading nowhere, until Fawcett's call on the evening of 14 June.

"Sit down," he said. "I've got big news. We got 'em, Lar. I can't believe it, but we really *got* 'em." I listened intently as he continued:

"Bob Todd sent me this today. It's a document that confirms a lot of what you said happened." He read me the cover letter; it was from Colonel Peter Bent of the 513th Combat Support Group and stated in part that, although the Eighty-first Tactical Fighter Wing no longer kept any record of the incident in its files, Her Majesty's government had kindly provided a copy of the attached memo. The document was titled "Unexplained Lights" and was on official air force letterhead. Written two weeks after the fact by Deputy Base Commander Lieutenant Colonel Charles I. Halt, it described numerous details of the incident, much of which confirmed my account. The paper mentioned beams of light shooting down from above, background radiation readings, damage to the trees, and impressions in the ground at the site. Halt closed by stating that "numerous individuals" including himself, had witnessed the events in Rendlesham Forest.

Over the next weeks, many people in the UFO field began to hear about the Bentwaters incident, the Halt document, and the witness who'd blown the whistle—me. I made an argreement with Fawcett and Greenwood to speak about the event if my real name were not used. Barry came up with the pseudonym "Art Wallace"; I hated the name, but wanted to protect my privacy and that of my family. I remembered quite clearly the debriefer's threat that bullets were cheap. In reality, I knew hiding behind another name was useless. I knew that anyone who *really* wanted to find out who Art Wallace was—for whatever reason—would.

Fawcett and Greenwood wanted to keep me and the Bentwaters incident as the cherry on top of *Clear Intent*, and my family was becoming nervous as hell. By this time, Barry had established contact with a UFO writer and researcher in England named Jenny Randles. I had seen her name in the *Omni* article; she was the one who suggested that a nuclear-armed aircraft had crashed in Rendlesham Forest and that the UFO incident had just been a cover story—created by the U.S. Air Force! I had to laugh at that one.

I eventually learned that Jenny and two other women from Suffolk—Brenda Butler and Dot Street—had been investigating the incident since early 1981. They had even spoken with air force and civilian witnesses. Greenwood was excited at the prospect of speaking with them on what he called "an intriguing case."

The English research team included quite a number of people; even a lawyer was involved. CAUS offered to help them in any way possible, so Greenwood sent Randles a copy of the Halt document, still unavailable in England. I felt that since they had invested so much time, we should help them out—who knew what they would turn up?

Late that June, I spoke at a UFO conference in Beverly, Massachusetts. There I met Greenwood and other UFO researchers. My old air force buddy, Steve LaPlume, lived nearby, and I invited him to come. Steve pulled up on his Harley Davidson, and we had a great reunion. Fawcett planned to break the Bentwaters incident during his lecture and asked Steve and me to tell our stories, to which Steve reluctantly agreed. By the time I was to speak, I was scared senseless. Introduced by my real name (so much for Art Wallace), I launched into an edited version of events. Steve then told about his involvement, which was minimal. He also spoke about his sighting on Woodbridge base two weeks after the December 1980 incidents.

There was a writer-researcher there I liked right off named Budd Hopkins. He'd written a book called *Missing Time* and spoke about people who'd been abducted by aliens. His lecture bothered me a great deal. That afternoon I told him about the August 1974 experience I had had with my mother in upstate New York and gave him her phone number should he want to talk to her about it. Later, I met two women who claimed to have been abducted; they seemed very sane and strangely familiar.

The conference itself was sponsored by the Massachusetts chapter of the Mutual UFO Network (MUFON), the largest UFO organization in the country. On the way home, Fawcett told me that MUFON did not like UFO stories involving aliens and attacked people who told them. He hoped that in the future things would change in that respect. Fawcett's comments only increased my resolve not to talk about the aliens I had seen in the woods that night.

The end of September led to more meetings with Fawcett. He tape-recorded my account again, and when I asked him why, he said he'd lost the first one. Dot Street called me from England again, but I remained guarded. Also calling from the U.K. that week was Keith Beabey, a reporter with the *News of the World*, a tabloid with the largest circulation in Britain.

Sunday night, 2 October, Greenwood called to say the *News of the World* had broken the story in England. Their front-page headline read "UFO Lands in Suffolk: And That's Official." I was shocked. Barry had found some copies of the paper in Boston and was sending one to me. The story included a copy of the Halt document and statements by Art

Wallace, distorted beyond belief. There was also a copy of my drawing of the craft and a large photo of Gordon Williams; he had verified the landing, but stated that he was not himself involved! Coverage continued onto the next page and included a picture of Fawcett, along with his supporting statements.

In the weeks that followed, most British papers carried their own versions of the story, including several treatments in the official U.S. military daily *Stars and Stripes*. A science writer named Ian Ridpath and local forestry worker Vince Thurkettle came up with a brilliant explanation for the events: the security police had mistaken the Orford lighthouse for a UFO and panicked. The paper ate it up.

In America, Rupert Murdoch's *Star* was the only paper to grab the story, which was no surprise, since he owned the *News of the World* as well. I wasn't happy to see my story in this paper next to a feature on J. R. Ewing of *Dallas* fame. Who would take it seriously? Bentwaters coverage had taken off like a flash fire; most people in the U.K. were now familiar with it. The story was finally out of my hands.

Within days, Fawcett and I were invited to tape an interview for the BBC program *Breakfast Time* at its New York studio in Rockefeller Center. I insisted on being shadowed, or blacked out, for the program, to which their interviewer Bob Friend agreed. After discussing some details of what I'd experienced, Friend asked me to comment on some of the wilder rumors surrounding the incident: was it true of we'd given the aliens assistance in repairing their craft? "No!" I said. "Where would we get the parts from, UFO supply?" The reporter laughed. I added that the claim about Gordon Williams shaking hands with the beings was untrue as well. The program aired in England the next morning, and I hoped it would put an end to all the nonsense once and for all.

In the car on the way back to Connecticut, Fawcett confronted me: "You saw the aliens, didn't you, Lar? You remember the whole thing." I realized I'd slipped up during the interview, so I came clean and told him what I really remembered. At least it was off my chest now. As uncomfortable as I was confirming that element of the story, Larry seemed to accept my account.

I told Cindy the entire story the next day. She had never given the subject of UFOs much thought, but nevertheless believed me. Cin said she found it all rather scary and expressed concern for my personal safety, just as my family had. I tried to keep that thought out of my mind.

In late October 1983, I met a young Texas blues guitarist named Stevie Ray Vaughan. After his show in a very small club, I told him he was soon to be a star; hell, he played better than Jimi Hendrix. Stevie smiled and said he just liked to play. That meeting was the start of a long friendship between us. He also believed in UFOs and wanted me to show him one. "Teach me to play like you, and I'll try to work something out," I bargained.

In November, we found out that Brenda Butler and Dot Street had sold the Halt document to the *News of the World* for two thousand pounds—nearly five grand here. CAUS, solely responsible for obtaining the document with the information I had provided, had sent them the copy gratis solely to assist in their research. After that, we broke off all contact with them.

A similar incident followed later that month, when a rather insignificant New York City PR man called me to offer his services as a middleman. His plan was to sell the Halt document to the *National Enquirer* for twenty-five hundred dollars; fifteen hundred for him, one thousand for me. I declined, as the document was not mine to sell. I also still believed I would hurt my credibility if I accepted money for anything having to do with Bentwaters or UFOs. The guy hounded me until I told him to shove off. Later, he bad-mouthed me to anybody who would listen, but few did. My integrity intact, I pressed on.

I spent Christmas in Glens Falls with my mother and sister. Cindy spent the holiday with her family. I had no idea what the new year held for me, but I knew I wanted to get engaged. Cindy was the one for me, and I didn't want her to get away. In UFOland, I was the current hype; with Cin, I was just me, and that was all she wanted.

On Christmas Eve, my mother and I watched Fawcett promote *Clear Intent* on the *Merv Griffin Show*. When Larry told Merv about the aliens I had seen in Rendlesham Forest, some of the audience laughed, and Zsa Zsa Gabor feigned surprise. Then Merv leaned in toward Larry with his fist under his chin and said, "Ooooo!" Bentwaters had now gone Hollywood.

1983 Developments |

March 1983
In England, Jenny Randles reviews more of the Bentwaters rumors in an article titled "Impact—and After." The author sees only two possibilities:

Either a conventional aircraft was forced to land in Rendlesham Forest or an un-
conventional one did so . . . It [is] conceivable that in December 1980 an American aircraft did crash in Rendlesham Forest and the fact was covered up—possibly
because the aircraft was carrying a nuclear device. In which case the UFO landing
story must have been used deliberately as a convenient distraction from the disturbing truth.[14]

March 1983

Omni's "UFO Update" is on the Bentwaters incident. Brenda Butler's
RAF contact is named as Woodbridge British Liaison Officer Squadron
Leader Donald Moreland. Though the magazine alleges that Base Commander Conrad "spoke" with aliens, he "claims that he never observed
any aliens, but he did interview two of the eyewitnesses, and concludes,
'Those lads saw something, but I don't know what it was.' " (The following year, Adrian Bustinza confirms that he was one of the two eyewitnesses Conrad interviewed.) The "UFO Update" concludes, "The
alien spaceship, she [Randles] suggests, is just a fiction leaked by the
U.S. Air Force to cover up the crash of a plane carrying nuclear
bombs."[15]

March 1983

"Rendlesham Revisited" appears in *Probe*, a magazine published in Bristol, England. Authors Ian Mrzyglod and Martin Shipp, assisted by Butler and Street, visit Rendlesham Forest in late September 1982 to
determine if the case warrants serious investigation. They conclude that
it does not:

SCUFORI (Swindon Center for UFO Research and Investigation) did not find out
whether or not anything came down in the forest, be it an aircraft or a UFO, but
as nothing is ever likely to emerge from this case, does it really matter?[16]

8 April 1983

Acting on information supplied by Larry Warren, CAUS attorney files
a Bentwaters-related FOIA request.

20 April 1983

Harry Harris telephones Captain Kathleen McCollom, chief of the
Eighty-first Tactical Fighter Wing's public affairs division. After they
talk, he writes her, "re: Incident in Rendlesham Forest during December, 1980":

Further to our . . . conversation of today I would be grateful to receive your comments as to whether or not a U.F.O. or "flying saucer" landed in Rendlesham Forest during the month of December 1980 and that this "vehicle" was surrounded by American Air Force and other military personnel who were in communication with the "crew" of this craft.

I do not feel that the issue of whether or not this incident occurred "off base" or "on base" is really relevant . . . but merely as to whether or not the event occurred, irrespective of who had jurisdiction. . . . Please indicate why American Air Force Personnel removed the radar tape from the civilian air base at Watton near Norwich and indicate if this tape may be available for the inspection of those whom I represent.[17]

26 April 1983
Captain McCollom responds:

I have no way of verifying the information you require. I was not an eye witness to the events that you say took place, and do not know of anyone who was.

As you probably know, the Air Force discontinued is "Project Blue Book" investigation in 1969 and no longer has any official interest in these phenomena. I therefore have no photographs, documents, or any sorts of records that could provide any of the information you need.[18]

Forty-eight hours later, Bentwaters Base Commander Colonel Henry Cochran addresses CAUS's FOIA request. The colonel's statement reads:

Reference your letter dated April 8, 1983 requesting information about known aircraft activity near RAF Bentwaters. There was allegedly some strange activity near RAF Bentwaters at the approximate time in question, but not on land under Air Force jurisdiction and therefore no official investigation was conducted by the 81st Tactical Fighter Wing. Thus, the records you requested do not exist.

Regarding the other statements in your letter; no photos of the alleged aircraft were taken by the Air Force. Also, there is no requirement under the Freedom of Information Act to create a record for the purpose of fulfilling a request. I can assure you that if there were such records we would provide them to you.[19]

8 September 1983
Larry Fawcett writes Larry Warren:

Thank you for the pictures. Per our conversation on the phone the other day I am looking forward to your letter to me telling the whole story of Bentwaters. We have now learned a lot about the incident based on the information supplied by you. . . . [20]

8. | THE STORY BREAKS

2 October 1983

With Sunday morning's *News of the World* headline proclaiming "UFO Lands in Suffolk: And That's Official," the Bentwaters incident breaks in the English media. It is the first in a blizzard of related articles and features a photo of Gordon Williams ("No Hoax Says Air Chief"). The text above the headline reads: "Colonel's top secret report tells the facts. Mystery craft in exploding wall of color. Animals flee from strange glowing object."

The front page also carries Airman Art Wallace's drawing of the vehicle and part of Colonel Halt's memorandum:

> [Halt] declined comment on the memo but added "This is a very delicate situation. I have been told very clearly that I could jeopardize my career if I talk to you about it."
>
> Brig. Gen. Gordon Williams, back in the states says, "I recall Lt. Col. Halt's report. I don't know exactly what happened. It is all there. He is not a man who would hoax the Ministry of Defence or the American Air Force. . . ." Despite the official silence . . . reporters discovered that the UFO was tracked on radar by RAF Watten, 50 miles from where it landed. . . . USAF intelligence officers later checked the tapes of all radar installations in the area.

Squadron Leader Donald Moreland recalls:

The Colonel [Halt] sat in my office and was a very worried man. The first I knew of these events was when he came to me and related what he had seen. I know Col. Halt well and respect him and I fully believe he was telling me the truth. Whatever it was, it was able to perform feats in the air which no known aircraft is capable of doing. I put the events the Colonel related to me down to inexplicable phenomena.

Keith Beabey reports:

The Colonel's report confirms the strange events in the forest that night, but lacks the eyewitness detail given to us by Art Wallace, a USAF Security Policeman, now back in America as a civilian. He was sent to the site in a convoy of military vehicles from nearby Bentwaters and describes what he saw: "We looked up in the sky and saw a red ball of light coming towards us from over the trees. There was no noise, no sound at all, we were all mesmerized. All of a sudden, the red light exploded. The place was filled with an explosion of colors, all kinds of colors. We were momentarily blinded and when the colors died down, there was a machine."

Art said there were beings in the craft, but he could not see them as he was on the wrong side. "But others did, they said there were three, wearing silver suits." Art Wallace—we have changed his name for security reasons—tells his story on Page 3 today.

Bob Smith's article comes in from New York City and headlines page three. He has just interviewed Art Wallace by telephone:

UFO Lands in Suffolk: The Airman's Story
　　The Forest Exploded with Blinding Light
　　The first thought to penetrate U.S. Airman Art Wallace's brain as he saw Britain's first authenticated UFO landing was that he was seeing something from Star Wars. To Art, the machine that landed silently in a forest in an explosion of red light looked like "the spaceship from the movie."
　　He told me: "It appeared to have a triangular shape and was covered with pipes and valves and things. It was about 20 ft. across the bottom with sloping sides up to the top 12 ft. to 15 ft. high . . . certainly big enough to handle people."
　　Art's rendezvous with the unbelievable came in the early hours of December 27, 1980, after he was ordered into a jeep at RAF Bentwaters, Suffolk, where he was a security guard.

The jeep drove in convoy towards nearby RAF Woodbridge, then pulled up on the edge of lonely Tangham Wood, said Art. "We were all told to hand in our weapons. I had an M-16 rifle. Then we took lights into the woods. Amazing things seemed to happen even then. I noticed animals running in panic from the forest. Fuel gauges on the vehicles registered empty when we knew they were full. As we approached a clearing we could see some very bright lights. We were a bit shook up to come across a U.S. medic treating one of our security police who had appeared to be broken down and was crying.

"The clearing was full of RAF and USAF security people—about 200 of them. Several movie cameras had been set up and choppers were flying above.

"Then we saw an object. It appeared to be resting on the ground and looked like a giant aspirin. It was transparent. We were in awe, never having seen anything like this. Nearby, there was an airman carrying a radio. Suddenly we heard a chopper pilot telling him: 'Here it comes.'

"We looked up and saw a red ball of light coming towards us from over the trees. In the distance, it looked about 100 ft. high and appeared to be coming in to land. It came down right over the transparent on the ground. There was no sound at all.

"We were all mesmerized. All of a sudden, the red light exploded. The place was filled with an explosion of all kinds of colours. We were blinded. When the colours died down, we looked again, and there was a machine there.

"A Captain motioned us to approach the ship. We walked up close enough to touch it. It was giving off a metallic bluish light. There were about three groups of four security men each circling the thing. I could see our shadows on the craft. As we walked, they moved.

"But when we stopped, the shadows seemed to take another pace. It was weird. Suddenly a green light came on at the top of the spaceship. It moved down the side of the craft until it reached our heads then bounced from one to the other along the side. Just like the ball bounces in a video game.

"Then I realized the vehicle was inhabited. There were beings aboard. I didn't see them because I was on the other side of the craft. But others did. They said there were three, and they were wearing silver suits. I had a strange feeling and seemed to black out.

"The next thing I knew, it was about 5 a.m. and I was waking up, lying half across my bunk. I still had my uniform on and was up to my knees in mud.

"To this day, I don't know how I got back to the barracks, or what happened after I saw the green light bounce off our shadows. My roommate said I'd been brought into the room by some people—he didn't know who—and just dumped on the bed.

"Later that day, myself and some of the guys who had been at the field were given the once-over with a geiger counter but we were never told why or what the results were.

"We were all called to the base security office at Bentwaters and told what we'd seen had been classified top secret. Several civilians were doing all the talking. We took them for CIA. They said if we ever told the story, no one would believe us. One guy added that if we did talk, then bullets were cheap. I thought, 'This guy is actually threatening our lives. He obviously means it.'

"Looking back, the one thing that bothers me is that the officers and civilians present seemed to know all about it—they weren't all that surprised."

Art Wallace—that isn't his real name—was honourably discharged from the USAF in June, 1981. He is now aged 22. If named, he could be jailed for saying what he saw.

2 October 1983

London's *Sunday Express* features Bentwaters in "I Saw UFO Land—American Officer." The article quotes:

Sir John Nott, who became Minister of Defence within a fortnight of the reported sighting, said last night: "I know nothing about it. Certainly I never saw any reports about a UFO landing. I don't believe in UFOs anyway."

Another former minister of Defence, Sir Ian Gilmour, said: "I should think this is absolute rubbish."

On 3 October, an air force spokesman begins to exercise some damage control. While acknowledging that *whatever* Lieutenant Colonel Halt and his men witnessed in those woods actually happened, the air force considers any talk of "aliens" to be "fanciful."

"It *Was* a UFO" in the next day's *Ipswich Evening Star* observes:

An official report spelling out how a spaceship landed in Suffolk is genuine, the Americans confirmed today. But they poured scorn on another, even more astonishing claim . . . that the craft was manned by little silvery creatures. That part of the Great Suffolk Mystery was unlikely, Fanciful and Outlandish, they said.

At the public affairs department, Capt. Kathy McCollom told the *Star*, "Yes, it is a genuine report. But it doesn't explain what these lights were.

"All we did was a memo as a courtesy for the Ministry of Defence. We have never investigated it, and we aren't interested in things that happen off base."

But Capt. McCollom described as "fanciful" other reports said to come from an anonymous airman on the patrol that night.

He claims other members of the patrol saw "little silver men" inside the space-ship and ever since had been sworn to secrecy by the Americans.

The reporter adds:

Forester Vince Thurkettle, 27, who lives a few hundred yards from the landing site . . . "I saw nothing at the time, but the next day a chap came around asking questions about a UFO but wouldn't say who he was. A few weeks later I discovered three oval depressions in the ground as though something had landed. But they could just as easily been rabbit scrapes."

. . . Last night Suffolk Police said their records revealed that in the early hours of December 26, the law enforcement desk reported seeing unusual lights in the sky and said they had sent troops to investigate.

3 October 1983

On Monday, the *Express* leads its coverage with "I know UFO secrets, says peer":

Civil servants were keeping quiet last night about reports that a UFO with 3 silver-suited aliens on board had landed in Suffolk.

The Ministry of Defence confirmed that details of a landing had been reported to it, but an official said he could not reveal the contents of the report. "It's a matter of confidentiality," he added. . . . The MoD said: "The report is on file. The Ministry keeps these reports for statistical purposes, it does not act upon them."

But a senior member of the House of Lords accused Whitehall of "cover-up, one big cover-up."

Lord Clancarty (who is author of a number of scholarly UFO books) said: "Not only am I personally convinced that a UFO landed there—I already heard something about it.

But an *Express* skeptic fumes:

According to some "eyewitnesses" a UFO landed in Suffolk, 1980. We think that's about as unlikely as Elsie Tanner getting into a nunnery. [Elsie Tanner is a British soap opera character of somewhat dubious morals.]

Talk of an "exploding wall of color" and of animals fleeing in terror from a strange glowing object suggest it was just Boy George holding a private, outdoors practice session.

Also that Monday, the *East Anglian Daily Times* headlines: "UFO Sighting in Suffolk 'Verified.' " They also review the Halt memo, the account of the "ex-serviceman now living back in America," Butler and Street's research, Thurkettle's account, and the Suffolk police's findings.

4 October 1983
The Suffolk *Evening Star* runs this item in a box:

> Comment: UFO—mystic
>
> Man would have to be somewhat arrogant to deny any possibility of life on other planets. What makes us hope we are alone? Probably the fear that would be generated by having to acknowledge the alternatives.
>
> But if there is life out there and it is capable of visiting our Earth as regularly as the UFO spotters would have us believe, then it is far more sophisticated than we are.
>
> So why do they insist on behaving like something out of a 1950s sci-fi horror? The affair at RAF Woodbridge is ludicrous not because one finds it impossible to believe in other planetary life.
>
> No, it seems so ludicrous because one finds it hard to believe that sophisticated beings from other planets would have so much in common with a Hollywood B movie script.

5 October 1983
The next morning, *Stars and Stripes* fires its first salvo at the British press and the statement of "a former Air Force Security policeman now living in the United States":

> RAF Bentwaters. England—"UFO Lands in Suffolk" screamed the headline in Britain's biggest-selling Sunday newspaper. And, if the main headline in 2-inch letters didn't sufficiently alarm its 4.1 million readers, the *News of the World* Sunday newspaper trumpeted, "And That's Official" in a subheadline. That was followed by smaller headlines. . . .
>
> The headlines, a related photo and two stories took up about four-fifths of the paper's front page, all that space devoted to an incredible yarn about three beings in silver spacesuits landing in a pine forest in the East Anglia region of England three years ago.
>
> The story said that, despite a massive cover-up by the U.S. Air Force, the paper's investigators have proof that "the mystery craft came to Earth in a red ball of light at 3 a.m. on Dec. 27, 1980."

The paper reproduced in part a report—which it claimed was confidential—by [Col. Halt]. The report describes how some Air Force personnel claimed to have seen a mysterious craft come down to Earth in a red ball of light.

The newspaper said that the landing happened in a forest called Tangham Wood, half a mile from RAF Woodbridge and that about 200 British and American military and civilian personnel saw the unidentified flying object.

The newspaper, which is similar to the American weekly *The National Enquirer*, also had a long account on Page 3 from a former Air Force security policeman now living in the United States. He said that he saw the Star Wars–like craft and that there were creatures aboard. The *News . . .* claimed that the sighting had been successfully covered up by Air Force officials and their counterparts in Britain's Ministry of Defence until a copy of Halt's report on the incident fell into the hands of the American chief of CAUS (Citizens Against UFO Secrecy).

Air Force officials at RAF Bentwaters and at 3rd Air Force headquarters at RAF Mildenhall, England, Monday strongly denied there had been any cover up. They said they had cooperated on queries dealing with the incident in the three years since it happened.

Air Force Capt. Kathleen McCollom, Chief of the Public Affairs division here, confirmed that sightings of the strange lights were reported near RAF Woodbridge in December 1980 but that the sightings occurred off base, and the small number of Air Force personnel involved were off duty at the time.

"There was never any official investigation of the sightings. No documents relating to the sightings were ever classified (as the paper said) and there are no more documents . . . relating to the sightings," she said. "The people who saw the lights don't want to comment on it, and I have to respect their privacy.

"Colonel Halt doesn't want to talk to anybody about it," she said. "There really is nothing new about this case. I've been answering queries about it for nearly three years although we have no official interest in it. . . ."

She said the Air Force had no more information to add to the case. She said that reports of the sightings have been exaggerated to a comical degree.

Air Force Lt. Col. Doug Kennett, director of the office of public affairs for 3rd Air Force HQ denied that Air Force officials have in any way tried to cover up the affair, and said that the service has cooperated fully in aiding UFO investigators in their search for any evidence concerning the reported strange sightings.

Kennett said the Air Force had responded to a half-dozen Freedom of Information Act requests from CAUS alone since last April and had managed to track down Halt's memorandum to the MoD and had supplied it to the organization.

"People think that we've got some top secret report that we are holding judiciously, but we have given them everything we have on it." He said quotes attributed by the newspaper to Halt are untrue. "He never talked to them."

That same day, this editorial appears in the *East Anglian Daily Times*:

A Lofty Disdain

The most remarkable (possibly the only remarkable) feature of the story about the Woodbridge UFO is in the reaction of the nearby U.S. Air Force. According to a spokeswoman, the USAF has not investigated unidentified flying objects in its area for some years.

Further, if some strange-looking craft did in fact land within 20 yards of the base, decanting a few strange-looking people in the process, this would still have been no concern of the USAF since the landing was outside its perimeter. It would therefore be a matter for the British.

Now if these strange things were indeed visitors from some other part of the universe, this lofty disdain would be well justified. After all, if a little green man landed in England demanding, "Take me to your leader," it would be reasonable to suppose that he would be wanting Margaret Thatcher rather than the local U.S. base commander.

On the other hand, the bulk of expert opinion has it that most [UFOs] . . . could perfectly well be identified if anybody took the time and trouble. These are balloons and helicopters and low-flying planes and quite possibly test missiles of one kind or another.

Some of these, one would have thought, would have been of passing interest to an air base in the flight path. When a U.S. radar operator reports that something is approaching the base that he can't identify, is he really supposed to report it to Woodbridge police station?

Possibly so. There was a rather puzzling occasion some time ago when an exceptionally low-flying plane woke up practically everybody for miles around Woodbridge, and the USAF said that they had noticed nothing at all. Maybe a natural disbelief in UFOs is sometimes taken to extremes?

7 October 1983

Two days later, the *Woodbridge Reporter*: "Little Silver Men in Spaceship in Rendlesham Forest?" summarizes the accounts and allegations. Airman Art Wallace's drawing of the craft appears at the top of the page.

While some East Anglian families may be discussing the article over dinner, a number of their neighbors stand outside and watch things fly over their homes. Most of the witnesses are residents of the quiet coastal hamlets of Hollesley and Alderton, six and seven miles, respectively, southeast of Woodbridge. Some of these locations are as close as three miles to the December 1980 site.

At about 7:45 P.M., 37-year-old Sandra Button sees three lights forming a triangle in the sky as she walks down the path of her garden toward the baker's van at the front of the house. She stops and just stares. Within five minutes, she is joined by a neighbor:

> They were still there, they were high up over the marshes. We watched them for about 20 minutes and they did not move.

Mr. Button and the couple's three children soon join the two women, and all continue to watch together. The baker turns off his engine, "but there was nothing, just a deathly silence." Then, the center light dims, the thing rises, comes toward them, and passes slowly over. It is last seen heading north toward RAF Woodbridge and RAF Bentwaters. Mrs. Button says:

> As the lights rose we could see small red and green lights, and we could make out three triangular shapes. There was a weird humming noise as they passed overhead. My husband was very skeptical about it all until he heard the noise. It was unlike anything we had heard before—in no way was it a plane.

Baker Ron Maco hasn't moved from his truck:

> We froze [when it came in over the trees]. The lights were in a triangle and remained perfectly still. . . . Whatever was in the sky over us, the lights beamed down and we heard a high-pitched whine.

Half an hour later and two miles north, William Wright is preparing for a fishing trip when he sees lights from his garden, three large white lights forming a triangle that alter slightly as they move toward him. A small red light is apparent behind each large white light as they slowly pass over his house:

> The lights were constant, they were not flashing. There had been no noise at all, but as they came nearer I heard a sort of drone, unlike the noise of jets, which we are used to. . . . I am keeping an open mind on the subject. We see a lot of aircraft in this area but this did not have the same speed or noise or feel about it.

At the same time and very close by, two frightened women sit in a car that has suddenly stopped working. Leiston residents Debbie Foreman and Pauline Osborne also watch the lights pass over:

The headlights on the car dimmed, and the engine cut out. Until then the car had behaved quite normally. But everything seemed to go wrong.

While many local residents are too frightened to talk to reporters, others demand a meeting with American air force officials from RAF Woodbridge. The RAF Bentwaters public affairs office is unable to comment on the sightings, but spokeswoman Captain Kathy McCollom notes that a C-130 Hercules transport aircraft was due at Bentwaters during this time.[21]

Bentwaters, the news story, is now a week old.

9. | THE STORY CONTINUES

9 October 1983

Today's *News of the World* carries three new stories by Ian MaCaskill and Keith Beabey. "Sketches That Were Hidden Away" reviews the accounts of several independent civilian witnesses. First is Leslie Frost, an engineer living in Suffolk. In August 1980, he had observed several unknown craft, one of which he describes as "a triangular smaller machine along the lines of the [Wallace] illustration in last Sunday's *News of the World*."

Graham Herring of Southampton observed an object hovering near his home on Hinkler Road in July 1983. The citizens-band-radio operator then sketched several pictures of it on the first thing he could get his hands on, his CB logbook.

> Shortly afterward two men came to my home and said they were from the Ministry (of Defence). They were very interested in my sketches of the UFO and asked if they could borrow them to show some experts. They promised they would return them—but they never did.

In "The Sinister Plot to Hush Up The Truth," an unnamed former senior Ministry of Defence official is quoted as saying:

Secret service agents "invented" a plane crash as part of an elaborate plot to hush up the UFO incident at 3 A.M. on December 27, 1980.

An American airman is convinced he was brainwashed by interrogators to blot out all memory of the alien craft.

The Defence Ministry official was an Assistant Under-Secretary of State—a post that allows access to top-secret papers. He is still bound by the Official Secrets Act, so he cannot be named. He said: "It is in the public interest to push this hard. What worries me is not what the Ministry may be concealing. It's the alarming possibility that they may be trying to brush something under the carpet, something stupendous which has got them as baffled as the rest of us."

. . . What the man from the Ministry really thinks happened is amazing. He reckons top-secret space experiments could have been carried out over England— and something may have gone drastically wrong. "Those of us who have been following the UFO phenomena in recent years were aware of this incident. . . . There was sufficient unease on the American side to suggest that something very significant had happened. . . . Now questions need to be pressed vigorously in the House of Commons—and they should be answered."

He revealed in an exclusive that every year there are 10 to 15 visual or radar "telling signals" over Britain. All are reported to the Ministry of Defence's special UFO unit. "But after the reports arrive there you never find out what happened. . . . It's my contention that there is a deliberate cover up by governments in the United States and here."

The American airman convinced he'd been brainwashed is the subject of the smallest article titled "Man Who Never Was":

The man whose eyewitness account of the UFO landing first broke the official secrecy barrier, has told of how he was involved in the giant cover-up that followed. And when he later tried to rejoin the U.S. Air Force, there was no record of his existence.

Airman First Class Art Wallace—an assumed name—told us how he saw the strange triangular-shaped craft come in to land. He said he was under strict orders not to talk about about it.

"It seems far-fetched in the cold light of day," he said, "but I have a feeling I was drugged in some way. After the forest incident I woke up in the barracks without knowing how I got there."

Wallace said he remembers thinking a few days later that he was in an underground cavern being shown films of American astronauts on the moon. In the background, there were strange spacecraft. But, he says, it was all part of the bizarre brainwashing efforts of U.S. intelligence agents.

The lengths the American secret service seem to have gone to cover up the landing of the space ship are extraordinary.

Art Wallace said that, after leaving the Air Force, he was unable to find a job and tried to re-enlist. But he was told that he could not—since there was no record of him ever having been in the USAF.

A colleague, John Burroughs, who also witnessed the landing of the brilliantly lit craft, had never existed either, according to Air Force records. Yet Burroughs did speak to Lieutenant Larry Fawcett, 44, deputy police chief of Coventry, Connecticut, who is also deputy director of Citizens Against UFO Secrecy—and confirmed the evidence given by Art Wallace.

10 October 1983

On Monday, "Bentwaters 'UFO' Simply a Lighthouse, Paper Says," appears in *Stars and Stripes*:

London (AP)—A newspaper's claim that a UFO landed in Britain in a ball of red light was dismissed by a rival publication Sunday, saying that the light was from a lighthouse.

The mass-circulation *News of the World* claimed a week ago that the UFO had three beings inside it in silver suits when it came down in a forest near RAF Bentwaters in Suffolk . . . at the end of 1980.

The tabloid *Sunday People* sent a reporter to the site and quoted Vince Thurkettle, an officer for the state-run Forestry Commission, as saying: "The light from the Orford lighthouse, on the coast, can be seen through the trees."

That afternoon's *Ipswich Evening Star* reports that Suffolk UFO investigators say they have been deluged with information from locals:

The new interest follows the publication of USAF official reports of the sightings. Ms. Butler said the local researchers would be taking full reports from all the local people who were puzzled by what they saw almost three years ago.

The *Manchester Evening News*, Wednesday, 12 October 1983, reports:

Space Craft Landing—Call for Inquiry

A team of Manchester UFO researchers is to call for a public inquiry by a High Court judge into reports of "flying saucer" near an air base in Suffolk. Speaking for the group, Jenny Randles states: "We are so convinced that the evidence we have makes a case that we are fully prepared to hand it over to an independent panel of scientists . . . we already have a case which demands an answer."

. . . Three days later there was another sighting of the UFO, also in Rendlesham Forest near the NATO air base, by USAF and RAF men, say the researchers, who include Det. Chief Inspector Norman Collinson, deputy head of the Greater Manchester Police fraud squad, and Altrincham solicitor Mr. Harry Harris.

16 October 1983

It is announced from the floor of the House of Commons that Tory M.P. Sir Patrick Wall will question Defence Minister Michael Heseltine on the Rendlesham Forest incidents. Sir Patrick, senior member of the eleven-man Select Committee on Defence, is quoted as saying, "There is so much evidence, there must be something in the UFO theory and whatever is known should be made public."[22]

It is two weeks since the story broke.

19 October 1983

Bentwaters public affairs chief Captain McCollom writes English UFO researcher Mark Ian Birdsall that she is

. . . not in a position to verify or disprove anything printed about our supposed UFO sightings. There was no official investigation of any kind done so I have no documents to refer to. . . . In short, we have no official interest in what may have happened, especially since the lights were seen off base. There is no further information I can provide.

20 October 1983

Next day, the Bentwaters story is picked up in the States for the first time since its brief mention in *Omni*. The *Star*'s full-page article is titled "UFO Landing Documented for the First Time by Stunned U.S. Air Force Brass in Top-Secret Report—Officers tell of amazing sight as huge red ball exploded, leaving craft carrying 3 aliens." The reporter notes Halt's incident as coincident with Airman Art Wallace's:

As Lt. Col. Halt and the others were being treated to the extraordinary display, another craft had landed near a party sent to investigate.

Security guard Airman Art Wallace (not his real name) told how he was in a convoy of jeeps sent to observe the strange lights. "We saw an object . . ." [followed by two paragraphs of previously reported Art Wallace testimony].

The next afternoon in London, Tory M.P. Sir Patrick Wall states:

I want the full facts to come to light. I do not expect we will be told everything that happened but it should highlight the issues.[23]

24 October 1983

Monday night, 24 October, the House of Commons meets in late session. M.P.s who had not yet seen a copy of Colonel Halt's memo would be most familiar with it before session's end. During the proceedings, Sir Patrick Wall asks Armed Forces Minister John Bradley if he has seen the memo and if Her Majesty's government "will now release reports and documents concerning unexplained incidents in the U.K."

Mr. Bradley answers:

Subject to normal security constraints, I am ready to give information about any such reported sightings that are found to be a matter of concern from a defence standpoint, but there has been none to date.[24]

6 November 1983

The *News of the World* runs an article on the incident under what is surely the most lurid headline to date: "Bug-Eyed Alien Greets Air Chief." Relative to Art Wallace, the update is a stew of inaccuracies and distortions:

Amazing new facts about the night a UFO came to Britain have been revealed by the U.S. serviceman who saw the craft land.

The secrets were locked away in 22-year-old Art Wallace's mind. But following hypnosis, he has now given us:

A full description of the aliens who manned the ship;

Details of how a senior American officer actually communicated with one of the beings;

Evidence that the U.S. Air Force may have helped repair the damaged craft.

. . . Since Wallace—now back in the U.S.—revealed to us what he saw that terrifying night, his life has been threatened.

Recently, he received a phone call at his home and an unidentified man told him, "If you don't shut your mouth then it will be shut for you."

This follows a frightening meeting he had with several men he believes were from the CIA, during which he was warned that "bullets are cheap."

During his session with two top hypnotists, Wallace . . . not only confirmed his original story but made some astonishing new revelations. He now says he remembers seeing a face-to-face meeting between one of the aliens and the officer who was in charge of the U.S. base.

The alien was between three and four feet tall, with a very large head and huge saucer-like eyes. . . . It appeared to have greyish skin and was wearing what looked like a dark jumpsuit and the outline of its figure glowed.

Wallace was unable to hear any voices as Wing Commander, now Brigadier General, Gordon Williams and the being communicated with much hand waving and pointing at the strange triangular craft. . . . The four aliens appeared to be floating just above the surface of the ground and at one point, became alarmed and formed themselves into a defensive line. One of them floated over the UFO near to where Wallace was standing and he blacked out. The next thing he remembers, he was back in his barracks.

Wallace believes the craft needed repairs after hitting a tree.

He was told later by some of his pals on the base that a U.S. transport plane flew in from Germany just hours after the UFO landed, and was immediately surrounded by armed military police. A package from the plane was put in a jeep which then drove off towards the landing site at Tangham Wood. Later that day, the craft is gone.

The base's deputy commander, Lt. Col. Charles Halt, admits there is "one hell of a lot more" to come out.[25]

Writing from his Whitehall office the next day, Defense Minister Heseltine privately assures the Right Honorable M.P. Merlyn Rees:

. . . that there is not a grain of truth in the allegation that there has been a "cover up" about alleged UFO sightings.

As you will recall from your time as Minister for the Royal Air Force, reports of alleged sightings are examined by operations staff to see whether there is any interest from a defence point of view. No such interest was found in the case of the incident reported . . . or in any of the other sightings reported in the UK. In the News of the World incident, there was in fact no question of any contact with "alien beings," nor was any unidentified object seen on radar.

My Department's interest remains solely in the implications for the air defence of the U.K.

21 November 1983

The following week in Beverly, Massachusetts, about fifteen people gather in Marge Christensen's living room to meet Art Wallace; it is his first public appearance. Larry Fawcett, Dot Street, and a local reporter named Andrea Atkins are present. Atkins writes in the Beverly *Times:*

Wallace says he has gotten accustomed to skepticism about his incredible story. . . . "I know I wasn't crazy. I know it happened. I know it's hard for people to accept." . . .

Fawcett and Mrs. Christensen . . . said yesterday that Wallace's sighting is significant because two days after it occurred, British researchers, none of whom knew the American Wallace, were told the same story about what went on in the woods near Woodbridge.

. . . The incident, he said, has changed his life, made him wary of phone calls and talking with the media. He said his family worries about his safety. But he is even angrier with people who attempt to dismiss what he claims he saw.[26]

December 1983

The New York–based Scientific Bureau of Investigation becomes the first American UFO organization to publish on the Bentwaters incidents; it is the cover story of their quarterly, *The SBI Report*. On 20 December, the *American Examiner* runs "UFOs Are Terrorizing America's Air Force—Spacecraft buzz base in English countryside." The full-page story adds nothing new.

27 December 1983

On the third anniversary of the Bentwaters incident, army staff sergeant and military UFO researcher Clifford E. Stone writes to air force headquarters in Europe under the Freedom of Information Act requesting records of the events.

10. | *1984—*
LOOKING FOR OTHER WITNESSES

Nineteen eighty-four, George Orwell's year. Mid-January. It didn't seem that Big Brother was watching everyone, but I knew he was watching me.

When the phone rang, Scott picked up, said, "Hello," listened, and handed it to me. "It sounds like the police," he said. Fully expecting a UFO researcher on the other end of the line, I said a cautious hello. "Hi, Larry. How far are you planning to go with this Bentwaters story?" "Who is this?" I asked. "Larry, I'm Jim Greenfield.[27] I'm an agent for the National Security Agency. Right now I'm representing the Department of the Air Force. There's a little concern here about what you're telling CAUS."

It's hard to explain, but I just knew this guy was for real. I knew they'd gotten my records in 1981 and had expected them to get in touch with me sooner or later. I answered, "I'm going to keep going until I find out what happened in England." Greenfield responded that he only wanted to know my intentions; he wasn't worried about UFOs as much as what I knew about the nuclear capability at the bases. It was felt that, because I had an ax to grind, I might want to say something that would hurt our country. I told him that was definitely not the case and that my knowledge of alleged nukes at Bentwaters was not an issue.

He told me he'd heard that I had pictures of the UFO at Bentwaters; I told him I didn't. Then he asked if I would like to see pictures of that UFO someday. "Anytime you want," I said. "I'll look at them now, but how about letting the public see them, too?" "No go," he responded, "You should know better." He ended the conversation abruptly. "Watch your back, Larry. We'll talk again."

I didn't like this at all. What did they want from me? Obviously, a line of communication, but why? I wondered if the NSA was in some way on my side but doubted it and kept the call to myself. I believed that one of the SPs involved in the incident did have personal film of the UFO, but it sure wasn't me. How long would it be before Greenfield called back? I did want to see those pictures, if he had them. Those pictures were like the carrot on the stick for me.

I spoke to Steve LaPlume later that month. He was off to South America to do some mercenary work; he'd wanted to do that kind of thing since our days at Bentwaters. He told me that he had trained at camps in Georgia and now had a contract to train contra rebels in Honduras. We planned a get-together for the spring when he returned to the States.

I worked with guitarist Stevie Ray Vaughan when he was in the East. His career had really taken off, and, thanks in part to his music, blues were enjoying a resurgence. Cindy and I were practically living together now, but at times I continued to feel some kind of nonhuman presence around me.

The controversy surrounding the Bentwaters incident increased day by day. Fawcett had introduced the case at a conference in Lincoln, Nebraska, and, with a wide array of researchers in attendance, the videotape of my entire BBC interview was shown. After viewing it, Randles stated that it was much more convincing than the edited version she'd seen on English TV.

Late spring found me at another MUFON conference in Beverly, Massachusetts, but the infighting among researchers was more prevalent than the research, and I spent most of the weekend depressed. I did get to meet John Schussler, a NASA employee from Houston. He remarked on the coincidental timing of Bentwaters with the 29 December 1980 Cash–Landrum incident near Huffman, Texas.[28] Some folks were wondering if the UFO we'd seen in England was the same object they'd seen in Texas. I doubted it.

People I'd never met were now attacking me. An editor at *Aviation*

Week Magazine, a noted UFO debunker, led the charge when he told WTNH's Al Terzi that I might be a drug addict. Rumors about me began to circulate in the UFO field: among them, that I had never been in the air force. Of course, such remarks were never made to my face, only behind my back. Each was more ridiculous than the last, and I laughed them off as well as I could.

Fawcett continued to remind me that I should keep my non-Bentwaters UFO-related experiences to myself; they would cause too many problems and hurt the case. He was now busy trying to reach Adrian Bustinza, who was living in Texas. When the air force location service told Larry they had no record of an Adrian Bustinza, I didn't wonder too much about where those records had ended up.

But Larry had located Greg Battram at home in the Midwest and interviewed him by phone. Greg confirmed almost every detail of my account—right through to the next morning's telephone call to my mother. Greg's support meant a lot to me.

Cindy and I were engaged in April, and we set the date for May 1985. I was happy—my family all liked her, and she took good care of me. Though the UFO stuff overshadowed my life, I promised her that I'd walk away from it soon and put my energy into our lives and marriage. Still, the compulsion to tell what had happened at Bentwaters continued to ride me like an addiction.

New revelations made walking away more difficult than ever. Fawcett called to say that he had just done a phone interview with Adrian Bustinza on 20 April 1984. He'd asked many questions and recorded the call with Adrian's permission. Although Adrian confirmed a great deal of what I'd told Fawcett, he denied having been in the underground facility, but said he knew of other guys who had been, like me. That was just how I'd handled it when I first talked about that experience: it hadn't happened to me, it happened to a guy I knew—Adrian! I certainly couldn't blame him for being on the defensive now. Later, when Fawcett played the tape for me, Busty sounded nervous at just the mention of the facility. I understood how he felt, but his reaction left me out on a limb.

Fawcett and Greenwood's book, *Clear Intent* was released early that summer and managed to get some press attention. It included my Bentwaters account. In general, the book did a fine job. It showed proof, through documents released by the Freedom of Information Act, that the UFO cover-up was both real and continuing. Greenwood and Fawcett gave me a signed copy.

Interest in Bentwaters continued to grow, especially in England and America. Chrissie Hynde of the rock group Pretenders penned "Show Me," a song about the *News of the World's* Bentwaters coverage, that became a top-ten hit. At the same time, Minolta ran an amusing television commercial: a group of U.S. military personnel are midencounter with a landed UFO and its little alien pilots in a pine forest. Then the soldiers move in with cameras—Minoltas, of course. Before long, the little aliens are posing for pictures with the troops, and everyone is having a great time. The spot ends with the voice-over saying something like: "You don't have to be from this neck of the woods to use the Minolta SX-70." Though I laughed when I saw it, I was left feeling a little angry.

Cindy was now gaining a greater awareness of the UFO subject and my part in it; I don't think she liked what she saw, and we had fights about it regularly. I wasn't helping matters by sounding off on the topic to anyone who'd listen. I felt that I was indestructible. I'd *prove* Bentwaters had happened, at any cost. That included the cost to my family, my friends, and me.

My anger was changing me. I remembered the younger Larry as a nicer guy; now I was anything but. I justified the change as necessary; I had to be tougher as attacks on me continued. My real fear was of some government reprisal. But I didn't talk about it and slid into a lethal depression, finding solace in the bottle more often than I cared to admit. I never really slept well anymore and dreamed of Bentwaters and the underground facility often. There were constant invasion dreams, and occasionally I fought desperately to keep those things with jet-black, slanted eyes away from me.

One night, those creatures were in our apartment. I woke up and turned to Cindy and tried to wake her too, but she was out. Then a voice in my head echoed: "You are our puppet." I leaped from the bed and ran straight into our solid-oak bedroom door. I smashed my nose and Cindy woke up, scared. I told her I'd had a bad dream.

Over the preceding year, I'd begun to have an unusual medical problem. The skin at the base of my neck and the top of my back would first start to get hot, then I would begin to bleed through the skin. It would happen without warning and ruined a dozen shirts that year.

Late one June night as Cindy and I sat watching TV, she suddenly moved back and said, "My God, Larry, you're bleeding again." The back of my yellow T-shirt was already red. That was it for her: "We are going to the hospital," she said. Cindy was an occupational therapist at one of the hospitals in New Britain and called their emergency room immediately. She knew the nurse who answered and described the situation as best she could. The nurse expressed concern over the amount of blood I was losing and told Cin to get me to the ER. I couldn't stop the bleeding and was getting weak.

Once in the ER, we waited to be seen by a doctor. When my turn came, I was shown into a small room and Cindy followed. She thought I had ruptured a blood vessel at the surface of my skin, and I hoped that was all it was. I hated hospitals and just wanted to get out of there.

A doctor entered the room and asked questions about the bleeding, such as how long had it been going on. I told him on and off for about a year. He took some blood and asked us to wait. He returned after about an hour and told us the tests were showing some strange things; he and some other doctors were going to do some more tests and again he asked us to wait.

Cindy was concerned, but I had now stopped the bleeding by applying direct pressure. After almost four hours, three doctors entered the room. The oldest of them said he had some questions for me and that I shouldn't be alarmed. "Were you in Vietnam?" he asked. I said "No, I was too young." "When you were in the service, did you work around any nuclear devices?" "Yes," I answered. "Larry," he said, "our tests show that you may have been exposed to an unshielded nuclear device. Can you recall any time that this might have happened?" Cindy's face dropped. "Yes," I answered, "but you wouldn't believe me if I told you."

I was told that my white blood cells showed signs of having been heavily dosed by rads. One of the effects would be occasional hemorrhaging through the skin. All three doctors seemed puzzled; if I'd been so exposed, such effects shouldn't be showing up for twenty years or so. It had only been four years since Bentwaters.

The doctors asked me to keep them posted on any further developments and told Cindy to keep an eye on me. Then we drove home. I was scared. Were the other guys having health problems? Did the air force know they had brought us into a dangerous situation that night? Was I going to die because of it?

Fawcett called the week after the hospital visit to say that English UFO researcher Dot Street was visiting the States and wanted to meet with me; the book she'd coauthored was due out in 1984 in the U.K. I reluctantly agreed. She was staying with the Fawcetts, and we spent a day together later that week, talking for hours about details of the case.

Dot showed me a picture of one of her air force sources. I knew the guy and told her he'd worked the day shift in law enforcement; he hadn't been involved at all. Law enforcement had played a minimal role the night I'd been involved. She didn't like hearing that, but we got along well otherwise.

Street, Randles, and Butler had been on the case from day one. I did feel the women were purposely being led to think the Bentwaters UFO reports might be some cover story for the crash of a jet carrying nuclear bombs. A lot of folks in England were nervous about the alleged nuclear arsenal we kept there. In fact, two of the *Sky Crash* authors were affiliated with Britain's antinuclear movement. That notwithstanding, nothing had crashed at Bentwaters while I was there.

At about this time, I got a call at work from Jim Greenfield, the NSA agent. He asked if we could meet, and I said yes. We decided on Art Secondo's Hall of Fame, a sports bar in Southington. I told Cindy I was meeting a friend for a drink and left without volunteering any other information.

By ten o'clock the place was beginning to get crowded. I was on my third beer when a tall, well-dressed man sat down to my left. "How ya doing?" he said without introduction. He then produced a small, black portfolio, the kind that holds photographs. He opened it and slowly began to turn the pages. I looked, shocked to be facing actual color photos of the Bentwaters incident! Some were fogged and hazy, but others were not.

As I studied the pictures, I felt someone watching me. I looked up to see a man staring at me directly across the bar. Was he Greenfield's partner? As I turned back to the portfolio, it was closed in my face. Greenfield and the guy across the bar both got up and walked out. I waited another fifteen minutes before leaving for home. What had been the purpose of the meeting? Nothing made sense anymore.

In mid-August 1984, Fawcett called to find out if I would participate in a project about Bentwaters that CNN was planning. It was to be a three-part special investigation and sounded good. Chuck DeCaro, the network's military and technology correspondent, would be covering it. Fawcett had met him while promoting *Clear Intent* in Washington, D.C. Chuck was interested in Bentwaters because it was recent and most witnesses would still be alive. We spoke by phone soon after and set up an interview for the first week in September. I would supply names and photos of other witnesses, a copy of my service record, and details about the third night. Fawcett would assist Chuck with other information.

DeCaro and his camera crew arrived at my father's house the first Thursday afternoon of September. We spoke on camera about my experience in England. DeCaro told me he intended to speak with every witness he could. He also planned to submit questions to the Department of the Air Force about UFO activity around the bases. They were even going to be shooting on location in England. DeCaro was really intent on getting answers and was a reserve officer in the Special Forces, so I felt comfortable with him. We were to talk often during the six months of production.

Four days after my taping, Fawcett called to ask if I wanted to go to Japan. I said yes, and he told me they wanted me there for three weeks. I should expect a call from Nippon Television Network (NTV). I was excited beyond words, but Cindy was worried about my taking the time off work.

In August 1983, the *Hartford Courant* began reporting on a wave of UFO sightings over southern Connecticut and Westchester County in New York. Over the next year, a vast number of credible people had been reporting large boomerang-shaped objects in the region and now the sightings were increasing and even made the front page of the *New York Times* in September.

Bob Luca called in September 1984 to invite me to a UFO conference in Brewster, New York. It was being organized as a result of the large number of recent UFO sightings in the Hudson River valley and would feature talks by witnesses and video footage of the objects.

The location of the conference was a middle school, overrun with press and media. I was shocked to see NBC, ABC, and the *New York Times* all represented there. We needed the big news organizations on our side, now more than ever. Presenters included Dr. J. Allen Hynek, Budd Hopkins, and Philip Imbrogno, a local science instructor who had led the investigation of the Westchester sightings. Fawcett also spoke and focused on the government cover-up. I was still rather anonymous, so I was free to wander around and talk with people, which I enjoyed.

Over one thousand people of every description and educational level showed up that day, most with the hope of getting some answers to what they had been seeing in the skies over Westchester and Connecticut. One lesser-known speaker infuriated me. He stated that a credible UFO witness must have at least a bachelor's degree to be taken seriously. His view excluded many in the lecture hall, and witnesses with valuable stories to tell now reconsidered sharing them. I walked out of his lecture. I needed to get some air. I wondered how UFO research-ers who had never seen a UFO could be so judgmental of people who had.

Outside, I spoke with a group of people who'd also been turned off by that speaker. I said that a garbage man was just as qualified as a Ph.D. to report a UFO sighting. A man holding a set of photographs he'd taken of the Westchester boomerang approached me and said, "Thanks, Larry, I'm a garbage man!" He had been planning to show them to Dr. Hynek, but was now disgusted. They were the most detailed photos I had ever seen of a UFO's superstructure. He thanked me again and walked away. I don't think he showed them to Dr. Hynek, and, to the best of my knowledge, his amazing pictures never resur-faced. I wondered how many other people had hard photographic proof tucked away in a drawer at home out of fear of being ridiculed by half-witted UFO researchers.

Al Terzi, a reporter and news anchor for Connecticut's ABC affiliate WTNH, was out on the lawn conducting interviews with witnesses and conference speakers. Fawcett had introduced us the previous spring, and Al had been doing his own research into the Bentwaters events ever since. He even wanted to go to England with a film crew and produce a news feature on it for WTNH. Al asked if I'd like to comment on the conference for the six o'clock news, which I did.

As we spoke, he changed the subject to my involvement at Bentwa-ters. By now there was a large crowd watching, and when the interview ended I was mobbed with questions and requests to retell my story. When my voice finally gave out, I broke away from the ring of people.

A science writer from the *New York Tribune* named Antonio Huneeus introduced himself, and we talked for a while. He then introduced me to a New York City–based UFO researcher and police detective named Pete Mazzola and another man named Peter Robbins. I met a lot of brave people that day, all with the same objective: we just wanted to know what was going on.

NTV producer Junishi Yaoi soon called, and we negotiated the deal. He liked to be called Jim and spoke English very well. He offered to pay me five hundred dollars and expenses. I wasn't a great business-man, but asked if my brother Scott could come with me (Cindy couldn't take time off work). Jim said that would be impossible; but would I accept one thousand dollars plus expenses? Get paid to visit Japan? This was too good to be true, so I agreed. By now I felt I'd earned it.

Jim and his crew would be coming to the States in a few weeks to interview me. He also arranged for a hypnotic regression with Pat Gegleardo, a hypnotherapist and respected psychic. She had found a number of crime victims for the Connecticut state police over the years.

When Jim's crew arrived at my father's house in Southington, my father, Sandy, Scott, and Bill were impressed with how professional and efficient they were. Jim and I hit it off right away. After a brief interview, he asked if I'd heard the tape. "What tape?" I asked. Jim described a tape in his possession, recorded by Lieutenant Colonel Halt during the third night of UFO activity near Woodbridge base.

I couldn't believe it! He had it with him and let me listen to it. It ran about twenty minutes. Though heavily edited, it sounded like an on-site account of part of what I'd witnessed. I asked Jim how he had gotten hold of it. He told me that a friend of Lieutenant Colonel Halt's, an officer, had given a copy to a lawyer in England named Harry Harris. Harris, in turn, had sold the tape to Jim and his network for two thousand dollars. I wanted a copy; it could only strengthen my case. Jim promised me one when I got to Japan.

My flight to Japan landed at Narita Airport on 10 October. Once deplaned, a moving sidewalk rolled me along for a quarter mile. At the far end of the terminal, I walked past some news crews to the baggage pickup. Feeling like I was being followed, I turned around and saw that I was—by news crews! At least fifty reporters and cameramen were coming at me, some holding my photo—I guess so they would know me when they saw me. I heard: "Art Wallace!" "Art Wallace!," being yelled at me in distinctly Japanese Accents. I hadn't used the name Art Wallace for many months, but was too stunned to correct anyone. A reporter asked how I liked Japan; I told him it had a nice airport. I got my bag, then spotted Mishima, part of Jim's NTV crew. He got me through customs quick.

As we drove toward Tokyo, Mishima explained that NTV had promoted my visit heavily over the preceding few weeks, so I should not be surprised if people reacted to me as if I were a celebrity. I couldn't get over it. Once in Tokyo, Mishima pointed up to a large billboard at the top of a building. It was a promotion for *The 11:00 P.M. Wide Show,* Japan's version of *The Tonight Show.* On it was a giant picture of my face, looking slightly Asian. It was outrageous. I checked into my hotel completely exhausted.

Jim picked me up and we walked to another hotel for my first press conference. I looked at this trip as a challenge and just hoped I could communicate my experience to the Japanese. It was amazing how responsive the Japanese people were to the subject of UFOs. Most Asian countries were represented at the press conference, as well as Australia and New Zealand.

Before entering the room, I was asked to put on a pair of Ray-Ban Wayfarer sunglasses. Asking why, I was told that Japanese people liked mystery. I felt like a jerk, but wore them through the questioning with minimal trauma. I went sight-seeing that afternoon and saw everything I could of the city.

The next morning, everyone at the hotel seemed to be smiling at me and know who I was: my picture was on the front page of several city newspapers. I was assigned a translator and made my first Japanese television appearance. The more TV programs I did, the more people recognized me on the street; some asked for my autograph.

I was introduced to Uri Geller in Tokyo, and we ended up having quite a talk. He took UFOs very seriously and asked my thoughts on what we should do about the government cover-up. "Just keep fighting the fight," I said. Later he bent one of my house keys—the nerve of some psychics. I made some more TV appearances and was given a better translator. Masako and her family owned a fish store in a working-class part of Tokyo. Masako was great and honored me with an invitation to visit her family home, a rare experience for an American. There, I traded cigarettes with her father. A few days later, I shaved off my mustache and made the papers again. The press wondered if this act had some deep meaning.

Things got even sillier the last week, when I played myself in a low-budget film about the Bentwaters incident. NTV's special-effects team built a model of the UFO and spray-painted three Gumby dolls silver—yes, it was bad. The actors Jim had hired were mostly French and German models. Lieutenant Colonel Halt was played by the president of A.M.F., Japan; I was told he took acting jobs for a kick. When the actors showed up for work in World War II–era army uniforms, I refused to go any farther until they were wearing USAF security police uniforms. Within an hour, they were. The film was shot in a pine forest that really looked like Rendlesham, unless you looked up—the forest was at the base of Mount Fuji.

The 11:00 P.M. Wide Show was my last appearance on Japanese TV. I was not comfortable with this show from the start. The host had no lenses in his glasses, and he kept making pointed-ear and antenna-on-head gestures with his hands when he talked about the three beings.

On top of this, my legs wouldn't fit under the table, and the Halt tape refused to play on the show's recorder; everything went wrong.

The next morning, I drove to Narita Airport with Jim. When we said good-bye, he gave me four beautiful copper cups as a gift. He also gave me a copy of the Halt tape. On the flight to New York, I watched a squadron of Soviet MIGs fly between us and the coast of the Soviet Union. The recent KAL disaster made the sight of those Migs particularly unnerving. Cindy met me at the shuttle terminal in Waterbury. I had missed her a lot and had spent most of my thousand dollars on gifts for her and my family.

In December, I gave a copy of the Halt tape to Fawcett, who in turn passed it on to CNN's Chuck DeCaro. The Bentwaters *Special Assignment* was due for airing in February 1985. Chuck called soon after he'd finished doing the principal interviews. Though all our accounts were mutually supportive, the other witnesses he'd spoken with were apprehensive about going public. Their families were worried for their safety. As a result, all but me would appear with their faces blacked out. But their statements and the Halt tape added new dimensions to the investigation, and our case was growing stronger every day. Chuck said that after each taping, he had tested my story on each witness, beings and all; they all said I wasn't lying.

Cindy and I spent Christmas at my mother's. I was glad the year was coming to a close and hoped 1985 would be a good year. After all, I'd be getting married in May, when I planned to give the UFO quest up for good. I'd accomplished enough toward getting Bentwaters into the public eye, and that's all I had ever wanted to achieve.

1984 Developments |

13 January 1984

The Department of the Air Force's headquarters in Europe sends Staff Sergeant Clifford Stone this letter:

Dear Mr. Stone,

This is in response to your 27 December 1983 Freedom of Information Act Request concerning alleged UFO sightings in Europe during December 1980. We are furnishing you with a copy of the only records in the possession of the United

States Air Force in Europe documenting this incident. Search and copy fees have been waived.

Sincerely,
(signed) Albert G. Stewart, Colonel, USAF
Director of Administration[29]

The records attached to the letter consist of a single page—the Halt memorandum.

7 February 1984
With a phone number supplied by Larry Warren, Larry Fawcett places a call to the home of Greg Battram. Some of that conversation follows:

GB. I was in the air force up to this point a little over a year. I had been in England about two months.

LF. OK, you were stationed at Bentwaters or Woodbridge?

GB. At Bentwaters.

LF. Were you attached to the Eighty-first Police Security Squadron?

GB. Yes.

LF. What was your job there, Greg?

GB. I was in the planning and program section.

LF. Go ahead.

GB. We had an alert over there for exercises and things about once or twice a month. And during those times, all the back-office people would go on a security post, additional posting and stuff out there. So, the night we saw the UFO, we were out there on duty, on one of these exercises, and it was nighttime. Nothing going on but we all still had to be there, and we were driving around on Woodbridge base on a perimeter patrol, and we saw some lights up in the sky, and it looked a lot different from any other aircraft we had ever seen.

We watched them for a while and then they disappeared . . . in a clearing of a forest and that's when we saw the object or whatever. We thought it was a fire at first. When we saw that, we thought, oh, boy, we could have some problems out here, so we called Central Security Control and told them we wanted to go out and see what it was. They said go ahead and they would notify the base fire department and the British authorities. So we took off out the back gate, there at Woodbridge, and headed toward the forest.

LF. Who was with you, Greg?

GB. I can't remember the names of those guys. Three other guys in the truck.

LF. OK.

GB. We got out there and parked the truck on the side of the road and went walking in toward the clearing. Just as we got about fifty yards away, we started to feel the hair on our necks and arms and stuff stand up.

LF. Yes.

GB. And it felt really strange. And we could hear a thrumming kind of sound.

LF. A what kind of sound?

GB. A thrumming noise coming out of the forest, from the direction of that object. It had like a ground fog all around it.

LF. OK.

GB. We couldn't really see a distinct shape, but there were alternating colors in it and the whole bit. It was really strange. The closer we got, the worse the static electricity feeling got, and we just said, "Fuck," and we turned around and took off.

LF. Did you have weapons with you?

GB. Yes.

LF. You did?

GB. Yes. Guaranteed. I didn't know what the fuck was in there, and I was not taking any chances.

LF. How big was this thing?

GB. Oh! Shoot. I would say it was, it could have been, the fog itself was like one hundred feet across.

LF. Yes.

GB. I really couldn't see the thing. Inside, it seemed like there was a denser section to the fog, about thirty to fifty feet maybe across.

LF. I see.

GB. It seemed like that, and when we left we met up with Lieutenant Englund as I remember it . . . anyway he was the only officer I knew; and some security police come over from Bentwaters. I think Larry was with them.

LF. Yes.

GB. We just told them the whole bit and he said, "OK, head on back." So we did.

LF.   Could you see all the light-alls they had out there?

GB.   I could see a couple of them as they were bringing them out.

LF.   OK. Were there a lot of personnel going out there?

GB.   Well, it seemed like it. I saw twenty to thirty people.

LF.   When did you hook up with Larry? When he tried to call his mother that time?

GB.   Shortly after that we were, I guess, sitting in one of our rooms or in the snack bar or one of the two. He decided he was going to call his mom, and I said, I'll go with you. We walked down to the phones by the base exchange. He tried one phone and didn't have that good of a connection, so he tried the other and got through.

    I think it was like, when he mentioned this to his mother, the phones just clicked off, and we couldn't figure out what the fuck it was. So we tried the other phone, and it didn't work either. We didn't put these two things together at the time. Then, when Larry first called me it was really crazy, because we started remembering all these crazy things. There were a lot of things I had forgotten about over there that we started talking about, and we remembered it, or he would bring up a name and I would remember it. It was interesting.

LF.   Was there a lot of commotion about this in the next couple of days after that?

GB.   Not really officially, I think. Not that you could really see. We got talked to the next day, and [they] said "be quiet."

LF.   Because Larry, Bustinza was telling me they were called down to the communications shack and all were debriefed on what they had seen and so forth.

GB.   Yes, because we had a meeting, the planning and program section did. Every commander of every squadron or tenant-organization section was there. It was like the base security council met. Then there were some other people that I had never seen before, and they turned out to be from Washington.

LF.   From where?

GB.   From Washington apparently.

LF.   And they debriefed you?

GB.   Yes, they gave their little speech, it was all discussed at the meeting. Get the word out to everyone, don't spread any rumors and that kind of stuff. And calm it down and talk it down.

LF. Did you hear any conversation by any of the airmen besides Larry, talking about seeing little creatures?

GB. I heard that from a couple of people. You could hear it in the conversation, but they thought they had seen something. I mean, the way the rumor was going around, it was like a big joke, "You saw little green men, too."

LF. Did Larry tell you that he had seen them?

GB. You know I can't remember whether he did or not at the time. But we got to talking again recently about this, when he first called, and he mentioned that. It didn't seem like a shock or anything, like I had not heard it before. So it's possible he did.

LF. OK. So you did hear that while you were on base.

GB. Yes.

LF. And this incident was in December, right?

GB. Yes.

LF. OK.

GB. It seemed like a week before New Year's. Something like that, it seemed real close to it.

LF. Were there any other sightings after that, Greg, that you heard of?

GB. The stories went on for a while like they did before that night. We heard a lot of stories about people seeing lights at night and strange things. We thought they were all on dope.

LF. Yes.

GB. That's why it was strange that night, because it was the second night we had been out on this alert. I had thought the night before, now I get to see if these guys are really high or if they're really seeing something. The night it happened, it was like—holy shit! There must be something in the water.

LF. So in other words, when you came into the field, you came one way, and Larry and his groups were coming another way really.

GB. Yes. Well, we were already there, because it was right off Woodbridge.

LF. Were you picking up any chatter on the radios about this?

GB. No. We couldn't get through; the closer we got, the worse it got.

LF. . . . When the thing was in the field, you really couldn't get a shape to it, other than lights on the bottom and all kinds of colors were in it.

GB. It seemed to be alternating, mostly between oranges, reds, blues, and whites.

LF.   You are definitely sure there was something solid there?

GB.   Yes, because I don't [know] if it was more a sight or a feeling, but it was a denser section to that fog bank. Like it just didn't fit.

LF.   In other words, there was no fog anywhere else but actually where the thing was?

GB.   Oh, yes, it was right there. Strange . . .

LF.   Now Bustinza told us that the secretary of the air force flew in there a couple of days after.

GB.   Oh, I do remember him.

LF.   You do?

GB.   I remember talking to him. That was interesting though.

LF.   How about Burroughs? Did you know Burroughs at all?

GB.   I remember him a little bit, but I can't place a face.

LF.   OK.

GB.   I remember the name right off the bat.[30]

February 1984

Clear Intent is released in the United States. It devotes five pages to the Bentwaters incident, scrupulously built around Art Wallace's account. The authors quote from current RAF Bentwaters Commander Colonel Henry J. Cochran's response to CAUS's FOIA:

> There was allegedly some strange activity near RAF Bentwaters at the approximate time in question but not on land under U.S. Air Force jurisdiction and, therefore, no official investigation was conducted by the 81st Tactical Fighter Wing. Thus, the records you request do not exist. (p. 213)

But if no records existed, how did Colonel Cochran know something had happened?

> . . . in a June 14, 1983 letter from Col. Peter Bent, Commander of the 513th CSG, an utterly stunning admission was made. Col. Bent said:
> "The Air Force file copy had been properly disposed of in accordance with Air Force Regulations. Fortunately, through diligent inquiry and the gracious consent of Her Majesty's government, the British Ministry of Defence and the Royal Air Force, the U.S. Air Force was provided a copy for you."

For Greenwood and Fawcett, the first released copy of Colonel Halt's report "reads like science fiction." They conclude that:

Outside of some small variation in detail, the story in the document is amazingly similar to what Art Wallace described. The letter was certainly part of a more detailed file, since it was clear an official investigation *was* conducted. (p. 216)

20 April 1984

With another of the phone numbers supplied by Warren, Fawcett is able to reach Adrian Bustinza at his home. Citing Warren as his introduction, Fawcett finds the witness willing to talk.

LF. How long have you been out of the service?

AB. Oh, going on about two years. About a year and two or three months.

LF. How long were you in?

AB. Six years.

LF. Six years? How come you didn't make a career out of it?

AB. Oh, I don't know.

LF. Larry Warren told me you were a career man.

AB. No.

LF. No.

AB. They all thought I was, I guess.

LF. Larry had told me here in the beginning that he was at Bentwaters during the time of the incident and that he was on a guard post and a jeep pulled up with a Lieutenant Englund and I believe yourself was in the jeep.

AB. Right.

LF. Larry was told to get into the jeep and from there you drove down to the motor pool, I believe.

AB. Right.

LF. And Lieutenant Englund told you to fill the light-alls.

AB. With gas.

LF. With gas. Now Larry said there was something screwy. He said, "We filled these things up." And I think it was either Lieutenant Englund or Captain Verrano that was there.

AB. It was, well, Lieutenant Englund was the one that was there.

LF. OK.

AB. Captain Verrano was on day shift at that time.

LF. OK. He said that the light-alls were filled and Englund kept saying they weren't or something to that effect.

AB. Right.

LF. Does that sound right?

AB.   Yes.

LF.   He said the damned things were filled to overflowing and they
      kept saying they weren't filled. Is that right?

AB.   Yes, that's correct.

LF.   OK.

AB.   So we went ahead, and we checked them. We made sure they
      were full, and they were full. And then we took them up back to
      the field, and they wouldn't work. And they were functioning
      perfect when we tried them out.

LF.   OK. Let me go on. You know, you can stop me if it's different,
      OK?

AB.   OK.

LF.   Larry said from there you jumped in the jeep and went to the
      gate of Bentwaters.

AB.   Right.

LF.   There you met a couple of other vehicles.

AB.   Correct.

LF.   From there you went out the gate to Bentwaters toward Wood-
      bridge.

AB.   Right.

LF.   OK. As you got past the east gate in Woodbridge, I believe, he
      said you turned off, like, a logging road.

AB.   Right.

LF.   He said there were military police in the street. There were flares
      down, and they were blocking traffic.

AB.   Right.

LF.   OK. From there you took a right and went up into the wooded
      area.

AB.   Correct.

LF.   He says when you got to like a sort of staging point up in there,
      there were other vehicles there when you got there.

AB.   Right.

LF.   OK. You got out of the vehicles. They took the weapons away
      from you.

AB.   Well, they didn't take mine.

LF.   They didn't take yours?

AB.   No, sir.

LF.   OK. Well . . .

AB.   They, well, let me see—no, mine wasn't taken away, but I had a
      side arm also.

LF. You had a side arm?

AB. They did take our big weapons away, which were M16s.

LF. OK. Before I go any further on this point, Larry had said when he was at the guard post something very funny was happening. The animals were running out of the woods.

AB. Yes.

LF. A lot of deer.

AB. A lot of deer were running out of the woods and not only the deer, the rabbits. You know, I mean it was natural for the rabbits to run out of the fields but, you know, when the lights hit them— not just by themselves.

LF. I see.

AB. And there was a lot of deer out in the roads,'cause I remember Lieutenant Englund cautioned me to drive with caution on the way over there. There was animals all over the road.

LF. OK. Now he said there was a Major Zickler there also.

AB. Yes, that was our squadron commander.

LF. In fact, Larry said when he stepped out of the jeep he fell into mud up to his waist.

AB. True.

LF. Everybody was laughing.

AB. Yeah.

LF. Now Larry said they broke up into about four-man teams.

AB. Right.

LF. And you started to go into the woods like in a line.

AB. Correct.

LF. And there was John Burroughs there?

AB. John Burroughs, correct.

LF. All right. Sergeant Medina?

AB. Right.

LF. A Captain Verrano?

AB. Captain Verrano, yeah, station commander.

LF. Ball, Sergeant Ball?

AB. Yeah, Master Sergeant Ball, my flight chief.

LF. Mark Thompson?

AB. Oh, yeah, that crazy guy, yeah.

LF. Sergeant Combs?

AB. Sergeant Combs, law enforcement?

LF. Yeah. Airman Palmer?

AB. Palmer. Law enforcement, too.

LF.   OK. From that point, you went into the woods in a line, I guess. Were there any bobbies there or British police or anything?

AB.   Not at the beginning.

LF.   Not at the beginning?

AB.   No.

LF.   OK. As you were going through now, Larry said all of a sudden, they could see lights coming through the woods and he could also hear helicopters over above.

AB.   Yes, a squadron, pararescue squadron was activated.

LF.   Pararescue. Where were they from? Woodbridge?

AB.   Woodbridge . . . they weren't very far away as a matter of fact.

LF.   Do you know how many were up at the time?

AB.   I recall Major Zickler said, scramble two, I believe he said.

LF.   Two?

AB.   Two. I think that's what he prescribed, two.

LF.   OK. As we're going into the field now, Larry said he could see lights coming through the field.

AB.   Right.

LF.   You got to sort of like a barbed-wire fence, I think he said, or a stone fence or something.

AB.   A barbed-wire fence.

LF.   And at this point Larry could hear the helicopters talking with the ground radios.

AB.   Right. They flew by the officers there.

LF.   OK. As you got into the field, Larry said the field was ringed by military people and British personnel.

AB.   Yes.

LF.   Is that right?

AB.   Yes.

LF.   How many do you figure there were?

AB.   Oh, I estimate at least thirty people.

LF.   Thirty?

AB.   At least thirty.

LF.   Now, Larry said that he saw movie-picture cameras.

AB.   Movie-picture cameras?

LF.   Yeah. You know, they were taking pictures.

AB.   Well, yeah they were, but I didn't know they were movie pictures or not. I did see a couple flashes.

LF.   OK. Larry says at this point, when you came to the field, there was like a large aspirin-shaped transparent thing in the middle of the field.

AB. OK, that's the yellow mist I was talking about.

LF. Right. All of a sudden he could hear the helicopter or somebody say, "Here it comes." And they looked up, and over the pine trees came a red ball of light. And this red ball of light like went over the top of this mist in the middle of the field and all of a sudden it exploded into a lot of colors, but there was no sound. Do you remember that?

AB. Yes, I remember that. That's the main, the cream of the crop I would say.

LF. Well, you know that I know what I'm talking about then?

AB. Yes.

LF. OK. After the colors dissipated, Larry said, there, was this machine there. This "thing," what he called it. Now, he drew several pictures for us, and he said that you were told to get going closer to it. He—I believe he said it was him, might have been Zickler, I'm not sure—and two other guys walked out into the field toward this thing. Is that correct?

AB. Yes, sir, that's correct.

LF. You get up next to this machine, very close, and as you started to walk you could see your shadows on it, and when you stopped, the shadows continued a little bit. Now, Larry says at this point a light came down from the top of the thing and sort of like jumped from head to head on the shadows, and at this point, Larry says he can't remember anything. And the next thing you know, he woke up. He was in his barracks on his bed. He was covered with mud, and he asked his roommate what time he was brought in. They said around four o'clock in the morning. Now, he said that the next day he was told to go down in the security shack, I guess, whatever you have there.

AB. Security control.

LF. He was debriefed and told basically not to say anything about the incident, that they're to go on with their lives and to forget about it.

AB. Right.

LF. Larry said that either that day or the next day, he got a call to go outside his barracks. That he would be picked up by an automobile, and him, and I believe he said, three or four other guys were out there. Now this vehicle pulls up. Now here's where it gets crazy. This vehicle pulls up and a couple of Chinese-looking guys get out, as he describes them. Oriental types, and he's told to get into the back of the vehicle; he says it was very strange inside. The only way he could describe it, you ever see the green lights from the dash? was like this vehicle. He got inside the vehicle, and they started to drive, and the next thing he knew he was underground somewhere. I don't know if you know any of this. Are you there?

AB. Yeah, I'm with you. I don't want to say anything else. I'm with you.

LF. OK. Now, from this point, he was taken underground, he got out and they walked along a catwalk inside. Now, he said this cave was man-made, you could see it was man-made. And as they were walking along, he could look down and he could see people down below; he said also there was one of these machines down there that they saw in the field. Does that sound anything?

AB. The underground part. I really don't know anything about the underground part.

LF. OK. Now, let me get back to the field part, OK? We put Larry under regressive hypnosis. Now, what came out under hypnosis was, while he was in the field and he was standing next to that machine, he was like petrified—frozen—that he couldn't move, you know? And he could see beings, small type of creatures. And they were talking to an officer there. He gave me the officer's name [Williams], I can't remember who the hell it was now. It was a big guy whoever it was.

AB. Lieutenant Colonel Halt.

LF. Halt. OK. And he said the beings were conversing with Halt. And at this point, something happened on the other side of the craft because all the beings like got defensive. They all lined up. Larry said he could hear a commotion on the other side of this machine, and all the beings' eyes got real big, and they all lined up in a straight line, real quick, like a defensive move. And then they dissipated a little bit, you know. It seemed to calm down whatever was going on on the other side of the ship. At this point, one of the beings floated over the top and came over by him, and that's the last thing he remembers. Does it sound anything like you remember?

AB. OK. Oh, boy, let me see. I remember the conversation. I don't remember word-for-word conversation, OK?

LF. Yeah.

AB. What was going on, I was shocked.

LF. You saw the beings?

AB. I just couldn't believe what was going on. I thought I was in a dreamworld or something.

LF. OK. Do you remember any of the conversation between Halt and the beings?

AB. No, I don't. To be honest with you, I don't. I was just in the feeling of insecurity with it. When you feel helpless . . .

LF. Yeah.

AB. . . . totally helpless. Even though there was plenty of personnel there and they want you to feel secure, and considering the kind of job we did, one would feel secure, but you feel like your whole body, your whole privacy has been invaded.

LF. Right.

AB. No escape, you know?

LF. Boy, Larry said the same thing.

AB. Right.

LF. If it wasn't for Larry, I wouldn't have been able to sue the government to get the documentation of this incident. Let me go on a little further now. Larry said that something happened to their machine. Do you remember that?

AB. Yeah.

LF. And our government helped them repair that machine. They flew a piece in from Germany, I believe.

AB. Hold on, let me see. Colonel Halt, when we approached the machine, I remember Colonel Halt said—I remember Larry. I don't know why they picked Larry, but I remember Larry was going up there, and I was so scared I don't know what to think. I was in a foreign country, you know.

LF. Yeah. Larry said you made a comment, and you said something like, "Oh, no, not again!" Yes. And Larry said, "What do you mean?" And you said, "I went through this." See Larry had it mixed up though. He said, "I went through this in Alaska once before."

AB. Yeah, OK. It wasn't Alaska. When I was talking to them and I was telling them about it, I had just come from Alaska TDY.

LF. Yeah.

AB. It was in California where it actually happened.

LF. This was at Davis?

AB. Mather Air Force Base. Yeah.

LF. OK. So go ahead, you started to say something.

AB. I said "Oh, no, not again." Colonel Halt said—he mentioned a couple of names to me. We walked up toward the craft.

LF. Yeah.

AB. When we walked up there, Colonel Halt started talking, and it was like, it was instant communication between personnel.

LF. Between the men?

AB. The men.

LF. How about the beings?

AB. To tell the truth, I remember seeing the craft. I remember Colonel Halt talking, and I remember looking to who he was talking to and I couldn't see nobody.

LF. You couldn't see nobody?

AB. I couldn't see what, I mean, who he was talking to, and for a minute there I thought everybody there was going crazy here or something, you know. And I do remember him saying he would contact the electronics division, which would be CRF, I think it was, the call letters for the group. And they would possibly have to get the part from another world. And I just looked at, I couldn't hold my, you know. Who are you talking to, what are you talking about, you know?

LF. Right.

AB. It was like, when something like that's happening right before your eyes, you want to try to keep track of everything, but it's hard because everything is happening so fast.

LF. Yeah.

AB. More or less, it was like Larry says. I remember that, and then after that, you know, I woke up in the morning.

LF. You don't know how you got out of the field?

AB. I don't know, well, yes, I remember. I got back in the jeep and lieutenant who was in the jeep, they kept telling us that we were better off not talking to anybody about this at all.

LF. I see.

AB. Not even among ourselves. He said people would think different about us and everybody. Lieutenant looked at me, he said, "You're a supervisor, you ought to know better." And he said,

"You keep an eye on these guys. If anybody says anything, you report to Colonel Halt."

LF.   OK.

AB.   And then personnel affairs would handle the whole situation.

LF.   OK. Now, you did see Halt talking to somebody though, but you could not see who he was talking to.

AB.   Right.

LF.   What, do you remember, basically, what was he saying? Just that we can get parts from the electronics division or we'd try to get parts?

AB.   The electronics division, that's all. I'm sure, I remember. Because I looked at him real funny, I remember, I said, "Electronics division, who is he talking to, what is he talking to?" I asked myself those questions.

LF.   What about the other guys with you? Did they see anything? Besides Larry?

AB.   I really, Burroughs, I think. See, I'm trying to debate; Burroughs . . . I'm not sure. I remember somebody taking pictures, right?

LF.   Yeah. Well, we know that.

AB.   The guys used to have pretty good confidence in me out there, and, I don't know. One of the guys told me that he had taken a picture. They confiscated the cameras from some of the personnel there and the film. I can't remember if it's Burroughs or the other guy—they said, "I switched the film, I got to get my film out of the camera."

LF.   That's what I heard. Larry had told me he thought you did it.

AB.   No, I was on duty that night, and I didn't have my camera with me. I wish I could have done something like that.

LF.   Now, according to Larry, they flew a piece in from Germany, and it landed at Bentwaters. Do you remember that?

AB.   Yeah. When the plane flew in, I remember they called for security right off the bat. And I happened to be on duty, and I set the security.

LF.   Was that the same day?

AB.   No, because we had been working days then. It was in the swing, so it had to be about three or four days later. Because then we went on three-day break.

LF.   Well, then, how long was that machine there then?

AB.   I really don't know. I mean, as far as out in the field?

LF.   Yeah.

AB. When we came in contact with it. Two nights.

LF. Two nights it was there.

AB. Uh-huh. I went on my three days off after that.

LF. OK.

AB. See because Larry's shift and my shift intermixed.

LF. OK.

AB. When they were working days, we were interlapping with each other.

LF. OK. Let me go on a little further now. Larry said after the morning when he woke up, he went to that briefing in the, what is it . . .

AB. The CFC briefing.

LF. Yeah, CFC, that's it. And they were shown a film in there. The guy said, "Once you see this film, you'll know why all the secrecy." Why it's necessary for all the secrecy. And they began showing film clips. World War II vintage it started out, showing a flight of aircraft, and over above was a bunch of flying disks. Then they showed another film, which was Korean War vintage where a MIG—a Chinese MIG—was flying, and UFOs came up alongside of it, and it tipped, and the MIG went down and crashed. Then they showed another film clip from Vietnam, showed a disk coming up out of the jungle sort of like. Almost like what you've seen in the field there.

AB. Right.

LF. Then they showed another film which was the Apollo landings, and there were these disks on the moon. Did you see that film also?

AB. No, sir. I did not see that.

LF. You didn't. Did you ever hear anybody say they saw that film?

AB. Yes. I recall I was having a conversation, this is after the incident happened, a couple of days afterward. I was having a conversation with somebody, and we were up in his room; it was one of these individuals that was there, as a matter of fact.

LF. OK.

AB. And he said he had been taken in to look at that, they had been showing these films. And he was asking me if I had been, you know, seen these films. And I said, no. I said, I haven't. I said, "but they got you all upset." I can't remember his name . . . he wasn't a real good acquaintance of mine. But he said that he'd been taken, like in the underground or something like that, and was watching. They were showing some films that they had told him not to say anything to the others, but he figured since I was one of the individuals that walked up to the craft, that I would have been one of the first ones that got shown. They either just kind of ignored me, period, or forgot about me. But I don't think they would have forgotten about me like that. You know?

LF. Uh-huh.

AB. But to tell the truth, they didn't do much with me. I got debriefed a lot—I did get debriefed a lot. Major Zickler and Lieutenant Colonel Halt, and I even had three meetings with the base commander himself.

LF. Who was that?

AB. The base commander at the time was . . .

LF. I had his name, Larry gave it to me. But I don't have it in front of me.

AB. It would be Colonel . . . God, I can't even remember his name.

LF. Was it Gordon Williams?[31]

AB. Williams, Colonel Williams.

LF. That's it. Well, he's now a brigadier general.

AB. Is he really?

LF. Yeah. Now, what did he say to you? When you went into the office, what happened?

AB. He told me he wasn't fully aware of what was going on. But that he had gotten, from higher-up officials, a briefing of what was more or less going on. And they had told him to bring in indicviduals individually and give them a briefing as to how to communicate with the press if at any chance we were approached by the press off base.

LF. Did they ever tell you what this machine was?

AB. No, they didn't. Colonel Williams's words were, quote unquote, "Whatever you saw out there, I don't want to personally know anything about it. That's between you and whoever's handling the case." Well, no one ever told me what that machine was. I just took it for granted, since it was nothing I had ever seen, I took it for granted—I labeled it a UFO. What I thought afterward was that these supposedly UFOs, with beings and stuff, they're far more intelligent supposedly than we are, how is the air force going to help them fix the machine? How are they going to help?

I remember the words Colonel Halt said: "We'll get you the parts from our electronics division." And that kept ringing a bell and ringing a bell, like how can we help them? You know?

LF. Adrian, describe what the machine looked like.

AB. That I won't forget. It was the first time I've seen one like it. It was circular shaped . . . it looked like a pancake. It was thick in the middle, and it would narrow out toward the edges. I seen lights, all kind of lights. It would have been a beautiful sight, you know. The lights were so bright that I could only see certain parts of the craft, and there were a bunch of little gadgets on it, too, like some planes got, and other little gadgets that I never even seen on aircraft before.

LF. Was it made of metal?

AB. I would assume.

LF. OK. About how close did you get to this thing?

AB. I'd say I was about, within six to ten feet of it.

LF. And how big was it?

AB. It wasn't a humongous thing, but it was of a very good size.

LF. Compare it with the size of, say, a Chevy or a Dodge or something like that. Make a comparison with something in size—a truck, tractor trailer in length.

AB. About as wide as an A-10. From what I could see in the beginning, it was very big, but I couldn't really tell exactly how big . . . as big as a medium-sized house, I would say.

LF. And larger than maybe twelve feet?

AB. Yes, in height, definitely yes.

LF. And how big are the A-10s in length?

AB. About forty feet.

LF. Did you hear any sounds when you were up near it?

AB. The only sound that I heard was like a rumble, like when you hear a jet pass over. But I don't know whether it was the choppers or it was the sound coming out of the machine down there.

LF. You didn't see any engines on this machine, right?

AB. No, I didn't.

LF. When it moved, when it took off, did you hear anything or feel anything?

AB. When it took off, it was, like, hovering. It went up and, like, took off at about a forty-five-degree angle, and if you would have blinked, you would have missed it.

LF. That fast?

AB. That fast. And we got a cold draft of air that lasted about a good ten seconds. You know, like when you get a good blow of dust or wind. No noise though; I do remember that.

LF. OK. When it took off, were you able to see the bottom of it?

AB. No, I can't say I did.

LF. Did the colors change at all?

AB. The colors were constantly changing while I was there. I remember, it was different colors, and they just, like, go on and off or go to a lower shade.

LF. When the machine was down on the ground, what color was the body of the machine?

AB. I'd say like a blackish grayish.

LF. But it was metal, you're sure of that?

AB. I'm pretty sure, it had to be metal, yeah.

LF. Black or grayish. And did the machine glow at all when it took off? Did the lights change?

AB. The lights, yes. That's what it did. It turned, like, into a ball of light.

LF. The whole machine?

AB. The whole machine. And it was like a glow around it, and it just took off.

LF. How long was it on the ground there. Do you remember?

AB. I don't remember how long.

LF. But you did see it take off?

AB. Yes, I did.

LF. And it was after they fixed it? Did you see them fix it there?

AB. No, I didn't see them fix it.

LF. What makes you think that airplane that came in from Germany had parts of that machine?

AB. Well, because I've never seen a C-130 come in and get security the way this plane got security. Planes are constantly coming in and out, and C-130s always landed at Woodbridge. Next thing, we got top aid security on it, and guess who gets called.

LF. OK. So, how long do you think the whole incident, landing, took while you were in that field?

AB. Oh, I'd say I was in that field a good three, four hours.

LF. Were there British military personnel there?

AB. I don't recall British military personnel, but I do recall the bobbies.

LF. What were they doing?

AB. They were in the background. As a matter of fact, I don't think they were even close enough to see there was a craft. They were in the wooded area. I guess they were like a perimeter security.

LF. OK.

AB. It flew toward the wooded area. You know I didn't like when I saw it up close. I couldn't understand how a big thing—that big—could go in. It seemed like this thing was going dashing in between the trees. We were chasing it for a while.

LF. OK. Let me get into a little bit more, and then I'll let you go. Larry also told me something really screwy happened after they showed him the films.[32] Larry said all of a sudden there was a shadow, appeared behind the screen, and he could hear voices in his head, like somebody was talking to him, saying something like, "We've been here a long time. The governments, all the powers of the world, know about us. Your government isn't what it looks to be. We are in charge." Like Larry could ask questions in his mind, and answers would come to him. Did you ever hear anything like that before?

AB. No. It was really funny that, ever since then, I don't [know] whether I went through something like that and then I never realized it, but I get dreams every now and then, you know, like someone was talking to me. I don't know whether it's something I'm trying to remember that happened, that I wasn't aware of, or maybe they're just dreams, I don't know. The government is capable of so many things. I've been on the inside, and I've seen what they can do to the outside.

LF. Larry told me he was threatened. They told Larry that bullets are very cheap if he opened his mouth. Do you remember anything like that? Any threatening of any of the witnesses?

AB. No. They just warned me. They told me, this is a warning. You know better. I figured it was all CIA work.

LF. Oh, that's another question I wanted to ask you. Were there any civilians during this time there? Like CIA or FBI people?

AB. There was a lot of plains. There were about eight plainclothesmen. Right after this incident, the air force secretary came to visit the base.

LF. And that was right after the incident?

AB. Yes, sir. And then we had a visit from Major, Commander Bouchard, that was his [the secretary's] personal bodyguard.

LF. Did he talk about the incident?

AB.   No. He said, "I understand you were involved in the incident, too?" I just kind of played dumb and said, "I don't recall what incident you're talking about." He said, "Well, we'll just leave it at that then."

LF.   OK. Can you think of anything else that might be important?

AB.   After that incident I was sent on three different TDYs. Nobody who's right off the rank could go on a TDY like that, if you know where I'm coming from.

LF.   Did Larry disappear for a couple of days?

AB.   About a week's period.

LF.   He was off the base? You didn't know where he was?

AB.   Right. I remember I looked for him, and I was going to ask him, I needed to talk to somebody—I couldn't find him.

LF.   OK, well Larry said when he came out of the underground complex, it was by the photo lab.

AB.   By the photo lab, right.

LF.   He said there's an exit there from the underground complex by the photo lab.

AB.   OK, I know about that. I know about that underground thing there.

LF.   You do?

AB.   Yes, it's Intelligence.

LF.   It's Intelligence.

AB.   One night I was with _____. I was making a security check of the Intelligence building, which we always did. The door was open, the windows were open, like somebody had been looking for something. We made a check, and I secured the building. Checked everything around the building, and at one point, I saw a shadow. I reported seeing it. By the time I had done my sweep, _____ came back and did their second sweep. Intelligence was called out [and] made a sweep of the building and everything. Their papers had been ruffled, and one of the safes was open. When they relieved me of my post, they told me Intelligence wanted to talk to me, and they took me down there to the bottom. The reason I know about the bottom is because that's where they supposedly kept all their crypto material.

LF.   How big is this place underground?

AB.   It's about, I'd say it would hold a good five hundred people in case of, like a shelter.

LF.   It's like a shelter? OK. The thing at the California base matters. What happened there?

AB. There, we didn't really see much . . . we were all out on the perimeter. The alert pad and bright lights lit up the whole area, and there was something in the middle of the pad but hovering about, oh, forty, fifty feet above in the air. Real shiny lights. You couldn't even look up at it really—bright, bright lights all around. And then it just disappeared. We called it in, they just started laughing at us.

LF. What was your unit at the time?

AB. 320 SPS.

LF. What year was that, do you remember?

AB. '77, '78, or '79.

LF. You don't remember exactly?

AB. I don't remember exactly. I put that one way behind me. It was one of the first times and the last one for me until I went to Bentwaters.

LF. Remember when you were telling me the helicopters came in from Woodbridge? What outfit was that there?

AB. 67 ARRS.

LF. The other thing, you were talking with the electronics division, CRS, right?

AB. Yes.[33]

Warren and Robbins's copy of the transcript ends here.

26 April 1984

In Lincoln, Nebraska, a researcher named Ray Boeche is actively developing a series of Bentwaters-related leads. Today, he places a call to John Burroughs:

JB. Hello?

RB. Yeah, John, this is Ray Boeche in Lincoln, Nebraska.

JB. Yeah.

RB. I was talking to Adrian Bustinza and Larry Warren, and they said that they'd been stationed with you at RAF Bentwaters.

JB. Yeah, I was at RAF Bentwaters, yeah.

RB. Yeah. What we're in the process of doing here is looking to an event that happened there in December of 1980—the UFO landing on the base.

JB. Yeah, what about it?

RB. Well, we'd talked to Larry and talked to Adrian, and they suggested we talk to you.

JB. OK, who are you again?

RB. Ray Boeche.

JB. Who are you with?

RB. Well, I'm with an organization called Citizens Against UFO Secrecy.

JB. Yeah.

RB. It's a public service organization.

JB. Before I can tell you anything about that or say anything more about that, I'm gonna have to contact my squadron, because I'm really not allowed, you understand.

RB. Yeah, I understand that.

JB. I'm not trying to hold anything back against you, but I've got to, you know, go through legal channels, before I can talk to you on that; now I'm not saying I won't talk to you, but I have to talk to somebody up there first.

RB. Yeah . . . yeah, that's perfectly understandable.

JB. Who'd you talk to earlier?

RB. Adrian Bustinza . . .

JB. Yeah.

RB. and Larry Warren.

JB. Those names don't, aren't really familiar.

RB. They were both with the security police over there.

JB. OK. Let me call my orderly room and talk to squadron commander.

RB. OK.

JB. After I talk to them and have them tell me what I should say, if I can say anything.

RB. OK.

JB. Now, I gotta do that because I'm still in the military; if I was a civilian that'd be a different story.

RB. Yeah, that's understandable.

JB. I'm gonna find out what I need to do before I can say anything. Once I left there, I was pretty much told not to say anything, but that was a long time ago.

RB. I certainly appreciate your situation.

JB. As soon as I get an answer I'll call and let you know. I'll let you know the answer tomorrow 'cause I'm leaving for Canada for a month tomorrow.

RB. I appreciate that.

JB. OK, bye.

RB. Thanks a lot.[34]

The next day, Ray calls again:

RB. John, this is Ray Boeche.

JB. Yeah, how ya doing?

RB. Real good, how are you?

JB. Pretty good.

RB. Wondered if you got hold of your security officer?

JB. OK, I didn't get a complete answer yet, OK?

RB. OK.

JB. They're checking on stuff and all that—they're not sure. They want to contact them over there.

RB. OK.

JB. Why don't you send me some stuff on you guys. I'll get it when I get back from Canada.

RB. OK.

JB. I'll look at what you have, and then they'll give me an answer, and then I'll get back in touch with you, OK?

RB. OK, that sounds good. I will send you some of our material. I'll send you a copy of a document that we got through the Freedom of Information Act. It was written by Lieutenant Colonel Halt, who was the deputy base commander.

JB. Is that how you got hold of all this?

RB. Yeah.

JB. What did they tell you about it, what did they exactly say?

RB. Just said that he believed that you had hitched a ride out to the site. That you weren't on duty and that you'd hitched a ride out to the site.

JB. Well, OK, all I can say right now is that there's a lot more to it than that.

RB. Yeah. One thing I guess I should have mentioned yesterday: we work real hard to maintain anonymity of anybody we talk to.

JB. Right. I understand that, but it's a sticky situation. The government claims there's no such thing, and then they've got people working for the government who say there is.

RB. Yeah. I appreciate your situation 100 percent.

JB. If they clear me to talk to you, I'll say what went on. I don't know what they told you, but what little was told you, there's a lot more to it. But it depends on what they tell me. All I'm saying right now is that there was me and two other individuals that were involved in the whole thing from the start.

RB. All right, have a good trip to Canada.

JB. Thanks a lot. I'll talk to you in about a month or so.

RB. I appreciate that, John, thank you.

JB. You're welcome.

RB. Good-bye.

JB. Bye.[35]

Summer 1984

East Anglia. A young couple in Haverhill leave their home at 7:00 P.M. for what should be an hour-and-a-half drive to Sudbury. Once on the A1092, both observe a bright ball of light following them. As the light overflies the car, its motor and lights fail. The circular glow continues on for another hundred yards, then stops to hover in the road.

The couple step from the vehicle and are enveloped by an immediate sense of calm. Both remember the engine starting after a brief adjustment, then being back on the road to Sudbury. They arrive at their destination at 1:30 A.M. Neither is able to account for nearly five of the preceding six and a half hours.[36]

17 July 1984

Statutory Declaration

I, Gordon Levitt, of 24 Munday Lane, Orford, in the county of Suffolk, Department Manager, do solemnly and sincerely declare as follows:

1. I make this declaration realizing that it is a document on oath and in the knowledge that it may be shown to the general public.

2. On or about the night of 28 or 29 December 1980 at approximately 7 pm to 8pm, whilst residing at White Lodge, Sudbourne, in the county of Suffolk, I was in the garden putting my dog into its shed. When my attention was aroused by some unknown means. I looked toward the coast and observed a light which moved on a steady path towards me. My dog also reacted and its attention became focused on the object.

   The phenomenon glowed with a phosphorescence and was unlike any conventional object with which I am familiar. It descended and hovered for a few seconds immediately above us at a height of no more than twice the rooftop of the house and its size, were the object to be placed on the ground, would be similar in size to the rooftop. The object then moved away and disappeared over the woods in the direction of Butley, Rendlesham Forest and RAF Wood-bridge.

3. The following day there were still evident signs of distress in my dog. It cowered within its kennel and was not keen to come out. Having told my wife, June, immediately following the experience, I subsequently discussed it with several friends, including Ron Macro, a baker from Kesgrave in the county of Suffolk.

4. I exhibit here, marked "A," a drawing of the object which I saw. And I Make this solemn declaration conscientiously believing the same to be true and by virtue of the provisions of the Statutory Declarations Act, 1835.

Declared at Orford, in
the county of Suffolk
this 17th day of July
1984.

Before me,
(signed) Harry Harris
A solicitor.[37]

Summer 1984

Leeds, England. UFO researcher Mark Ian Birdsall writes a series of letters to British and American government and military agencies. His search for information on the particulars of the Bentwaters incidents has been intelligently mounted but gently rebuffed at every turn. During August alone, Birdsall's queries are put down by both the American defense attaché and the Eighty-first's new chief of public affairs.

Reassigned to the States, Captain Kathleen McCollom is replaced by Captain Victor Warzinski as chief of base public affairs division. Where McCollom's UFO-related statements were terse, reserved, and businesslike, Warzinski appears to enjoy parrying with researchers and journalists. On 20 August, he writes Birdsall:

1. Thanks for your amusing letter dated 15 August 1984.

2. Regarding your question why so many people were reassigned "so quickly" after the event. You should know that our people serve established tour lengths overseas. . . .

   Those witnessing the incident were already programmed to move to a new assignment upon completion of their tour here, and for some, this came rather quickly. In another instance, "prime witness" Colonel Halt was only reassigned this past summer.

3. Regarding your questions about who believes whom, I don't know that anyone has drawn any official conclusions. Colonel Halt informed the MoD of what he saw. The MoD chose not to investigate the matter. The USAF quit investigating UFOS years ago at the completion of the Project Blue Book study.

    There's a hint there that the matter did not merit investigation. The only thing that ever brought the issue to light was a rather fanciful story published two years after the event by a couple of people who make a living selling this sort of copy.

4. Was the Woodbridge incident genuine? Was it a CIA hoax? Or was it simply an unexplained incident blown completely out of proportion, like the fisherman's tale of the "one that got away" that keeps getting bigger and bigger with each retelling?

5. Please take another look at your "massive evidence" and tell me if any official government source (or even *credible* witness) ever drew a conclusion in favor of an extraterrestrial visitation.[38]

Ted Turner's fledgling television news organization budgets about $200,000 for the first CNN *Special Assignment*. The three-part feature will look into the Bentwaters incidents, and an investigative reporter specializing in defense and technology issues is assigned to the project. The reporter, Chuck DeCaro, soon develops a series of incident-related questions, which the network then submits to the air force.[39]

21 August 1984
The day before writing to Birdsall, a less glib Captain Warzinski sends a message to USAFE headquarters in Ramstein. Its subject:

Interim Feedback, CNN Query . . . re UFO sighting

1. Still researching answers to most questions raised in reference message. Since four years have passed since subject incident, many of the contacts and principals have since departed. Much of what remains is only hearsay and second hand reporting. Very little supporting documentation available. However, here is what we have been able to establish thus far.

    Questions 6, 7, & 18: General Williams is presently assigned to AFISC at Norton AFB, CA. Suggest OSAF/PA, refer these questions to his serving PA office.

    Questions 12, 18, & 19: Colonel Halt is presently assigned with AFLC at Tinker AFB, OK. Suggest OSAF/PA, discuss his desire to go on record and grant interviews to credible press. He had indicated a desire to do so while assigned here. We discouraged this at the time, feeling it would only fan the fire. Interview could not be advantageous. He would basically say he saw lights he could not explain. Does not mean he's drawn a conclusion in favor of UFOs. I also understand Halt could have a cassette tape which he made during the incident on a portable recorder.

Questions 9, 10, 11, and 12: Whereabouts of Major Zickler, Lt. Englund and Sgt. Burroughs unknown at this location. Suggest OSAF/PAM ask AFMPC to initiate personnel search.

Question 16: 3AF/PA has letter on file from OSI Commander during period of incident saying OSI did not do any investigation. Matter was referred to British MoD who would have jurisdiction. I have another letter from MoD saying the incident "was not considered to indicate anything of defence interest." Full text of letter will be transmitted if you desire.

Question 19: 3AF/PA also has a letter on file written by Col. Cochran, the Base CC at the time, saying no audiovisual documentation was done, nor was any report or investigation initiated by the USAF.

Question 20: Base newspaper files and independent confirmation indicate that first visit to Bentwaters by Secretary of the Air Force (SECAF) following incident was 24 Sept 81. Article only mentions his wife accompanying, but I'd expect some of his senior staff also accompanied. Other stops on the SECAF's itinerary were other UK and GE bases. Visit was the SECAF's first official visit overseas since taking post earlier that summer, and was concerned mainly with people and quality of life issues.

2. Have also found the original copy of Col. Halt's report. Has USAFE seen full text yet?

3. Bentwaters POC is Capt. Warzinski . . . 21 Aug 84

24 August, 1984

A second message is sent to USAFE headquarters by Captain Warzinski. It also concerns CNN queries:

1. Have been unable to find many more answers to questions posed in reference A. As mentioned in reference B, most people concerned with this incident have since departed this installation. Virtually no documentation of incident has been retained. Previous Freedom of Information requests have discovered no "hidden" files. The best source for possible answers to these questions, Col. Halt, was reassigned to Tinker AFB this summer. Suggest SAF/PA work with him to flesh out hard answers. Based on what we have been able to establish locally, here are our proposed answers:

Question 1: Col. Halt's report made reference to two sightings.

Question 2: Col. Halt's report said the first sighting took place at approximately 3 a.m. on 27 Dec 80. The second sighting is said to have taken place at an unspecified time during the night of 29 Dec 80.

Question 3: Unknown. Halt's report makes no mention of any cordons. No other documentation can be found on this subject.

Question 4: Unknown. Col. Halt's report only makes reference to Security Police personnel. The local Disaster Preparedness and Bioenvironmental Office say they were not notified of the incident. A letter written by the Base Commander during the incident says no audiovisual documentation was done, no investigations initiated, or reports accomplished.

Question 5: Unknown. Due to lack of any documentation, beyond Col. Halt's report to the British Ministry of Defence, no other reports were initiated or completed.

Question 6: Gen. Williams did not witness the incident. Col. Halt wrote the report as the senior ranking person present at the incident simply as a courtesy to the British MoD, who would have jurisdiction for handling the matter. . . .

Question 7: Suggest you ask Gen. Williams. Incidently, Williams has been quoted in one British paper as saying "I recall the report. I don't know exactly what happened. [Halt] is not a man who would hoax the British MoD or Dept. of Air Force. I have nothing to add to the subject."

Question 8: Unknown. Halt's report refers to "numerous individuals" including himself witnessing the activities, but does not elaborate further.

Question 9: Unknown. Major Zickler is no longer assigned to this installation.

Question 10: Unknown. Sgt. Burroughs is no longer assigned to this installation. (Incidentally, we think Sgt. Burroughs is the anonymous airman who gave the interesting account to the press of seeing little silver men, discussions between the silver men and the USAF people, dancing balls of light on people's foreheads, and blacking out to unexplainably awaken caked with mud in his dorm room to be later visited by black-coated hush men, etc.)

Questions 11 through 17 are repeats from the message of 21 August 1984, but not question 18:

This is strictly a personal interpretation but Williams probably did not wish to be involved with the incident, Halt then made his report to the MoD and had nothing further to say and we feel that Burroughs did give off the record interviews.

Question 19: The Base Commander at the time said that no documentation was done. We have heard that Col. Halt did make a cassette recording while observing the incident, however the disposition of this tape is unknown.

Warzinski concludes:

> Wish we could have been of more assistance. Advise SAF/PAM contact Col. Halt and work up appropriate PA guidance. As far as we are concerned, we have told everything we know.[40]

Autumn 1984

The USAF responds to CNN's information request:

Q 1. Exactly how many "unexplained lights" sightings occurred?

A 1. Col Halt's report made reference to two alleged sightings.

Q 2. Over the course of how many days did incidents occur?

A 2. Col Halt's report said the first alleged sighting took place at approximately 3:00 a.m. on 27 Dec 1980. The second alleged sighting is said to have taken place at an unspecified time during the night of 29 Dec 1980.

Q 3. Did USAF Security Police cordon off the area specified in Col Halt's report?

A 3. Col Halt's report makes no mention of any cordons nor is there any other documentation on this.

Q 4. Which units were involved in the sightings? Were AAVS units there?

A 4. Col Halt's report only makes reference to security police personnel.

Q 5. Was there a "Helping Hand," "Covered Wagon," "Faded Giant," or "Broken Arrow" report or reports generated by the incident?

A 5. Col Halt's report makes no mention of such reporting. In addition, RAF Bentwaters Disaster Preparedness and Bioenvironmental Office say they were not notified of the alleged incident.

Q 6. Did General Gordon Williams witness the incident? If so, why did Col Halt write a report?

A 6. General Williams did not witness the alleged incident. Col Halt wrote the report as the senior ranking USAF person present at the alleged incident as a courtesy to the British Ministry of Defence who would have jurisdiction for handling it. The Ministry of Defence said the matter did not have any defense implications and chose not to investigate the alleged incident further.

Q 7. Will General Williams write an official statement about his involvement with the incident for CNN?

A 7. General Williams did not witness the alleged incident, therefore, it would not be appropriate for him to write a statement.

Q 8. How many USAF personnel witnessed the sightings?

A 8. The number of people witnessing the alleged sightings is unknown.

Q 9. Did Security Police Maj Zickler witness the incident(s)?

A 9. Unknown.

Q10. Did Sgt Burroughs witness the incident(s)?

A10. Unknown.

Q11. Was there a Lt Englund in the Security Police unit at Bentwaters? Did he witness the incident?

A11. Unknown.

Q12. What are the current units and duty stations of Williams, Halt, Burroughs, Zickler, and Englund?

A12. Williams is currently assigned with the Air Force Inspection and Safety Center at Norton AFB, Calif. Col Halt is currently assigned with the Oklahoma City Air Logistics Center at Tinker AFB, Okla. Sgt Burroughs is currently assigned to Luke AFB. The location of the others is unknown.

Q13. Were there USAF Disaster Preparedness, EOD, or Nuclear Weapons management teams dispatched to the sight of the incident? Are there copies of their reports in USAF files? If so, which units have the files?

A13. Col Halt's report makes no mention of such involvement. No such reports are on file with these organizations.

Q14. What units or what personnel took the radioactivity readings referred to in Lt Col Halt's report? What unit or personnel established the geometry of the indentations on the ground? Where are their official measurements and reports?

A14. Unknown.

Q15. Were there any non-NATO personnel interviewed or seen at the site of the incident? Could these personnel have been associated with the explained lights?

A15. Unknown.

Q16. Were USAF OSI personnel dispatched to the incident site? Did OSI personnel interview Lt Col Halt, Airman Larry Warren, Airman Steve La Plume, Gen Williams, Maj Zickler, Lt Englund, or Sgt Burroughs?

A16. The British MoD would have jurisdiction for any such investigation. OSI was not informed of the alleged incident and did not investigate or compile a report.

Q17. Will the USAF provide a list of USAF personnel who witnessed the incident(s)?

A17. No, because it is unknown who witnessed the alleged incident.

Q18. What are the reasons that Gen Williams, Col Halt, and Sgt Burroughs gave for not granting official interviews?

A18. The individuals have declined interviews for personal reasons.

Q19. Are there any photographs, tape recordings, videotapes, drawings, or descriptions of any kind in USAF files? If not, to what agency or agencies have the files been transferred?

A19. There was no audiovisual documentation done.

Q20. Did the Secretary of the Air Force visit Bentwaters immediately after the incident?

A20. No. Secretary of the Air Force's first visit to RAF Bentwaters was in September, 1981.[41]

8 October 1984

Chuck DeCaro writes to Major John Kirkwood, an officer with the Pentagon's Office of Public Affairs Media Relations Division. The reporter is angry:

Dear Major Kirkwood:

Reference the "answers" to CNN's questions about the Bentwaters Incident—apparently not an alleged incident as the Air Force insists—CNN has found them evasive, insipid and totally unsatisfactory: they are obvious, sophomoric attempts to avoid the issue and they should be a personal embarrassment to you. The USAF didn't even have enough guts to put the answers on official letterhead!!

Nevertheless CNN would like the following data about the incident:

1. Who was the Security Police Squadron Commander at Bentwaters?
2. Who was the Security Police Squadron Commander at Woodbridge?
3. Please provide a roster of all personnel in each of the above units.
4. Who was the SP duty officer and NCOIC on 27, 28, 29 Dec 80.
5. Please ask Col Halt what unit identified the radioactive foot-prints left by the "lights." Please provide a roster of all personnel in that unit. If Col Halt cannot "remember" please provide the Table of organization and Equipment for Woodbridge and Bentwaters, so that units possessing the appropriate equipment might be identified by process of elimination.

6. Please provide a copy of vehicle and equipment checkout from the motorpools at RAF Bentwaters and RAF Woodbridge for 27, 28, 29 Dec 80.

7. Please contact Sergeant Burroughs (Luke AFB) and ask him if he was present at the incident(s). Please ask if he would answer written questions about the incidents. Ask if he would consent to an interview at this time.

8. Ask Col. Halt if he would answer written questions about the incident or consent to an interview.

9. Ref Q-15, on my earlier letter. If the area in question was being guarded or patrolled by a number of SPs how could the USAF not know if any non-NATO personnel were in the area? Are you saying that the USAF SPs were so incompetent that they couldn't stop an outsider?

10. Was the alert or defense condition at Woodbridge or Bentwaters elevated at all during the initial or following incidents?

11. Ask Col. Halt if any of his personal family members witnessed the later incidents. Were any photos taken through the telephoto lens mentioned in Col Halt's report? If so where are those photos . . . ?

12. What were the names of the original SPs who were sent on foot to investigate the lights? Were they later interviewed by the OSI?

13. Did USAF Disaster Preparedness, EOD, or Nuclear weapons teams from Woodbridge or Bentwaters, or any other USAF base or station participate in investigating the incident or its aftermath?

I hope that in light of all the time the USAF spent in "carefully" answering the original questions, I trust that it will not take the USAF another two months to "research" and "coordinate" the answers.

Thank you.

(signed) Chuck DeCaro[42]

25 October 1984

Former Bentwaters base commander Sam Morgan is now working at the space command headquarters in Colorado. He confirms that the excerpted twenty minutes of audiotape alleged to have been made by Lieutenant Colonel Halt and his men the night of 27 December 1980 are very real indeed. The fact is made public at the London press conference on the release of *Sky Crash*.[43]

The bookstore at RAF Bentwaters is among the first in England to stock *Sky Crash* and sales are brisk. Master Sergeant Howard Varney buys his copy there and remembers:

That's *all* that anybody talked about! There was no other conversation on the base for a month. Any conversation you had with anybody—did you read this? Did you hear about this? *What about this?* You know? That's all everybody talked about. In shops, at work. It's the only conversation that people were having.[44]

26 October 1984

While *Sky Crash* brings some sober musings in the English press, its multiple scenarios allow commentary to fragment, as in the *Evening Star*'s Friday editorial:

These ladies, it should be remembered, offer the spaceship theory as only one of a range of possibilities. The others, which include weapons testing, and the recovery of part of a Russian satellite, sound much more plausible and would better explain the official silence. They might even prefer us to believe the UFO theory![45]

In the same edition, *East Anglia Daily Times* reporter David Green relates a lesser-known investigation:

Reports were last coming of a seemingly inexplicable occurrence near the River Alde at Snape, only a few miles from the USAF base at Bentwaters. It was the second strange happening in the Bentwaters area in the past four years and follows the apparent sighting of a UFO by American airmen.

Several people visiting the famous maltings concert hall are certain they saw a number of highly paid barristers sitting on the stage listening to a man reading from a thick document.

"One minute they were there, two years later they had gone," one woman told me after treatment for shock. "They all had pin-stripe suits and were yawning. It was horrible," said an ashen-faced off-duty policeman who asked not to be named.

Some residents say they are sceptical over the alleged "sighting," having lived near the concert hall for many years and never heard or seen anything worth mentioning. They pointed out most of the so-called eye witnesses had just stumbled out of the Plough and Sail pub 300 yards away.

A Ministry of Defence spokesman refused to take the incident seriously. "It is probably just another prank by the French security services," he said.[46]

Colonel Halt visits friends on RAF Woodbridge this week. He is traveling back from Saudi Arabia to his new assignment, Tinker AFB in Oklahoma.[47]

27 October 1984

Jenny Randles writes to the Bentwaters public relations chief concerning particulars of her own and Birdsall's investigations. Captain Warzinski responds 5 November:

Thank you for your letter of . . .

My response [to Birdsall] indicated neither government has drawn any conclusions because neither government felt the matter merited investigation. The final line of the paragraph reflected my personal scepticisms about the subject of UFOs in general, and the conclusions offered about this incident in particular.

I still regard "various alarming scenarios . . . [which] . . . span across witchcraft, drugs, space warfare and a near nuclear holocaust!" to quote the advance publicity flier for *Sky Crash*, as "fanciful." I still regard Art Wallace's story, as reported in the *News of the World*, as "fanciful." I still regard quite a bit more that has been written and said about this incident, by a number of people besides yourselves, as "fanciful." The word is used as it is defined: imaginative; not necessarily supported by facts. . . .

I'll grant that the Rendlesham Forest incident could leave some room for conjecture. However I hope you'll pardon my telling you that I'm still a sceptic who needs to be convinced that anything more than an unexplained light sighting took place four years ago in that forest.

Col. Halt's report to the MoD absolved the USAF of any further interest in the matter. This is where the situation has stood these past four years, and I do not expect it to change any time in the future.

However, I do not wish to establish an adversary relationship with you. I do wish to help you where I can, and am willing to attempt to answer any specific questions you may have on the subject. I look forward to hearing from you.[48]

6 November 1984

The following day, Captain Warzinski receives this cable from air force headquarters in Germany:

Subject: CNN Queries, RAF Bentwaters UFO Incident

Reference: OSAF/PAM Letter, 29 Oct 84, CNN Query on incident at RAF Bentwaters 1980.

1. Questions 1 and 2: Commander of the 81st Police Squadron at the time was Major Malcolm Zickler [sic], . . . 81 SPS provides security for both bases.
2. Questions 3, 4 and 6: Am unable to provide requested information. Such records have long since been destroyed in keeping with routine administrative practices.
3. Question 10: No.
4. Question 12: Names of original patrolmen first sent to investigate the lights are unknown at this location. Perhaps Col. Halt can provide answer. No one was later interviewed by OSI, as they did not conduct any investigation.
5. Question 13: There was no USAF investigation of any nature concerning this incident or its aftermath. Col. Halt's report referred the matter to British Ministry of Defence who had juristiction. MoD chose not to investigate, saying the incident "was not considered to indicate anything of defence interest."
6. We are using following statement in response to local queries about the incident: "We are aware of the book and its accusations. It would be inappropriate for us to comment on these speculations. Nor will we be drawn into a discussion about the motivations behind the book. A report of the incident was referred to the British MoD, who, failing to find any defense implication, chose not to investigate. Current USAF policy is that we no longer investigate UFO sightings and have not done so for many years. Everyone who was involved with the incident has since been reassigned from this installation. In short, we have no official interest in what may have happened, especially since the incident did not take place on the installation."

In the meantime, Randles has written back to Warzinski:

Which *specific* elements of what has been written and said . . . are in your view "fanciful"[?] . . . I am not denying that you could have a point. Certainly the suggestion that Art Wallace has exaggerated somewhat is one of the few things upon which I and your former intelligence officer, Colonel Halt, appear to agree. However, that Art Wallace is basically telling it like it is appears to be supported by a lot more evidence than I have so far seen you come up with to denounce it.

Just as a thought . . . if this could be arranged at some future point, would you be willing to face Art Wallace in your office and tell him, in our presence, that you regard what he is saying as "fanciful" and that he is blowing up a light into the claims he is making? If you have any real support for your beliefs I guess you would be willing to do that. . . .

Of course the case does *not* rely upon the testimony of Art Wallace. . . .

Captain Warzinski makes no direct mention of Wallace in his 19 November response; he doesn't have to:

> While I'm in the process of discounting little silver men teaching space psychology in our underground complex, I'm also establishing myself as an authority who knows what did actually happen. And I'll admit I don't know exactly what happened.

23 November 1984

From the office of the secretary of the air force comes this letter:

Dear Mr. DeCaro,

In response to your written query dated October 8, 1984, we have obtained the following information:

1. Due to the size and proximity, normally one individual serves as commander of the Security Police units at RAF Woodbridge and RAF Bentwaters. During the period of the alleged sighting it was Maj. Malcolm F. Zickler.
2. Officials at the United States Air Forces in Europe Headquarters indicate they are unable to provide information on questions 3, 4, and 6 . . . because such records have long since been destroyed in keeping with routine administrative practices.
3. Colonel Halt and Sergeant Burroughs were contacted concerning your request for information. Both individuals declined to respond orally or in writing to your questions.
4. The answer to question 10 is no.
5. In response to question 12, the names of patrolmen are unknown. OSI did not conduct an investigation.
6. In response to question 13, there was no USAF investigation of the alleged incident.

(signed)
Joseph G. Wojtecki, Lt Col, USAF
Chief, Pictorial/Broadcast Branch
Media Relations Division
Office of Public Affairs[49]

3 December 1984

Following up on his brief conversation with Warren and the 1974 UFO incident with his mother, writer-researcher Budd Hopkins telephones

Joann Warren in Glens Falls, New York. As his call finds her in the middle of preparing for her daughter's wedding shower, Joann asks Budd to call back at a less hectic time. Several days later, he does:

JW. I didn't know you, and it's not that I mistrust you or anything like that, sir, but I have to be very careful.

BH. There's no reason not to take precautions and be careful.

JW. Well, Larry said if you're Budd Hopkins and you're the one who wrote the book *Missing Time* that I should speak to you.

BH. (*Laughs*) Well, I am Budd Hopkins.

JW. Budd, what did you want to know? When it happened? What happened?

BH. Well, exactly what the story was.

JW. Well, it was unbelievable, absolutely unbelievable, and I can remember it like it was yesterday, and I'll never forget it as long as I live. This happened in 1974, 19 August, I believe. My son was here. We have two bedrooms in this apartment, and I have the back bedroom. My bed was under the window, two large windows together. I don't know how Larry got into the bedroom—he had slept in the front bedroom. But he had brought his sleeping bag in, and he put it beside the bed, and my daughter was in the double bed with myself. Now, I don't know why, but through the night, I woke up out of a sound dead sleep, like something was watching me.

BH. Uh-huh.

JW. I sat up in the bed—now believe me, I never had had any thoughts this way at all. I never thought UFOs. I turned around, and there was this bright, bright light—it almost killed my eyes. Yet, Budd, when I remember, it did not illuminate the room.

BH. Uh-huh.

JW. It was outside the window, I couldn't tell how close, how far away, but if you saw the backyard, you'd understand what I mean because we have pine trees out there. We have big pine trees. I saw this, I was absolutely amazed. I was spellbound. I don't know how much time went by, I have no idea whatever. I saw a shape; as bright as that light was and it really burnt my eyes—but I tried to wake my daughter. I couldn't wake her.

BH. And she wouldn't wake up.

JW. She wouldn't wake up.

BH. Now this would be unusual?

JW. It was just unusual to the point where she would stir, but I couldn't wake her up. I could not wake her up.

BH. Yeah.

JW. Then all of a sudden, up comes Larry from the side of the bed. Now, I did not know he was in there. I said to Larry, "Larry, Larry," and it was a little frightening for me, and yet it was a funny feeling for me, it was like slow motion.

BH. Yeah.

JW. So Larry got up and he looked—now he saw it, he saw it—he couldn't stay awake. He went down and went back to sleep. Now this is the most unusual thing I've ever heard of, absolutely unusual.

BH. Yeah—you'd think he'd be galvanized into action.

JW. Now, as a time period, I don't know how long this went on, but I could draw this for you. I saw the outline and it was like two diamonds.

BH. Two diamonds?

JW. Two large diamonds, connected by a long pipe.

BH. Uh-huh. Now, were they glowing and giving the source of the light?

JW. It was bright—it was just so bright, but I cannot remember the room being illuminated, lit up. I can't remember that at all.

BH. Yeah.

JW. Now I watched this and watched this. It was there, it was there, but I stayed right where I was, and I don't know how much time went by—I have no idea, until eventually I fell off to sleep, but I can never say I watched it till it was gone because it was always there.

BH. Yeah, right.

JW. Now the funniest thing is what happened the next night. My friend from next door, Sue Hickerson, she heard on the radio all these people calling the radio station about these things flying in the air.

BH. Uh-huh.

JW. So we turn on the radio. You could go out in your yard and watch these things! The radio station was saying to keep their cars away from the radio station. Now, it was all this big deal. This went on all evening. The very next day, if you called the radio station, you didn't get any information at all.

BH. Really.

JW.   Nothing, absolutely nothing. It was not just I that saw it or Larry or my friend next door—half the town saw that the night of the twentieth. But my thing happened on the night of the nineteenth, and I'll never forget it as long as I live. All I know is that I was sound asleep. For some reason I sat up in that bed, and I felt someone was watching me.

BH.   So it was between the pine trees and the house.

JW.   It was between the pine trees and the house, it's only a couple of feet.

BH.   Now when he got up, did he actually stand up out of his sleeping bag?

JW.   No, I can remember that so well. When I tried to wake my daughter, all of a sudden he came up from the side of the bed. I did not know he was there.

BH.   Yeah.

JW.   I thought he was in the front bedroom. OK, why was he in my room? He had a bed in the other room. I don't know why.

BH.   When you woke up in the morning and even during the night this was happening, how did you feel physically?

JW.   Ah, slow motion.

BH.   Slow motion?

JW.   It was just slow motion, it was . . . somebody's watching me. I was afraid, in a way, but I wasn't really fearful.

BH.   But did anything, recollections pop into mind?

JW.   Yeah. I don't know if I was out or just dreaming about this or just thinking about it. It was like being in a huge metal room with a deck.

BH.   With a deck?

JW.   With big tanks and these hoses all over the floor—hoses—going up into the tanks. And, it's like the big oil tanks with the ladders down the side? I don't know where I was. It was . . . in the room, or in whatever it was, but I remember these tanks so well, and remember an upper deck going around something and I could see some windows and it had a rail but was metal—everything was metal, except for the hoses. The hoses were not metal, and they were black, and there was a lot of hoses, all over the floor.

BH.   They looked like regular hoses then, except they were black.

JW.   Very large, very large hoses, and there was water, and I remember that so well.

BH. You never had any memories, dreams, odd dreams of somebody coming in the room or some odd figure, not that we all don't have dreams somewhat like that, you know.

JW. Well, that's one of the problems now.

BH. Uh-huh.

JW. That's one of my problems and has been for the last few years.

BH. What's that?

JW. I've even changed my bedroom, I'm sleeping in the front of the house now. I do have that problem.

BH. What exactly?

JW. Well, I was in the bed one night. I had my door open on the hall, and we have a streetlight out front. The light comes in a little so you can see things, and I was half asleep, and I woke up, and I just saw down the end of the bed, and it looked like a every dark spot.

BH. Uh-huh.

JW. Well, I sort of roused myself a little bit, and I looked, and I couldn't see through it. Now, I looked to the right, I bent over and looked to the right—this frightened me, and I could see the light from the right—and I tried to look to the left, but I could not see any light though the middle. It was a little bit frightening, that if I had gotten on my knees and got up, and if I crawled down the end of that bed, I know—and I *know* this—I would have come face to face with someone, or something. I know I would have. I've had things like this happen since that.

BH. I've been doing this kind of research for years, and you're not telling me anything I haven't heard before, in any way.

JW. Well, I have a dear friend—of course, she moved down South—I could talk to her about these things, but you can't talk to people about these things!

BH. That is quite true, but what you're telling me is the kind of thing that I've heard many times and often as a part of a pattern, that's quite clear. I'm curious, had you actually gone to sleep [first] when you woke up and felt this dark shape by the foot of the bed?

JW. I don't remember. I think I was asleep.

BH. But something woke you up?

JW. But something woke me up. Or else I was halfway asleep. I had a fear that time, that frightened me—but not like it should.

BH. How do you mean? Not as much as it should?

JW. I should have been scared to death. It was frightening, but not really.

BH. How did this end?

JW. I just turned over, as quietly as I could and tried to forget about it, tried to go to sleep, tried to force myself asleep. I just turned over and forced myself to go to sleep, but I went to sleep. Now, come on, I would never go to sleep.

BH. Yeah, of course if you had somebody who was in the room there.

JW. I would never go to sleep. And I've always associated that with what happened in '74, and maybe it has nothing to do with it.

BH. Yeah.

JW. Now, it hasn't happened in a long while, but it has happened since. The fear part of it just left me. I don't have a fear about it so much. Since the children don't live here anymore, I go in the front bedroom. I don't seem to have any problem in the front bedroom at all. Not as of yet anyhow.

BH. Now, when the children, I take it you have two children?

JW. Yes, right.

BH. When they were little, did you ever have anything odd happen to either of them, where they came back with an odd story or [having] gotten lost in a funny way.

JW. Oh, Larry, Larry's always been—he was the one, you know, always that these things would, ah—he was into this. Of course, you know what's happened to Larry since.

BH. Yeah, right.

JW. But I just never thought that it would happen to *me*. We saw them, the neighbors saw them. You could go out, right in the front here where the parking lot is and could see these things zooming all over the place and stopping, zoom here and zoom there, and you could see them. And mine happened the night before. That's made me wonder. If it happened to me, I wonder if it happened to anybody else.

BH. Yeah, it's quite possible. People don't tend to report these things. Just one last thing on the whole business with Larry's [Bentwaters] situation, his recollections—I'm sure he's filled you in on everything that a . . .

JW. Uh-huh.

BH. What is your feeling about the apparent status of all this and Larry's role in it? Do you feel that he's in danger or . . .

JW. I've never, no. Isn't that awful? I talked to his dad at one time, and they were very frightened when he was going to Japan. I'm his mother, and I suppose I should feel this fear. I suppose at times I do get nervous about it, Budd, but something happened to that boy and it truly happened to him.

BH. Yeah, right.

JW. And, my God, if someone doesn't take a stand, no one's ever going to take a stand, and I push Larry 100 percent and not into danger, I hope.

BH. No, I think you're right. I don't think there is a problem in that way because I don't think the government can afford even the illusion that they're taking them seriously, if they did anything, you know.

JW. Oh, especially not now.

BH. Yeah, all it would do is to underline to the world the reality of the situation, and their only way out is to ignore him. Hope that people will lose interest. But just in terms of your feelings when Larry was little and so on. You find this really a complete break with Larry's . . . I mean Larry never presented any wild story to you.

JW. Oh, no. Oh, my gosh! Oh, no, absolutely not. This thing from England, and that's what your talking about . . .

BH. Yes, the Rendlesham thing.

JW. Oh, no, never. I don't think I'll ever forget the night he called me and—no, absolutely not.

BH. He called you, and he was cut off.

JW. Oh, yes, he certainly was, sir, he certainly was.[50]

11. | *1985—*
JUST LIKE REGULAR PEOPLE

By January, my concerns had shifted from UFOs to my impending marriage. Cindy was far more important to me than Bentwaters, and I really wanted the marriage to work. By now, she was disgusted with the whole subject of UFOs and scared by my involvement. I wanted to walk away from it all, but every time I tried, a new development would pull me back in.

The on-site tape made by Lieutenant Colonel Halt, which I'd brought back from Japan, was really causing a stir in the UFO community. Those who'd heard it were blown away by its science fiction–like quality, so I wasn't surprised to hear that skeptics had already begun their assault on it. Charges ranged from Halt's having staged it to my having recorded it with some friends. By now, I was used to such rumors and attacks, but they still did their damage. Any witness, considering the pros and cons of coming forward, might think twice after learning how witnesses were treated. It seemed to me that the best defense our government had against UFO witnesses was to let them go public, knowing full well that the UFO research community would chew them up and spit 'em out as soon as they did.

On the bright side, though, Bentwaters was now producing a constant flow of new leads, almost on a weekly basis. I'd continued to speak off and on with Chuck DeCaro and tried to help with any outstanding details I could. My family and I anxiously awaited the CNN broadcast.

Late in February 1985, I received a call from Lee Spiegel, a producer with WNBC radio in New York. Lee got my number from Fawcett because he had important information to share with me. He was very interested in the Bentwaters story and was investigating it for his network. He had just spoken with Colonel Halt! Lee was calling from Tinker AFB in Oklahoma, where Halt was now stationed. Spiegel said he'd interviewed the officer at his home and that Halt had been very candid about the events of December 1980. However, when Lee finally asked him about Colonel Williams and the beings, Colonel Halt grew defensive, then asked Lee to have his crew step outside. It was at this point the former deputy based commander made some off-the-record comments.

According to Spiegel, Halt had told him that beings *had* been observed on the third night of UFO activity and that Gordon Williams had been involved that night. He also said that "a lot more" happened than people realized. Colonel Halt would only tell what he knew of the whole story if Congress subpoenaed him to testify. It was too bad the interview was off the record.

Halt also commented on the two books that recounted the incident, *Clear Intent* and *Sky Crash*, which I hadn't seen yet. He apparently liked Fawcett's and Greenwood's book and felt the Bentwaters part was much closer to the truth than *Sky Crash* depicted it; Lee told me Halt couldn't say enough negatives about its three authors.

Spiegel concluded the call by saying that perhaps I could be a guest on his radio show in the future. I took his number, and he told me he would call again but never did. When I tried to call him, I was told that he was no longer at that number. We never spoke again.

The first part of CNN's *Special Assignment* would be airing on Monday, 25 February. I had been driving Cin batty with the tension I was feeling over it. The night before, DeCaro called me at Cindy's apartment. When I asked him what the other witnesses were saying, he told me I would be pretty much out on a limb. Although they'd said, "Warren isn't lying," off the record, none would confirm or deny the part about the beings on TV. I froze. I'd hoped this show was going to be the big one, the one to break the wall of silence. "I'm sorry, Larry," Chuck said, "but my producer won't allow me to say the guys backed you up because it was told to me off the record."[51]

He added that the broadcasts had drawn the attention of the National Security Council. They had sent an air force officer to CNN's Washington facility to preview the show. He took notes as he watched, then left. Chuck thanked me for the assistance I'd given over the last six months. He would call again to find out how I'd liked the shows. I hung up, looked at Cindy, and said, "I'm screwed again!" She just shook her head; she had heard that song before.

The next morning, I could hardly focus on work. I knew part one of *Special Assignment* was having its first airing that afternoon. That night, I watched it with Cindy. The first show dealt with local witnesses Jerry Harris and Gordon Levitt, who dismissed the lighthouse theory outright. Master Sergeant Gulias described the three depressions in the perfect twelve-foot triangle—and the official explanation that they'd been made by burrowing animals. The entire Halt document was read by DeCaro, complete with a courtroom artist's renderings. The piece ended with a teaser for an interview with "Airman Greg," Greg Battram. Not bad, I thought. One down and three to go.

The next part featured interviews with Greg and other witnesses. Though faces were obscured and, in one case, a voice disguised, I recognized Master Sergeant Ball, Sergeant Gulias, and Captain Verrano. All things considered, the guys said a lot. Captain Verrano verified that motion-picture film of the UFO had been taken to a waiting aircraft by Gordon Williams, then flown on to Germany. I'd said that from the start. Sergeant Gulias said: "We saw flying objects containing maybe people or a different life-form." And Greg said, "I think I saw a UFO. Some kind of a spaceship from someplace not of this earth." Master Sergeant Ball said "I didn't believe in UFOs. I was skeptical. Now I believe there may have been someone else there." *Wow, good for them!* I thought. It took guts to refer to the beings at all.

The lighthouse theory was addressed by forester Vince Thurkettle, but his explanation was ridiculous. Master Sergeant Ball countered: "I never once saw a lighthouse that moved, and this object moved because we followed it. No way could it have been the Orford lighthouse." Next followed an attempt to synchronize the lighthouse's flashing to the reaction of the men recorded on Lieutenant Colonel Halt's tape. Though DeCaro was filmed walking in the Rendlesham Forest, it wasn't near the site I'd been involved in; the farmer's field was not shown once. But parts of Lieutenant Colonel Halt's tape were played and had quite an impact.

Thursday night was my turn. Bernard Shaw introduced the final *Special Assignment* with something like, "This airman may be alone when he claims he saw UFOs at RAF Bentwaters, but he also claims to have seen alien beings as well.'' Alone? What about the other guys who saw UFOs, and said so on the show?

DeCaro then amended the situation somewhat: "Warren's descriptions of the transformed object match what three airmen reportedly saw at the same location the night before. But Warren's story takes an even stranger twist.''

And there I was, under my own name, the only witness not blacked out, directly answering DeCaro's questions about the life-forms we saw. CNN placed my experience on the second night of events, when it had been on the third. Why did the media insist on revising history? Apart from the error of referring to Gordon Williams as a lieutenant colonel, I stated only what I knew to be true.

At the end of my interview, DeCaro's voice came in again: "CNN has contacted two airmen who Warren said were present that night. Both say that something happened, but neither confirm nor deny Warren's story.''

Then Gulias, who had helped investigate one of the landing sites, made his final statement. He felt his superiors had little interest in getting to the bottom of things: "Things seemed to be clamped down quite suddenly and nobody was talking to anybody else about it. And when I tried to find or ask specific questions about things, nobody knew anything.''

DeCaro closed the final segment from the steps of the Pentagon. He talked about the slowness of the air force responses to CNN and their misleading answers, such as: "There was no audio-visual documentation done.'' He then dropped a big one:"CNN has also found an officer who says he drove the base commander to a waiting aircraft to deliver what he was told was a motion-picture film of one of the UFOs,'' followed by the officer's statement. He had been told the film was on its way to Germany.

DeCaro concluded: "If they were merely Keystone Cops who were hallucinating, as one critic suggests, then what are the national security implications of those same airmen guarding a strategically important air base where nuclear weapons are reportedly stored? If they weren't hallucinating, then what are the implications of what they did see? When CNN recently asked the air force about the possible existence of movie film of the Bentwaters UFO, the official air force response was, 'The U.S. Air Force stopped investigating UFOs in 1969.' "

Though television, especially the big four news networks, seemed always to be having their strings pulled on this subject, the broadcasts were not bad at all. In Cindy's opinion, though, I had been hung out to dry.

The next day, I was on the phone to Greg Battram in Saint Louis. I was glad to find he was doing well and happy in his new career. We reminisced over some of the funnier memories we'd shared of the security-police academy and Bentwaters. Greg had completed his four-year tour without any other strange incidents.

When I asked Greg what he'd thought of the CNN shows, he simply said he hoped he wouldn't have any trouble from the federal government as a result. He remembered the call I'd made to my mother in great detail. Though we had a laugh about having survived Bentwaters, some of the gut feelings we'd had at the time came back; it was unnerving. Greg told me he'd seen me in the back of a pickup truck en route to the landing site, while he and others ran the other way! I remembered those guys running out of the forest and, in hindsight, wished I'd been running with them.

Fawcett and I spoke later about the way the story had been messed with. He told me not to worry: HBO had just approached him with plans for an *America Undercover* special about Bentwaters and other UFO sightings. A producer would be calling me soon to set up an interview.

Al Terzi had been keeping in touch from WTNH in New Haven; his interest in the story just seemed to grow. I had Cindy put him and his wife on our wedding guest list, along with Fawcett and Greenwood. Cin was worried that her wedding day would turn into a UFO conference, but I assured her that it would not.

At the start of March, I heard a disturbing rumor; its source was said to be the *Air Force Times*, the service branch's official newspaper. Ex-Wing Commander Gordon Williams had died suddenly. No one in air force or UFO circles could confirm the rumor.

One night when I'd run out of cigarettes, I left the apartment and headed up Allen Street toward the drugstore at the corner. As I walked, I looked up to see what appeared to be a rock-concert lighting system hanging above the trees. It was about half a mile up the street and moving in my direction: it was huge.

There was a kid on the pay phone outside the drugstore, and I grabbed his arm and pointed at the thing. He yelled into the receiver that a UFO was coming and hung up. We just stood there and watched this thing coast over, long as a football field. It had six giant red lights surrounded by small starlike lights across the front, and a mist or fog appeared to blow off them.

As the object moved closer, cars stopped to watch, even a New Britain police car. I ran into the drugstore and yelled for everyone to come out. A bunch of us stood and stared at it. One man said that it might be a Skycrane, but as the thing came over, it was obviously no helicopter; he ran to his car and drove off.

Though it was overcast, we could all see the body of the craft without much trouble. It was round in front and had a long tail with a pulsating red glow at the end. It had to be three hundred yards long. When it passed over, the ground rumbled, as if little New Britain had a subway. I crossed the street and had a beer in our neighborhood bar. This was not a bunch of ultralight aircraft flying in formation, no way. Then I ran home and told Cindy; she was mad she hadn't seen it.

I called the New Britain police to ask if any cops had seen it. The dispatcher admitted that indeed numerous police officers had. Next I called Al Terzi. He was at home in Southington, the direction the thing had been headed. He checked outside but never saw it.

When I got off the phone, I wrote down all the details I could remember. The next day, I found that many people I worked with had seen it, too. A local newspaper carried a front-page story on the sighting, including a description of how police officers had watched the craft take water from a pond near Interstate 84. The *Hartford Courant* featured coverage of the event as well.

Cindy and I were married in May 1985. Despite the polka band at the reception and my best man, John Strough, getting locked out of his hotel room, all went well. After a draining day, relatives and guests dispersed to area hotels, and we headed back to my dad's house, where Fawcett was giving a lecture on UFOs to all of my relatives. Cin looked at me and said, "Let's go home."

The next day we left JFK Airport for London. My dad had gotten us the tickets as a wedding present. Though her first choice for a honeymoon had been Bermuda, Cindy gave in to my wish to show her London. She'd never visited England, and I insisted. But London was expensive, and after I'd shown her my old haunts, we were both wishing we had gone to the islands instead.

In a London bookstore, I found a copy of *Sky Crash*. I knew what I was in for when I opened it. The very first sentence on the flyleaf read: " 'They don't know my real name . . . if they find out they will ruin me.

They will blow my head off in the street or something. If my name was used, I think I am a dead man.' Witness Art Wallace.'' I'd never said that; even the inflection was not mine.

Though we had fun in London, I couldn't forget that we were only seventy miles from RAF Bentwaters and Woodbridge. Toward the end of our stay, I took Cindy on a day trip to Suffolk. There, we met a sergeant who was stationed at Bentwaters. When we began to talk, I asked him if he'd heard anything of what had happened out in those woods four and a half years earlier. "It's all anyone talks about around here" was his answer. He got very excited when I told him that I'd been involved and offered to drive us out to the area. We accepted.

We drove to within half a mile or less of the farmer's field and got out of the car. The ground was very soft and wet. We walked through the forest for a while. Cin said she felt weird "being where it all happened." I took a few snapshots for no reason at all—just some trees, I thought.

We returned to the States shortly after and settled into married life. From where I stood, things were starting out well, but Cin was still angry at my choice of honeymoon locations.

In June 1985, I attended another meeting of Massachusetts MUFON. It was here I was introduced to a writer named Whitley Strieber, his wife, and young son. Whitley was very curious about Bentwaters. He told me he had also had some UFO experiences—Strieber had been abducted and was writing a book about his experience called *Communion*. I wished him luck. He said I should write a book, but I brushed off the thought. I couldn't change a flat tire, let alone write a book.

But another writer there also felt I should start thinking about a book. His name was Bill Heizerling, and we planned to keep in touch. I intended to give up all UFO stuff within the year anyway. After all, I'd promised my wife.

Not long after, I spoke with Larry Bryant, a first-class FOIA specialist working with CAUS. Larry suggested I write a letter to the editor of the *Air Force Times*. If it were printed, other witnesses might come forward. It was a great idea, and within a week I'd drafted, typed, and retyped the letter, then sent it off. Not surprisingly, the letter was never printed.

Fawcett called to advise me not to concern myself about *America Undercover*. HBO had decided not to deal with Bentwaters on the program. He'd also learned that Connecticut senator Christopher Dodd was interested in the case. I reached his office and was soon talking to the senator about my involvement. But he lost interest faster than anyone I'd ever spoken with about it. His Hartford office wouldn't even forward my messages to him. Once again, I was not surprised.

Something that did surprise me was included in our honeymoon pictures. I'd picked them up at Fotomat and was going through them with the cashier when she asked, "Whose your friend?" I was shocked to see what appeared to be the hazy image of an alien, large eyes and all. When I showed Cin later, she was blown away by it. The picture was one of two I'd snapped in Rendlesham Forest. Eventually, I gave a copy to Greenwood and a copy to Hopkins for their personal files.

DeCaro called in September to ask if I'd want to do a second CNN *Special Assignment* on Bentwaters. I agreed instantly. But there was a stipulation: I'd have to take a lie-detector test, and he wanted to film it. "Any time, any place," I said. Chuck said he'd call back with the details.

When he did, there was a problem. When the polygraph operator (the only one in the state) found out the nature of the examination, he wanted no part of it. Shortly thereafter, CNN had a change of heart, and the follow-up was abandoned. Soon after, DeCaro left the network to start his own news-gathering business.

Heizerling kept in touch from Vermont and really pushed me to think about a book. I'd finally gotten through *Sky Crash* and was disgusted with most of what I'd read. The actual story was complex and difficult enough, but so-called interviews with me were so distorted that no reader would ever believe Art Wallace—it was a mess.

Stevie Ray Vaughan came by whenever he was in Connecticut, and it was always great to spend time with him. He had made it his business to learn about the incidents since we'd met, and by now he was a committed Bentwaters fan and also on my case to write a book. I listened as Stevie talked, but it was still difficult to imagine myself as an author.

On the night of 10 October, Cindy and I watched HBO's *America Undercover*, "UFO's: What's Going On?" I was impressed by a few of the people they had on, but especially by Travis Walton—boy, had he been through the mill. I looked on him as a true pioneer and inspiration. Then suddenly, the program introduced the Bentwaters incident. They played some of Lieutenant Colonel Halt's tape, then beat that old dead-dog lighthouse theory to death with some Ph.D. I'd never heard of. He supported his view by misquoting the Halt tape. Lawyer

Peter Gersten, however, did a great job discussing the air force's refusal to release six Bentwaters-related documents, on national security grounds. That bit of information surprised me.

Next was a clip from my 1983 BBC interview with Bob Friend, but HBO had edited it: what I said had *not* happened was presented as though it had. I seemed to be saying we had helped repair the UFO and that one of the aliens had even shaken Gordon Williams's hand. I recognized the edits: I'd been trained in television production. A sloppy cut-and-paste job made me look like a fool.

Cindy said, "This isn't fair." I was beyond words. I soon called HBO's New York office, stated my business, and asked to speak with the producer of the *America Undercover* program they'd just shown. I asked why they had edited my interview like that, why they hadn't simply called me—I would have done an interview with them.

The producer said as far as the edits were concerned, HBO had the rights to use that footage in any way they wanted to. After all, HBO was in the entertainment business. I slammed down the receiver and called Fawcett and blew my top. He said, "Don't worry, Lar, you'll get another chance to be on TV."

I felt used. The month before, I'd been told that Bentwaters wouldn't be on the show. I ended our conversation and our affiliation when I hung up the phone. It was sad because I had come to like Larry and his family very much, but now I knew that I didn't need anyone to manage my story. If I was going to stay in the fight, I'd have to do it on my own.

I sat for a while, then called Travis Walton in Arizona. We talked about our experiences and how lousy we thought most UFO investigators were. Then he gave me some advice: "Larry, quit the UFO game before it ruins your life." I agreed. Travis already had ten years under his belt as a ufological punching bag. By year's end, it seemed I had managed to quit.

1985 Developments |

January 1985

In England, debunker Ian Ridpath still champions the Bentwaters lighthouse theory. As for the Halt memo, the deputy base commander had the date wrong: the true date must have been 26 December 1980, not 27 December. How does Ridpath know? A meteorite passed over the twin-base area the night of 26 December. Halt's triangular series of depressions are recognized as "rabbit diggings." Also, there was no unusual radiation at the site, and the "starlike objects" observed by Halt and his men were just that—stars.[52]

11 April 1985

A letter to the Honorable James J. Exon, United States Senate, from the office of the secretary of the air force:

Dear Senator Exon,

This is in response to your inquiry on behalf of Messrs. Ray Boeche and Scott Colborn who requested information on unidentified flying objects (UFOs).

Regarding the incident at RAF Woodbridge, United Kingdom, in 1981, several base personnel reported seeing an unidentified object; however, we have no information that movies, plaster casts, or other such items were ever made. The Air Force stopped investigating UFOs in 1969, and all records of past investigations subsequently were sent to the National Archives. Those records are available for public inspection.

We have included additional information on the Air Force's past involvement in UFO investigations. We trust this information is useful.[53]

The letter is signed by a lieutenant colonel, name obscured due to a poor copy.

26 August 1985

A letter to the editor of the *Air Force Times* from Larry Warren:

When I was on duty as an Airman First Class with the 81st Security Police at RAF Bentwaters/Woodbridge Air Base, England, I happened to be one of the witnesses to events which remain disturbing to this day.

The events . . . have left me in the middle of the controversy, where I find that the Air Force ostensibly has washed its hands of the case and that the major news media generally have been uninspired to dirty their hands with.

To help me ease out of the middle, I ask that any *Air Force Times* readers with documentable evidence of the various events surrounding the case, or evidence of actual participation in the events, contact me immediately, so that, in a united effort, we might proceed with the necessary strategy for any upcoming Congressional inquiry and FOIA litigation.

With your sworn testimony, either as a voluntary submission or as a response to subpoena, we can help compel the government's full accountability on what exactly occurred on that very strange night in 1980.

The adage "there's strength in numbers" certainly would apply to such a high visibility, multiple witness event like ours. NOW is the time to come forward (confidentially, through me, if you prefer) so that we can add your voice to mine in the appropriate forum. The government has the answers to the questions we have been asking ourselves for the past five years, now is the time for answers.

Let's separate fact from fiction. You can reach me through the Editor of the *Air Force Times.*

The *Air Force Times* does not print the letter.

Mid-1985

In London, Quartet Books publishes *A Secret Property*, a novel based in part on the Bentwaters incidents. Its author, Ralph Noyes, enlisted in the RAF in 1940 and saw active duty in the Far East and North Africa. Discharged in 1946, he entered the British civil service in 1949 and served in the Air Ministry and the Ministry of Defence for the next twenty-eight years. His interest in UFOs developed between 1969 and late 1972 as head of a MOD division that brought him in contact with the UFO problem. Wishing to pursue a career as a writer, he took early retirement in 1977 and left the service in the grade of under secretary of state. The back dust jacket of *A Secret Property* is a collage of UFO news clippings around Larry Warren's sketch of the Bentwaters craft.[54]

Airman Terry Bastian is on active duty at a base in the States, but as leave approaches, he plans a vacation near his previous assignment, RAF Bentwaters. There, he stays at Wood Hall, a fine old Tudor house near Shottisham. Wood Hall is only a few miles due south of RAF Woodbridge. Like many couples who maintain B and B's Terry's hosts are outgoing and friendly. When a conversation turns to the events of December 1980, Terry is surprised by the couple's reaction:

They indicated to me that they'd both *seen* the actual ship—it had actually passed over their hotel, on the way to Woodbridge. The husband, he followed it over to the next field, as far as he could over toward Woodbridge. He didn't indicate how much he's seen after that, but they were very adamant that, yes, it did occur and they were trying to persuade me as much as possible.[55]

17 November 1985

Researcher William Heizerling writes Larry Warren:

It is my opinion, and that of many others, that the Rendlesham case is perhaps one of the most significant, multiple-witness UFO events ever to happen.

Since its occurrence, many conflicting reports have emerged concerning what really happened, charges, counter-charges, denials, etc. . . . which must be addressed soon if truly meaningful evidence is to emanate from this case. . . .

Needless to say, your first-hand account is of the utmost urgency, Larry. What you have to say will play a pivotal role in the final analysis and significance of the Rendlesham case.

Both Dr. Hynek and Dr. Smith have become extremely interested in this case, partly as a result of meeting and talking with you. . . . They urged me, as an intermediary, to get your written report to them as soon as possible. . . .

. . . I *urge* you to get your account to me as quickly as possible. This case is too big and too important for procrastination—especially on your part, since you are the one expert witness whose information is privy to us. Your report, in fact, may be one of the most important pieces of information pertaining to the UFO phenomenon. . . . [56]

12.

1986–1987—
"YOU SHOULD WRITE A BOOK!"

The fifth anniversary of the Bentwaters incidents had just passed. Though I'd promised Cin otherwise, I was still involved and, in my opinion, not doing a very good job of lifting the veil of government secrecy concerning UFOs. That I'd previously thought I could now made me laugh a little. Nobody was cracking this thing, but it didn't seem to matter. Who needed answers when they had "entertainment?"

Bill Heizerling continued to call. More than ever now, he wanted me to write up my recollections for publication. Dr. J. Allen Hynek and Willy Smith of the Center for UFO Studies in Chicago had already requested copies of my account. But I was hesitant to give any written account to anyone. Why bother? Someone would only find a way to use it against me. But Bill wanted to take it a step farther—perhaps we could write the book together.

I'd thought about this the past year but knew from experience that any partnership was risky, especially for witnesses, so I remained distant from Bill's suggestion. I had other priorities: my job and my marriage were beginning to suffer from my preoccupation with Bentwaters. But truth kept me on the front lines. And the Bentwaters incidents continued to be distorted by people who had not even been there!

On 28 January 1986, I watched the launch of the space shuttle *Chal-*

lenger on a small TV monitor across the hall from my office. Though shuttle launchs were routine by now, this mission was special. With a New Hampshire schoolteacher on board, children all over the country would be tuned in. After watching the craft lift off without incident, I returned to my paperwork. Moments later there was a commotion in the hall, where people appeared confused and upset. I looked back at the TV as the two booster rockets flew erratically—the *Challenger* was gone. No one was clear on what had happened, but by 11:50 A.M. the entire country was in shock—we'd lost all seven astronauts in a split second.

My marriage and job now seemed secure, but Bentwaters was still my shadow. February 1986 brought my second firsthand contact with the NSA's agent Jim Greenfield. Again, the meeting was set up by phone. The place would be a restaurant in Brookfield, Connecticut. I wanted to tell Cindy, but had second thoughts. Why frighten her? She was having enough trouble with my nightmares, mood swings, and flash-backs.

The meeting took place on a Saturday at noon. Greenfield and another, unnamed man were late, but once they were seated, the conversation was as casual and relaxed as our earlier talk had been. Jim asked how I was adapting to married life and laughed when I said it was easier than military life. "Larry, we want to offer you a deal."

My red flag went up, "What deal?" I asked. "Larry, you could help us out a lot by changing the course you're on." "Go on," I said. "Listen," Jim began, "in all the years you've been trying to change the world with this thing, don't you feel you've been ripped off by these assholes you've been dealing with?" I thought about it for a second and agreed. "But the truth is the truth, Jim, and in time this will all come out."

"Well, Larry, let me tell you, it won't. You see, a lot of people are concerned with the suggestion that Williams was present at the landing site." "But he was!" I insisted, "I saw him there." Jim only added, "They don't like talk of aliens either. It makes them nervous." "Well, Jim, it makes me nervous, too, but I saw them."

The other guy sat quietly through the meeting, but the look on his face was nasty.

"Larry, back off on those elements, please. It serves no one, especially yourself. Lots could come your way." My military records could be "cleaned up," maybe a VA home loan could be secured for me, even some cash down the line. I wasn't eligible for a VA loan; I hadn't been in the service long enough. It seemed funny that Cindy and I had just been talking about buying a home. I finished my cheeseburger in silence.

I took a breath and looked Jim in the eye. "It's true that a lot of people in the UFO field are assholes. But if people like me don't take a stand, more people will be fucked up by this stuff. Some will probably even die. Thanks for the offer, but I can't lie to myself. The last time we spoke, you told me you were just a messenger, that you didn't know the details of Bentwaters, but you do. Shit, Jim, you know everything about me. I'll stick to my guns, and you guys stick to yours." He didn't say anything as I excused myself and got up to leave. As I did, Jim said, "Larry, we will."

I left the restaurant and drove home. I knew I was in trouble, but didn't know what to expect from the NSA now. I wasn't keeping my promise to Cindy, either, and was beginning to feel that promise could never be kept: the more public I was, the safer I'd be.

In June, I presented a paper at the annual Massachusetts MUFON conference in Beverly. Dr. Hynek was there, as were lawyer and researcher Bob Bletchman, Heizerling, Hopkins, and Debby Tomey. Debby was a terrific woman from Indiana who had had the courage to come forward about her UFO abduction experiences. Her story would be featured in Budd's new book, *Intruders.* Despite my complaints about some researchers, over the years I'd made a lot of friends in the field, and it was always good to see them.

I presented my paper at a private conference dinner. It was hard to stand up there and tell the story, reliving it as I spoke. I desperately wanted people to visualize what I had seen in England. The talk was well received. I only wished that Cindy had been there to hear it, but she would never go to a conference with me; she wanted no part of it.

The next afternoon, I spoke at length with Dr. Hynek. We had met and spoken before, but this time he seemed particularly interested in what I had to say. As we talked, I noticed he did not look well. The previous evening, he'd been helped from the stage during his lecture; Dr. David Jacobs presented his paper for him. It was sad. Hell, Dr. Hynek had been involved since the 1940s—he was a living legend in the UFO field. Hynek had even played himself in *Close Encounters of the Third Kind!* He was obviously very ill.

I even got the normally serious scientist to laugh a few times. As our talk ended, he put a hand on my shoulder and told me he was impressed with my story. I was actually shocked when he said, "Larry, you're doing the right thing. Keep at it." I said I would try my best. Looking almost a little sad, he smiled at me, then walked away. I sensed he knew a lot more than he admitted in public.

I returned home, suddenly excited about the prospect of doing a book on Bentwaters as I had seen it, as it had happened to me. I was my own free agent, and it was five and a half years after the fact. The time seemed right.

Though I hadn't any idea of how to start, and an overall concept remained elusive, the title came like a bullet: *Left at East Gate.* It was what the law-enforcement cop at the roadblock had said to us before we headed into the twilight zone. Three books had already published variations of my experience, and not one of them had got it right. This one would have to be different. People, not technology, would be its focal point.

Cin was as supportive as possible, but not happy with my decision. By fall 1986, she was growing more distant, but I guess she could have said the same of me. I couldn't blame her. In my life, a nonhuman presence continued its periodic visitations, and now even Cindy sensed the little bastards in the house from time to time.

October brought good news, though: my confirmation as a speaker at MUFON's 1987 international UFO symposium in Washington, D.C. And I had done it on my own. As the year drew to a close, I started work on *East Gate.* I knew I wanted it to read like a novel, while remaining absolutely factual. I also knew I would have to find a coauthor who could not only write, but who wouldn't bail out when he realized what he had gotten himself into.

In mid-November, a letter arrived from the headquarters of the Air Force Accounting and Finance Center in Denver. It was another request for $95.42, the remainder of the three-hundred-dollar fine I'd received for calling my mother the morning after the incident. They were giving me sixty days to prove the debt was not valid. Otherwise, it would be turned over to the IRS. I decided to call Denver.

Once connected with an officer, I asked him why I was being charged the amount. I'd never paid a bill that didn't tell me what I was being charged for. The officer checked the record and said no reason was given. He thought it might be from a fine.

I thanked him, started on a letter to the Air Force Accounting and Finance Center and mailed it off the next day. I'd asked them to forward a new bill stating the reason for the charge. If they would do this, I would be glad to remit the $95.42. It was the last I heard from them.

WTIC radio in Hartford reunited Fawcett and me via the *Mark Davis Show* in late spring. Fawcett was the guest that night. After listening to several incorrect statements about Bentwaters, I called in to correct them, and Davis kept me on the air for the rest of the show.

That fall, Greenwood began to correspond with Colonel Halt, now stationed in Belgium. In December, Greenwood sent me a copy of a tape Halt had sent him. Greenwood had sent Halt a tape of my June MUFON lecture and asked him to comment on it. Halt responded that I was a professional entertainer, then went on to confirm many elements of my account. He didn't comment on aliens and ended the tape with an aside that I may have left the service because of drug use or homosexuality. Cindy and I saw the new year in together watching the ball drop in Times Square on TV.

I had been speaking with Whitley Strieber by phone from time to time, mostly about our recurrent interactions with nonhuman beings. I told him I just wanted to know what they wanted with me. Long past its original release, his book *Communion* remained a best-seller and seemed to be bringing more people forward, people who had also had the experience. It made me give some extra thought to how I had been keeping that part of my life separate—and secret—from my Bentwaters involvement. I had to talk about that in the book, no matter how it would be received.

I decided against Heizerling as a coauthor. While a nice guy, a good writer, and certainly supportive, he represented mainstream ufology to me. It was nothing personal, but I just didn't feel he was the person to take on this project.

Real estate people kept me occupied for most of January, February, and March 1987. We found a house in Bristol, Connecticut, and our loan approval was just around the corner. Though UFOs were not the only source of stress in our relationship, we both thought getting the house could help solve the problems in our marriage. We moved in the second week of June, and Cindy had a field day planning our home's decor. We spent twenty-four hours straight painting before the furniture arrived. No more landlords or rent increases. It was going to be tough, but it was ours!

On Thursday morning 25 June 1987, I drove to New Haven and caught an Amtrak train to Washington. Passing through New York, then Philadelphia, I couldn't help but wonder when the UFO phenomenon was going to get the attention it deserved; forty years seemed long enough. As the train rolled south, my concerns shifted. I wanted to make the best presentation I could and deal with some things I'd not talked about in the past. MUFON's director Walt Andrus had told me I'd have forty-five minutes to speak, and I planned to fill every one of them. What I couldn't cover, *Left at East Gate* would.

1986 Developments |

June 1986

An emotionally unstable man sits at a table in Framingham, Massachusetts, typing out a rambling six-page letter to Pat Robertson. He writes the well-known televangelist about Einstein's unified theory, that Jesus equated himself with the unified field, and that "Jesus Christ is part of the mystery of the Great Pyramid and the Great Pyramid is part of the mystery of Jesus Christ." Other revelations are addressed.

Robertson is encouraged to charge himself with an additional Christian mission: "In my estimation, you above all others, are the one *to open the eyes of the Christian community to the fact that some UFOs and their occupants are part of the Christian mission.*"

The way to begin going about this? Easy, contact Larry Warren:

> Recently I spoke with a man who had a very close encounter. He would be a good candidate for a guest on your show. His name is Larry Warren and he openly admitted that his life has changed in a positive way spiritually since his UFO experience six years ago. When I approached him about my idea of suggesting to you about his appearing on the "700 Club," he was quite willing and enthusiastic. He was familiar with you and watches the "700 Club."
>
> You can read about the Rendlesham Forest Incident in note 15 of the notebook attached to this sign. Larry Warren is the "Art Wallace" who came forward to leak the story to the public. He no longer cares if his real name is used since he has been given an honorable discharge from the U.S. Air Force.[57]

After a brief synopsis, the writer notes "that one thing the UFO encounter taught him [Warren] was, 'There definitely is a God.'" The writer closes this part of his letter with Larry's home address and phone number, strongly suggesting "you grab this opportunity and call or write Larry Warren and invite him on your program. The potential could prove to be as wide as the universe."

A copy of this letter is supplied to Connecticut Police Lieutenant Fawcett by the New Haven office of the FBI, following the writer's eventual threat on Warren's life.

8 October 1986
A computer at the Denver headquarters of Air Force Accounting and Finance prints out a letter to Warren. It arrives at his New Britain, address the following week:

Balance Due $95.42

Date Due 01/26/82

Account No. [Warren's Social Security number]

Letter Date 10/08/86
  We attempted to contact you about your debt with us but were unsuccessful. We reported your name and account information to a credit bureau. Such a report could adversely affect your credit rating. Additionally, we must take action to offset the amount of your debt and administrative costs against your federal income tax refund for the current year.
  . . . To stop our referral of your debt to the Internal Revenue Service IRS, you have 60 days from the date of this letter to send us written evidence proving this debt is not valid. Any false statements or representations you make may subject you to civil or criminal penalties under the applicable Statutory Authority. . . . We urge you to contact this office immediately to settle your debt.
Sincerely
Robert J. Grandinetti
Chief, Accounts Receivable Branch
Directorate of Settlement and Adjudication[58]

PART 2
Notes

1. Review of *DeGaulle: The Rebel*, by Jean Lacouture, *New York Times Book Review*, 11 November 1990, p. 58.
2. The Armed Forces Security Service is a field arm of the National Security Agency.
3. Letter on file.
4. Jenny Randles, "Impact—and After," *The Unexplained* (March 1983).
5. Document on file.
6. Letter on file.
7. Randles, "Impact—and After."
8. Document on file.
9. Report on file. Environmental medicine generally refers to nuclear exposure.
10. Randles, "Impact—and After."
11. Terry Bastian and Brian Downing, interview by John Timmerman, San Diego, California, September 1991.
12. "Crashed UFO in England," *Frontiers of Science* (May–June 1982), p. 11. Credit: Budd Hopkins.
13. J. Bamford, *The Puzzle Palace* (Boston: Houghton, Mifflin, 1982), pp. 1–4.
14. Randles, "Impact—and After."
15. "UFO Update," *Omni*, March 1983.
16. *Probe* 3, no. 4 (March 1983).
17. Letter on file.
18. Letter on file.
19. Letter on file.
20. Letter on file.
21. *East Anglian Daily Times*, 12 October 1983, p. 6; K. Beabey, "A Flying Triangle of Fear," *News of the World*, 23 October 1983.
22. H. Dehn, "Mystery Light Puzzles DJ David," *News of the World*, 16 October 1983.
23. "MP Demands Facts over UFO Reports," *Evening Star*, 20 October 1983.
24. "Suffolk 'UFO Sighting' Raised in Commons," *East Anglian Daily Times*, 25 October 1983.
25. B. Smith, "Bug-Eyed Alien Meets Air Chief," *News of the World*, 6 November 1983. This is the only occasion where a journalist alleges that "Art Wallace says" there were *four* aliens and *armed* military police. This seems more a case of sloppy journalism on Smith's part than an instance of Art Wallace contradicting himself on two otherwise absolutely consistent details.
26. "UFO Group Attempts to Enlighten Public," *Beverly (Mass.) Times*, 21 November 1983.
27. A pseudonym for what surely was a pseudonym.
28. The Cash–Landrum UFO incident occurred in Texas within twelve hours of the third night's incident at RAF Bentwaters. Two women—Vicky Cash and Betty Landrum—and Betty's grandson, Colby, saw a huge, toplike UFO while driving in rural Texas. When the object, escorted by numerous black helicopters, approached the vehicle, its occupants suffered radiation burns. Soon after, both women were diagnosed with cancer.
29. Letter on file. Credit: C. Stone.

30. Transcript on file. Credit: Barry Greenwood.

31. In a phone conversation with Fawcett in mid-1992, I asked him about that part of the interview where he asks Adrian if it had been Colonel Halt he had seen in the field, not Colonel Williams. Fawcett had described the officer in question as "a big guy, whoever it was." It was Williams who stood about six feet five inches, not Halt. I told Fawcett that I knew from conducting my own interviews how easy it is to confuse a detail, even an important one, during a particularly exciting Q & A session. Was that what had happened here? Had he meant Williams and said Halt? I told him I had assumed this to be the case after reading it. He didn't say yes, but I did interpret the sound to be affirmative and the point not debated. But the continuing references to Halt instead of to Williams are unfortunate. A minute but possible error in transcription: On page 25 of the longhand portion of the Fawcett–Bustinza transcript supplied by Ray Boeche, the word "canvas" appears in a context that makes me suspect Bustinza said "camos" or "cammies": "They all had canvas on, so you can't really tell the names."

32. Fawcett seems to be combining parts of two events here: the end of the debriefing and one of Warren's memories from the underground.

33. Transcript on file. Credit: Barry Greenwood and Ray Boeche.

34. Transcripts on file. Credit: Barry Greenwood.

35. Transcripts on file. Credit: Barry Greenwood.

36. Andrew Clark, "Have 'Space People' Visited East Anglia? Mystery Sightings 'Too Many to Be Dismissed,' " *East Anglian Daily Times*, 25 April 1989, pp. 18–19.

37. Statement on file.

38. Letter from Captain Warzinski to M. I. Birdsall, dated 1 August 1984. Letter from A. B. Rowley, Chief Warrant Officer, U.S. Navy, Operations Coordinator Defense Attaché Office, American Embassy, London, to Birdsall, dated 13 August 1984. Letter from Rowley to Birdsall date 22 August 1984. Letter from Warzinski to Birdsall, dated 22 August 1984. Credit: Antonio Huneeus.

39. Chuck DeCaro, interview by Peter Robbins, 12 February 1994.

40. USAFHQ message, 24 August 1984, on file.

41. *Rendlesham Revisited: Documents from the 81st Tactical Fighter Wing, USAF* (Quest Publications International, 1992).

42. Letter on file. From *Rendlesham Revisited*.

43. "New UFO Evidence Revealed" and "Recording of UFO Sighting 'Not a Hoax,' " *East Anglian Daily Times*, 25 October 1984; "UFO Tape 'Is Not a Hoax,' " *Evening Star*, 25 October 1984. Credit: Barry Greenwood.

44. Howard and Grace Varney, interview by Peter Robbins, Glens Falls, N.Y., 24 August 1991.

45. "Comment—Unidentified Official Secret," *Evening Star*, 26 October 1984, p. 4; "This Is Weird . . . Unreal,' " *Evening Star*, 26 October 1984.

46. "After UFOs . . . Yawning Men in Pinstripe Suits," *East Anglian Daily Times*, 29 October 1984.

47. "UFO Man on Visit to Base," *Evening Star*, 31 October 1984; "Base Visit for Man in UFO Mystery," *East Anglian Daily Times*, 31 October 1984.

48. Letter on file.

49. Letter on file.

50. Recording on file.

51. CNN's special report on the Bentwaters incident was produced by Ed Turner (no relation to CNN founder Ted Turner).

52. "The Woodbridge UFO Incident," *The Guardian* (January 1985); repr., *The Skeptical Inquirer* (fall 1986).

53. Letter on file.

54. Ralph Noyes, *A Secret Property* (New York: Quartet Books Limited, 1985).

55. Terry Bastian and Brian Downing, interview by John Timmerman, San Bernadino, California, 21 September 1991.

56. Letter on file.

57. Letter on file.

58. Letter on file.

PART 3

THE RETURN, RESEARCH, AND RESPONSE

1. 1987—
WALL OF DENIAL

25 June 1987, the train slid into an enclosed platform, then squealed to a halt. I gathered my belongings and stepped off the train into Washington's Union Station and a sea of people. The weather was oppressive; temperature and humidity ranged in the high nineties. I'd expected the Capitol to have clean streets and an invisible homeless population, but I found the opposite to be true. I hailed a black-and-white cab and asked the driver to take me to the American University campus.

As we drove, I could see the dome of the Capitol Building and the Washington Monument. However, the only monuments in the District of Columbia that truly interested me were the Vietnam Memorial and JFK's grave; I felt they were in some way connected and planned to visit them when I had some free time. We passed countless federal buildings, and I found myself wondering which one contained the vault where files and photographs of the Bentwaters incidents were stored. How many other secrets were locked away here?

After arriving at the campus, I checked into the dorm where the conference speakers were being housed. Later that afternoon, I attended a press conference. I entered the small lecture hall and took a seat in the last row. The major news media had representatives there, asking a panel of UFO researchers their thoughts on the phenomena. However, attention soon turned to a man in the front row named John Lear. The son of William Lear, inventor of the Lear jet, John Lear was a distinguished pilot who held well over one hundred airspeed records. He had flown for the CIA's Air America during Vietnam, had extensive intelligence-community ties, and recently made an unsuccessful bid for the Nevada state senate. He was very much against government secrecy concerning UFOs; when he spoke, people paid attention.

I sat listening to the press question him; the man was interesting. But I almost fell out of my chair when Lear answered a question about the origin of his interest in the subject: it was Bentwaters. An A-10 pilot, stationed there when I was, had confirmed to Lear that a major UFO incident had taken place near there in late 1980. The incident had involved a contact with the UFO's occupants. A cover-up had followed. I knew I would have to spend some time with Lear.

I did have a problem with MUFON director Walt Andrus. He and the *National Enquirer* had claimed the results of a bogus voice-stress analysis proved I was lying during part of my CNN interview. I was told that he had written a letter to Phil Klass to let the debunker know that MUFON did not support the validity of the Bentwaters case. He also stated that I must have been exaggerating the part about aliens. We had never even met, but Andrus had not let that stand in the way of passing judgment on my account. I couldn't help feeling the man was uncomfortable with the fact that UFOs were piloted by living things.

That evening I attended a reception for the high-visibility speakers— authors Gary Kinder, Strieber, and Hopkins. Entering the room, I was suddenly surrounded by a Japanese film crew headed by my old friend Jim Yaoi. It was great to see him again. The camera turned to me, and Jim asked some questions. I looked up to see everyone looking at us and wondering who the young upstart was. I was amazed that Bentwaters was still famous in Japan. In America, the incident was already considered old news by many researchers.

As the weekend progressed, speakers and researchers from around the world networked with each other. Even Rhode Island Senator Claiborne Pell seemed to mix easily with the crowd. Forty years after the cover-up had begun, the conference that marked it was shaping up as a massive success. Even the poorly air-conditioned lecture halls stayed full, with every seat taken for most speakers' presentations.

I felt very involved, yet out of place. I called Cindy to see how she was. While I was busy with UFOs again, she was putting our new house in order. Cindy didn't sound happy, and I couldn't blame her. She just said, "Get home soon."

I spent part of Saturday with Chuck DeCaro. No longer with CNN, Chuck had started his own news-gathering business in Virginia. As always, he seemed supportive of what I was trying to do, and we caught up on Bentwaters over lunch. I found out that Chuck felt a little burned over the *Special Assignment* story, too. As I already knew, anyone too close to the Bentwaters story was screwed. Later, he gave a great talk at the conference, explaining the approach CNN had taken with the Bentwaters story. He then ran the *Special Assignment* program for the audience to see for themselves. His unscheduled lecture angered some MUFON members, but I didn't care and was grateful DeCaro had taken the time for me.

I had been looking forward to meeting Jenny Randles at the conference, but when someone finally introduced us, she literally ran away. It was disappointing. I really wanted to discuss the problems I'd had with *Sky Crash* with her. I was later told she'd been scared to meet me because she heard about my reaction to the book, which I was now calling "Sky Trash."

For me, the most depressing part of the conference was the presence of the New Age movement. I knew my experiences with nonhumans had never been pleasant or spiritually fulfilling, and that movement's welcome-the-space-brothers, channeling-crystal bullshit really got to me. I felt their cultlike, glazed-eyed attitude was not helping the subject of UFOs to be taken more seriously by the general public. I had hoped the New Agers would have gone to Shirley MacLaine's seminar, also in town that weekend, and left us alone. Having these people run around the conference marking forty years of the government cover-up of UFOs set us back fifty years.

That evening, John Lear, Charlie Hickson, and I went out for drinks at a bar in Georgetown. Charlie was a true legend in the UFO field and someone I had admired for a long time. Almost fifteen years earlier, he had had the courage to come forward and report his UFO abduction near Pascagoula, Mississippi. Calvin Parker had been abducted with him and suffered a nervous breakdown as a result. Charlie said Calvin had never been the same since the 1973 incident. As we talked about the UFO situation, our volume increased. I'm sure more than one congressman or senator heard us carrying on; hell, Tip O'Neill was at the bar just feet away from our table.

We returned to the campus in time to catch a late session in one of the lecture halls. I listened for a while, then wandered out into the hallway. Through the doors of a large lecture hall, I could hear the big event of the weekend: the abduction panel discussion. I walked in and took a seat. The moderator was Dr. David Jacobs of Temple University. Seated on stage were Debby Tomey, whom I'd met in Beverly, Massachusetts, and Strieber; I didn't know the others.

Things got off to a ridiculous start with Strieber reading off a list of charges against Klass, who was standing at the front of the stage taking pictures. Then Klass yelled something back about demanding equal time—it was both funny and depressing.

At this point, I almost left to hit the hay. As a rule, I rarely listened to lectures by UFO researchers because they're often boring—if you've been to a conference on UFOs, you know what I mean. But *these* people had been through the real deal. I wanted to hear some of their stories, but Strieber seemed to be dominating the microphone, so I slipped out into the hall.

A British researcher approached as the door closed behind me. Drunk and arrogant, he informed me: "You Yanks misidentified a Harrier Jump Jet at Bentwaters for a UFO!" "What about the pilots?" I asked. He just stared at me with a grin on his face. I was sick of shitheads like this and told him to "piss off!" As I started to walk away, a voice coming from the stage stopped me in my tracks. It was calm, articulate, and sincere. I immediately reentered the conference hall.

The speaker was seated near the center of the stage and talking about the childhood UFO incident he'd had with his sister. He was the only one on the panel not claiming to have been abducted by aliens, but it seemed his sister had been. In any case, the man had had one hell of a sighting and experience. He talked about how his sister had never forgotten parts of the incident, while he had blanked it all out for fifteen years, and described the trauma that remembering it had produced in his life.

The most impressive thing about this guy was the way he seemed to have overcome the negative aspects of his experience. When Jacobs introduced the panel at the end, it was Peter Robbins who generated the largest round of applause—we all had been right there with him when he spoke. I've got to meet that guy, I thought.

I returned to my overly air-conditioned room and made some notes and changes on my typed lecture paper. If I could affect the audience the way Robbins had, I could call the conference a success.

Early the next morning, Sunday, I took a stroll around the campus.

Since my talk was scheduled for two o'clock, I had time to visit the Vietnam Memorial. I arrived there early enough to experience it alone. Surrounded by the seamless black granite and too many ghosts, I was overwhelmed.

Back on campus, the last day of the conference was packed. On the steps outside the lecture hall where I was due to present my paper, I ran into Klass. I found him polite and friendly, asking if he might interview me. I agreed and out came the tape recorder. We spoke on the steps there for about an hour. Many of his questions were very good, and I had no answer for some. When he asked me if I'd ever been abducted, I said no.

Thinking back on Fawcett's advice, I didn't volunteer anything about my other experiences; why even bother with this guy? When he finished, we shook hands and parted ways. I was later told Klass thought I must be a "drug-addicted hippie," because of my background in the music business.

It was now time to present my paper. I approached the stage with a hall full of people. I was excited and began my talk. Shortly after I'd started, one of Andrus's assistants walked up to the podium and interrupted me midsentence. My forty-five minutes had been cut to fifteen. I was furious. I was now being censored by the same people who accused the government of covering up the truth about UFOs.

Making it clear to the audience that it was now impossible to present what I'd written, I put my paper aside and let loose on how witnesses were often dealt with by UFO researchers and organizations, including MUFON. Andrus suddenly left the hall. I said that, without witnesses who were willing to come forward, there would be no UFO cases and, finally, no researchers. Egos wouldn't solve this mystery, but the people who had experienced it might. I closed with the offer to present the paper outside for anyone who wanted to listen. About 150 people followed me out the door.

I returned to the conference hall later, and standing alone in the hallway, I again heard that voice that had struck me earlier. "Hi, Larry." I turned to see Robbins across the hall and walked right over to him: "You're Peter! Man, I loved what you had to say last night."

We began to talk. He told me that we'd met in 1983, but I probably wouldn't remember. He was right, I didn't. But I did begin to size him up as my coauthor then and there. I didn't know the guy at all, but I did know he was the person I was going to ask; it was just one of those things. We hit it off great and made plans to get together in July.

It was good to get back to Cindy and our new home. The house needed a lot of work. Both of us fixed the pool and completed the painting. Cin had the interior of the house looking great.

Every other night, I'd call Robbins in Manhattan. We talked about UFOs, of course, but lots of other things as well. Toward the end of the week, he invited me to spend the Fourth of July weekend in the city. I loved New York, and Cindy didn't mind. With me out of her way for a few days, she could get other projects accomplished, so I accepted.

Peter lived in a great neighborhood near the UN, a quick walk from Grand Central. I was at his door by 11:00 A.M. Peter greeted me warmly, and by late afternoon, we were deep into a discussion about Bentwaters. I didn't trust anyone enough to tell them about the more personal things that had happened to me from childhood on, but I did feel comfortable enough to let him record me as I went over my Bentwaters experience in detail, minus the underground complex, the NSA, and a few other personal details. I was glad his exposure to the nasty politics surrounding the incident had been limited.

When we'd get away from UFOs for a while, Peter talked about himself and his family. I already knew who his sister was. I recognized her from photos in his apartment, lots of rock fans would have. Helen Wheels had gold and platinum songwriting credits with the Blue Oyster Cult, but as a performer, she was something else. I'd seen the Helen Wheels Band blow the Ramones off Hartford's Agora Ballroom stage earlier that year. She was the sister who'd been through the UFO abduction. I looked forward to meeting Helen; both she and her brother had been there and back like me. I could relate to these people and felt I had nothing to prove to either of them.

As the weekend progressed, I told Peter my rough plans for *Left at East Gate*. He seemed interested. Before leaving that Sunday night, I asked him to be my coauthor. I warned him that he should expect attacks from other researchers just by associating with me and that the closer he came to some of the truths about Bentwaters, the more likely he would come under some sort of government surveillance.

Peter seemed to be turning the proposal over in his mind. He said he'd been looking for a serious writing project, and though he had no more knowledge about Bentwaters than most other researchers, he had followed developments in the case since late 1983. He also said he understood the implications of my warning, but I didn't think he really did. He had no idea what he was getting himself into; I only hoped he could handle it if the heat were turned up. I told him I was willing to split whatever profit we made on the project fifty-fifty. We shook hands on it before I returned to Connecticut. I finally had a coauthor!

We both felt the best way to start would be for me to bring him through the last seven years of my life, beginning at Bentwaters. He would eventually have to know every inch of the story; there was no other way. Everything would have to be put on hold, though, because Peter had a summer job in Maine that started the next week. He'd be gone until Labor Day, but now that we were set, I could wait.

At summer's end, Cin and I spent Labor Day weekend at my mother's. As we drove home, we talked and listened to old Motown songs on the radio. But while we were driving south on Route 8 in northern Connecticut, things suddenly changed.

We had just passed Torrington when I began to feel strange. Just ahead, above some hills, I saw what looked like three brightly lit planets. Then I lost them behind a hill, then they were back: large stationary objects, orange in color.

"Cin, look at this!" I yelled. Cindy looked, saw them, then looked away. No one in the cars around us seemed to be reacting to the UFOs, but I felt connected to these objects—*how could anybody not notice them?* I wondered. "Cin, please look!" I yelled, but she covered her face with her hands and said, "No! I don't want to see it!" That's when I lost it. "Goddamn it, you bitch, please see this is real! Don't let me be alone in this!" Cindy started to cry, but kept shielding her eyes. I felt betrayed in some way. UFOs had so drastically affected my life, and she was too scared to even look.

I continued to watch them as I drove. One suddenly took off southward, and the second one just blinked out. When the third one began to lose altitude, I screamed at it, "You bastards, let her see you!" Now, with no cars in sight, I pulled off onto the shoulder of the highway. Cindy kept hiding her face, and I got out of the car to get a better look. Directly above us, perhaps a thousand feet, was a triangular craft with three lights on its underside.

Again I pleaded with my wife, "Come out here and look at this thing!" "No!" was all she said. I looked up and screamed, "What do you bastards want from me!?" followed by a torrent of profanity. The object then began flashing its lights, as if it were mocking me. My wife told me to get back in the car. I did, but at that moment, I knew my marriage was in trouble. I had no control over the situation. Those little jerks in the UFO had something to do with this, and I cursed them as we drove home in silence.

Later, at home, I went out for a run to blow off steam. At the end of my driveway, I looked up and saw a huge cigar-shaped object moving west. It seemed to have windows. I just shook my head and began to jog, but soon felt as though I was being followed. I stopped and turned around in time to see a bright white light coming down the road at eye level. Flying a few feet over my head, there was no structure to it, only light. Down the street it went, until it came to a stand of pine trees, where it shot straight up and out of sight. *What a weird night,* I thought as I ran back home. That was the beginning of the worst week of nonhuman visitations I have ever experienced. I was careful not to go into too much of it when I called Peter. I didn't want to scare him away.

Beginning in September 1987, I spent about one weekend a month at Peter's apartment. Each trip, I'd bring him more of what I'd collected over the years: letters, documents, articles, papers, videotapes, and the part of my service record I'd walked away with in 1981.

I would open up a little more on each visit as well. Peter had had his recorder on since our first interview. It never seemed to be off when we were talking about Bentwaters, even when we were covering territory we'd been over before. It pissed me off a lot when he'd backtrack, and he did so often. I couldn't blame the guy; he was testing me and trying to cover his ass at the same time. I'd have done the same thing in his place. But if he could just hang in there, I knew I could prove it all to him. I just needed time.

By now, NSA agent Jim Greenfield had expressed interest in Peter. He'd even given me permission to pursue the book with him—without reprisal from the agency. However, my distrust of Greenfield had grown immensely since our contact had begun. I knew that if they got their claws into Peter, our book would fail. So I decided not to tell Peter of the agency's interest. I intended to protect the project at any cost.

At home, Cindy and I hardly spoke. When we did, it was usually in the form of an argument. The nonhuman intrusions were becoming more intense and terrifying. Cindy never woke up during the bedroom visitations, which only increased my frustration. Talking to her about it was out of the question.

Each day, I grew more agitated. I drank and began to screw up at work. I wasn't sleeping at night and began to feel as though *they* were robbing me of my sanity. By the end of that week, I knew something was about to snap and that I could not stop it.

On a Monday night, Cin and I began arguing over a bill. It quickly escalated into a violent shouting match, then I pushed her. Cindy told me to "grow up" and slapped my face. That was when I hit her. Later, she lay down on our bed and cried. Her lip was bleeding, and she was bruised. I wanted to die. I loved her, yet I could have killed her.

Though Cindy should have had me arrested, she did nothing, but for her it was over. Soon the divorce was planned, and we lived like roommates from then on. It was terrible. At times, we both forgot what had happened and laughed together. Then reality would kick in, and we'd return to our own corners.

By legal agreement, I was to move out on or about 1 May 1988. I planned to move to New York City. All of my family thought New York was a bad idea. They also thought what I had done to Cindy was beneath contempt. On that point, I couldn't have agreed more. I tried to erase that event from my mind. I was such a selfish bastard, all I could really focus on now was the book.

Peter had come a long way since July 1987. By now, he'd read almost everything I had given him, amassed dozens of hours of interviews with me, and was familiar with all the Suffolk locations from the maps I'd drawn and supplied. In fact, Peter was ready to start writing his part of the book, except for one thing. We talked about it the next weekend I was in the city.

I told him that he now probably knew more about the Bentwaters incidents than any civilian in the UFO research community, but that I'd come to feel we still had something important to do. I had to take him to England. He had to go back to Bentwaters with me, back to the landing site. He had to feel the place, walk the walk, as they say. Peter heard me out, then said, "When do we go?" I had two weeks of vacation coming to me, so we agreed to go in February 1988.

In December, I took out a loan to cover expenses for the trip while Peter secured our flights on Virgin Atlantic Airlines. Our plans were coming together well, but I spent Christmas at my mother's, wondering if there was anything I could do to save my marriage. Though it was too late now, part of me couldn't accept the fact that I'd destroyed the best thing in my life. It was the worst Christmas I could remember.

New Year's Eve—seven years after Bentwaters, and my life was once again in turmoil. Our trip was only six weeks away, and I still hadn't been able to tell Peter a number of things about Bentwaters. I really wanted to, but could he handle them? I just didn't know, so I decided to wait until we were in the shadow of the twin bases. Once there, the information might be easier for him to take.

2. 1987— GETTING INVOLVED

My name is Peter Robbins. My interest in the subject of UFOs began in 1975 with the return of a childhood memory of an incident that took place in June 1961 and involved my younger sister Helen. It happened in Rockville Centre, New York, outside the house on Harvard Avenue where my sisters and I grew up.

It had been a beautiful morning. Helen and I were playing out by the rock garden on the front lawn when I noticed some "things" in the sky. They were coming down at a very high rate of speed. "Look!" I yelled and pointed skyward. Neither of us said a word for the duration. We watched the things come to an abrupt stop over the Parkers' house across the street. What they were I did not know, but I could certainly see what they looked like—five, silvery-white, disk-shaped objects. Each was about the size of a commercial airplane at several thousand feet, or a smaller, private plane at several hundred. The five held in a precise, military V-type formation. Around the edge of each were regularly spaced, pale-yellow lights that appeared to be windows.

The two of us just stood there, about six feet apart, and looked at them. Instantly apparent were all the things they were not. They were not airplanes, helicopters, balloons, blimps, or dirigibles. They were not clouds, birds, kites, or reflections from the ground. All these rejections flashed through my mind in a matter of seconds. There was nothing ambiguous about the objects. They were there, and I was transfixed.

Though no science-fiction buff, as a fourteen-year-old American boy, I would have to have been deaf, dumb, and blind not to have seen a flying-saucer movie or two by 1961. Flying saucers were just what these things were. For some seconds, I told myself I must be misinterpreting some type of conventional objects, but I couldn't hold the thought. I started to repeat the phrase, "secret government test planes, secret government test planes," but that didn't take either.

This was impossible. Everyone—adults and children—knew they were fantasy; you just knew it. But it seemed we were wrong. They were real. Five of them were above the Parkers' house.

I was starting to lose it. Helen could keep watching if she wanted, but I was getting out of there. Wheeling 180 degrees, I began to run toward the front door. Then several things happened at once. First, I forgot about the things in the sky—forgot about them! Something more immediate was happening.

As I'd started to run, everything around me seemed to slow. I took a few seconds to realize that it was me slowing down and not my surroundings. There was nothing frightening about any of this. On the contrary, whatever was going on now only fascinated me. It was like moving through molasses, and the novelty was overwhelming. Motor functions and coordination now gone, I was falling and couldn't have cared less. My thoughts were simple: how pretty Mom's hydrangea bushes looked, how busy the ants were at the walkway crack I was slowly collapsing toward, and how beautiful a morning it had been. Everything went blue for a second, then everything went black. I think I was unconscious before I hit the ground.

I don't know how long I lay there, but when I did come to, they were gone. Helen and I never talked about it, which was just how I wanted it. All I wanted was to forget the whole episode, and within a week or two, I had. Completely. Almost fifteen years passed before my sister and I discussed the incident.

During that memorable telephone conversation, Helen confirmed everything I'd remembered with no prompting. She also told me that if I had not made this call to discuss the memory, she would have introduced the topic, and soon. My sister—who had never forgotten the incident—also remembered being taken up into one of the things and going through what we would now call a classic UFO abduction experience. It is fair to say that I began my own investigation of the subject that afternoon.

One Monday morning a dozen years later, two friends and I left New York City for a five-day visit to New Hampshire. The fortieth anniversary of Kenneth Arnold's Washington State UFO sighting—24 June 1947—fell during that *week. Because the event signaled the start of our so-called modern UFO era, that evening's* Nightline *devoted some minutes to it. Treatment and discussion were brief, but the show was memorable for its respectful take on the subject.*

Richard and Cornel and I left New Hampshire that Friday evening. I was home by 2:00 A.M., got a couple of hours' sleep, and was up again at 5:30. By 6:00, I'd showered, shaved, repacked my bag, and had a cup of coffee. On Second Avenue I hailed a cab to LaGuardia where I boarded the next shuttle for Washington, D.C. A cab took me from Dulles International Airport to the campus of American University. I made my way to the hall where MUFON's conference activities were centered.

That weekend had me thinking as much about the nature of good research as it did about the nature of UFOs. Research: "to look again." It was amazing what a determined, independent investigator could come up with. Budd Hopkins's and David Jacobs's abduction research was both grounded and pioneering, as was the paper that nuclear physicist Stanton Friedman delivered. It addressed the extraordinary double life of Dr. Donald K. Menzel of Harvard University and the National Security Council, an astronomer and early UFO debunker. Not only was Friedman's talk riveting, it was also gilt-edged. He'd received permission from Harvard, the National Archives, and Menzel's widow to review the astronomer's papers at length.

Other presentations stayed with me for other reasons. One was Larry Warren's. Having him on the program made me think back; we had met briefly in 1984, at the end of a major UFO wave over Westchester County. Thousands of county residents had seen UFOs over the preceding months. As a result, many of these individuals had successfully pushed to have a daylong conference on the subject. Pete Mazzola had driven Antonio Huneeus and me to the conference high school where it would be held.

By mid-afternoon, Antonio, Pete, and I were ready for a break. A crowd had formed on the lawn, and we headed toward it. "Who is the guy talking?" one of us asked. "Larry Warren," someone said. " 'Art Wallace' from the Bentwaters incident." Now, that was a name we knew.

For a controversial witness, Warren appeared straightforward enough. He seemed to be answering the questions as best he could and didn't put on airs. If what he was saying was true, he had a lot of guts to come forward. If he was relating a delusion or just plain lying, he certainly was good at it.

So here, in Washington, I was looking forward to a real *talk from this guy—a* vocal *military witness to a UFO incident is a rare commodity.*

Warren held my interest from the start, so it was all the more frustrating when a man stepped up and interrupted him midsentence. The talk was being cut short. I assumed it was because a number of the previous speakers had run over their allotted times. Whatever the reason, I was disappointed, as were many others in the audience. Warren seemed flustered for a moment, but continued, his anger apparent. It was a shame, I thought, this guy was interesting.

A nearby area had been set aside for vendors, and I made my way from the abbreviated Warren lecture to the booksellers' tables. UFO researcher Leonard Stringfield stood talking and laughing with Hopkins next to a table stacked with Stringfield's books and reports. Hopkins introduced us. Before moving on, Stringfield inscribed a copy of one of his books for me.

I also purchased a copy of Jenny Randles's latest, The UFO Conspiracy. *By chance, I was carrying the book with me when I spotted the author later. Asking if I might join her for a minute, she was kind enough to take the time to listen to what I was saying, then write in my copy of* The UFO Conspiracy: *"To Peter, I hope you find what you are looking for."*

MUFON had scheduled a panel discussion for that night. The moderator would be Dr. David Jacobs, whom I knew through Budd. The Temple University history professor taught the country's most outstanding university course on the history of UFOs and had written The UFO Controversy in America,[1] *an evenhanded look at UFOs and society's response to them.*

But what interested me most about the panel was its composition. With the exception of Jacobs, all panelists had been through an abduction experience. I was looking forward to hearing them, but wished someone on the panel would be speaking as a family member of one of these folks—someone like me.

Shortly before the discussion was scheduled to begin, I walked up to Jacobs, busy on stage, and asked to be put on the panel, giving him my reasons. He explained the impracticalities of my impulse: the program and the stage were set; there were only so many mikes, and the participants were already listed in the conference's proceedings.

I agreed with his points, then asked again. Three or four minutes before introductions were made, an extra chair was placed on stage and I was seated with the others.

The next afternoon, I saw Larry Warren in a hallway and introduced myself. After talking a while, we exchanged addresses and phone numbers and agreed to meet again soon. I would get to record his account of the incident and conduct whatever type of interview I wanted. "Soon" turned out to be the following weekend.

Larry arrived Friday afternoon, 3 July 1987. Though glad to see him, I really didn't know whom I had invited to my apartment. Only two things seemed certain about Larry Warren: he had been through something in December 1980, and he was still very angry about it. What had he been through in England? What effect had it had on his life? What effect did it have on his present state of mind? More, how curious was I to find out? At once both open and guarded, things lay behind things with him.

He had brought along a pile of reading for me, all of it on Bentwaters. We talked our way through a number of subjects over a great Japanese dinner. The conversation continued late into the night, and the next morning over breakfast, we picked up where we'd left off. His account of the incident was riveting, never more so than the few times he veered away from giving me a direct answer. My impression of him was consistent: I was not being lied to, but he had more to tell. What, though, was I to make of the information he was giving me?

Not counting breaks, our first interview ran the full weekend. That Sunday afternoon, I finally asked him why he was telling me all this? Larry answered that he was looking for someone to write a book with and thought I might be that person. After hearing me speak in Washington, he'd decided to ask if I was interested.

I understood that all his cards were not on the table. If I accepted the offer, what exactly would I be agreeing to? After all, the guy was talking about being a principal in his own book, and that could get touchy. And was an independent coauthor with latitude what he really had in mind? What if the trail led somewhere he didn't want it to go? What if I found out he had been wrong about things, or that he'd been lied to, or that he'd lied? The man might even be some kind of Bentwaters wanna-be—on base that night but not involved, then telling the stories he'd heard as though they'd happened to him. Any of these scenarios were possible, but I didn't think any of them were likely.

I asked the questions I had to and got more encouraging answers than I'd expected. What Larry proposed was simply that he tell his own story, in his own terms. I would be free to chronicle, support, or refute whatever I could about the incidents and his part in them. Though we should stay open to the other's suggestions, each of us would have our own last word on anything we wanted to include. When the book sold, we would split whatever it made.

Larry's offer was worth considering, but there was risk attached. Such a collaboration would be like starting a small business with a stranger; but that was the least of it.

Those of us who had made it our business to look into such things knew that a storm of controversy had already swirled around the Bentwaters incidents for several years. Having one of the witnesses, or alleged witnesses, as coauthor was asking for trouble. Larry couldn't have agreed more. Such a book could take some time to complete, maybe even a year or two. Given the circumstances, could we both stay with it that long?

Another sticking point: I didn't see myself well suited to the job. Larry should have been looking for a different sort of writer; perhaps one who had actually written a book. If it had been me, I would have tried to enlist a good investigative reporter. What he did not need was a coauthor who also had a UFO incident in his past. I just didn't think the coincidence would wash with a lot of people. But all these objections were subordinate to a larger question: if I agreed, how far was I willing to go for this story? If only a tenth of what he claimed were true . . .

What if, what if—my aunt Dolly used to say that you could drive yourself crazy with them. There were risks involved, and I was weighing them. Late that afternoon, we shook hands on it, then he left for home.

Whatever value Larry's testimony might prove to have, this investigation would be rooted squarely in postwar history. As far as I was concerned, there was no other place to start. By mid-September 1987, I was reading about little else but RAF Bentwaters, RAF Woodbridge, the history of Suffolk, the history of the air force, the U.S. and U.K.'s special relationship, British and American intelligence operations, and whatever had been published on the Bentwaters incident.

Some of these texts, papers, and articles were instructive, some confounding; some were both. I read through the minutes of the British UFO Research Association's (BUFORA) spring 1984 meeting on the incidents. Member Jenny Randles reported first:

The Sky Crash *team's original source had been an unnamed American air force officer who'd told them a structured craft, visible on radar, had "come down" in Rendlesham Forest on 29 December 1980. That claim was confirmed by a local farmer who also wished to have his identity protected. The officer said specifically: "Entities had been seen repairing the craft and there had been conversations between them and the U.S. Air Force officers."*

Only days later, another air force witness came forward by statement. Back home now and having no interest in going public, he stated there had been no fewer than eight radar-detected UFOs near RAF Woodbridge at the time.

Randles's co-researchers Dot Street and Brenda Butler soon established a contact on the air base who confirmed most of the details of the earlier stories, but wouldn't allow himself to be named either. Wasn't there *anyone except Larry who would go on record about this? I thought as I read.*

The women then made contact with RAF Woodbridge Squadron Leader Donald Moreland, but he would neither confirm nor deny the events. One point of Randles's had eluded me from the start:

The lecture and discussion did produce one very important point. The usual story (crashed UFO and aliens engaged in conversation) was given much more prominence than that of a crashed missile or aircraft.[2]

Why should a crashed missile or aircraft be given any prominence? Crashes, certainly those of known missiles and aircraft, produce explosions, and an explosion would have been impossible to keep from local residents. None of the authors' military witnesses nor any East Anglia resident ever reported an explosion or ground shock. No rumor of any crater in the woods, no fire damage or cordoned-off location. No military leak or local account of a crash site restored to precrash appearance—nothing.

Harry Harris spoke next. His findings were that a UFO had landed in Rendlesham Forest, and that, if the accounts were false, a good number of people had put considerable effort into creating the impression one had landed.

A statement from Keith Beabey, the News of the World *reporter who'd originally broken the story, was read into the record. He was "now totally convinced that the facts were true, that Halt's letter was genuine and that much of the story had still to be revealed." Beabey was also convinced that the testimony of Art Wallace was true.*

Science writer and editor Ian Ridpath differed from the other presenters. He had also visited East Anglia and spent time with Vince Thurkettle, the first to postulate the lighthouse theory. Ridpath agreed with Thurkettle. He also held that what the airmen had really witnessed was a meteor; one had, in fact, passed over the area the night of 26–27 December. The British Astronomical Society had confirmed it as "white or yellow" and "bright as the moon." If you had been in the area, looking up in the right direction at just the right moment, you'd have seen it blaze by—for a maximum of six seconds.

Ridpath then enumerated the four points that he felt "demolished" the case:

1. Whilst the depression . . . gave a high radiation count, no control sample had been taken, thus making it impossible to judge the significance of the radiation.
2. Col. Halt had mentioned in his letter a bright white light seen among the trees which later broke into five white objects resembling stars. They resembled stars because that's what they were.
3. If Col. Halt believed that what he saw was a space craft, or even an unidentified aerial object, why had he not sent up planes to intercept it?
4. The object witnessed at 3 am on Dec 27th was the meteor. The airmen saw it in conjunction with the light from Orford Ness and misinterpreted both. The UFO was nothing more than a misidentification of explicable lights coupled with human error.[3]

Though familiar with Halt's memo, Ridpath never suggests questioning the officer's word. But if the colonel's account was even remotely accurate, Ridpath's theories had to go out the window. For example, Halt writes: "The object was hovering or on legs. It maneuvered through the trees and disappeared. At this time, the animals on a nearby farm went into a frenzy. The object was briefly sighted approximately one hour later near the back gate." So why even suggest it was a meteor or star?

Ridpath's four points struck me only as evasive and clever. They implied an attitude contemptuous of anything outside his limited agenda. Dismissing them, I moved on. But what about the possibilities Randles suggested?

A crash could happen. I imagined they did happen. A missile test gone wrong. An American aircraft down in the countryside, possibly armed, possibly nuclear? At best, such an event could result in a destructive near tragedy. At worst, the thought was positively chilling. In any case, it was worthy of some sober reflection—but why here? Nothing pointed toward either of these frightening possibilities. Despite information to the contrary, Randles chose to state and reiterate this theory, and I could only speculate as to why.

1987 Developments |

Fall 1987

Colonel Charles I. Halt, now stationed in Belgium, receives a cassette tape in the mail. An American researcher has sent it with a request for some comment. The officer listens to the tape—Larry Warren speaking on Bentwaters—then records a response for the researcher, excerpts of which follow:

There were at least three different nights where something did happen. I can tell you very specifically that the event I witnessed, that the portion I saw and participated in did happen on the late evening of 26 December and early in the morning of 27 December, the following morning was a Saturday morning. . . .

[Gordon Williams] asked me for the tape so that he can take it for the Third Air Force and play it for Major General Beasley, who was the Third Air Force commander, the senior air force officer in England.

. . . Gordon Williams was not there, the only time he responded was after the incident, he expressed an interest in being involved if anything happened in the future. I know Gordon Williams wasn't involved and had no prior knowledge, [but] he did get very interested. . . .

I also know that the initial incident happened two nights prior, which would make it Christmas Eve, that was the initial landing, so to speak, the incident where Burroughs, Penniston, and Parker, the three security policemen went off base. Captain Mike Verrano was involved in the first incident during the day, he went to the landing site and made some observations, pictures on the ground, he was a player early on. When the contact was made with the base commander, it wasn't Colonel Williams, contact was actually made with myself and Col. Ted Conrad, the base commander. . . .

His [Larry's] recollection of what happened on the pickup truck fits in well with what I know having taken place up to this point. . . . Contact at the Woody Bar, 9:30, 10, Lieutenant Englund came, and he said the UFOs are acting tonight, or something to that effect, I was elected to kind of debunk this UFO business.

So I took my vehicle, changed clothes, and collected my small tape recorder. It was pretty cool, clear, basically a moonless night, very dark. They collected me in a jeep, Lieutenant Englund was there, we proceeded to the woods—I am sure there was a roadblock, although I don't recall seeing any—went through Woodbridge base and up to the scene. He [Larry] is correct—during the first landing, people went, on foot.

[John Burroughs] had a burning desire to get closer or to get more involved in the incident, especially after his involvement in the initial incident. He spent many nights in the woods hoping to reestablish contact with whatever it was, so Burroughs was there.

. . . I am familiar with the lighthouse. The lighthouse was approximately 20 to 30 degrees off to the right from where we saw the object in the sky, just above the ground, I should say. It definitely was not the lighthouse. The object moved, it was physically moving from side to side. The objects we saw in the sky were not meteors in that they stood in the same position and moved horizontally and occasionally vertically. They did not fall down toward us, although there were some beams of light that did come down, these came down as beams, and the main object stayed reasonably stationary in the sky.

. . . I don't recall anybody taking pictures, I saw nobody with a tripod. Neville had a camera, and his film came all fogged. . . .

. . . I would suspect anything he [Larry] says as far as his discharge and the reasons therefore, it just doesn't add up.[4]

I did little reading when Larry was in town. My days were spent asking him the questions I'd thought of since our last interview, the tape always running. Mid-November's visit was no different in this respect, but at one point, in response to a question, Larry made a sketch for me. It was an overview of the Capel Green area during the third night's UFO incident. It showed the scene, and the craft, as if viewed from above.[5]

I read Sky Crash *in December. The text on the jacket opened:*

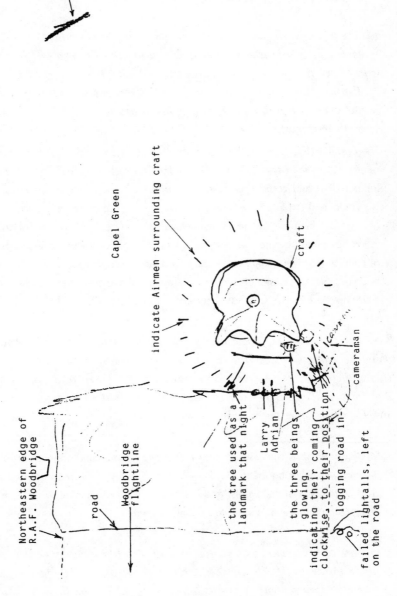

drawing, Larry Warren Nov., 1987

"They don't have my real name . . . if they find out they will ruin me. They will blow my head off in the street or something. If my real name is used I think I am a dead man." Witness Art Wallace.

Why begin a book by quoting a witness you identify as questionable? Because with the exception of Colonel Charles Halt, there was no one else to quote! The authors seemed to want it both ways.

While the findings of some writer-researchers irritated me, others caught and held my interest. Two Nebraskans, Ray Boeche and Scott Colborn of Lincoln, were a case in point. Boeche's paper "Bentwaters—What Do We Know Now?"[6] assisted by Colborn, showed what some dedicated digging could establish. Boeche, a twenty-year veteran of the work, begins his abstract:

The premier UFO case of the last several years undoubtedly has been the event referred to as the Bentwaters Incident or the Rendlesham Forest Case. Its tale of a landed UFO and contact with the occupants by high-ranking officers of the U.S. Air Force had captured the interest of the UFOlogical community and the public at large. At this point, some 17 eyewitnesses have been found, official documentation has been obtained, and more is being sought at the present time. Because of conflicting government responses, and a very evasive approach to this case by a United States Senator, it would appear that the Government is attempting to cover up the full story of what occurred on that night in December of 1980.[7]

Boeche cites two of the eyewitnesses among his principal sources, both airmen whom he refers to as A and B, an officer involved in a command capacity during the event, FOIA evidence, congressional inquiry, and close contact with other principal researchers in an investigation that took almost three years to complete. The paper opens with an eerie familiarity:

Many of the close witnesses to the events have experienced ongoing problems in dealing with what happened to them during that night. . . . They are troubled by vivid nightmares of the events, and are fearful of government reprisals if their role in exposing these events were to become known.[8]

A promise of anonymity was given the airmen before either gave Boeche a statement. In December 1980, Airman A had been acting security police commander at RAF Woodbridge; both A and B were among the first on the scene and already present when Colonel Halt arrived. The three then returned to RAF Bentwaters where they refueled two light-alls and took them back to the area of the sighting. Airman A notes:

> In the process of checking out the light-alls, everything was functioning. When we got out there to the sight of the object, we had trouble turning them on. Our truck wouldn't run either. It was kind of like all the energy had been drained out of them.[9]

Leaving the malfunctioning units behind, A and B joined in the search for the object and observed it moving through the trees. At this point, they came upon the strange ground fog, a yellowish mist sitting several feet off the ground. Both then heard the sounds of animals from a nearby farm; both men judged the animals to be panicked. Airman A not only remembers the episode but also recalls that he "was kind of glad it happened. It gave me back a sense of reality." Then:

> Suddenly the object was just there. It was a dark silver-colored metal, with plenty of rainbow-colored lights on it. I couldn't tell if something was breaking the light up, like a prism, or if that was the actual color of the lights.[10]

With the airmen then ordered to surround the object, A noticed two English policemen standing off to the side, one of them taking pictures. A and another airman were then ordered by Colonel Halt to confiscate the bobby's film, which they did. Two air force law-enforcement officers also had cameras and stood close by photographing: they were not disturbed. The object disappeared about half an hour later, too quickly to assess how:

> It was a really scary feeling. You feel useless, like you can't do anything. I was just frozen in place at first. My life actually passed in front of my eyes.[11]

Neither A nor B seems willing to discuss the subject of the alleged beings. When pressed by Boeche, however, A states "I saw something very strange, stranger than the craft landing, and all the rest."

Airman B corroborates all aspects of A's account. Like A, B neither confirms or denies the presence of beings; the closest he gets is to say, "A lot more happened out there than anyone knows about."

The officer then reviews Airman A's statement, saying that it confirms his own recollections of that night; he had observed the filming as well. The officer also remembers Lieutenant Colonel Gordon Williams being present and involved:

The colonel was driven directly to a waiting fighter at RAF Bentwaters with a canister of film of a landed UFO. The film was given directly to a waiting fighter pilot for transport to Air Force Headquarters at Ramstine [sic] Air Force Base in West Germany. I have no idea of what became of the film[12]

This officer's statements agree with Larry's and contradict two significant air force denials: that Williams was not present and that the event went unfilmed. The author then turns his attention to the likelihood of some official cover-up.

25 March 1985. As a result of one of his inquiries, Boeche received a phone call from a respected records-management official with the air force. She told him, "I've been told that photos were taken, and that some of them, but not all, were fogged. However, our records here do not show the existence of any photographs at all."

She suggested that he direct an FOIA request to airforce headquarters in Europe; he did, specifically asking Ramstein for access to any stills or movie film of the incident. The air force response ignored the request, which Boeche appealed Other FOIA actions were initiated, but no matter how well worded the requests, no significant information was gained. Boeche again appealed and won release of a single document that revealed nothing new. Growing frustrated with the paper chase, Boeche tried to contact Lieutenant Colonel Halt, without success.

Now moving into the most provocative part of his investigation, Boeche telephoned the office of Nebraska senator James J. Exon. A former governor and relatively conservative Democrat, Exon had a good reputation among constituents as a man willing to help "to the best of his ability."

Several weeks later, Boeche and Colborn met with the senator. He told them that if such an incident had occurred, he would have been made aware of it as a member of the Senate Armed Services Committee. Boeche reminded Exon of an earlier, documented UFO incident of which the senator had been unaware.[13] Exon acknowledged that something could have happened without his awareness. They gave him copies of all they'd received, including Colonel Halt's tape, and left with the senator's promise to look into the matter. He would also discuss the allegations with other committee members and let the researchers know what he could turn up.

The senator's first letter arrived on 2 April 1985. He had found out nothing:

Frankly, I am not convinced that the incidents you are concerned with did, in fact, occur. Nor have I found any evidence of a cover-up by the government. . . . If you have any evidence to substantiate the validity of the tape previously provided, I would appreciate your forwarding that information.[14]

A week later, Boeche successfully placed a call to Colonel Halt. After listening to Boeche explain his circumstances, Halt told Boeche he was "quite willing" to discuss the matter with Senator Exon. Boeche then asked Halt about the existence of soil samples and plaster casts of the landing marks at the site. Halt answered that one of the soil samples was sitting "on my desk in front of me" and "I don't have them [the casts] here, but I could put my hands on them without much trouble."

When told that Boeche had talked to an officer who stated that Wing Commander Gordon Williams had not only been present, but had been driven back to Bentwaters with film of the landed UFO, Halt stated, "Yes, I can verify that for the senator—I could substantiate that for him." But on 11 April 1985, the air force wrote the senator: "We have no information that movies, plaster casts, or other such items were ever made." Somebody was not telling Senator Exon the truth. It was either Colonel Halt or the air force, and the colonel had the plaster casts.

Boeche's exchange with Halt was immediately communicated to Exon's Washington office; a defense aide assured the researcher that the senator would be apprised. Boeche attempted to reach General Gordon Williams at Norton AFB in California, but a Major Verke there told him the general was out of town. When Boeche called back, Verke told him: "The general has no comment."

By now Exon had spoken with Halt. On 13 June 1985, Boeche again spoke with the senator's defense aide: Exon "will not discuss the content of his call to Colonel Halt with anyone." Asked if this might imply some meaningful confirmation by the colonel, the aide replied it was probably significant "since he won't discuss it." The officer added that Senator Exon would pass along information "after he decides what he can tell you." The same day, and presumably following this call, the senator wrote Boeche: "While additional information other than that you have obtained may exist, I can find no evidence of a cover-up of UFO incidents by any department or agency of the U.S. Government."

On 27 June 1985, the senator's defense aide received another call from Boeche. His notes of that conversation illustrated how seriously the senator had come to take the matter:

I don't think that he's trying to deny the existence of UFOs or anything like that. I don't know what he found out, and neither does anyone else in the office—he did the whole thing himself. . . . This is very unusual for him to take this much of a personal interest in a subject, and for him to spend so much time on it. He wrote all of the letters and made all of the phone calls.

Again, I was not privy to any of the information. I know he talked to Halt several times. I know he agreed when he talked with Colonel Halt that what was discussed between the two of them was between the two of them only, and none of us in the office were privy to any of it. . . . I think he talked to everybody in DOD that there was to talk to. I've never seen him do the whole thing himself like this—it's just unusual.[15]

At work on a Bentwaters article for Fate magazine, Boeche called the Washington office again and was told by a senior aide, "You've gotten all the information you're going to get. . . . Senator Exon will not say anything more."

Boeche then telephoned the senator's local office, where he was cut off by another angry aide: "You're not going to pin him down in a national magazine! That's unfair, that's so unfair! He's not involved with this at all!"

On 14 August 1985, Boeche is told that another meeting with the senator would be "impossible." A final letter from Exon notes: "I do hope you recognize that we have put in more time on this matter than any other case since I have been a United States Senator."

Ray Boeche concludes his paper with the suggestion that readers send their senators the information in the article and ask for some answers.

3. Early 1988— WALKING THE TIGHTROPE

Living in a house that's no longer yours is a miserable experience. Cindy and I were living apart now, but under the same roof. I slept in the guest bedroom. Throughout January 1988, I threw myself into my work to keep my domestic situation off my mind. When I visited the city almost every other weekend, Peter had me drawing maps of the landing site. The farmhouse, the field, that ancient oak tree were images burned into my mind forever. I had always found it strange that CNN, authors, and researchers had never actually found it. I wanted to give Peter as clear a lay of the land as possible and drew the sketches as accurately as I could.

By 1 February, our funds had been secured for the trip to England. We'd both come to feel the book's credibility depended on our going back to England and doing a certain amount of background research together. Peter planned to bring a good 35 mm camera and black-and-white film because we both wanted *Left at East Gate* to have photos of the base and the site of the incident.

I was still hesitant about telling him I had ended up under the air base the day after the incident. He was aware that I had originally admitted the experience, but I claimed to have done so only to get Bustinza's story out. There was so much I still wanted Peter to know, but I held back. At this early stage, he could still easily bail out, and might well do so if he knew what I knew.

I arrived in New York with a large suitcase and a bad cold. Peter gave me lots of homemade chicken soup and many cups of tea. By the next morning, I felt fine. We wouldn't be leaving for the U.K. until 17 February, and Peter had arranged for us, Budd Hopkins, and Antonio Huneeus to make presentations at the American College of Orgonomy in Princeton, New Jersey. He said the audience would be made up almost entirely of psychologists, psychiatrists, medical doctors, and scientists.

As a science writer for the *New York Tribune*, Huneeus had contributed hundreds of UFO-related articles to the national and international press over the years. He was also an old friend of Peter's and the first writer in the States to interview me, in 1983. Peter invited him over for dinner that evening and made a great meal.

Afterward, we talked about UFOs well into the night, often laughing our heads off at Antonio's stories, like the South American account of an alien getting itself caught between a refrigerator and a wall before disappearing in frustration. That one killed me.

Over the preceding months, Peter and I had found we had something other than UFOs in common—a fondness for bad science-fiction films, B movies, and the Marx Brothers. We both knew that a sense of humor could be a lifesaver.

For Peter and most of the other people around me, I joked, put on a happy face, and tried to seem stable. At the same time, however, I knew I was beginning a downhill slide and had no idea how to stop it. But as long as Peter thought I was fine, that was all that mattered. My routine, when I stayed with him, was to ask for the apartment key at about 11:00 P.M. and then disappear into the void of New York nightlife, where I boozed it up at the Limelight or the Hard Rock Cafe.

Peter, Antonio, and I took a bus out to Princeton on Saturday morning. Budd was driving and would meet us there. When Peter told me of his interest in Wilhelm Reich and the science he'd pioneered called orgonomy, I had felt only a slight curiosity. However, going through a college fund-raising brochure as the bus rolled through New Jersey, I found a picture of a Reich cloud buster, an unusual-looking device that could alter the weather. It was also said that the device could attract UFOs. Peter knew several cloud-buster operators and had seen one demonstrated; he said they really worked. He also told me that Reich had published his weather data and UFO findings (concluding that some were extraterrestrial devices) in the fifties and had been heavily discredited for it.

As I carefully studied the picture, I tried to figure out why it looked so damn familiar. Christ, we had had those things at Bentwaters! I'd seen the same kind of device on the base back in 1980, but had thought it some kind of communications device. Peter seemed shocked when I told him and started bombarding me with questions. All I could tell him was that the things I'd seen were made up of long pipes, painted black, and mounted on concrete bases. They had a multitude of large cables running from them into concrete framed wells dispersed around the base. There was no question in my mind that they looked like the one in the picture. Peter seemed intrigued and disturbed by my observation.

The miniconference went very well; the audience received our presentations with open minds. Budd's talk was about the UFO abduction phenomenon, while Antonio zoned in on the world UFO picture with a vast slide presentation. I spoke on Bentwaters, and Peter moderated.

Later, Budd showed us some amazing Polaroid pictures taken within the past two weeks by a man in Gulf Breeze, Florida. They showed clear-cut craft with what could only be described as portholes. Budd was looking into the case and very excited about it—so were we.

My greatest fear in talking to so many mental-health professionals about my experience at Bentwaters had been that when I finished, they would rush me, put me in a straitjacket, and lock me up. But that didn't happen. In fact, most of them seemed very moved. It was the first time I had addressed a non-UFO audience, and their reaction made me feel great. With at least ten of the doctors joining us for dinner after, Peter told them about my having seen cloudbusters on the base. Dr. Richard Blasband, who had worked with the devices for years, said it didn't surprise him at all: even a large cloudbuster was easy enough to build, and Reich had kept the air force apprised of his weather-modification work. Their application at Bentwaters may have been to keep a window clear in adverse weather conditions, thus allowing aircraft to complete their missions unhindered.

Back in the city, Peter called to confirm our flight and continued with his last-minute preparations—everything was on schedule. Although we hadn't made any reservations in London or Suffolk, we both felt confident that we'd be OK. I called Cindy in Connecticut, just to say hi. Although we were headed for divorce, neither of us seemed fully to accept it yet. Wednesday morning, 17 February, Peter and I were on our way to the U.K.

London's Gatwick Airport welcomed us with gray skies and a light rain. We got through customs without a hitch, although we had made a lot of jokes prior to touchdown about being denied entry to the country. Our first night was spent in a rather unspectacular south London hotel, where once again, Peter, mini tape recorder in hand, continued his endless interview. After a couple of hours of that, I suggested we head out and find a nice traditional pub and unwind. We found one nearby, right across from the building where penicillin was discovered. Laughing, we wondered if there was any connection between the two.

Back in our small hotel room, Peter continued going over his notes. He was still working away when my mind drifted back to December 1980, and I fell asleep.

4. 18 February 1988—
MORNING AND AFTERNOON

*M*y *travel alarm went off at about 7:30* A.M. *Waking, I asked Larry to turn on the radio and tune in some news. He clicked the dial and the old, vacuum-tube model began to warm up. Growing louder, the clipped, cheery voice of the morning DJ was finishing the on-the-half-hour news brief. We stared at each other as we realized we had tuned in to a report in progress of a UFO sighting in the English Midlands. I grabbed the recorder on my nightstand and pushed record.*

DJ.   Sergeant Steve Godwin, who was on patrol in Warham in the West Midlands, claimed, "It was far bigger than a plane." Senior police officers are studying their reports. This could be a breakthrough, folks! Don't be surprised tomorrow if you see huge headlines all over the papers, [*with great mock seriousness*] "Unidentified Flying Object Confirmed." I very much doubt it though, but rhythm and blues are with us forever. [*A guitar track rises, then the voice-over*] Who's Paul Jones got on that blues-and-rhythm program tonight? Oh, look at this, it's . . .

LW.   Isn't that something?

PR.   We fucking need this?

We arrived at Ipswich station early in the afternoon and changed to a local train. It took us to the village of Woodbridge. Larry, by far the more adept in the use of the English pay phone, was elected to find one, then locate a bed-and-breakfast with a vacancy. I stood guard over our luggage.

Larry made some calls and quickly found out that the base was undergoing a great deal of construction. That meant bringing in civilian contractors—lots of them. It seemed the local inns and B and Bs were booked solid, at least Monday through Thursday; today was Thursday.

Following some brainstorming, we decided to have lunch at the pub across the street. After replenishing his coin pile, Larry continued making calls; twenty minutes later, he had a place for us. Due to a last-minute cancellation, a room had come open at the Old House, a B and B in the nearby village of Eyke. Our hostess, Mrs. Warnock, had asked Larry to give her about an hour and a half before we arrived. We sat talking until afternoon closing at three, then sat on the bench by the entrance to the pub.

The taxi stand was just across the road, so we decided to spend the remaining time right where we were. The afternoon was brisk, sunless, and windy. Knowing that home and hearth lay only a twenty-minute cab ride away did much for our spirits. Over the next hour, A-10 aircraft regularly passed overhead. "Tank busters," Larry called them. Slow, low-flying, and loud, A-10s were to be our most-sighted (and most-heard) aircraft that week. Larry told me they were based at Bentwaters. Bentwaters: we were finally here.

At a few minutes past four, we caught a cab to the village of Eyke. Larry chatted with our driver and discovered he'd been driving in 1980. Did he remember the UFO uproar back then? The driver nodded yes.

He remembered the Japanese television news crew and "these women—Londoners, eh, too!"[16] The condescending spin he put on the word "Londoners" made us laugh.

D.   They wrote a little book on it, too, I think.

LW. I was here at the time this supposedly happened.

D.   All these flashing lights they saw, might have something to do with—drinking [*laughter*], you know.

PR. Makes 'em flash brighter!

D.   People are, you know, smoking, and they're seeing lights on. I knew a guy who used to try and indoctrinate *me* into it!

PR. Oh, he really believed it?

D.   I didn't want to know, you know.

From Woodbridge, to Melton, through Bromeswell. We soon passed an inn on the left called the Cherry Tree. This was a location—*the spot where Larry and another airman had tried to hitch a ride the evening of the incident.*

Driving into Eyke, our cab pulled up in front of an old three-story house near the center of the village. Just across the road stood an Anglican church and a small cemetery. Paying our driver, we unloaded the bags by the front door, rang the bell, and watched the cab drive off in the direction of the base.

Shortly, a woman in muddy wellies came around the far side of the house. We both liked Jan Warnock immediately and followed her to the back of the house. We should call her Jan. We shouldn't use the front door, no one else did. We should use the rear entrance. We walked through a small storm porch and entered a combination dining room, sitting room, and library. It featured a full brick hearth that someone must have spent a lot of time restoring. I was glad to learn that the cozy room was for guests' use. We followed Jan up the stairs, down a hallway, and into our bedroom. Larry was delighted to park his heavy suitcase and flopped down on the nearest bed, declaring it his.

Large and comfortable, our room ran from the front to the rear of the house with a bed, standing wardrobe, and window at either end. The opposite wall held a small sink stand and a counter, on which stood cups, spoons, tea bags, sugar, a drain board, and an electric kettle. Jan told us when breakfast was served and asked what we liked. Both charming and considerate, she departed only to return shortly with some biscuits and a pitcher of milk.

Jan and her husband, Tony—an instructor of biology at a nearby school—seemed to us a keenly intelligent and interesting couple on whose doorstep fate had kindly deposited us. In any case, it was a relief to be somewhere central to the business at hand.

I put some water on for tea and began to unpack. It was now past four. Since this morning, I'd been looking forward to getting settled and to work. Now I was just tired.

The kettle's whistle brought me to the counter, where I brewed our first of many pots of tea that week. Larry seemed withdrawn, and I could only guess what he was thinking. After thanking me for the cup, he didn't say anything for awhile. He was here again, where it had happened. What was that like? Not taking his mood personally was easy for me.

I took out our area map, spread it open on my bed, and began to study it. Dumb luck had brought us to one of the two villages best situated to both the Woodbridge and Bentwaters bases. The other village, Butley, was located four miles to the east. Eyke was closer to Bentwaters, walking or driving.

It was early evening now. I checked my notebooks and tape recorders. Larry *had the TV on but didn't seem to be watching. The idea of spending our first night in really appealed to me. We could use the sleep and get an early start in the morning.*

Neither of us had said a word for some time now, and I decided to pick up our eight-month-long interview again. For all intents and purposes, once I asked him the first question, we could have been back in my living room. Larry answered as if he had been waiting for me to begin:

PR.   When Adrian and you finally talked about this, was he, you know . . .

LW.   Was he serious?

PR.   I'm sure he was serious, but . . . was it like: "Is somebody gonna hear this, or I gotta talk to somebody about this, or I think I'm going out of my mind, or I got a secret I want to tell you"?

LW.   A little of everything. I had to pull it out of him.

PR.   When you say "pull," you knew that there was more than he was telling you?

LW.   Exactly. I knew the night he slipped that thing [note] under my door.

PR.   We did get a good transcript of Adrian and the car and kind of feeling drugged or going unconscious in the car and waking up and there.

LW.   Yeah . . . had the feeling of going down.

PR.   Right.

LW.   Descending.

PR.   But, what, when you finally started to "pull" it out of him, was he telling you?

LW.   That this happened in this room, with this voice telling him from behind the screen in a whole room of people.

PR.   Did he have any idea, or did you ask him, why he, of all people, was chosen? I mean, he wasn't somebody who affected policy, he wasn't somebody who was going . . .

LW.   . . . talked to everyone in the room; there were other air force guys just like Adrian in, sitting in chairs, but he couldn't turn his head either way.

PR.   . . . no real restraints, just the ones that keep you held, without any real thing being there.

LW.   Right, and it wasn't human, what talked to him.

PR.   The talk itself you mean?

LW.   It was telepathy. [*Several quiet seconds..*]

PR.   Any other details about what information they gave him?

LW.   Yes. Religion, the whole nine yards. I've gone through that I think.

He had, but I was back on it. There was something about that part of his story that had never felt quite right.

PR.   Religion. That doesn't sound familiar. What do you mean?

LW.   It is. I did say it, it's about how the church and all this are just plastic entities and, if all this were known, organized religion's gone. It's hard to remember the conversation now, years later.

Less significant details still had me curious as well.

PR.   Did you go out there with a thermos of coffee, a sandwich, or . . .

LW.   No, they come out with a truck and bring you meals. It sucked. Green eggs, that was a big joke. They come right out of a can or some kind of thing. Green eggs—wasn't good. It was good regular food, but they put it in these metal things that would turn it green.

PR.   Ahh!

After another anecdote, Larry directed a serious look at me:

LW.   I know how little you knew about this when you came into it. I want you to be aware that for every good person, there are going to be three that are going to wait to cut it down and cut everything about it down.

PR.   That's why it has to be so candid.

LW.   And the thing is, you are going to start getting cut down.

PR.   I know that.

LW.   Completely.

PR.   I'm aware . . . I can't say that I don't have a problem with that, but I fully anticipate that. [It's] part of the package.

LW.   [*Flatly.*] Anticipate it.

It was growing dark out; we talked about writing and the tone we wanted to set:

PR.   We are not out to bring down the government.

LW.   No.

PR.   We are here to try and shed a little more light on why there's so much terror of the truth.

LW.   Yes. All I have ever done is told someone else's part of this, in the first person—because I was asked to.[17] The only other thing I ever did was not tell the complete truth and then told it later. I held back, if anything. I never, never added anything that wasn't true. But I waited for the time to be right. Whether it was or wasn't, the future will decide.

With his voice trailing off, Larry walked to the front window and looked out:

LW.   There's the old forest out there.

PR.   Ummm.

LW.   You want to go tonight?

Good Lord. Did he mean go out to the base—out to the forest—tonight? Yes, that was what he meant. My thoughts had been turning to a home-cooked meal, some good conversation, a warm fire, some BBC, a few pages of reading, and an early lights-out. That's what I had been thinking. What I said was, "Ah, it's OK with me."

What the hell. We were here to work. Wasn't that what he was suggesting we do?

LW.   I think we should head out there. We can hitchhike tonight and, uh, take a look.

PR.   Bring your flashlight.

LW.   Yep.

PR.   I'll bring some extra batteries.

Other than adding another layer or two of clothing, my preparations consisted of a miniature load: small notebook and pens, adjustable-beam flashlight, two recorders, extra microcassettes, and fresh batteries. There seemed no reason to bring the camera. I'd planned to shoot only daylight film, and black-and-white at that. We had no fancy equipment—just a borrowed Nikon body and a normal lens—no flash, no tripod, no color. Besides, under the circumstances, couldn't just bringing a camera onto the base at night get us into trouble? Then again, air force security probably didn't give prizes to the person caught with the most tape recorders in a restricted area. For me, though, the recorders were essential. Who knew what memories this evening might jog in Larry? I wanted to be able to let the machines run and sort out the material later. Besides that, what would there possibly be to photograph at night that couldn't be better captured in day-light?

I noticed I was coming into a good second wind; nothing like anticipation and anxiety to get the juices going again. It was then I noticed something I hadn't before: it was about Larry's hair.[18]

PR.   Now that I look closely, there's a sense of gray.

LW.   Yeah, I have it. I haven't done anything. In a few days, you wait, it's going to get worse! [*Laughs.*]

PR.   You said other guys also had the same problem?

LW.   Other people were gray, right after. Gray. Literally. That's no joke. It did happen and [to] a lot of people—it happened to me, and it was kind of strange that it happened right then and there. Dress a little warm, I suggest hiking boots tonight if we're gonna . . . [*sees them on me*] Good deal, yeah.

I turned off the recorder. It was already past six when we said our good-byes to the Warnocks and left the Old House. Heading northeast along the A1152, it was already dark.

5. | 18 February 1988— EVENING

We *didn't say much to each other for the first few minutes, our eyes and moods adjusting to the moonless night. As the base lights grew visible in the distance, Larry stopped and began to point out some of the areas glowing on the horizon:*

LW. If you look, you can see the beginning of one of the nuke-proof bomb shelters. The WSA is right out there. And those lights blinking?[19] That's a security patrol right there. [*The vehicle proceeded along the road defining the base perimeter. It was for SP use only.*]

PR. It's moving, yeah.

LW. See that light hovering way out over there?

PR. Sure do.

LW. I don't know what that is. I have no idea.

PR. [*Jokingly*] Maybe it's our friend from this morning [the radio report of a UFO].

LW. [*Indicating*] That's the WSA.[20] We can't get to it.

PR. Oh, no, right. OK, here come two . . . [*We watch the A-10s land.*]

LW. Look around. Take in the atmosphere. This is what it was like that night we saw it. [*A momentary quiet.*]

PR. And we have a moonless night tonight, too. Just like then.

LW. It comes back. I mean, it was there. I was on that flight line that night. Now at the opposite end of the forest, you can see flight lights, the runway lights. The other end, that is so secure over there, it is so fortified. It looks like a simple little airport, right? But that's an air base. We're far away from it [about a mile]. Security police patrol, you see them every now and then. No vehicles other than their maintenance trucks are allowed to drive that road. I'm so, "feeling" right now. Thoughts, everything. Like half horrified and half elated to be here and see this. [*Another A-10 comes in for a landing.*] I'm thinking about what happened here.

PR. Oh, it's spooky. It is extremely exciting, and at the same time, I am feeling a rational fear, I think.

LW. Are you feeling eerie?

PR. Not yet. I'm on the edge of eerie.

Recorder off, we continued along the road. Then, a quarter mile from the base perimeter, a light, no bigger than a star, shot through the sky above us. The possibility of its being a meteorite evaporated as it stopped, began to move back and forth, pulsated a few times, changed color, hooked around, and took off. Start to finish, the whole thing lasted maybe ten seconds. It broke the mood for me:

PR. Stop! It's changing speed and direction!

LW. I know. See? They're here.

PR. Oh, my God!

LW. No one will believe this.

PR. It's, it's . . .

LW. They're here. All the time.

PR. It's dimming! It changed color!

LW. I know.

We pause to watch. It then blinked out—it just disappeared.

PR. Oh, fuck. See if we got any other pals up here, wait a minute. [*Searching the sky for a possible second one.*] That was a son of a bitch.

LW. I know. One of the many things you're about to see, no doubt.

We continued to look up for what seemed a long while.

LW.   You saw a UFO. You're probably going to see something else while you're here. You're probably going to see one of them flying. I mean, you're going to see the actual ship, I don't doubt it, they fly 'em. You see 'em, you see 'em. A lot of stories around here other than mine.

PR.   Well, that was a kick in the head. You know, they're going to think we're lying. I don't care. I did not anticipate having to deal with this. Something we have to tell the truth about.

LW.   I know. They don't phase me too much. I see them land in front of me and that's it.

PR.   It went reddish, then it went whitish again, and then it did that dovetail thing and blinked out.

LW.   Fucked-up. Fucked-up.

PR.   We just have to continue.

Walking quietly now with flashlights off, we came to a sign; its black letters read: "Ministry of Defence Air—This is a prohibited place within the meaning of the Official Secrets Acts. Unauthorized persons entering this area may be arrested and prosecuted."

We walked past the sign and entered the base residential area. For the next hour, I got the tour.

LW.   These are barracks as they used to be. This housing [*indicating*] they were starting while I was here. They were just plain bland row houses. They've done it up nicely. Look through one of the windows, you'll see how the rooms work. This is a bunk situation, [you can] tell the new guys, their walls are bare. [*Indicating*] These are family housing areas. Change, change, change, looks nothing like when I was stationed here.

PR.   That's yours that they built that new structure on?

LW.   That was my barracks.

PR.   Son of a gun.

LW.   My Aston Martin used to be parked right in front of those lights. Greg Battram's car was parked right over there. People still don't know about decibels [rock was blaring from a window]. That was our dayroom, the phone was in there where we had to make that call to whatever that was [psychologist].[21] [*Pause.*] How ya' doin? [*I nod.*]

Larry Warren's swearing in, U.S.A.F., 22 July, 1980 Jeff Lindsay on left).

Sign on flight line at RAF Bentwaters, December 1980.

Main gate of RAF Bentwaters, morning of incident, 28 December, 1980. Note sign declaring "Alert Condition".

Guard shack at East Gate (where it all began).

Larry Warren the day of Colonel Gordon Williams's change of command ceremony, March 1981. The white ascot represents a special security detail.

Heading back to the USA May 1981. Larry Warren (top center) with Greg Battram (top left), Larry Walls (right), and two members of "D" Flight.

Capel Green, site of the incident. Craft's point of contact clearly visible as discolored area in the far right middle ground (1988).

Capel Green, 1990. Ten years after incident, site remained mysteriously discolored.

Parking lot on Bentwaters from which Larry Warren and others were forcibly taken to an underground facility on the Bentwaters Flightline, 29 December, 1980.

Dispersed in the aftermath. Incident witness Adrian Bustinza is suddenly sent on a temporary duty assignment to Egypt, photographed by fellow exile and witness Larry Warren.

Earthen bunker concealing an unspecified underground facility at RAF Bentwaters (note blowers for ventilation).

Enlargement of sign outside bunker depicted in photo above.

Controlled Area

It is unlawful to enter this area without permission of the Installation Commander.
Sec. 21, Internal Security Act of 1950; 50 U.S.C. 797

While on this Installation all personnel and the property under their control are subject to search.

LARRY WARREN

Building housing base photo lab from which Larry Warren emerged from the underground facility, 31 December 1980.

Larry Warren's account of the Bentwaters incident gains widespread publicity: a Tokyo television broadcast in 1984.

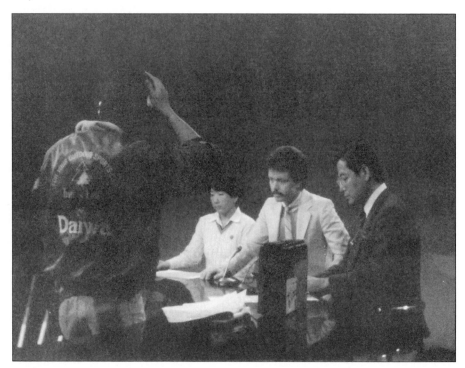

Enter Peter Robbins, with ufologist Dr. J. Allen Hynek, Westchester, New York, 1984.

Larry Warren with longtime friend and Bentwaters fan, the late guitar great, Stevie Ray Vaughan.

Larry Warren reliving the incident at researcher Peter Robbins's request, eight years later, February 1988.

Soil samples from Capel Green. Soil on right from UFO landing site. Note difference in color and texture.

One effect on Rendlesham Forest of "freak storm" of undetermined origin, October 1987, five months later.

Rendlesham Forest, before the "storm."

Rendlesham Forest after.

"Weapons Storage Area," formerly housing nuclear arsenal at RAF Bentwaters. Photo taken with 200mm. Telephoto lens.

MINISTRY OF DEFENCE
AIR
THIS IS A PROHIBITED PLACE
WITHIN THE MEANING OF THE
OFFICIAL SECRETS ACTS
UNAUTHORISED PERSONS ENTERING
THE AREA MAY BE ARRESTED
AND PROSECUTED

Capel Green 1995 showing landing site still blighted fifteen years after Larry Warren's experience.

ANTHONY JAMES

Peter Robbins and Larry Warren in March 1994, at the sight of the third night's incident.

At the mess hall, Larry had me look through a window; there was the security police table where he and the other cops had sat the morning after. Other memories came and went. But the spell was broken as we turned a corner to face a Burger King, identical to thousands dotting the States. It seemed a little surreal, but no dinner and several hours walking had left us hungry, so in we went.

The restaurant was warm, noisy, and crowded. Airmen, airwomen, and air-children sat at the bright formica tables, eating, drinking, talking, and laughing. Though many wore camouflage or fatigues, others wore civilian clothes, and no one paid us much mind. Looking at the posted menu, I noticed they only accepted American money. I had none on me, but Larry had a couple of bucks, enough for two burgers and two drinks. A smiling, young American woman in Burger King uniform took our order. We found a table and waited for them to call our number.

"See that kid?" Larry said, pointing across the room. "That was me eight years ago." The airman was leaning against the far wall waiting for his order. He was wearing an SP flash on his camouflaged shoulder and looked to be about nineteen or twenty. Larry decided he'd try striking up a conversation with the guy and left the table.

A woman's voice called our number. I picked up our order, came back to the table, and was starting to eat as Larry returned with the security police officer; his name was Mike. A polite Midwesterner, the airman, first class, slid in across from me as Larry introduced us. For the next few minutes, they talked about the base, the service, and the security police. The acronyms and abbreviations flew by as the two established some trust and commonality.

"We're here working on a book about some things that happened to me while I was stationed here," Larry said to Mike. "My friend has never been in the service, doesn't know what it's like, and I want him to have some idea. You know how, when you get to a new base, you hear stories about it from the older guys?" Mike nodded; he knew. "They've probably changed since '80 or '81, but what do you hear now? What kind of stuff do they tell you when you get to the base now?"

Without malice, Larry had set him up. What would Mike say? He looked down at the table for a moment, then looked up. "There's only one legend here," he said. "It's about what happened to the SPs in the woods a couple of years ago.[22] I don't know how you guys feel about this stuff, but we take it seriously. Older guys tell the new guys about it, like one at a time in their rooms with the doors closed. It's not a joke here.

"A bunch of SPs were taken off guard mount. They were taken to an area a few miles from here. There was a thing there, a machine, of undetermined origin. They were ordered to surround it. There were beings and everything. They say

the CO actually communicated with them. Everything was hushed up. The men were sent all over the place after. The CO was transferred and promoted. They say some of the men went crazy or had nervous breakdowns, that there was a suicide."

Straight-faced and hardly believing I was hearing this, I looked away from Mike; Larry was calm. "I didn't mean to put you through anything, man, I could see it wasn't easy for you to say that and appreciate your honesty. It's just that the book we're working on is about that, and I had to have Peter hear it from someone else. You see, I was one of the SPs in those woods that night, and it did happen. That and more."

Watching Mike's face drain of color made me feel like I was on the scene of an accident. "It's getting kind of close in here," he said. "Can we get out of here?"

Once outside, the airman had multiple questions for Larry: "Did they display any hostile behavior? Did they communicate? What was the ship like? How were you briefed?" I didn't want to interrupt but was eager to tape them. I took out a recorder. "Is it all right with you if I turn this on?" "Sure," said Mike.

M.   We hear about this all the time, but it's just too hard, you start getting a little annoyed and suddenly you got people there . . .

   I was scared to death because they said that it was an offense to talk about these things. Out in those woods, they cut that forest down.

   I knew—I know what it is, the forest is ripped apart after that windstorm happened.[23]

LW.   I heard about that.

M.   The windstorm destroyed our security. We have backup now, but we had special holes, we were in DFPs, we were in holes all night and shit—but [*now almost whispering*] when I went out, I know that something happened. Something did happen.

LW.   It's a weird place here, isn't it?

M.   Yeah. It's very mysterious out there at night, we'd all feel it. There's like—Butley Village . . .

LW.   Then they said we saw the Orford lighthouse in the trees, blinking?

M.   That's one explanation that I heard. Somebody got the recording of CNN's tape and played it back on TV, and it said, "Well, sir, I see it flying around now—oh, it's gone—oh, there it is again." They said that it coincided with the lighthouse's actions.

PR.   Well, for a few seconds it did.

M.   Rumor can travel if somebody wants to spread something. You could change around the whole story.

LW.   Oh, yeah. But, it's good to hear it's still actively [discussed]. East End Charlie was the thing when I got here.[24]

M.   Oh, East End Charlie was a big deal. The girls . . . [*Larry laughs.*] We had this one kid who . . .

LW.   You know the story about him? How he was shot down . . .

M.   He was shot down, they found him and burned him, yeah.

LW.   Townspeople, I heard, burned him.

M.   Did you hear about that church down there, too?[25]

LW.   I hate that place. They had a [human] sacrifice there in 1968.

M.   I know! [*I gasp; both men's voices drop, sounding momentarily guarded, compressed.*] [Inaudible] killed himself over there.

LW.   Yeah.

M.   And that's why over the past year hardly anyone's in there now.

LW.   Did they have you guys, tell you about the druids? All those people with the hoods and candles, they go in the woods. They'd say, "Ya see 'em, don't shoot 'em." They used to tell us that. I never saw it.

M.   They still *do* that shit! I was out there one night with my buddy from Charlie Flight. We took a starlight scope from out of the armorer's, and we were watching out there these people dancing wildly. We were gonna jump the fence to see what's going on, but you don't know when those people are gonna freak out.

LW.   There's just something, something *weird* with this whole area. I still, I feel it now.

M.   Well, they say this is where witchcraft originated. And they say it's the most haunted area in England, therefore the world. A lot of weird shit.

LW.   The black dog . . . you ever hear about that?

M.   No.

LW.   There was a big black dog that runs around with red eyes . . . that's another tale. There's a lady with no face. That is *awful*, I *hated* that story!

M.   There's the cab driver swears to God [*his voice drops*] . . .

LW.   [*Laughing.*] Doesn't surprise me.

M.   He still drives, and you ask him about it, and he, swear to God, he gets all pale?

LW.   Well, I'm telling you I saw all this, but there's *something* about this area. There's just something about it.

M.   But Butley Village especially. You go there and practically every-
       body in that village practices witchcraft, a lot of people do.

LW.   Yeah. [*Turning to me*] I didn't tell you that. It, it's weird.

M.   Butley Village is strange.

LW.   And they stare at you.

M.   Yeah!

LW.   You go in there and they're like this . . . just dead expressions.

M.   Yeah, I went to a pub there, *once*, once. I was with a friend of
       mine. He just *couldn't*, I didn't feel like I belonged.

LW.   No. No, you don't.

M.   People are afraid to face the truth, that's the way it is.

LW.   Smart guy.

*At about 9:15 P.M., we said good night and left Mike waiting for his ride back
to RAF Woodbridge. Larry and I walked quietly off the base.*

LW.   Nice kid.

PR.   Very nice.

LW.   Real bright kid, reminds me of my brother-in-law, but, Peter, he
       knows about the underground. He got off that subject *real* quick
       [before I had turned on the recorder].

PR.   Did you hear how his voice dropped?

LW.   Yeah.

PR.   Pshewww . . .

LW.   We should let people hear these tapes.

PR.   Oh, yeah.

LW.   I'll tell you what, I'm so amazingly glad that you have been able
       to see all this. And this is just starters. I saw his jacket, and it was
       a cop. The best way to approach 'em is just to start talking. He
       was curious.

PR.   And you know what was amazing, too, was that the story he orig-
       inally told us, just the brief . . .

LW.   You probably were a little confused with a little of, some of the
       phrases we were bouncing back and . . .

PR.   At this point, a lot of it is making sense to me, it's like not speak-
       ing French too well, but you understand it pretty good.

LW.   Yeah.

PR.   But the way that he put together the original story, he had so
       many of the details *right*!

LW.   Well, he was a good kid to ask.

PR.   Yeah, and I think it was just a good way to test the water, too, nobody's going to freak out when you get into that stuff—it's *fascinating*.

LW.   No, not here, not on base, because, it's like you said, I asked him about the local lore, and he brought it up.

PR.   Man, yeah, filled in some spots for me, too.

LW.   I forgot about the lady without the face, the way I heard that . . .

PR.   And I "forgot" about the w, wi, willage, village of witches!

LW.   Oh, yeah, well, that's . . . I never, well, I didn't remember to tell you that.

PR.   Well, thanks a lot.

LW.   They're down that way though.

PR.   OK, so let's keep going down *this* way then.

LW.   It is like the *Village of the Damned.*

PR.   [*Under my breath*] Shit.

LW.   There is weird shit here. [*I sigh.*] WSA, you can see the pines lit up behind it.

PR.   Yeah. Quite a view.

LW.   So, what do you think?

PR.   Hey, we're on a roll.

6. | *18 February 1988—* NIGHT

*O*nce off the base and out of range of its lights, the road and surroundings quickly returned to an inky black. Even with flashlights, we felt somewhat reckless walking along the A1152. The northern part of Rendlesham Forest lay several hundred yards beyond the farmer's field to our left, so we headed into the darkness for a better look. With the forest's outline now clearly visible, a light over the trees caught my attention. I pointed it out to Larry, switched on the recorder, and checked my watch. It was almost exactly 9:30.

PR.   That's not a light on a tower. I mean, it's just a red light standing there.

LW.   No, that I'm not talking about . . .

PR.   No, I'm talking about the one to the right, the one that's just above the horizon skyline.

LW.   Yeah.

PR.   Now, you're sure that there's not . . .

LW.   There's no tower there. Bentwaters' towers aren't lit.

PR.   Oh, fuck.

LW.   And the flight tower, the air-traffic control tower is pretty small.

PR.   Well, let's walk slow. I want to see if that thing decides to go somewhere else. Jesus God. Those pine trees are eighty to a hundred feet tall?

LW. Yeah. Look at it! Look at it!

PR. Yeah, yeah, yeah.

LW. It's hanging in the sky, moving like a pendulum.

PR. And it's got a definite shape, I mean, it's not a star or anything like that, it's elongated. We don't have anything that does that, do we?

LW. No. Not on this base. Maybe the one under it. Look at that, Peter, it is just moving back and forth, this is too much. Do you have the tape going?

PR. Yeah.

LW. We're observing a light on the horizon. Take it over, just describe it.

PR. It's big. Well, it's bigger than a star. Its glowing fairly reddish but like almost pink or salmon. It's elongated, it's not round.

LW. That's near, near the Woodbridge base?

PR. Yeah, it's near the Woodbridge base. And [*to the recorder*] Larry says the pines are eighty to one hundred feet high.

LW. It's moving back and forth.

PR. Yeah, oh my . . .

LW. . . . It's moving back and forth.

PR. It is and then it just goes back again, like a fraction of an inch.

LW. This thing here . . .

PR. It did it again!

LW. Look at this! This is unbelievable! We are seeing a UFO back here back at RAF Bentwaters all over again. This is the second one we've seen this evening. I know it sounds like I'm imitating the Halt tape, but this is happening right here, and it is out in the direction of Woodbridge. It is not an aircraft at all. This thing is gaining altitude now—look at that!

PR. Oh, shit.

LW. Look at that! It's gaining altitude. *This thing is not an airp . . . LOOOOK!*

PR. Oh, my God, it's *bigger*!

LW. *It's taking off, it's going off!* It's almo . . . *Look at that!*

PR. Jesus Christ.

LW. We are seeing this thing that is unbelievable.

PR. Same color, it's in color.

LW. Oh, it's swingin'. Look at this shit.

PR.   Yeah, yeah, yeah.

LW.   It's swingin', swingin', swinging—in an arc?

PR.   It looks like it's turning or[ange], oh, jeez, it just changed.

LW.   *Look at this.* Now I can't tell if it's gaining altitude or *losing.* Let's take a walk out in the field.

PR.   OK.

LW.   Let's do it carefully. Why don't we turn the flashlight out. [*We walk forward into the field.*]

PR.   Good night.

LW.   Peter, look at that, that is fucked up.

PR.   Yeah.

LW.   Actually, keep your light off now until we really need it because it's blocking all the ambient [light]. We're seeing a hovering object that is *massive.*

PR.   It's got to be, it's got to be, I mean, how big is that thing? You know, this sounds really funny, but it looks like a tipped ellipse.

LW.   Yes, it does.

PR.   Oh, man.

LW.   Um hum. Yeah.

PR.   So, it's like sort of reddish in the middle and less reddish at the edges.

LW.   Wow.

PR.   It just changed! It's a circle now.

LW.   We got an actual UFO sighting happening right here.

PR.   It's just grown again.

LW.   Yeah. This thing is changing shape, it's moving back and forth, it is *not* a helicopter.

PR.   I can't take my eyes off of it. We're walking further into the field.

LW.   And this is a, a farmer's field, but we're not in Rendlesham Forest.

PR.   It's, for the record, 9:34 P.M.

LW.   This is *real,* too, this is . . .

PR.   18 February.

LW.   In the background, you can hear the engines of the A-10 aircrafts at Bentwaters air base, which is the flight line for the U-2.

PR.   Dead ahead, over the Rendlesham Forest. [Inaudible.] So, about how many miles out there are they [UFO lights]?

LW.   About five miles out, ten miles out. I can't get a fix on it, it's weird, it changed.

PR.   It just got bigger though.

LW. I know, but it *changed.*

PR. Yeah, yeah.

LW. I see range lights here.

PR. Where?

LW. Heading out, oh, a good four hundred yards, set of range lights for a, the Bentwaters flight line. Hopefully, we're not walking in a restricted area.

PR. Yeah, or a minefield.

LW. Well, hopefully we're not in a minefield. OK . . .

PR. And that's a police patrol. Son of a gun.

LW. I think that's a police patrol right there [*indicating*], but what they're doing, they're aiming up that way. [Inaudible] Now we're seeing security police literally, this sounds ridiculous.

PR. They're watching it.

LW. A security-police patrol is watching. Possibly watching an [inaudible] object in the sky.

PR. Genuinely, that is what it looks like from here.

LW. That is, that's what it is.

PR. Almost the exact, really, almost the exact same spot it was when we first saw it. And *it is big.*

LW. It's orange, right?

PR. It is. It's now orange, it really looks like a disk now. *Now it just turned.* Oh, Jeeeesus.

LW. It is a *disk.* It is an *actual disk,* in our eyes.

PR. We're looking right at it.

LW. Two eyes, four eyes can't be playing tricks.

PR. Well, sure they can, but I don't think they are, I don't think they are, I mean we're biased to this stuff, but we're standing right *here.*

LW. This is literally public. We have seen *two* already tonight. This is the second one.

PR. Oh, man. . . . [*Cross talk, quietly, nervous laughter.*]

LW. Bury me with my boots on . . . [inaudible] and an SP patrol. You see the cop? There was, there was a shadow. He just, the light . . .

PR. . . . walked in front of the light, yeah. Those red lights that . . .

LW. Those are range lights. That's not really security. Look, look, the police, see the lights going on out there? The police have another one.

PR. Yeah.

LW. Here he comes right around the corner, whatever is over there,

I *hope* that's a police patrol. [A second SP vehicle's headlights come into view on the base perimeter road.]

PR.   It is *so bright*, and it's right on the horizon. There's no . . .

LW.   There's an SP patrol, it's moving out of the field, it's heading in the same direction as the other vehicle. They're probably getting a fix on it, too, and coming to have a look because they're heading down the same direction over the hill.

PR.   Let's see if they pull up.

LW.   Let's keep our voices down because we don't know what . . .

PR.   They're heading back toward the road slowly.

LW.   See, the perspective here: that is over Rendlesham, that is not. As you can see, these range lights are very close, that's way out there.

PR.   Yeah. Again, it really is in almost the exact same spot when we first observed it.

LW.   But there was movement, I saw movement.

PR.   Oh, yeah, and I saw it change from a circle, which might have meant a turn or just a pulsation change. It is still glowing.

LW.   I see movement though.

PR.   And now it's a circle again, and now it's moving. Oh, my gosh, do you see it going up?

LW.   Yeah. Yeah.

PR.   If you don't, tell me.

LW.   But I see movement.

PR.   Yeah, no—it's like it changed angles and then came back again. Just keep walking this way.

[*Tape runs out, I change it.*]

PR.   OK, this one's going now.

LW.   Look, it's dim, it's dim. Now [*urgently*]. There's an SP patrol right out there. They're the only people allowed out there. Security patrol, they've got headlights, I don't know where some of them . . . Oh! . . . uh-oh . . . uh-oh. Don't run, just walk.

PR.   Yeah.

LW.   I don't know what that is, but it's probably for us.

PR.   Keep the light off.

LW.   No, keep it on. It's better.

PR.   It's still there.

LW.   It's dimming out though.

PR.   *Wait a minute!* It really is dimmer. It's . . . it's smaller. [*Fifteen second pause.*]

PR.   It is smaller, and it's paler, and it's still that vague, very washed out sort of red.

LW.   It's moving, it is moving. I'm judging against the tree, it's right to the left of the tree, and it does move next to it very slightly.

PR.   Yeah. But it's essentially maintaining a hover *all* of these minutes.

LW.   It's a *circle*, I mean, you can see it right through the trees.

PR.   Yeah.

LW.   I see what Halt meant on that tape.

PR.   That was a good description, yeah.

LW.   I think nobody's going to believe this!

PR.   Hey, do you know what? I don't even care. I don't even care. I mean . . .

LW.   Let's take a walk.

PR.   Yeah.

LW.   Unbelievable. Look at this, *look at this.*

PR.   It's white!!! It's . . .

LW.   Look, it's changed, it literally has changed. It's dropping, *it's dropping.*

PR.   It is! It's at the tree line right now.

LW.   *It's below the tree line!*

PR.   Yeah, it is. It's in front of the forest now.

LW.   Oh, my God.

PR.   What the hell is going on out there?

LW.   *Look it . . .* oh, my God. It's down on the trees! *It's down in the trees!!*

PR.   It's moving.

LW.   This is unbelievable—we are seeing an object hovering near the ground. It is . . . this is unbelievable. This is amazing! *Look . . .* it came back out away from the trees.

PR.   Yeah, yeah, yeah.

LW.   You're seeing what I'm seeing?

PR.   No, I am. I mean, we're bo . . .

LW.   This is so fucked up. Peter, I can't believe this shit.

PR.   Yeah, I know, I know, I keep doing reality checks with my eyes, ah, all systems are OK.

LW.   But we're seeing the same thing?

PR.   Yeah, yeah, yeah.

LW.   That's promising.

LW. This thing is below the tree line now, and it was above. [*Pause. To the object.*] Go down!

PR. Yeah. Do something!

LW. It's safe to say that if that was a plane, it would have landed a long time ago. It's *sneaking* into the trees, it's gradually . . .

PR. It's subtle.

LW. . . . moving itself in. It will bounce out . . . *now* it bounced back through the trees!

PR. Let's just say for the sake of argument . . .

LW. Yeah.

PR. . . . that that's just some advanced helicopter. Could it maintain that extraordinarily flat, still hover without any real modulation? I mean, can *any* helicopter just hang like, you know, like a fake flying saucer on a string?

LW. They wouldn't do it. I've never seen that happen. We'd hear the chopper.

PR. From here we would, yeah.

LW. There's no small helicopters on this base.

PR. And there're no quiet helicopters.

LW. CH-53s, they're giant. Biggest in the world, and you hear 'em, you hear 'em. They're not even running right now,'cause you'd hear them all the way out here. *This* is light over the *forest*, it's over the woods, over Rendlesham Forest.

PR. And it's still at about the tree line, just below.

LW. Jesus Christ, this is too much. Halt said, in '81, one came right over the base, it was a giant one and did a figure eight.

PR. The SPs still in the same spot.

LW. You can see his lights are on. But *another* vehicle went down that way. Then it faded.

PR. Yeah.

LW. You have a light?

PR. Yeah. It's just . . . there. It's just . . .

LW. We'll have to send a free copy to the underground complex.

PR. [Laughs.]

LW. "For all of you in the underground complex—a complimentary copy."

PR. Right. "Thank you for not taking our enzymes."

LW. I don't know, man. I'm kind of afraid.

PR. I keep on thinking . . .

LW. I don't want to get fucking abducted here.

PR.   ... this would be a bad night to start out a trip to Mars.

LW.   I'm going to cut this for a minute.

[*Tape off/tape on midsighting*]

PR.   *It's in the forest!*

LW.   *It's in the forest!*

PR.   *It's in the trees!* It's dropped ... it's dropped tremendously. It's moved.

LW.   Now wait a minute ... Peter! Peter! [*Fearful and urgent.*]

PR.   Sh, sh, shhh ... sh, sh, sh, shhh ...

LW.   Peter, this fuckin' thing has moved into the woods, it's coming closer.

PR.   It *is* closer, isn't it.

LW.   It's coming toward us, I can't believe this shit.

PR.   We're seeing it clear as a bell, we're seeing the tree line above it. It did it instantly. It ...

LW.   People, please believe, whoever hears this tape, we are seeing a UFO subtly move, a spacesh ... It's coming to us.

PR.   It's something.

LW.   Oh, my God.

PR.   It's still small, it's still not the size that it was when we first saw it.

LW.   Look, look, look! ... God.

PR.   Pshewwww ...

LW.   Oh, shit, look, there's a police patrol coming down, look! They're looking, they're looking for it. *Look at this! Look at this!* It's going ... *Oh,* ... *my* ... God, ... Peter, I don't believe that this is happening.

PR.   It is happening.

LW.   Look at the little bastard! It's a ...

PR.   It's rising.

LW.   It *is* rising. The police patrol is coming toward it.

PR.   And it's ... it's gone up a fraction.

LW.   Oh, my God! Oh, my God!

PR.   It's ... [*Long pause.*] You know, we have to be real careful about talking to any guys on base about this.

LW.   Don't talk to anybody about this.

PR.   Mum's the word.

LW.   They're here, right?

PR.   Oh, yeah.

LW.   I'm in a vacuum.

PR.   It's risen again. Let's just stand right here.

LW.   What is it about me?

PR.   They like you.

LW.   You know what you're seeing out there? You're having a Bentwaters incident all over again. I had to make it real to somebody.

PR.   You're doing a good job.

LW.   It's kind of on the horizon again.

PR.   Yeah, it's really like sitting *just* at the tree line.

LW.   Let's take some steps. Don't look back. Don't look at the cars, they can see the reflection in your glasses.

PR.   It's risen again.

LW.   It's risen, and it's moved to the right.

PR.   [*Gasps.*]

LW.   They're so familiar to me.

PR.   It's gotten smaller.

LW.   I have no fear of it.

PR.   Jesus.

LW.   What just happened?

PR.   I mean . . . I don't know. We're backing up.

LW.   It's going down a little bit.

PR.   It's at the tree line again.

LW.   They're closer than you think.

PR.   I'm having trouble gauging distance. That looks like it's sitting right at the tree-top line. It's below the line . . . no . . . [*exasperated*] I don't know. It *is* below the line again.

LW.   It's so dim.

PR.   It's as dim as it's been. It was like five times brighter maybe. It's, oh, my God, it's going out. It's getting smaller, it's like when you turn off an old TV, it's got that one little dot left in the middle? I can't even make out a color [*very frustrating for me to admit*], whether it's white, I think it's still off-red.

LW.   No, it's only white.

PR.   Shit.

LW.   [*Suddenly.*] Those blue lights are off.

PR.   Huhhhhh! They *all* went off while we turned around! The blue lights are specifically the landing field lights?

LW.   Yes, they only go on if a plane is landing.

PR.   But no plane landed. Oh, shit.

LW.   And there were only a few of them right in front of us. That was *it.*

PR.   And you can't miss them. They're bright cobalt blue. They're gone.

LW.   I see movement. It moves, it really does move. There's no question about it.

PR.   Yeah. No, we both agree on that.

LW.   There's nothing, certainly nothing natural out there. I'm getting the horrible feeling that those lights went on for us, man, they did.

PR.   Or they went on for *it.*

LW.   That's a worse scenario.

PR.   Let's just back up some. [*Long pause.*] It's gone, Larry, or, yeah, it's gone, isn't it? [*Pause.*]

LW.   No.

PR.   Oh, shit, no, there it is. Oh, boy, but it's so tiny. And it's well in front of the trees.

LW.   We have to take a walk.

PR.   Yeah. We've been amazingly lucky so far.

LW.   Yeah.

[*Tape off/tape on*]

PR.   That's a very weird light.

LW.   Yeah, it is.

PR.   It's like there's something in there that's shining up into the sky.

LW.   Yeah.

PR.   And that's right out in the forest, isn't it?

LW.   Yeah. Exactly.

PR.   [*Out in the field, in front of the forest, something is beginning to move.*] What the hell is going on?

LW.   It looks like, I see figures or something in it, do you? Movement?

PR.   I see some wavering at the base, but I don't see any kind of articulation.

LW.   Well, wait . . . wavering.

PR.   This is too odd.

LW.   This is unreal.

PR.   We got to remember that we're coming into that real bad stretch up here.

LW.   Well, let's do something. Let's go in the field.

PR. OK. Now we're off the base, right here?

LW. Well, we're on a farmer's field.

PR. But I mean we're not on a, the base.

LW. No.

PR. OK. Good.

LW. I don't know what that is.

PR. Oh *lookit*, you can see the pinpoint of something that's causing it. But what's causing it?

LW. *Look! Look! Look! Look!* It's in the trees!

PR. Yeah. Turn off the light, turn off the light.

LW. Look.

PR. Yeah, I saw it move.

LW. Going right through the trees I saw it, a *tail* on it.

PR. [*Simultaneously.*] Yeah, yeah, yeah. [*Pause.*] No, it just went . . . Oh, Jesus.

LW. Look, it's going right through the trees!

PR. Taillights just went on over there, or they looked like taillights.

LW. No, they're not, they're some kind of . . .

PR. Look! There's light in the middle. Closer.

LW. Yep.

PR. Oh, Jesus.

LW. Peter.

PR. There are three of them. Two of them look like they're on the ground.

LW. [*Amazed.*] We might be seeing a landing.

PR. Yeah, but . . .

LW. *Look! Look!* Right through the trees.

PR. I see it. *A fourth!*

LW. *No, moving.* You see it moving?

PR. I saw it, I saw it. That's what I mean, it just went . . . it just hid behind the tree.

LW. I *told* you this fuckin' place does this.

PR. I really don't want to go too close to these ones.

LW. Something's turned on out there.

PR. I know.

LW. Do you see that?

PR. That same weird kind of . . .

LW. Orange-gray.

PR. Yeah, right.

LW. Yellow-green, white-green, or something. Whitish green? Dim, powerful, dim, powerful.

LW/PR. Hold on a minute.

PR. One . . . two, three . . . there are four that we can see right now. One that is casting a tremendous glow.

LW. Well, fuck all that.

PR. *Oh, my God.*

LW. What's happening?

PR. What's that big thing over there? Or is it two together.

LW. No, hold on, hold on.

PR. What are those fucking two things right there?

LW. I don't know, it just turned on.

PR. It just looks like a happy face.

LW. No.

PR. With no smile.

LW. No. One appeared and the other appeared.

PR. Something's going on in these woods.

LW. Something *is* going on in these woods. There's a lot of activity. Those woods are dead woods. That's just forest.

PR. One, two, three, four, and the one on the right is still a *mother.* It is . . . it's defined mostly by two lights. [*Pause. We hear a long scream from the direction of the woods.*]

LW. A woman's scream it sounds like. Halt has statements saying that that's what happened.

PR. It was a high-pitched sound. It didn't sound like an animal.

LW. [*Frustrated.*] This is so strange, cause you can't get a fix.

PR. No. [*Another scream.*] Sh . . . !

LW. I heard it again, that scream.

PR. Yeah, it's going on. But the car sounds are blocking it. *What is that thing on the right?*

LW. [*Shocked.*] I don't know, man, but it just kind of came on.

PR. It's now two very clear . . . [*A third scream.*] That sounded like it could have been . . .

LW. A chicken.

PR. A rooster. I think it was, I hope it is. But roosters don't crow at ten o'clock at night.[26] Let's keep walking this way. It will bring us closer and keep us away at the same time.

LW. I'm telling you this place is fucked up. There *is* something wrong here. Do you feel it?

PR. I feel a lot.

LW. I mean, we're seeing fireworks fly through the *woods*.[27]

PR. Yeah.

PR. There's a third light on it, Larry!

LW. There is, all of a sudden. It's three. It's so weird.

PR. And it's slightly . . . Hey, look! I don't know if I'm imagining things.

LW. I know.

PR. You see how it's a little bit lower?

LW. I know.

PR. So it could be . . .

LW. Peter, we're right next to a main road but . . .

PR. It doesn't matter.

LW. Out in these woods, it's like watching a movie of science fiction!

PR. It doesn't matter. I mean, I know this could be an illusion, I'm saying it right here . . .

LW. I know, but . . .

PR. [*Quickly, urgently*] But it could be . . . It looks like the curve, it looks like the curve. And it looks like thr . . .

LW. It's three, I see the third one. It's a kind of curve.

PR. Yeah, the third one is just very, very pale right now.

LW. It's a *round curve*.

PR. OK, let's get a fix on the other ones again. We've got one, two . . . now there *were* four, now there're three again.

LW. Could that . . . ?

PR. I mean, three separate individual things. The glow . . .

LW. *Look*, another one's flying through the trees. *Look*!

PR. Yeah. I saw it. I saw it.

LW. *Look!*

PR. *There it goes*! Look at this. Is that a plane?

LW. No.

PR. Is there any chance . . .

LW. No, there are not . . . sh! That's not a plane. You've heard an A-10, and that's not what they sound like.

PR. And that doesn't sound like a rooster now. And *now it's one light*.

LW. I know.

PR. And now its *one* light. [almost angrily] The thing that was *three* lights is one right now.

LW. I know, I know. We got landed UFOs right out here.

PR.   Wheww, we got somethin'. [*Pause. A fourth scream.*] I *hope* that's an animal.

LW.   I see it, another flash. There's a lot of light out there in the forest.

PR.   Yeah.

LW.   That's that beam. That big thing.

PR.   Yeah. There is no moon out tonight. There is no ambient light at all. [*A fifth scream.*] That's a dog, I hope.

LW.   It sounds like, a weird animal.

PR.   Well, if there's something out there . . .

LW.   . . . with the body of a crab and the head of a social worker.[28] [*Laughter.*]

PR.   If there's something out there, then animals can flip out. Ah, the thing that was three is one—pale again.

LW.   I know. Oh, my God, it was like a . . . This is fucked up. And we want to go in those fuckin' woods tonight?

PR.   Uhhhh. [*Sixth scream.*]

LW.   Listen to the animals freaking out!

PR.   I, I don't think our tape is strong enough to pick it up, I wish it was, because this is a real animal reaction to *something*. [The sounds are clear on the tape.]

LW.   And this, we're possibly looking at two . . . some weird activity in the woods. We're seeing balls of light flying through the trees that are green and white . . . and this . . .

PR.   It's pinkish—orange.

LW.   That is like . . . there was three! I'm going to . . .

PR.   But Larry, the thing . . .

LW.   I know.

PR.   . . . that was three lights is now one pale dot.

LW.   I know. And it started as one.

PR.   That's right.

LW.   And it was a lot brighter than that, too. Look! I saw a shift in light out there.

PR.   I don't fuckin' believe this.

LW.   And you know enough about this stuff so you don't overreact . . . but this, we're seeing phenomena. We're seeing some weird shit.

PR.   Yeah. This is really rich.

LW.   I didn't notice *anything* coming out here like that, except for that first thing we saw in the air.

PR. Yeah. Well, that was wild enough. I would have been happy with that one for the rest of the year.

LW. But we're having . . . a lot more, and aircraft don't come in like that. I don't know what that is but it's coming down through the trees *and gone.*

PR. What the hell is in there?

LW. I don't know. I don't know. That's the second farmer's field. That's really the edge of the woods of the second farmer's field.

PR. Yes.

LW. I need a light . . . actually. . . . Listen! Look! I saw something flash. Yeah, there it is—it was red, now it's . . . If that's a plane, how come we don't see it coming in to land?

PR. Oh, Larry, there's no chance it's a plane. There's no chance. It can't be. Planes don't do that. *Wait!* Something's . . . you see it?

LW. Yes.

PR. . . . pulsating in the forest?

LW. Yeah. Yeah, *Oh, my God!* Oh, my *God.* Look! *Look!*

PR. It's up.

LW. [*In total disbelief.*] *It's flying!*

PR. Yeah.

LW. *Look!* It's going up . . . up . . .

The tape ran out here. By the time I'd replaced it, a bright wall of light was illuminating the woods.

LW. It's just like a, a wall. I don't know what the fuck that could be.

PR. OK, now, look at the . . . I just saw one come off and on.

LW. [*The huge glow suddenly increased in intensity.*] *Look, look!*

PR. [*Excitedly.*] Yeah, yeah, *it's glowing,* it's glowing, that whole area's lighting up. *Oh, my God.*

LW. That's a car.

PR. Oh, thank God. [*Nervous laughter.*]

LW. I *think* it's a car. [It is not.]

PR. It looks like a car now, yeah, there, it's . . .

LW. *Wait* a minute. There's a hill there. [There is no hill.] Now, if that keeps going up in the air, then this is fucked up.

PR. OK, if it keeps going up in the air, then it's not a car.

LW. But watch what it does.

PR. It just disappeared.

LW. But they had three taillights. [*A silence.*] Who the fuck knows, I mean, my imagination's going crazy.

We continue walking in silence, almost half a minute without a word.

LW. [*Suddenly.*] Did that area just light up more, that whole area?

LW. Yeah.

PR. I mean, like *a lot* of light. A *tremendous* amount of light on the horizon. It is *glowing*—behind the forest, it is *really glowing.* [*Frustrated.*] *How the hell* can this stuff go on, like right here, and that it's like it's some big joke? I mean, doesn't anybody see this stuff?

LW. They do. It's all secret. That gives more credence to the joint. Well, if that was a car, it didn't do what the other cars did, but what it did do was have three taillights and just went up and stopped and was gone.

PR. Yeah. I, ah, don't know what to think about that.

LW. I don't either.

PR. Wait a minute, the one . . .

LW. I don't know. We should start walking.

PR. Yeah. I'm right behind you.

LW. I see like two eyes it looks like. Now, now could something like that . . . No, look.

PR. Oh—it's back.

LW. Is that a house?! It doesn't make sense.

PR. No, *that's* a house.

LW. It *is* a house, right?

PR. No, I mean that's a house right in front of us. [There is no house.]

LW. *Look! Look!*

PR. *Yeah, yeah, yeah, there it goes!*

LW. *It's back.*

PR. Yep.

LW. This is too . . . It *can't* be an illusion, it's nothing. There're no lights.

PR. Oh, no, no. There's not an illusion. It's just a matter of *what* the hell it is we're seeing. And look at *that* now, it's like one light on top of another. It wasn't like that a minute ago. *That's new.*

LW. I know. I know. They sit—one's sitting right on top of the other. It's so weird, it really is so weird. That's an SP flight right there.

PR. Yeah. Now . . .

PR/LW. It's one!

LW. I honestly don't know what to make of that. And that glow out there.

PR. [*Almost laughing.*] I was just going to say . . .

LW. I was *stationed* there, there was nothing *out* there, the base was over *there.*

PR. It looks like, there's a *city* over that rise. It goes from *there* to there on the horizon. *What the hell is out there?*

LW. [*Indicating.*] *That's* the WSA, that's at the end of the base.

PR. OK, but I mean there's buildings back behind those trees. *What the hell is behind these trees?*

LW. I don't know, there isn't supposed to be anything.

PR. [*Totally frustrated.*] I mean, but you know that there's not like a town just over that rise, right?

LW. I don't think so. The only town is Eyke near here.

PR. [*With some panic.*] Yeah, it came on suddenly, I mean it goes from *all* the way over there to all the way over there.

LW. I know. That's the forest, that's the center of the forest.

PR. [*Frightened.*] I don't want to go out there right now, I really . . . not on a bet. I don't care.

LW. Something wrong with this territory . . . another country.

PR. I'm turning this off for awhile.

[*Tape off/tape on*]

LW. OK. What are we looking at now?

PR. It's a very bright light. It's pulsating, it is white or white-yellow. It's elongated just below the horizon line, it's really active.

LW. It doesn't look like a marker but . . .

PR. Well, why would it be pulsating erratically?

LW. Look! It's bright.

PR. Yeah. Now the light's stable, now it's smaller.

LW. You can see trees lit up by it, look at that.

PR. Yeah.

LW. I see *movement* over there, *around* it.

PR. It's moving, or I'm moving.

LW. I don't know, I see movement.

PR. But it's definitely elongated, isn't it?

LW.   Yeah, *light* . . . it's too bright to tell.

PR.   But it pulses erratically, it's stable, and then it just pulses. *Now* it's really bright.

LW.   And people just go about their business.

PR.   Yeah.

LW.   *Look* at that.

PR.   That is one bright mother. Oh, gee, it's getting big.

LW.   Look, there's like a beam or searchlight on it, going into the woods to the left. What is this? There's like a beam on it. [*Pause.*] *Wowww.*

PR.   That's the brightest one we've seen. I keep like squinting and then opening my eyes as wide as I can.

LW.   It's easy to tell natural light, I mean look at those. They're on the air base. They're range lights.

PR.   They're not pulsing.

LW.   What the fuck is that thing?

PR.   They're not pulsing.

LW.   No.

PR.   Man, that's got . . . that's high on top in the middle, isn't it?

LW.   I don't know. I can't decipher it. It's too . . .

PR.   I know I . . .

LW.   It's like a prism.

PR.   Yeah.

LW.   Look at it though.

PR.   Shit.

LW.   Like a star.

PR.   Except it's in the woods.

LW.   Except that it's, unfortunately, it's probably on the ground.

PR.   Man, we could drive ourselves crazy with those things. Now, look at it now.

LW.   Yeah.

PR.   Let's keep walking.

LW.   Uh-huh.

PR.   Those lights are absolutely stable. This one's doing funny things.

[*Tape off/tape on. The sounds of wind and trudging.*]

PR.   Something just shot out. I just saw a little light come out of it.

LW.   Look at that, *Look* . . . at . . . *that.*

PR.   *Huge.* It's like magnesium.

LW.   Look—look at that light, in the trees now.

PR.   Yeah, yeah.

LW.   Look at that, it has an aura around it. You see that?

PR.   When my eyes are at a certain position.

LW.   Oh, *oh*, something else.

LW/PR. *Hello.*

PR.   This stuff's starting to seem normal. [*Laughter.*]

LW.   I know!

PR.   That's what's worrying me!

LW.   I know, I know. I mean, this is so bizarre. It looks like that has a hat on.

PR.   Now, we got *two* friends.

PR.   Shit. I mean, where we're looking, that's so-called publicly owned land.

LW.   That isn't even part of the base. Look at that, it's like *arc* light!

PR.   Yeah. It's really, really bright.

LW.   You can hardly look at it. It's like a *star*!

PR.   Yeah. Except it's much much much much much much brighter than the brightest star or planet.

LW.   Now, what's that, next to it? Those things are below the tree line.

PR.   It certainly is, you're right, you're right.

LW.   *Look at this,* I see the *beam,* the *light,* coming up in the sky from that . . .

PR.   Sheez.

LW.   Like the, rays from it or something.

PR.   Well, it's just a very bright light that's . . .

LW.   Look at, the orange one *changed.*

PR.   Yeah, yeah, it got smaller now.

LW.   Not really, it just, the light down here is *bright.* Look how bright it's getting. Do you see it?

PR.   Yeah.

LW.   It's getting bright. I've never seen anything like that.

PR.   Very different glow, and it's a different orange and a different size.

[*My attention is so fixed on what lies in front of us, that I am oblivious to figures approaching from the right.*]

LW. [*Suddenly.*] Let's go.

PR. Yeah, let's.

[*We begin to put some distance between ourselves and the location.*]

LW. *Look at that,* it got *bright.* Now it's red.

PR. Yes, it is *decidedly* red. And it's at a diagonal, am I right? Yeah.

LW. It's like a cigar! A little oblong . . .

PR. I didn't want to say it.

LW. No.

PR. Now, that could be a house right there with a light, that just went on?

LW. Peter, that isn't a house. That's that pumpkin head we saw before.

PR. *Oh,* it's back.

LW. Yeah.

PR. I mean, can you almost read . . .

LW. It's the same color.

PR. Yeah.

LW. Look at that other one, *look* . . .

PR. It's changed color, and it's glowing a little less intensely. The big one's still pretty big, but it's not as bright as it has been.

LW. Like *arc* light.

PR. Yeah, it really is a different quality.

LW. *Look* at it. I see the light beams change.

PR. Yeah, no, it's moving, it's pulsating on some level, whether something is causing the illusion or the actuality of pulsating, something's moving there.

LW. Absolutely no sound. No one walking in front of it.

PR. Happy Halloween. Let's walk along. OK, the pumpkin's now two lights, one larger on the right and smaller one on the left, or it's reflecting off of something. But it's split.

LW. It's too dull, it's that eerie color. You know, a window's a window. See the window way out in the distance on the Quonset huts?

PR. Yeah, yeah, that's a window. *That's* not a window.

LW. And that thing out there is just . . .

PR. Meanwhile, our cigar is a, like very pale, it's still at the diagonal.

LW. I see other lights, in between those two . . . little things that every now and then . . .

PR.   Yeah, yeah. In fact, look at the lower left-hand corner of our big light. [*Pause.*] Is there something like . . .

LW.   Like the wing?[29]

PR.   Well [*laughs*], I don't know. I don't know.

LW.   A delta?

PR.   Let's keep walking. Now *wait* a minute, now something just got real big, on that lower . . . The magnesium light is very dull now all of a sudden, within a moment, I mean compared to the way it's been.

LW.   It's like something, a stream between them. Come back *here.*

PR.   This is really strange.

LW.   Now I see it, I see it really well, it's in between orange.

PR.   Aha. It is orange. It's at the lower left of the bright light.

LW.   This is just so weird. I've worked out on that flight line, and I've never seen anything like that.

[*Tape off/tape on*]

LW.   This whole area. This a . . .

PR.   OK, what's going on right out there right now?

LW.   I don't know. It looks like I'm looking at a house but it *isn't.*

PR.   Keep walking.

LW.   It looks like two squares, doesn't it? That's a triangle with lights, two on the bottom.

PR.   Oh, yeah, they're small lights, but there they are. And the one on the left, too, appears to be blinking ever so slightly.

LW.   Why don't we walk down here. I don't know if . . . Peter, it's just weird, everything's weird from what went on here.

PR.   Yeah.

LW.   And there's one beam in the front, and it just went so far and went out.

PR.   It definitely had three red lights.

LW.   I never saw anything *like* that.

PR.   I'd be happy, you know, to find out that somebody makes a car with three red taillights, personally, but I don't know . . .

LW.   Where's the license go?

PR.   [*Laughs.*]

LW.   But *really*, it didn't look right, it just didn't look like a car. It went up to the tree line and then stopped. Now, what about these green and white things just whipping through?

PR.   That's "high strangeness" in air force-ese. Very. [*We reenter the village.*] It sure is nice to be back in this little town, very pretty.

I turned off the tape. We made our way back to the Old House, crept up the stairs and into our room. Totally exhausted, I was asleep within minutes.

7. | REMAINS OF THE WEEK

Friday 19 February

Despite our twilight-zone welcome to the neighborhood, I woke feeling rested. We would make no mention of our adventure to our hosts, but Larry felt they should have some idea of what we were doing here. I was not sure that was a good idea and sat down to breakfast hungry, but a little apprehensive.

The Warnocks joined us as we were finishing, and Larry was soon telling them about his service experience. Neither said a word until he'd finished, then Tony spoke up: "Well, finally, someone we can talk to about our experience!" With that, he and Jan launched into the details.

Almost fourteen years earlier, the couple were living in Sudbourne and one night hosted a dinner party. The party broke up late, about two, and they were waving good-bye to the last of the guests when "it" came into view. Jan saw it first, through the kitchen window: "This enormous orange light in the sky, and whatever it was, was getting nearer, and nearer." The glow was about the size of a Boeing 737. They watched from their bedroom as the glow went into the trees, then vanished. Within minutes, British jets and helicopters equipped with floodlights were buzzing the area.

Theirs was an earnest account of a memorable incident, something they had confided to almost no one. Despite this, Larry and I began to laugh. I don't know if it was the surprise of the coincidence that triggered this reaction, but it *was a relief to hear them laughing with us. We really had lucked out with this pair: Jan and Tony were genuinely interested in what we were doing here and would help us as they could. We had made two good friends.*

The conversation really opened up after that. Larry told them more about what had happened in 1980, but still nothing about the previous night's sightings. In turn, we learned that everything from the most advanced American spy planes to who-knew-what had flown over this little village since they'd been here.

Such things were not easily discussed in Eyke, and with the exception of two or three good friends, our hosts had never even tried. Despite its quiet, historic exterior, this village of eight hundred lay between two of NATO's most highly secured bases, and it was natural that locals might be guarded with strangers. Not many people here made fun of UFOs: they didn't talk about them at all.

But there was someone, Jan ventured, who might want to talk with us about the Bentwaters incidents. Al Brown was a retired American air force officer who had married a friend of theirs and lived close by. He was an authentic top-gun fighter pilot and had also been stationed at Bentwaters. In December 1980, he had been a squadron training commander there. Would we like her to ring him up? "Yes," we said.

Their brief conversation was upbeat but disappointing. The colonel would have liked to meet Larry, but unfortunately a business commitment would keep him out of town for the duration of our visit. It was too bad, but at least Jan had tried.

We were soon hiking through the Rendlesham Forest, or what was left of it. The freak storm had preceded us by four months. Both the Warnocks and Airman Mike had tried to give us an idea of what we were in for, but nothing really could have. What had been a beautiful forest was now a wasteland. Great tracts dating back hundreds of years simply were no more. We took in as much as we could, then headed back toward Eyke.

Jan made us a great dinner at the house that night, but it was difficult to unwind afterward. We stepped out for a smoke, began talking, and were soon walking out toward the base again. But this trip ended in a field at the north end of the village; I for one had no intention of going past that point tonight, and Larry had no problem with that. We scanned the sky and forest for the next hour, thankfully without results. The remainder of the week went by in jolts.

Saturday 20 February
Jan knocked a few times before inquiring, "Are you up yet?" Their friend, the colonel, was on the phone. He had changed an appointment and could now meet with us, but it would have to be soon, like in twenty minutes. Would that

be all right? Sure. Fine. Then we should be down for coffee in twenty minutes. Good morning!

Jan greeted me in the dining room with a pot of coffee. I poured myself a cup, but before I had time to drink it, the door opened and Tony walked in with Colonel Al Brown. I had to admit, the man looked the part of the former top gun and squadron commander he was. He had steel-gray hair, blue eyes, and one of those faces that wore its experiences like a map.

Before Tony could introduce us, Al nodded to me, crossed the room, and extended his hand. "Are you Larry?" he asked. "No, I'm Peter Robbins. I'm working on the book with him. Larry will be down in a minute." "Oh," said the colonel, obviously a little disappointed. But Larry was down in a minute, and I introduced the two as Tony exited. Once we were seated, I pulled back a bit; there wouldn't be much I could add to this conversation.

At Brown's request, Larry recounted the incident, minus some of the details I was now familiar with. Had the colonel known Colonel Williams back when? asked Larry. Sure, they had been close friends, still were. Still were? We had heard a rumor that Williams died. Oh, he had almost died, that was true enough, some kind of spider bite that got infected, it went back a few years, but he was fine now. Williams had also retired from the air force, but as a two-star general. He now lived in California and was an executive with a firm there. The former wing commander was fine and on a recent visit to England had even surprised the colonel by showing up in his kitchen one morning! As if to punctuate the statement, Brown took out his wallet and extracted Gordon Williams's business card from it.

The exchange proceeded on friendly, but guarded terms. It wasn't that the officer didn't accept the possibility of the incident, only that he had never seen any evidence of it. But what about the rumors that had swept the base that week? "You were a squadron commander," said Larry. "You must have been briefed."

It was as close as Larry had come to raising his voice. But the poker-faced officer just looked at him and said, "Nope, never heard a thing." That can't be right, I thought. The squadrons were briefed the next day, at least that was what our source had insisted last June.

Larry stared at the colonel a moment, then shook his head and smiled; it took a minute to get back on the track. As we continued to talk, the colonel mentioned that there had been rumors circulating around the country club, but no one had taken them very seriously.

Brown wished us well on our book. He did have to get going though, and we walked him to the door. That a former Bentwaters squadron commander might not wish to confide what he knew to us was hardly newsworthy. What had caught me off guard was that I liked the guy.

After breakfast, Tony began to tell us about some of the building that had been going on at Bentwaters. The contractors were all civilian, and a lot of them had stayed at the Old House. One memorable group never had a day off. They told the Warnocks that they were stopped daily by security, personally inspected, and had their vans checked—just for perimeter work! Their first actual day on base, all were held in isolation for three hours before being led to their jobs in secured hangars. Most people hereabouts felt the base housed more than it appeared to. "We don't know what's up there," said Tony, "I mean, we're all certain it's not just A-10s and, you know . . ."

Larry would be going back to the base alone today. We agreed that it would increase the chances of his getting to talk with other personnel. In the meantime, Tony and Jan would show me some of East Anglia. Jan and I dropped Larry off at the base entrance, then returned to the house to pick up Tony. From Eyke, we drove through Butley, then on to Sudbourne. Here, we stopped at the cottage they had seen the UFO from. Our turnaround point was Orford, where we paused for a view of the notorious lighthouse. Nearby Orford Castle was more interesting by far.

But the good company, fine weather, and historic sites were not enough to distract any of us from the storm's handiwork. Tony pulled the car over several times for me to better take in the war zones, but none was more affecting than our last stop. It was called "the thick," almost entirely made up of holly trees, many over five hundred years old, possibly the oldest in England. The Warnocks suggested I walk in for a better look.

The grove was exceedingly quiet, and the ancient hollies stately and beautiful, even without their leaves. The trunks were massive, some more than a yard across. It was only when I stopped looking up that I saw the trees on the ground. Some had been ripped out by their roots and fully overturned. Others leaned at fatal angles. The most unnerving ones had been impossibly cracked or snapped. A wind did this? *was all I could think as I got back into the car.*

There were other examples of the storm's velocity. Tony said it had ripped a slate tile off a roof and propelled it several hundred feet horizontally. The thing smashed through a neighbor's window and embedded itself hatchet-style in the living room wall. Falling trees brought down lines, leaving Eyke without power for six days. The Old House—fully booked at the time—stayed candlelit, cooked on bottled gas, and kept a fire roaring in the hearth. Two weeks passed before phones in the village worked normally again.

What had the official version been. On 16 October 1987, a "freak storm"—

the once-in-a-hundred-years kind—swept in from the southeast and cut a di-
agonal swath from Suffolk up through Wales. It arrived without any forecast or
prediction and whipped the Bentwaters area for about three hours. No rain
accompanied the winds, which were alleged to have peaked at 95 to 105 miles
an hour. But hundred-mile-an-hour winds don't flatten forests. I grew up next
to a state park and had seen what hurricanes could do to a forest. Often clocked
at ninety or ninety-five miles an hour, they always downed some trees, but never
flattened our trees to the horizon—not even remotely. Why was I spinning my
wheels about this? In terms of our book, why should this sad but unrelated
matter warrant any more than a footnote? It had nothing to do with our reasons
for being here and had already preoccupied too much of my time. But putting
this storm out of my mind was easier said than done, and I knew why.

Ever since Larry had seen that photograph of a Reich cloudbuster at my
apartment, he'd insisted the air force had scaled-up versions of them on Bent-
waters. It was a matter of record that Reich had kept the air force apprised of
his weather-modification work in the fifties. If that information had been di-
rected toward a project to develop the cloudbusters' potential by increasing their
size, it had succeeded. If Larry was correct, we might well be driving through
the result.

I knew how this sounded. Even a hint *that I took the possibility seriously*
could stress our already tenuous credibility to the breaking point. Unfortunately,
as a longtime student of the subject, I already did take it seriously. I had seen
one of these remarkable machines demonstrated several years earlier and knew
from my own experience how genuine their impact could be. There was no ques-
tion of "belief" for me: they worked. *A cloudbuster created atmosphere move-*
ment by literally drawing energy down from the atmosphere, then grounding it
harmlessly in moving or deep water.

The apparatus's appearance is simple and distinct. A series of fixed, long
pipes is connected to hollow lengths of industrial BX cable. When the ends of
the cables are placed into deep or running water, they act as conductors for the
energy being grounded in the water. The one I'd seen demonstrated was trailer
mounted and controlled remotely, but its operating principles were just as basic.
It sounded too simple, but the physics were just as demonstrable as water boiling
at 212 degrees Fahrenheit.

From what I had seen and studied, the atmospheric chaos a truly large cloud-
buster had the potential to create could easily drive an approaching weather
front into a frenzy, and perhaps had. If more than one device had been involved,
well . . . Suffolk's reputation as an exotic-weapons testing area didn't help to
calm my speculations any: if the air force had *tested some sort of super cloud-*
buster in England, it might well have been in East Anglia.

However, the case forming in my mind was built entirely on circumstantial evidence and speculation; the jury in me would need more. For starters, the technology was useless without water, and I had yet to see any of the deep wells that Larry said dotted the base.

I kept these thoughts to myself as the car wound its way through the countryside. Why muck up an otherwise wonderful afternoon? My hosts were such good company, and I had to admit it was good to get away from Larry for a few hours: his stress was infectious. We stopped at a pub for lunch, and arrived back at the Old House about three.

Larry returned about four and immediately suggested we take a little walk. As a result of asking one question too many on base, he had been picked up by a pair of LEs and escorted to the office of the deputy base commander. There he was briefly questioned, then politely released:

I told him I was involved in something here some years ago, something that happened at a high level, and he said, the UFO? and I said, yep. He goes, I don't know much about that.

Most of the individuals Larry had approached would not say much to him, but of those who were willing to talk, several cops and an airfield mechanic said they had also heard there was an underground facility at Bentwaters. The mechanic had been told by a pilot that well below the flight line, Bentwaters connected up with Woodbridge, Martlesham, and the North Sea. "Tunnels and trams, everything—just like Bustinza told me." Larry also made a sketch of an unusual-looking flash he'd seen on a pilot's flight suit. I don't need this, I thought. His drawing looked like a dark, hovering UFO on a pattern with writing above and below.

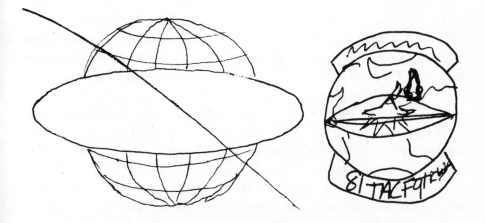

We stopped and turned in the road, then began to walk back toward the house. Jesus, was he telling it to me straight? After what I had already seen and heard here, you could have told me that Martians were marching out of the woods and I might have turned around to look. But if Larry were misleading me, I had yet to catch on. In the meantime, I would fight to remain objective but temper my responses with additional wariness.

Sunday 21 February

An item from the Warnock's family history seemed to nail down another of Larry's allegations. The couple and their three sons had moved to Eyke from Sudbourne in April 1980. One late night in December of that year, all five were wakened by the rumbling sounds of a military convoy. The vehicles were coming from the direction of the base and passed right in front of the Old House. Nothing like that had happened before, and it was a long time before anything like it happened again.

Next morning, a woman who lived up the street told some of the neighbors that the air force had had a close encounter the night before. She had been up late listening to the military transmissions on her shortwave radio. The woman was known to have eavesdropped in this manner before, but she was also something of a gossip and not above stretching the truth, so the case rested there.

Today's destination was the site of the December 1980 incident: Capel Green—a farmer's field at the eastern edge of the Rendlesham Forest. After a long walk, we saw the northeast corner of RAF Woodbridge. We were following the route that Larry and the others had driven that night. The Ministry of Defence sign posted behind the fence bore a warning identical to the one we had seen on our first night. The site where the unexploded-ordnance roadblock had been set up was just up the road and East Gate Road cut in at the south end of the fence line. Left at East Gate. Another hundred yards along was where they'd made the turn. We cut in through the underbrush.

An abandoned pillbox was our first landmark: Larry had passed it back in 1980. As the scrub pines diminished, we emerged through a grassy clearing onto a rise facing a field. When I saw the oak tree and the farmhouse, I knew we were there. Capel Green looked very much as it had been described to me.

Larry's right arm shot out in an automatic gesture as we stepped onto the rise. He was pointing into the tilled field. My eyes naturally followed. "It sat right there," he said. We both got very quiet. Larry was pointing at a large, roughly circular discoloration in the earth. "Of course, that's just a coincidence . . ." his voice trailed off.

The speed at which he'd indicated the marking in the field interested me as much as the marking itself. The man was sure that the thing he had seen that *night had been sitting on that exact spot. As a researcher, I was familiar with what we call trace cases, where soil or surroundings are affected or altered as the result of a close encounter, but visible traces after eight years? Maybe it was only some play of light. We still weren't close enough to say for sure. Some conventional explanation might account for the circular shape, but its effect was positively eerie. There was nothing else like it in the field. I took a photograph and we proceeded.*

For the first time since the night of the incident, my coauthor was back where it had happened. I reached into my pocket and offered him the other recorder. "Can you go out there and relive this?" I asked. He took the machine, hit record, and began to do just that.

It was an experience I would not soon forget. He walked me through it all, and the physical point-by-point description was accompanied by a detailed commentary. I kept my distance and just listened. By the time he'd finished, we were both pretty exhausted. Being here felt something like visiting a battlefield.

"How are you doing?" Larry asked. "Tired, and a little sad," I answered. He nodded that he understood. After labeling my film containers, I filled some with soil from the discolored area and others with earth from farther out in the field. We left by way of the logging road.

Our destination was the Cherry Tree, and we would hitchhike if possible. I was soon packed in between Larry and the driver of a small truck. He had heard the UFO rumors and remembered the 1983 news blitz as well. No, he didn't give the subject much thought, but did make a joke that wasn't very funny. Larry and I got out at the pub and thanked him for the ride. With a nod, he drove off. The pub, unfortunately, was locked tight. We had to remember they had afternoon closing here.

Back in Eyke, I told Tony what we'd observed at the field. He asked to see our samples, and I produced two of the earth-packed film canisters for his inspection. We sat down at the dining room table and dumped them onto sheets of typing paper: you did not have to be a scientist to see they were different. The dirt from the affected area was slightly darker, grittier, and drier. The unaffected sample felt moist.

A simple experiment seemed called for. How would the samples mix with water? I brought the soil out to a table in the garden, transferred equal amounts to two jar lids, then added equal small amounts of water to each. A few stirs and the "normal" earth quickly became good English mud. But no matter how I mixed the other one, the simple compound eluded me. Instead, the resistant little clumps sunk to the bottom, while the finer particles floated on the surface.

For the moment at least, there was no escaping the implications of what I was looking at: the soil from the epicenter of the third night's incident was different from the soil surrounding it. And I was as sure as I could be that Larry had identified the authentic location. The discoloration was exactly where he had placed a circled X on the map he'd given me last summer. It also matched up with the drawing he'd made in my living room last November. The soil would have to be professionally analyzed, of course, but it was now fair to say that these two humble jar lids might be holding physical evidence of the Bentwaters incident.

Monday 22 February

The first leg of today's walk took us along Bentwaters' northernmost flight line. The tarmac was active and secured only by a cyclone fence—a good place for some book-related brainstorming. Our ideas and expectations for Left at East Gate *were growing rapidly. We both wanted to write something that stood a chance of making a difference, but how could we structure a book of such varied perspectives? We had one first-person account, an interesting shared experience, a growing number of facts, and an endless amount of our own and other people's speculations. We were looking to achieve some sort of narrative balance.*

We were also looking for a well. It did not take long to find one, then another, and another. All had good-sized openings, and were squared off aboveground by low concrete barriers: ideal for a cloudbuster. Lift the metal grate away and one had only to drop the cables down. Yes, they were here all right; but they weren't proof, only provocative. Unless we could secure a more substantial lead, there would be no mention in the book of the storm, the cloud buster, or their chilling implications. At the least, we would have to find another witness.

There was also a decision to be made about Thursday night's incident. If we included a treatment, it would have to be the full treatment. Otherwise, it would be a joke: "Within hours of arriving in Suffolk, the pair claim to have seen no fewer than twenty-five UFOs near the site of the original incident." Oooh, boy. I briefly found myself wishing the episode had happened on the third night; anything would have sounded better than the first night. Too bad we were only interested in writing nonfiction.

Larry pointed out a low hilltop. If we could get ourselves up there, he said, we would have a clear view of Perimeter Post 18, and that was something we should photograph. All we had to do was go through the wire fence strung with MOD warning signs, walk across the field, and climb the hill.

Before I could offer an opinion, Larry was through the wire. I took a deep breath and followed him into the field, visions of land mines plaguing me right up to the top. I took the photos without incident, and we were soon back in the forest.

Half an hour later, we had reached a clearing at the edge of a farm. Here, a grassy hill stood above a small pond, complete with rowboat and cavorting ducks. The scene was out of a children's picture book, and we climbed the hill just for the pleasure of the view. "Isn't this lovely," I said. Then the world filled with noise.

Within seconds, the din was so loud that I could hardly hear myself screaming: "What is that?" "That" was directly over us, maybe a thousand feet up. Larry was now yelling back at me: "It's the Blackbird, the Blackbird! It's the SR-71!" Those huge engines, of course! It was an SR-71, and we were elated. The highly classified spy plane then banked, climbed, and made a second pass. Now smaller by the second, it disappeared on a western heading. Was I able to get a photograph of it? Right—if sharks could fly, I thought.

The SR bore no markings and was aerodynamically stunning—a flat, black rocketship of a thing. We knew the plane carried no weapons and that it had been deployed under President Kennedy, but at Mach 3, it was still considered the fastest thing we had in the air. This ship could climb at ten thousand feet per minute and, supposedly, photograph a license plate from eighty thousand feet. Its pilots had to go through astronaut training, and all missions were strictly controlled by the CIA.

I continued to look west, attempting to fix the sight in my mind. Larry told me he had once seen one make a night landing on the secured flight line at RAF Lakenheath in Norfolk; the plane was then lowered to a classified hangar. Our Blackbird had come off the Bentwaters flight line, apparently on a straight heading with us. Of all the luck! But now it was a memory, and the quiet returned. Larry looked down at the little scene again, then looked at me and said, "Isn't this lovely," and burst into laughter.

We had a final dinner at the Cherry Tree that evening. We were just finishing when the Warnocks' sons Richie and Pete entered. Jan had sent them along to see that we got back all right. Once home, I wished everyone good night and headed for our room. Larry spent another hour with the family, returning with a pitcher of milk for tea and a dozen new bits of information.

From a researcher's point of view, the week had been a gold mine. Almost too good to be true, and that's what was bothering me now. It sounded mad, of course, but could any of the week's incidents have been, well, less than spontaneous? Maybe I had worked in the theater for too long, but it was difficult to shake the feeling that some of our visit had been stage-managed. Larry had had some similar feelings—but he would, I told myself. It was easy for us to discuss the possibility into the small hours of the night.

Tuesday 23 February

Tony and Jan took their son Richie, Larry, and me on another drive. This one followed the route we had taken on Saturday, but added an extra stop—Capel Green. Today we walked in by way of the logging road. It was gratifying to note that as the field came into view, the usually reserved Tony caught sight of the discoloration, and said, "Shit!" It was the only time I heard him use such an expression.

From the site, it was back to the Old House for a final afternoon of talk and tea. Jan had dinner planned for eight that night; her mother and the boys would all be joining us. It was funny—while part of me couldn't wait to get back to New York, I was not at all ready to leave this place. I went upstairs to shower and change about seven.

By 7:15 I was happily washing off the soap and thinking about dinner. Then, boom! It sounded and felt as though something had slammed into us and rattled every Queen Anne brick in the building. An identical bang followed. What had happened? And why did I have to be in the shower when it did?

They might be sonic booms, of course—we were close to two air bases, but if they were, they were the loudest I'd ever heard. How fast or close would a plane have to be to make a sound like that? The next moment, Larry was knocking and calling through the bathroom door: "You won't believe what just went over the house!" Yes, I would, I thought.

At 7:15 precisely, two stealth-type aircraft had flown directly over the Old House. Larry had been reading by our rear window and pulled the curtains back in time to see the second one, then made a quick sketch of it. We showed it to Tony before dinner.

Like a good bird-watcher noting a species, our friend told us that those particular birds had been coming over for some time now. They must have been doing in excess of Mach 1 before they had even cleared the village! Was that possible? Apparently.

Everything about this plane was classified in the States, yet here in Eyke, the futuristic fighters were common knowledge. Considering the highly unusual airshow that had welcomed us to Suffolk, the stealths bracketed the week nicely.

The Warnocks proposed a toast to our success and safe return, and we proposed one to them. Under the circumstances, anyone able to put up with us for a week deserved knighthood.

8. 1988—
YOU DON'T KNOW WHAT YOU HAVE UNTIL YOU LOSE IT

After our return, I spent my remaining vacation time at Peter's apartment recovering from the trip. The first night back, we had dinner with his parents. They were terrific people, but I could only wonder what they thought their son had walked into. All I could think about was what had happened to us in England: our UFO sightings the first night in Suffolk, the confirmations we'd received from Mike, being picked up by law enforcement and questioned by the deputy base commander, seeing that SR-71, the terrible destruction of Rendlesham Forest—it was like reviewing a bad dream.

So much had happened in a week, and it would take some time to sink in. I remembered our last morning at Jan and Tony's. It had snowed overnight and a lone black chicken had stood in the snow-covered garden, looking dazed. I think we knew how that bird felt. If Peter had had any lingering doubts about my story before we'd gone to England, he didn't have them any longer.

One night, we attended a UFO-support-group meeting at Budd Hopkins's home, where we presented some of our findings from the trip. I was disappointed that some people didn't seem interested in our adventure, but had to remind myself that this was not your run-of-the-mill audience; one way or the other, everyone there had been through that mill themselves.

Back in Connecticut, nothing had improved between Cindy and me, but we remained civil to each other. Peter called to say that he'd had our photos from England developed and you could see the discoloration at the 1980 landing site very clearly.

After having put it off and off for nearly a year, I called Peter on the night of 28 April 1988. It was then I told him the rest of the story—my experience in the underground facility. He listened, barely asking a single question. All in all, he seemed to handle it quite well. For me, it was a relief to get it off my chest. It would be some time before I'd know how badly I had misjudged his reaction.

On 1 May, I moved out of Cindy's life and into New York City. Staying with Peter first and then finding a place on the West Side, I continued to agonize over our separation. I often called Cindy to ask if she would let me come home. Through tears, she always refused.

In July, Peter headed out to Oklahoma to teach painting for the summer. I found myself running with a music-industry crowd. Throughout the summer of 1988, the parties and self-abuse never stopped. I was completely out of my mind, depressed, usually drunk, and at times suicidal.

A close friend, a singer who had had her share of UFO experiences, was my only island of stability. She understood my pain and tried to be supportive, but every day I became more uncontrollable, "a member of the walking-wounded society," as she often said. Unfortunately, we were both lightning rods for UFOs, aliens, and paranormal experiences. Soon that was too much for either of us to handle, so we drifted apart.

I would often see UFOs over the city and had even seen one fly under the George Washington Bridge and continue on toward Westchester. I felt such craft used the bridge as some kind of navigation device. I continued to get hit, even in the middle of the world's most populated city. By late summer, I had started calling New York the devil's playground.

Now living in an apartment on Central Park West, I couldn't have felt any more isolated. Peter hardly called me anymore, and I didn't care. By now, I didn't give a damn about our book anyway. I got along well with my roommate, but he was worried about my behavior, and, eventually scared of me.

Every day brought more trouble for me. As the summer got hotter, my luck got worse; my apartment was robbed twice in the same week! What wasn't ripped off the first time was gone the next. When the NYPD arrived, they treated me like a criminal, suspecting me instead of investigating the theft. A few days later, I lost my job and now had no money. I had pissed away my settlement from Cindy and had nothing to fall back on. I unplugged the phone and locked myself in the apartment.

The following week, I finally hit bottom and attempted to kill myself by taking a bottle of my roommate's antidepressant prescription. I mixed this with a bottle of Jack Daniels and fell asleep.

I woke up early that night and remembered I'd been invited to a party on the East Side. I felt awful but went anyway. At the party, I got very sick—then remembered my stupid act of only hours earlier. At City Hospital, they discovered the drug I'd taken was out of date: I couldn't even kill myself properly. The worst aftereffect was a hangover that left me even more depressed.

One night in late August, Ray Gomez, a musician friend, finally dragged me out of the apartment. Over dinner, he begged me to get my act together before it was too late. Ray had beaten his own demons, and his words really hit home. He had had everything, then lost it, but was now trying to rebuild his life. I knew he was right. I had to do something before it was too late. Once back home, I plugged in my phone and pulled up the shades. Suddenly, the phone rang—a man named Curt Brubaker wanted me to come out to Los Angeles and participate in a live TV show. It was going to be called UFO Cover-up Live, hosted by M*A*S*H's Mike Farrell. Without thinking, I said, "Send me the tickets."

I met Brubaker at LAX. On the way to his Bel Air home, he asked me if I was lying. I was stunned. I told him he could have asked me that over the phone and saved himself a few dollars. "No," I said, I wasn't lying.

The next morning I met with John Burroughs. I hadn't known him well because he worked in law enforcement while I was in security, but I recognized him right away. Later, we spent several hours in Brubaker's living room hashing over the details of December 1980. John told me about the first night's events in great detail.

As I listened, I had the feeling that he and the other cops with him that night had experienced missing time, but didn't voice my suspicions. The man seemed nervous and had obviously not come to terms with his experiences. I couldn't blame him. I wasn't doing so well with mine. John told me about health problems he felt were directly related to the UFO. He said he had problems with his eyes and heart—man, that sounded familiar.

That afternoon I showed Burroughs the CNN program and provided him with a copy of Lieutenant Colonel Halt's tape and related material. All the while Brubaker listened closely. Since the drive from the airport, I'd felt that he had some hidden agenda. Both he and Burroughs seemed eager to gain my trust, but, considering John's continuing active-duty status, I remained cautious and told them only my public account.

Burroughs was interested in Peter's and my research into the incidents and wanted to know how far along the book had come. I didn't say. He even made a weak attempt surreptitiously to record me when I was describing the life-forms I'd seen. He could have just asked. I figured either Brubaker or Burrough's higher-ups had put him up to it.

We had lunch at Burbank Studios the next day. Producer Mike Seligman described his objectives for the TV show with as many schmoozy Hollywood adjectives as I'd ever heard. Because of his accent, I asked him if he was originally from Boston. For some reason, it was the wrong question to ask, and he suddenly became very abrupt with me. The last thing I needed was this guy's attitude. I told him he could shove his show; I didn't want any part of it. Burroughs agreed the program would not be a good forum for Bentwaters: lunch was over.

Before I flew back east, I called Peter in Oklahoma via a conference line. He felt the weekend had produced at least one positive outcome— two of the original Bentwaters witnesses had been brought together for the first time. By Sunday, even Brubaker seemed impressed by John and me. Nevertheless, I didn't trust him. When the program eventually aired, it was considered a farce by most in the UFO field. At least I'd made one good choice.

Soon after I'd returned to New York, I went to a get-together at Hopkins's. Peter was there, but we didn't have much to say to each other. A new NBC TV show was being filmed there called Unsolved Mysteries. The network was currently shooting a segment on UFO abductions for the premier episode. Sitting there listening, I felt like an outsider and ended up drinking wine by myself in Budd's kitchen.

Sharing a cab uptown later with Antonio Huneeus, I told him that I was sick of the book, sick of Peter, and very sick of New York. Antonio said it didn't surprise him. Even he had noticed a change in Peter, and they'd been friends since 1980. Peter seemed withdrawn and guarded and had been that way since we returned from England. I said that our relationship had deteriorated to the point where I just wanted to retrieve the documents I'd given him and end the association. He had been acting so differently toward me since the spring that I wasn't sure I could trust him. Antonio agreed that something was bothering the man. But what could I do to change things?

The next Saturday, Peter called. I was surprised, but invited him up to my apartment. He seemed to be in good spirits, and although we didn't talk about the book much, we went to the Hayden Planetarium to watch the space show. We both laughed when a flying saucer was projected onto the ceiling above us, but I wasn't laughing inside. I was feeling guilty for having pushed Peter into the Bentwaters investigation to begin with. After all the work we'd done, it now seemed to me that soon we would be parting ways for good.

We said good-bye in front of the planetarium. While walking back up Central Park West, I figured now was as good a time as any to dump Bentwaters and get the hell out of New York. A week later, I called my mother and asked if I could come to Glens Falls for a while to get my head together. She asked what bus I'd be on. Though I'd been having nightmares about living there again, I now had no choice. I'd be dead if I didn't get out of the city soon.

Halloween morning, I left the apartment keys and a note for my roommate, apologizing for my sudden departure. I'd packed everything I could carry into two suitcases. What didn't fit in, I left behind. With thirty dollars to my name, I headed down to the Port Authority Bus Terminal.

Exiting on the New Jersey side of the Lincoln Tunnel, I gazed back at the New York City skyline with anger and disappointment. I never wanted to see it again.

My sister picked me up in Glens Falls with my niece and nephew, both dressed in their Halloween costumes. I now had one dollar in my pocket and no idea where my life would go from here. My mother was shocked by my appearance. My weight had dropped considerably, and I knew I looked terrible.

But my stepmother, Sandy, had always told me I was the sort of person who could fall into a septic tank and come up with a diamond ring on his head; maybe she was right. Within the next two days, I had gotten a good job with a local radio station, bought a new car, and was on the road to recovery.

In November 1988, I visited Cindy in Connecticut. It was great to see her again. I believed we really missed each other; I know I'd missed her. Over dinner, I told her how the book had come to a standstill. She was glad and said she felt most of my (and our) problems had stemmed from Bentwaters. Cin hoped I really could walk away from it. Despite all the bad times, we still cared for each other. I just wished I'd never left.

Peter and I spoke a few times after the move. He was upset that I hadn't told him I was leaving the city, but he didn't mention the book. Neither did I. Things were pretty good for me now. I had some old friends to spend time with and some new ones as well. My health was returning, but the old pain remained.

That New Year's Eve was spent at my friend Ray Jett's house, playing music, laughing, and thanking God I'd survived my "lost weekend." But as far as Left at East Gate was concerned, I'd need to find the spark again.

9. | REMAINS OF THE YEAR

It snowed our last night in Suffolk. In the morning, I pulled back the heavy fabric of the window curtain to see Rendlesham Forest more white than green. Jan had breakfast waiting for us downstairs and had packed us each a lunch as well; we would not starve on our way to the airport. I think we all tried to keep the chat airy, but when it came time to go, good-byes were not easy. One of the best things about this trip had been the Warnocks, and I knew that I would miss them.

Tony drove us to Woodbridge Station. It was a particularly beautiful drive; the snow made everything look like an old-fashioned Christmas card. The three of us walked out to the railway platform together, and Tony shook our hands warmly before we boarded. Larry and I promised we'd keep in touch. Then the train pulled away.

The countryside rolled by for an hour or so. I stared out the window, thinking. On the outskirts of London, the train ground to a halt. A conductor soon entered our car and apologetically announced we'd be held here a while, then the engine was cut and all went quiet.

About half an hour passed before we shuddered to a start and began moving again. Up ahead, a full-scale bomb alert had Victoria Terminal in a high-tension grip. We got off the train into a sea of well-armed troops, bomb-sniffing dogs, and nervous travelers. I had never seen anything like it. But we moved through *the crowd quickly, hailed a cab out to Gatwick, and arrived back at Kennedy that night.*

It was good to be home. We returned with more experience and information than I had imagined possible—but it simplified nothing. I could not stop thinking about the UFOs we had seen only days earlier, but the idea of declaring myself a witness to yet another Bentwaters incident left me cold. I had wanted only to write a book, not become a character in it. But I had, and on our first night there. I was stuck with that fact.

Most of the first day back was spent going over what we had learned in England. The trip had given us a great deal of new information, and it would all need to be worked into book form. For the next few months at least, we had our work cut out for us.

That night, we had dinner with my parents. It was great to see them, but they hardly got a word in the whole evening; Larry and I were wound up tight as watch springs and rattled on about our adventures like mechanical mice on speed. Dad and Mom's curiosity about Bentwaters seemed more measured than it had been before I left. I could see the concern in their faces, but continued to chatter away about the trip.

Our contact sheets were ready for pickup at midweek. The lab I had taken them to specialized in black-and-white and had been recommended by my friend Stanley, a professional photographer. Considering the camera problems I'd had in England, some real anxiety attached itself to the moment: the pictures were irreplaceable. I first checked the contact sheets for two in particular. The shot of Capel Green turned up first. I went in for a better look with my loupe, and there it was: the discoloration in the field could be seen easily. What a relief! The "after" photograph Larry had asked me to take of the forest destruction looked sharp as well.

I circled those two images, along with several others, and ordered prints for the next day. With processing completed, there was a comparison to be made. Once home, I placed Larry's honeymoon snapshot on my desk, then lay the updated counterpart to its right. Bingo, I thought; he had nailed it. I had to hand it to the guy. With only a bend in the road for a landmark, he had placed us within twenty feet of where he had taken the original photo. Our camera angles were virtually the same as well.

That was my technical assessment; my reaction was to gasp. Side by side, the impact of the two pictures was shattering. Before the storm, after the storm, but a thousand words couldn't describe it. One was an image of cool, primeval lushness, the other, an image of total and utter destruction. Their only common feature was that bend in the road. I stared at the two pictures for several minutes before putting them away.

Larry had not had to talk about his marriage for me to know it was in trouble. Both parties seemed like victims to me. For the present at least, what Larry Warren had been through in 1980 had turned him into something of a loose cannon—as much in terms of being a whistle-blower as maintaining a stable marriage. From everything I had learned of the condition known as post-traumatic stress disorder, Larry displayed every symptom. Cindy might as well have married a Vietnam veteran. His problem did not seem to have anything to do with her, nor did its possible solution.

I spent a lot of that spring wearing headphones. Our English tapes added many hours to what we'd recorded since July, and over the next two months, I listened to all of them, repeatedly. I now had my own firsthand impressions of the bases and their surroundings and searched the tapes for any inconsistencies, no matter how subtle, in Larry's recorded remarks.

The search bore some interesting fruit. Things that had had little or no meaning to me earlier now assumed some significance. I continued to feel certain that Larry had not lied about his recollections, but there were still times he'd fade out, overreact or underreact, shift the conversation to something else—anything else—away from the given question.

My attitude was generally good, though. If I'd withdrawn some, it was because I had taken on a serious professional project and had plenty to keep me busy.

It was at about this time I first began to notice an odd click-and-beep on the phone. So this is how the paranoid fantasies begin, I thought. Was my phone being tapped? I doubted it. A serious bug is silent, otherwise it defeats its own purpose. Or did it? Was the intent some sort of harassment? Even sillier. Our modest endeavors hardly seemed worth the attention. Really, who would want to tap my phone? They were just erratic sounds and, given the complexities of New York City's telephone system, hardly reason for alarm.

I even maintained that attitude on the two occasions I found my mail had been opened. Personal letters had been slit along the top, then resealed by someone other than the senders—I checked on that. There was nothing special about the letters, and my mailbox didn't seem to have been tampered with; it was just odd.

I spent most of April 1988 alone in my apartment, a fair amount of that time at my typewriter, not typing. I couldn't concentrate on writing with a key element still missing. Frustrated, I turned to more suitable tasks. I had many notes on details that still had to be confirmed, followed up on, or developed. Each was its own small job and better suited to my current attention span. But even the humblest inquiries could develop profound implications.

An example was the navy intelligence officer Larry had always maintained was at his debriefing. That officer interested me. First, he exemplified the kind of detail a hoaxer would likely avoid. When stuck with a complicated account, why make it more complicated? That player seemed unnecessary and out of place. Why inject naval intelligence into Bentwaters when inventing an air force in-telligence officer was just as easy? Because there was something to it. That navy officer had been there. My military-intelligence reading had taught me that our current espionage establishment owed much of its form and content to navy thinking. Something connected naval intelligence to Bentwaters. I wanted to find out what it was.

Of the books I was reading, Duncan Campbell's The Unsinkable Aircraft Carrier: American Military Power in Britain *was one of the most compelling. I'd bought it at Larry's suggestion when we visited the RAF Bentwaters bookstore, and found it a real eye-opener. Campbell's text, maps, photographs, and flow-charts were helping me to understand more about the complexities of the military and intelligence communities here.*

One of the charts Campbell included laid out the navy's intelligence systems. Lines connected boxes representing agencies and offices. The line I was interested in following began with the box labeled "Naval Security Group SIGINT (Signals Intelligence)." It connected with another representing the "Special US Liaison Office, London (SUSLO)." The only other line intersecting SUSLO went straight to the National Security Agency: NSA and American naval intelligence were headquartered in the same building in London. It was something to think about. I drifted through April preoccupied by such details. Then things changed.

The call from Larry came about eight one night. I turned off the television immediately; it was something about his voice. There were a few things about Bentwaters he'd been wanting to tell me, and it was time I knew about them. Not that he hadn't trusted me, but "I just didn't know if you could handle it." He hoped I could now. Buckle your seat belt, I thought.

I had never recorded any of our telephone calls, but the impulse to grab a recorder, cassette, and phone jack was immediate. I didn't, though. I just kept my seat and listened. What Larry had to say might fill in that big blank, and I didn't want to miss a word.

One at a time, Larry calmly described a series of incidents I was not familiar with. The first began with a phone call, a car ride, and an elevator descent. As he talked, I watched the hair on my arms rise.

The underground was real, and Larry had been there. He was not sure for how long. Bustinza's standing account was actually a combination of both their memories: "A guy I knew" could mean "me," and I was walked through it all now. Other particulars followed. These included the beings he'd seen approach us in the field by the base that night and his contacts with NSA personnel. News that I'd been the subject of some agency background check, then OK'd to work with Larry, left me feeling momentarily nauseous. He was sure our phones were irregularly monitored and had been from the start. Other calls we'd made might have been similarly intercepted. What was left of my Bentwaters innocence drained away with each new revelation.

Was this really happening? I couldn't believe he was talking about this on the phone. Mightn't this be one of those monitored calls, I awkwardly suggested. If anyone were listening in, he offered, it was them, and they already knew all about it.

A warning bell was going off inside me. Forget about Larry. Given only what I'd experienced, learned, or thought I'd learned bout Bentwaters on my own, nothing he was saying sounded out of the question, and that was not a good feeling. If he was one of those rare people with the compulsion—and ability— to lie so spectacularly, I still wasn't getting it. And by this time, I was starting to wish I would get it: Larry as liar was preferable to these things being true.

Forget about the book. I had just been briefed on how far in over my head I had gotten myself. What frightened me most was I believed him. I never went to bed that night.

Over the next weeks and months, my behavior began to alter drastically. There was nothing self-willed about these changes, but I was nonetheless becoming someone I didn't know. The first thing to go was my sleep pattern, which I would have previously characterized as terrific. But overnight, I became a full-fledged insomniac. I lost interest in my teaching job of fifteen years and stopped socializing. Now afraid to compromise the privacy of people I cared about, I all but ignored my phone and rarely returned calls. One by one, my friends, professional associates, and family members were losing contact with me. I'm sure some took it personally. I made no attempt to explain myself. Every new estrangement created another void in my life, and each void was gobbled up by the black hole of Bentwaters.

Larry and I didn't speak again for a week. Though it had obviously never been his intention to cause me any harm or grief, he had, in fact, brought me into something well out of our control, and it was now catching up with both of us. Not that I disagreed with his method; had our situations been reversed, I'd never have told a potential collaborator everything up front.

Larry was not having a good time either. If I wanted out now, he would more than understand, but hoped it wouldn't come to that. There really had been no right time or right way to lay the full facts out. He had come close to telling me in England, but had decided against it after our UFO episode. That was probably a good judgment call; I might have blown a fuse. We needed to talk in person, and soon. He arrived back in the city on Tuesday, 10 May 1988.

For the next few days, I questioned and re-questioned him. But forty-eight hours later, I knew, or thought I knew, that the last toy had fallen out of the piñata. Whether I liked it or not, I believed him, and it made me angrier than I could say. I should demand a meeting with these NSA men, just them and me at the fast-food restaurant of their choice; Larry ought to be able to arrange it. And that's what I asked him to do.

But that kind of righteous indignation is hard to sustain. Within a day or two, I had modified my challenge out of existence. I had read far too much about the NSA to take anything about it lightly, least of all contact. Nobody had connected Bentwaters to the NSA that I was aware of, and I seriously questioned the wisdom of our attempting to be the first. Did these men really exist? Had Larry really met with them? I believed so, but had to admit I was too frightened to find out for sure. If they were an invention, I wasn't going to call his bluff. Day after day and face to face, Larry had stood his ground on all my questions and never broken a sweat—that had to be worth something.

Some details remind you to question everything. While reviewing his memories of the underground complex, Larry described what it had been like to stare down through that picture window at craft identical to the one he had seen in the field. I handed him a pencil and paper and asked him to draw it. This picture was immediately familiar to me. He had sketched its twin at the same small desk six months earlier. I took out the original drawing and compared the two: they were identical.

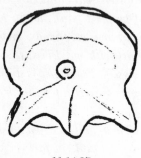 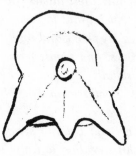

11-14-87   5-10-88

The implications gave me a momentary shiver. Larry had only seen the Capel Green craft from the side, and at a fairly fixed angle. Even as he was leaving the scene—when he stopped on the rise for a last look back, he still would have been seeing the thing from the same angle. So how had he arrived at this re-markable overview? I had never thought to ask at the time, but the answer now stared up at me from the desk: Larry had seen the craft from above, as well as from the side, or, worse, thought he had. I really didn't know if I could go on with this.

As the shock of April's call faded, misunderstandings between us became com-

mon; I think I was making sure of that. I was not interested in "collaborating" on this book, and was furious at having been cleared by anyone. I was also angry that the enjoyment had been taken out of my work. Illusion had been stripped away, or added to—either was sufficient grounds for jumping ship. The answers I was seeking would have to wait: I needed to back off from the project. "Take as much time as you need," said Larry, but he looked disappointed. We wished each other well and meant it. I would be in touch, but not for a while.

Time passes differently when your mooring lines are cut. Obsessed but uncommitted, without set hours and living off my savings, I began to write again, but not our book. What I was drafting would be called "Confidential;" its contents would be no one's business but my own and my editor's. By late spring, the stacks of paper that were Left at East Gate *had dust on the cover sheets. Work on the manuscript for "Confidential," though, was proceeding daily.*

The collapse of the Soviet Union now dominated world affairs, and in my own little world, its death throes were strangely welcome: something besides Bentwaters interested me again. The rise of Mikhail Gorbachev fascinated me. The speed at which this man was walking away from the cold war was positively astonishing. If nobody shot him, things could really get interesting. I was coming out of my funk.

Heading west in July, I threw myself into the teaching job I'd held two summers earlier. It was wonderful to be working with kids again and great to be back in Oklahoma. Larry kept in touch from New York and Los Angeles. Producer Curt Brubaker seemed interested in getting Larry's story for some kind of film treatment, but neither of us liked his proposition. Being a beggar didn't mean you couldn't be a chooser. Just before I returned to New York, Larry mentioned that there was something he wanted to talk about, but not on the phone. It could wait until I got home.

We met for lunch at my sister Helen's apartment the following week. Both of us still ambivalent about our book, it was time to go face to face again. Larry arrived upbeat, but seemed to be working pretty hard at it. He didn't look well, and Helen agreed.

At the kitchen table, Larry told us about several recent interactions with non-human beings—not fun stuff. What had he not wanted to talk about over the phone, I asked. Nothing, no big deal. He felt silly about it now, and we should just forget about it. "What was it?" I wanted to know. Nothing, just that he had come pretty close to killing himself the month before.

My sister and I were shocked. Had it really come to that? We didn't have to ask; we could see it had. What would happen to him if I walked away now? What would happen to me if I didn't? I was angry at myself for missing some sign of his distress and angry at him for almost leaving me alone with Pandora's

*steamer trunk. Larry tried to joke the whole episode off, but there was nothing
funny about it.*

*A few days later, I phoned Budd Hopkins and asked when he might have
some time to meet with me. Budd, a friend of fifteen years, knew Larry, had
interviewed his mother, and possessed a good working knowledge of the case. We
met at a diner near his lower Manhattan home soon after.*

*Over coffee, I laid out the situation as I perceived it and asked if he had any
suggestions on how best to proceed. "Carefully," he answered. What Larry remembered, said Budd, was likely a combination of real memories and programmed or screen memories. "But the government may have really done a job
on him," I mused. "The government and the aliens," Budd added. I hated that
idea, but at this point, nothing could have surprised me less.*

*In September 1988, I reached a decision I was not proud of. Over the coming
months, I would be recording some of my conversations with Larry, and I would
do so without his knowledge. It made me feel sneaky, but I was desperate. If
Larry Warren did not live to see the end of this project, which did suggest itself
as a real possibility, I would not be left holding the bag quite so alone. Tape
recorders, typewriter, coffee, cigarettes, and fear. Wasn't it great to feel like an
insider? Wasn't it exciting to be a writer?*

1988 Developments |

September 1988

*Robbins calls Warren to review some of the particulars of their February trip to
England and their April phone conversation. Warren is unaware that Robbins
is taping the call. It is the first of five such conversations he will record over the
next seven months.[30]*

LW. There's nothing honorable about any of them because they
don't particularly give a fuck. You know, they're not there for
me.

PR. I appreciate that.

LW. This is the way this stuff is—it wasn't my choice.

PR. No, I understand that.

LW. And when I told you about a call [from the NSA], the potential
of a call, I was led to assume—like I said, I've probably been lied
to more than you can *count* . . . In fact, I can *assure* you I have.
How you can come out of it unscathed is impossible. I'm like a
Vietnam vet in some ways. Though I didn't have to *kill*, people

died because of this. I was a pawn, and an unwilling pawn, and I had to . . . I was either mentally con . . . you know, either brain-washed at some point, to exercise certain control or power, but it wore off, it really did. You walked the walk, guy, I mean you're as far into this . . . and they're aware. I do go back to what they did, and what happened to me, and how I was used. And I can't prove a lot of it and I'm not allowed to prove a lot—I don't care. You know the thing is, Peter, I lost who I was. I don't think I gave my wife the benefit of who I was. I've lost every . . . She [Cindy] never met me when I was what I was. I had to live a lie of not being me, and I had to beat her over the head with this when I got mad or crazy or whatever. I never grew up after I was nineteen—some parts of me stopped.

PR.   You couldn't have told me, when we first met, that you'd been through this thing,'cause even if I'm one in a million, the kind of person that could grasp it in one sweep, it's just too much to ask of anybody. And so one of the things that I've been hearing in re-listening to some of the tapes that we made, is you, essentially, bringing me along.

LW.   Yeah.

PR.   And making observations about things that you knew perfectly well were true and then, and later in the week, saying "that fits in more with that." When we came back from there [England], it was like, things were much more profound and much deeper, for what was sort of privileged information. I felt for the first time this wasn't . . . it wasn't fun anymore. The experience of working on the project—which had been terribly exciting from the moment that we started, and a real detective story—and then thinking, my God, what are we putting ourselves on the mark for here? At different times, Larry's communicated to me that he's been made to feel that this is essentially protected, we can just move right into this and write about it.

LW.   Yeah, but that doesn't mean . . .

PR.   And then in the other extreme, of course, is they could care less, and this [book] is a big joke, and we're like little bugs.

LW.   Yeah!

PR.   And why are we pushing ourselves into a situation where we'll be made to look like idiots and go through more years of having our mail and our phones jerked around with? The reality is we know better than anybody, you can walk to a location, a mile down the road from Eyke, and in a field, have a pretty good chance of seeing something that is so beyond secret classification, there's just a number for it.

LW. Yeah [*Laughs*]

PR. How can you begin to even allude to that stuff and think that somehow they're going to allow you to print it, make money on it, draw attention to that area.

LW. Christ, I wonder, really, how much they know of what we have or what . . .

PR. Have you heard from anybody from the agency in the last couple of months?

LW. Well, not really.

PR. You know, it's a good thing that I *didn't* turn around and see little guys from the saucer walking up toward me. [*Nervous laughter.*] Much better I was squinting and looking in the distance. The other thing: how could that week really [have] *happened* like that?! It was too—I mean "good" is the wrong word—but to say too good to be true gives an idea.

LW. That's right.

PR. You know, even violating that [RAF Bentwaters security] area . . . as far as *I* was concerned, [the] seven, eight, nine, ten minutes that were very unnerving [were] when we were going across that perimeter area to that grassy knoll where we could look down on PP [Perimeter Post] 18.

LW. Yeah. Yeah, that was.

PR. That was not a healthy place to be! And anybody could have seen us and screamed "Halt," and should have . . . that should have fucked up. You should have had more of a problem when you were picked up by base security.

LW. Yeah.

PR. Instead of, hi, how you doing.

LW. No, they just wanted to know what I was doing . . . said, "Just don't bother anyone."

LW. I fell through a [figurative] trapdoor. Probably had a nervous breakdown where I didn't *stop* functioning.

PR. You know the great Greek tradition of killing the bearer of the bad news . . . I think—and I'm not saying I want out of this—I'm just realizing that this has affected me much more profoundly, at this point, than I could have *ever* imagined.

LW. I've got a psychologist telling me right now that it's posttraumatic this and that.

PR. Doesn't that make all the sense in the world?

LW. Yeah. This has been a nightmare, I'm sure it has been for you in some ways, too.

PR. Yeah, yeah.

LW. But for some reason it's . . . I mean, we'll be fine there.

PR. They told you they won't kill us?

LW. We won't be killed. [*Laughter.*] We won't be killed. I would have . . .

PR. You have the NSA's personal assurance on that? [*Laughter.*]

LW. No, but [*Laughter*], really we're still just . . .

PR. Small potatoes?

LW. Small potatoes. We're guys telling a story and a, we believe it and some nuts believe it and buy the book, hopefully many millions of nuts buy it. It wasn't by chance we saw what we saw over there.

PR. How could it *not* have been? I mean do you feel that, it was as deliberate as, that you were there with me and [they] open the door and launch the things?

LW. Well, I don't know. It's just a feeling. Like I said, you know I got hit for a solid week last year, as I call it, by something, someone, and there has been an interaction for a long time. I can't remember an awful lot of it, thank God. But then the little . . . I mean they came right *up* to us—they came right up to *you*, closer than me. It's just perception, you know? And it was plain as day—you could *hear* them! I mean that was the worst that the . . .

PR. But again, we had the *wind* going like a . . .

LW. Yeah. Oh, I heard them *literally* cracking that kind of brush or whatever, and that's where it caught my eye.

PR. Well, one thing for sure, *especially* if you are fixed on whatever the event is, tunnel vision can set in, and I *know*, as well as I *can* know, that that's exactly what was going on with me.

LW. Yeah.

PR. I have good peripheral vision, but I couldn't see *anything* except what was straight in front of me. If we were looking at almost anything else, I probably would have seen 'em, probably would have.

LW. You probably would have seen the movement; it was, there . . . I can remember what I saw just so damned . . . like the heads and in very dark kind of whatever clothing. But you know, I think these things obviously can take form, and I imagine their true form is something we maybe even, can't even understand.

PR. Yeah. Maybe the one that is presented in 80 percent of the archetypical-type cases is the one that they feel we can generally best handle.

LW. You know, you can cut this down and you're not lying, you're just not telling *everything.* Hey, the government does it every day. Obviously, there's certain things that can't go. It wouldn't be wise for us anyway, we'd be laughed at, completely. The only reason you could know is because of the fact that you *saw* enough. I talked to something, from somewhere else, under, in *full consciousness.* I wasn't manipulated other than the fact I couldn't turn my head. It said some very rational things, no big philosophical crap. You had to see more than just hear my words, you know what I mean? I didn't know how you'd be able to *do* that. I just knew one thing, we had to go to England for you to grasp any of this.

PR. That's right.

LW. And you did. I think back; that was a kind of really exciting time, you know, leading up to it, and when we were leaving.

PR. And how strangely innocent, like, *everything* was . . . before February!

LW. It changes lives.

PR. That's right.

September–October 1988

The *International UFO Reporter* publishes Benton Jamison's "A Fire in the Forest: New Light on the Rendlesham Landing." The author is a professor of mathematics at the State University of New York at Albany with "a longstanding interest in the question of government and military involvement in UFO investigation." In the article, Jamison notes:

> By coming forward, Warren provided not only a new twist to the Bentwaters case and names of previously unidentified participants, but the impetus for CAUS' investigation of the case. That investigation led to CAUS . . . obtaining the Halt memorandum from the Air Force. Had Warren stayed out in the cold, Halt's memo would most probably have stayed in the files.[31]

PART 3
Notes

1. David Jacobs, *The UFO Controversy in America* (Bloomington: Indiana University Press, 1975).
2. Jenny Randles. Minutes of the British UFO Research Association's spring 1984 meeting.
3. Ian Ridpath, ibid.
4. Copy on file. Tape supplied to Colonel Halt by researcher Don Worley. Worley's copy came from Larry Warren. Transcription and credit: Antonio Huneeus.
5. Original drawing on file.
6. *MUFON Symposium Proceedings* (1986).
7. Ibid.
8. Ibid.
9. Ibid.
10. Ibid.
11. Ibid.
12. Ibid.
13. Ibid.
14. Boeche, op. cit.
15. Ibid.
16. Probably referring to authors Jenny Randles, Brenda Butler, and Dot Street.
17. Adrian Bustinza's account to Warren.
18. Earlier in the narrative, it has been established that Larry and a number of the other men involved went gray overnight to varying degrees after the incident.
19. Referring to the sophisticated ultraviolet night-sighting apparatus.
20. The WSA tower was the first location to sight and report the unknown lights on the night in question.
21. After the incident, Warren and other men involved had to call this number daily and report how they were feeling, if they had any dreams, etc. We do not know who exactly this party was, but assume it was an air force-or intelligence-assigned psychologist.
22. "There's only one legend here" is exactly how Mike began. It turned out that there were several other stories of the area they shared.
23. Four months earlier.
24. East End Charlie was, in fact, a German fighter pilot who was unlucky enough to be shot down nearby and captured by enraged villagers, who then burned him alive. His ghost is said to still haunt the surrounding woods.
25. An abandoned tenth-century church at Bentwaters' northwest perimeter.
26. Roosters *do* crow at 10:00 P.M., but only the third scream sounded anything like a rooster.
27. Having the appearance of small, slow, green comets, moving horizontally through the woods and around the trees at slightly increasing angles.
28. A line from the film *Annie Hall.*
29. Referring to the mysterious "wing" that has been seen over Westchester, New York, since 1983.

30. Tapes on file. It was not until January 1991 that I told Larry about these recordings. He heard me out without a word—I thought with great interest, sympathy, and some sadness. After he'd listened to them for himself, he told me that he understood why I'd made them, said that he stood by every word, and again apologized for bringing me into this.

31. *International UFO Reporter* 13, no. 5 (1988), p. 14.

PART 4

COMING TO TERMS

1. | *1989–1990—*
BACK ON TRACK

My life had improved since last October. I found that living in upstate New York was better and safer than living in the city. I had also made some good friends, real people, far removed from show business and UFOs. It had been months since I'd last spoken with Peter, and I often wondered how he was doing. I doubted he still had any interest in writing the book. I knew that I didn't, but I did feel bad about having brought him in so deep. Few could handle all the madness that came with Bentwaters.

My family continued to attribute most of my current problems to Bentwaters, the book, and my obsession with it. For a while I tried to convince them (and myself) that I had given it all up but I hadn't. How could I give up my chance to set the record straight? If I didn't, others would continue to distort Bentwaters.

Few people in Glens Falls knew about my UFO background, and I liked it that way. I continued to have interactions with nonhumans at least every three months. There was really no walking away from it— even if I dumped the book, they would always be with me.

In early March 1989, I drove to Connecticut to visit Cindy. I wanted to let her know I was sorry for all the pain I'd caused her. I wanted to get on with my life and let her get on with hers. It was great to see her again, but bad memories kept the conversation tense. Cin asked if I was still writing the book with Peter. I said I was. She had thought I'd put Bentwaters behind me, and I could see the disappointment on her face as her defenses went up. After we'd said good-bye, I drove away from the house that used to be ours. It was the last time I saw her.

I called Peter that month, and after a few hours, we had the project back on line. We had both needed a break, I guess, but now it was time to get back to work.

Late that month, I visited John Lear at his home near Las Vegas. We were both guests on *Talk of the West*, a popular radio program in that part of the country. The show lasted a record six hours, and many military people called in to offer their support. Then John introduced me to Bob Lazar. Lazar said he was employed by the navy at Groom Lake, a supersecret government test site, deep in the Nellis Range. There were rumors that Groom Lake, or Area 51 as it was also known, housed alien technology. Lazar said the rumors were true. Whatever they had out there, I knew that our government was up to something unusual in the Nevada desert.

In May, I was off to Manhattan with my friend Ray Jett. Ray was attending a trade show at the Javits Center, and I had to get a guitar autographed by Julian Lennon for a promotion my radio station was sponsoring. Overall, the weekend was a good mix of business and pleasure and afforded me a chance to hook up with Peter again.

Ray and I were staying at the Days Inn on West Fifty-seventh Street, very close to Peter's new address. On Saturday, Peter arrived at the hotel with Antonio Huneeus, and we all had a great reunion. Antonio caught me up on all the latest UFO gossip, and once again, we proclaimed it all a hoax. We laughed a lot that day. Now, both Peter and I were excited about getting back to the book.

A mutual friend of Ray's and mine, Gus Russo, was also in town that weekend. Gus was a noted Kennedy-assassination researcher, and after a few hours, I was beginning to see how UFO and JFK-assassination research paralleled each other, at least insofar as the back stabbing and infighting were concerned!

The tension I'd felt with Peter was gone now, which was a relief. In the background, CNN's live coverage of the student resistance in Tiananmen Square was on, and after a while we stopped talking to watch; in our hearts, we were there with them. By the end of that weekend, the Chinese government sent in the army. Many were killed, and frightened old men had won again.

Peter and I still had a lot of research to complete before the book would look like a book. I had never thought the writing would be so hard. By now, most of our respective incomes were tapped by the project. But to us the truth was more important than money.

Soon Peter returned to Suffolk for some follow-up research, again staying with Jan and Tony. When he got back, I was glad to hear that the discoloration at the landing site was still present—this time in the grass rather than the dirt. He also had taken more soil samples for analysis.

Fourth of July weekend 1989, the radio station I was working for was promoting an antique-car show in downtown Glens Falls. The day was hot and humid; working outside was terrible! Later that morning, I thought I heard someone call my name. I looked up Glen Street and didn't see anyone I knew. Then a flash of light caught my eye. There above the First National Bank was a large cylinder—spinning on its axis and surrounded by a black Saturn-like ring. Watching it was difficult because its surface was highly reflective. The sight was amazing. Even time seemed to stand still at one point. On the street, people were uninterested, which seemed strange to me.

Another station employee watched the UFO with me. He had never seen anything like it before. A cloud bank eventually obscured the object from view, but soon two air force F-16s made a grid search over the Glens Falls area. I later learned, secondhand, that the FAA at Warren County Airport had tracked the object; the interceptors were scrambled from Pease AFB in New Hampshire.

By now, some of my friends had seen UFOs and had strange experiences with me. I continued to feel like a lightning rod and didn't like it at all. The year 1989 ended with a traditional New Year's blast at Ray Jett's, but I was frustrated by the lack of completion I felt concerning Bentwaters.

As the first six months of 1990 shot by, I was dating again, but relationships seemed to disintegrate when a woman found out about my UFO experiences. I made the mistake of trying to re-create Cindy in these relationships, but never could. After a number of these experiences, I put my focus back on *East Gate*. It was time to put up or shut up, and a lot of the energy I had lost in New York City had now returned.

By July 1990, divorce and all its negatives had caught up with me. My marriage was legally over, and that brought me down. I had written my first chapters with some hesitation. I knew that reliving the last nine years on paper would mean reliving a lot of the pain. That was going to be part of the challenge for me.

That month, I saw Stevie Ray Vaughan in northern Vermont. He was in the middle of a brief East Coast tour with Joe Cocker. I was glad to see Stevie finally getting the recognition he deserved. Backstage, he asked me how the book was going, I complained a bit about our slow progress, and he told me to hang in there.

He signed some photos for me. I had taken the pictures a few years earlier, and as we looked at them, Stevie said, "Man, Larry, I remember that day. My life was just getting better, and you were on a downward slide. I guess we're both survivors. Get that damned book out, I gotta read it." I promised him he'd get one of the first copies. Stevie smiled, then walked out on stage to the cheers of thousands.

At work a month later, I heard a news flash on the radio. Stevie Ray Vaughan had just been killed in a helicopter crash in East Troy, Wisconsin. He was just short of his thirty-sixth birthday. I was heartbroken. I'd lost a real friend. After attending his funeral in Dallas, I got back on track.

I spoke with Cindy that fall and tried to remain neutral when she told me about her plans to remarry. This news hurt, but at least it gave me some sense of completion. I wished her luck in her new life and tried to move forward with my own.

In late fall of 1990, I began to sift through boxes I'd packed away in 1981, hoping to find anything related to my time at Bentwaters. Tossing my old uniforms aside, I struck gold. There were the records I'd taken when I left the base. They confirmed my presence on D Flight at the time in question. There were also some medical records that confirmed the damage I'd suffered to my eyes in the flash before the UFO had appeared in Rendlesham Forest.

I'd also saved every letter that had been sent to me in the service and the ones I had sent to my mother. After reading through them, I found the one about that night. I also found my mother's reply—she mentioned the UFO in her letter. They were both postmarked January 1981, just after the incident. *This was great,* I thought. In the past, some critics of Bentwaters claimed I hadn't even been involved. These letters would shut them up for good.

Tension in the Middle East had increased with Iraq's invasion of Kuwait, and by all indications we were headed for a war that I strongly opposed. The holidays seemed rather solemn because of it, and I spent a strangely quiet New Year's Eve with friends. As I sat by Ray Jett's fireplace, it hit me that Bentwaters was now ten years past. I really couldn't believe it. At midnight, I raised a glass to Cindy and Stevie Ray, to a better year, and to the men of the Eighty-First Security Police, who turned left at East Gate and were never the same again.

2. | RETURN TO SUFFOLK

The main branch of the New York Public Library (NYPL) was completed in 1911 and still stands as one of the city's most beautiful buildings. It is also one of the world's most extensive research facilities open to the public. My grandfather had introduced me to its splendors when I was five, and now I was back as a regular. My refuge was the enormous second-floor reading room, a place where you could hide and seek at the same time.

Despite my ambivalence toward Left at East Gate, I was still going to the library, doing the background research. Sometimes I would bring my own books to read, but NYPL's newspaper morgue and microfilm files were an endless source of book-related facts and allowed me to focus the search on three favorite topics: the NSA, RAF Bentwaters, and the American presence in East Anglia. Each relevant item was put into treatment form or excerpted, then added to the time line.

Digging up a new fact was all well and good, but what had me going was how these pieces were fitting together. Even now, my notes on the history of the base and its environs were already overshadowed by the supersecret National Security Agency and its presence in the United Kingdom. The past, as they say, is indeed prologue.

In 1942, part of an old East Anglia village is leveled to make way for another American bomber-group base. In January 1943, the area is renamed Bentwaters, *after the old house that had stood on what became the main runway. Woodbridge airfield, under construction a few miles to the south, is completed first and activated that November.*

On 17 April 1944, RAF Bentwaters opens as a unit of bomber command's care and maintenance. The base, or station, is considered surplus to American needs, and work comes to a standstill in June 1944. Even so, the location proves most valuable. Bentwaters is close to the sea and becomes the site of one lifesaving emergency landing after another. In October 1944, Number 11 Group takes over and the station becomes the last RAF facility to assume a wartime operational role in England.

By that December, six units of Mustang III fighters are assigned to the base. These Lancaster bomber escorts fly their final operation against German U-boats off Denmark on 4 May 1945.[1] The base is used for bomber-escort training through August, then reequipped; in October, the first of the RAF's new Meteor III jets arrive.[2] The operational support unit stationed at Bentwaters is withdrawn in August 1949. The base is deactivated on 1 September 1945.

In June 1950, RAFs Lakenheath, Mildenhall, Scampton, and Marham become the first four U.S. Air Force B-29 bases in England. Three of the four are in East Anglia, Suffolk.[3]

The following month, RAF Bentwaters is reactivated on a care and maintenance basis.[4] The base is transferred to the U.S. Air Force in March 1951. The first F-86A Sabre jets in Europe arrive there in September. The planes now constitute the Ninety-first Squadron of the Eighty-first Fighter Interceptor Group, which is redesignated the Eighty-first Fighter Bomber Wing three years later.[5]

On October 24 (1952), President Harry S. Truman scratched his signature on the bottom of a seven-page presidential memorandum addressed to the Secretary of State Dean G. Acheson and Secretary of Defense Robert A. Lovett. Classified top secret and stamped with a code word that was itself classified, the order directed the establishment of an agency to be known as the National Security Agency. It was the birth certificate for America's newest and most secret agency, so secret in fact that only a handful in the government would be permitted to know of its existence.[6]

The National Security Agency comes into existence on election night, 4 November 1952, at 12:01 A.M. exactly. It receives no mention in the news, Congressional Record, Federal Register, *or* Government Organization Manual. *The new agency's ten thousand employees begin work that morning without generating even the hint of a rumor.[7]*

On 13 August 1956, at about 10:55 P.M., British radar operators and air-

traffic controllers in East Anglia observe many inexplicable radar traces crossing their screens. A ground-controlled approach (GCA) radar operator is first to pick up a fast-moving target thirty miles east of RAF Bentwaters. Whatever it is is heading in from the Channel at two thousand to four thousand miles per hour. There is no sonic boom as it passes directly over the base. Moments later, it is thirty miles to the west and beyond all radar contact.

The object is observed from both ground and air positions. One tower operator looks up to see a light "blurred out by its high speed." Ground control then alerts the pilot of an American C-47 flying four thousand feet over Bentwaters. Looking down, the pilot sees a fuzzy light speed by; it is heading toward RAF Lakenheath, and a warning is immediately sent from Bentwaters.

At Lakenheath, American ground observers look west to see several lights grow closer, stop, then exit at high speed. After base personnel watch two white lights approach each other and fly off as a pair, an air force officer telephones the chief controller at RAF Bentwaters. Reporting that something is "buzzing" their airfield, the chief controller has a de Havilland Venom fighter scrambled from RAF Waterbeach and vectored onto the UFO.

As the fighter closes on its target, the thing suddenly disappears and reappears behind the jet. On the ground, American airmen and officers watch the UFO "flip over" and get behind the aircraft. Another Venom fighter is scrambled. Marking its new location, the pilot attempts to maneuver himself behind the UFO but is unsuccessful. The thing departs shortly after.

Lakenheath's GCA radar operators, and radar traffic-control-center operators later testify to having recorded objects traveling at great speeds that had been able to stop instantaneously and alter their course instantaneously.[8]

As part of an NSA global plan, the first of ten COMINT communications-relay centers (CCRCs) is completed at Chicksands in Yorkshire during the autumn of 1956.[9] *In July 1958, the name of the Eighty-first Fighter Bomber Wing is officially changed to the Eighty-first Tactical Fighter Wing. The Bentwaters unit, now fully equipped with F-84s, receives its first F-101 Voodoos in December 1958.*[10]

In 1959, Pennsylvania Democrat Francis E. Walter, chairman of the House UnAmerican Activities Committee, reports:

The special functions of the National Security Agency and the role they play in the security of the United States are so highly sensitive that they are carefully guarded, not only from the public, but from other Government agencies as well. . . . The committee did not attempt to learn the details of the organizational structure or the products of the Agency, feeling it had no need for knowledge in these areas.[11]

In 1959, Congress passes Public Law 83–36. Section 6 of the statute grants the NSA authority to deny its own existence:

> Nothing in this Act or any other law . . . shall be construed to require the disclosure of the organization or any function of the National Security Agency, of any information with respect to the activities thereof, or of the names, titles, salaries or numbers of persons employed by such Agency. [12]

On 9 May 1963: the agency strengthens it control over it's employees:

> A 340 to 40 vote in the House gave the Secretary of Defense the same power [absolute] over NSA employees as the Director of the CIA has over his employees. Under the legislation . . . the Secretary of Defense was authorized to fire NSA employees without explanation and without appeal if he decided they were security risks. [13]

Edwin E. Willis, Louisiana Democrat, defended this bill on the grounds that:

> the NSA carries out the most delicate type of intelligence operations of our government. . . . The National Security Agency plays so highly specialized a role in the defense and security of the United States that no outsider can actually describe its activities. They are guarded not only from the public but from other governmental agencies as well. The Civil Service Commission, which audits all government positions, is not allowed to know what NSA employees do. [14]

Some Americans first learn of the NSA with the 1964 publication of David Wise and Thomas B. Ross's The Invisible Government:

> Probably the most secretive branch of the Invisible Government is the National Security Agency. Even more than the CIA, the NSA has sought to conceal the nature of its activities.
>
> . . . The only official description of its activities is contained in the U.S. Government Organization Manual, which states vaguely: "The National Security Agency performs highly specialized technical and coordinating functions relating to the national security."
>
> [NSA employees] "are subject to lie detector tests on application and intensive security indoctrination on acceptance. Periodically, the indoctrination briefing is repeated and employees are required to sign statements that they have re-read pertinent security regulations."
>
> The NSA has an unusually high rate of mental illness and suicide. [15]

In 1966, in the English Midlands:

Menwith is the most secret and recondite U.S. base in Britain. In a country where there are so many U.S. bases that no political embarrassment attaches to the opening of a new facility, every detail of Menwith Hill's operations have been kept an absolute secret. The official cover story is that the all-civilian base is a Department of Defense communications station [as at Chicksands, NSA facilities are always identified as Department of Defense][16]

The NSA abruptly takes over the tasks of Menwith Hill and Kirknewton inter-ception stations. These takeovers reflect a continuing tension between the NSA and such military agencies as the Air Force Security Service and the Army Security Agency.[17]

In 1968, an NSA employee writes and files a draft for a paper titled "UFO Hypothesis and Survival Questions:"

to consider some of the human survival implications suggested by the various prin-cipal hypotheses concerning the nature of the phenomena loosely categorized as UFO.[18]

Denver, 1969. The 1956 Bentwaters–Lakenheath UFO incident is reviewed by the joint air force/University of Colorado investigation team. After much study and analysis, the sightings are acknowledged as "the most puzzling and unusual case in the radio-visual files." A more detailed study of the incident is then carried out by Dr. James McDonald of the University of Arizona. The physicist concludes that "the apparently rational, intelligent behavior of the UFO suggests a mechanical device of unknown origin as the explanation."[19]

In September 1973, Bentwaters' 81st Tactical Fighter Wing completes its con-version to F-4D Phantoms. The base now also houses F-86Ds armed with "Mighty Mouse" rocket projectiles. The Phantoms are replaced with A-10 tank-buster aircraft in 1978.[20]

In January 1979, Citizens Against UFO Secrecy (CAUS) files a general request with the NSA "for all documents relating to or pertaining to Unidentified Flying Objects (UFOs) and the UFO phenomena." NSA's response acknowledges they are withholding 135 UFO-related documents on national-security grounds.[21]

In the spring of 1979, Chicksands Relay Center in East Anglia is expanded:

to accommodate a new undercover NSA team, working in their own compart-mented-off section of building 600. The team is disguised as DODJOCC—the De-partment of Defense Joint Operations Center, Chicksands. The presence of a civilian NSA team implies either that new developments at Chicksands are concerned in monitoring civilian diplomatic or commercial signals, or that the base's capacity for breaking codes and cyphers on site has been expanded. With over 1,250 military staff alone, Chicksands is the US Air Force's largest non-flying base in Britain.[22]

Autumn 1979, in Albany, New York, Larry Warren enlists in the Air Force.

It was terrific stuff, I thought, but to what purpose? What had become of Left at East Gate*?*

By autumn, the completed manuscript for "Confidential" *was with my close friend and confidante, Linda. Linda edited a scientific journal I'd recently been invited to contribute to and had an innate sense of the seriousness of our subject matter. The jumbled mass of typed and handwritten pages I'd given her in September was returned to me in October, edited and printed out in an edition of three. Alone in my living room, I carefully packed them in boxes, then added to each a set of supporting diskette files, audio tapes, key letters, documents, drawings, photographs, soil samples, a warning/disclaimer, and something approaching a will. The three packages were then placed with reliable parties and for all intents and purposes buried.*

Paranoid behavior? You bet. Overly dramatic? I didn't think so. I had never been more serious about anything in my life. If I did suffer some sort of mental collapse or worse, at least my family and friends would have a record as to why.

Over the preceding sixteen months, I had come to exist in an environment increasingly polluted by anxiety and frustration. But I had to admit that instead of withering in this mix, I had strangely acclimated to it. To be sure, it had changed me, but not necessarily for the worse. And it wasn't all about Larry anymore. Bentwaters had become personal. Unless some credible threat or reason interceded, I would honor my original agreement with Larry. My sense of humor was starting to return. The idea of "recommitting" myself to this book actually made me laugh. But our problems don't vanish with a simple change in attitude, no matter how heartfelt. I still hadn't slept well for a year and a half, and flashbacks of that first night in East Anglia still filled my dreams and waking hours. I knew it was fear that bred these disruptions. It was a fear I was ready to face, but how exactly could I translate that readiness into action?

The preceding spring, Dr. Giuseppe Cammarella, a psychiatrist and medical orgonomist practicing in Nice, France, had invited me to prepare two papers on Wilhelm Reich and UFOs for presentation in Nice in June 1990. I'd be the only speaker on the topic at the Fifth International Conference on the Life and Work of Dr. Wilhelm Reich. I had agreed on the spot. Reich's life and work had fascinated me since I was a teenager, and in recent years, I had done a good deal of relevent research.

Being given such an opportunity sent me into a frenzy of research and rewrites for the journal articles I'd been working on. But by spring of 1990, the papers were almost complete. Now that I was back on the case, this digression was fine with Larry. He also liked the idea hatching out of it. After Nice, I'd fly to Paris for a few days and from there make my way back to East Anglia.

I wrote to Jan and Tony Warnock in late March. Tony wrote back on 6 April 1990: "Delighted to get your letter: thought we had lost you forever. . . . Just turn up—it may mean the floor or the attic but you must come. Forget about any charges, just take us out for lunch one day. . . ." God bless the Warnocks, I thought.

I flew to France with several of the other conference speakers, and our plane arrived at Nice International Airport on Wednesday morning, 13 June. The conference, brilliantly organized by Dr. Cammarella—Joseph—and his wife, Moussia, drew two hundred people from close to twenty nations. While other speakers were put up at one of Nice's three-star hotels, I was given a choice: stay at a hotel with everyone else, or be a house guest of the Cammarellas. I moved in that afternoon and was quickly assimilated into the family.

The next week passed in a swirl of lectures, good company, sight-seeing, eating, drinking, and reflection. Then it was over. Saturday, 23 June, I waved good-bye to the Cammarellas and boarded the morning flight for Paris.

I landed at Orly an hour later. By noon, I'd already settled into my friend Kay's apartment and was out exploring the city's historic Eighteenth District. If I'd been charmed by Nice, I was overcome by Paris. My favorite French ufologist, Jean-Luc Rivera, arranged for Kay (now my simultaneous translator) and me to meet with some French researchers who were interested in Bentwaters. They also updated me on the major UFO wave still in progress over Belgium. Later, Jean-Luc took me out for a Moroccan dinner and introduced me to another quarter of the city. The Metro got me back to the Eighteenth District about midnight.

I wound my way back to rue Lecourbe in a kind or reverie. How could I possibly leave here—and tomorrow? At the moment, my choices appeared simple as a split-screen cartoon. On the left stood Paris, the Riviera, Monaco, and Nice: beautiful women, marvelous architecture, music, great friends, the best food, and a room with a view. On the right side of the screen: black-hole Disneyland. My flight home didn't depart Nice for another eight days. Kay was living with her fiancé, so I had the apartment to myself. I had at least fifteen friends in the city besides Jean-Luc and Kay, and most of them were actresses, so help me. I was leaving all this for what? Yes, I would miss seeing the Warnocks again, but they would understand. So would Larry. I might be obsessed, but I wasn't crazy.

As usual, I didn't sleep well that night, but this insomnia was special. To-night, the usual replays of our 1988 UFO incident were accompanied by an overwhelming desire to be back out in that field, facing Rendlesham Forest, the night, and the fear I had carried with me for over two years. Whether or not it would help to shake the monkey off my back, I had no idea, but by the time I did fall asleep, I wanted to be back in that field more than I wanted to stay in Paris.

The next morning, I boarded the boat to England and passed through Dover customs that afternoon. With no rail complications, I would be arriving at Woodbridge Station near midnight. I dialed the Old House and checked in with the Warnocks. Tony would be there to meet me at the station.

What a grand reunion! We talked all the way back to Eyke. Tea was up when we walked in, and Jan greeted me like the prodigal son. We talked until about one thirty, then turned in. The formal parlor was now my room, and I was delighted with the quarters. A year or two earlier, I would not have believed I could feel so, but it felt great to be back.

The next four days were extremely productive. With the help of my friends, I revisited Rendlesham Forest, the Oxford lighthouse, the site of Jan and Tony's UFO incident, the village of Butley, the Woodbridge perimeter, and RAF Ben-twaters. Pete Warnock and I even had a Coke at the base Burger King. Some airmen sat and talked at the table Larry and I had shared with Airman Mike that night in February 1988—the night I had returned to face.

I went back to Capel Green twice. First with Jan and Tony, and two days later with Pete. The field was now full of tall grass, almost all of which had already gone to hay. Outstanding in this lake of yellow were several still-green areas. The most pronounced patch was roughly oval and corresponded exactly with the soil discoloration we'd observed and photographed in 1988. New pic-tures were taken, and fresh soil samples packed up for the return.

Late Friday afternoon found a rather depressed me sitting in the Warnock's garden. I'd be leaving for London tomorrow, but still hadn't revisited that damned stretch of field. Tonight was my last chance, and I wasn't jumping at it. Each day, I planned my visit for that night, and each night I'd put it off until the next day. Now, my time was running out.

A voice brought me out of these thoughts. "Something wrong?" I looked up to see Richie and Pete standing there. "Actually, yes," I said, and proceeded to fill them in. My friends heard me out in silence, then offered a suggestion. "Would it help," Pete asked, "to have some company along?" "Yes, it would help to have some company!" Both volunteered on the spot and suggested we invite three friends of theirs whom I'd already met. "The more the merrier," I said. They made the necessary calls, and the plan was set. The five of us would wait until dark, then drive out toward the base.

Simon, Simon, and Paul pulled into the drive about 9:30. By ten, Simon one was negotiating his Austin through the tractor opening in the windbreak, the only place a vehicle could enter that field. He drove the car another fifty feet in, turned off the lights, and killed the engine: we had parked not fifteen feet from the RAF Bentwaters perimeter fence line. The six of us moved out into the darkness.

The ground was furrowed, and you had to lift your feet as you walked. We began just as Larry and I had, hiking along the inside of the windbreak, then establishing a position facing the forest. There it was: the tree line so familiar that I saw it in my sleep.

We scanned the distance for any sign of motion or activity, but all was still. Then we began to talk. My companions had all been students when the story broke and recalled the news blitz well. What exactly had brought me back to this place, one of the Simons asked. What had really happened out here in 1988? I was carrying the recorders Larry and I had with us that night, and the first of the tapes we'd made here. I walked the guys out toward the middle of the field, stopped, and set the scene for them. Despite the gentle weather, I was shaking as I pushed the play button.

The tape's effect on us was instantaneous; something like listening to a campfire ghost story, except that the ghosts had been here and were visible to the tellers as they spoke. Location, audio, the hour—it was the chance I'd wanted, and I was taking it. I could stop the recording whenever I wanted, but who wanted to? I let the tape run.

By the time I turned it off, we had all had enough. It was time to start back to the car. I felt great: with the help of these lads, I had faced the fear.

Momentarily lost in self-congratulation, I looked up to notice the others had left me some distance behind. But why had they stopped a dozen yards short of the car? Why weren't they going on? Looking past them, I understood why. Two tall, camouflage-clad air force security cops were checking our vehicle. One was examining the hood area, while the other stood by the boot. Both were armed and now looking at us. My friends and I stared at the SPs. No one moved for several long seconds, then I started toward the car.

If there was a problem here, it was my problem, and these guys should not have to be dragged into it. They lived here, for God's sake. I'd simply explain . . . wait a minute, what was I thinking? I was a walking amateur spy shop. Notebook, pens, compass, knife, two recorders (both holding very interesting tapes), and my Nikon with telephoto lens and high-speed film. If that wasn't enough to enliven an interrogation, maybe my shortwave radio would put it over the top.

I walked to within six feet of the sentries, made eye contact with the one by the hood, nodded, and waited for him to say something.

But nothing was said. We just stood there facing each other. Then the SP took a step back from the hood. That was it. It was over. Both men now moved off toward the perimeter, and we got back into the Austin without a word. Simon one turned the key and began backing up. The cops stayed in our headlights, not taking their eyes off us. We rolled back onto the road, turned, and headed toward Simon two's house in an explosion of loud giddiness. Back at the Old House, it was tea and talk into the wee hours.

The next afternoon, Richie stopped by to tell us that the break we'd entered the field through had been sealed. A crate big enough to hold a tractor now blocked the way. Apparently, no one would be following our tracks in for some time.

I left for London that evening. Four train rides, one Channel crossing, and a taxi ride later, I blearily lifted the latch on the Cammarellas' gate and walked down the drive to a hug and a kiss from Moussia, breakfast, and about five hours sleep. We spent the afternoon sight-seeing around Nice, and Joseph joined us for dinner that night. Twenty-four hours later, I was back in New York, sleeping better than I had in over two years.

3.

1989 DEVELOPMENTS

March 1989

The night before flying to Nevada, Larry Warren telephones Peter Robbins. Some of the business at hand is rather blunt:

LW. If, for any reason, something ever happened to me, Ok? And I'm not being dramatic, but if anything ever did . . . I am going to write a thing on this letter that this, my signature, immediately turns the entire, you know, should you want to do it. It's only up to you, however way you want to handle it.

PR. I think that's a sober and straightforward thing to do.

LW. I know my family wouldn't. You know, they just wouldn't be able to do it.

PR. Yes, I understand that.

LW. But, uh, you're the only person that can do it, if you want.

PR. So when do you leave?

LW. Tomorrow morning. I'm going to go out of Kennedy, and I can catch an 8:40 on America West, I've never heard of that airline.

PR. Well, as long as they've got a plane, that's good.

LW. And if it's black and unmarked, I can . . . (*Laughter.*) Or if it has no wings . . .

PR. Safety first! (*Laughter.*) It's one of our new round planes, you'll
like it.

LW. Try it, you'll like it.[23]

March 1989
Phoning from Nevada, Warren tells Robbins:

LW. I'm seeing stuff you won't believe out here, this is *amazing*. Peter,
I am—let me tell you what—a certain place?

PR. Yeah.

LW. . . . is . . .

PR. Buzzing.

LW. It, well, it is, I have to be very careful.

PR. I understand.

LW. They're there, and [*flustered*]—it's amazing—it really is.

PR. It sounds a lot like East Anglia area.

LW. Yep. Peter, you just won't imagine what is going on.

PR. Did you see stuff clearer than we saw?

LW. No. Kind of at a clip, ten miles. The whole area is amazingly
active, and I've talked to a few people and, oh, it's fascinating,
fascinating what's going on, what they have here. Nellis Air Force
Base is right down the road.

PR. Yes.

LW. But this area is bizarre. I know John [Lear] would like to talk to
you, will you be around tomorrow at any . . .

PR. I will.

LW. I'm watching a video right now of a regressive hypnosis of one
of these employees at Sandia.[24]

PR. I appreciate that it's difficult for you to talk.

LW. Well, I just wanted to tag with you. He is always unsure of his
phone situation, especially now with something that was, what
happened last night. I just don't know what the hell the situation
is on the phone. They're flying there and as real as the chair I'm
sitting in.[25]

25 April 1989
Today's *East Anglian Daily Times* carries an interview with Ron West, an
investigator with the British UFO Research Association. Based on his
twenty years' experience in the field, West firmly believes that East

Anglia is an important area for UFOs in Europe. "Part of the explanation is because of the high concentration of military airbases here."

A related article, "Glowing Object Seen at Airbase," appears on the next page:

> East Anglia's most famous UFO incident happened in Rendlesham Forest outside RAF Woodbridge in late 1980. Six witnesses have claimed that on December 27, 28 and 29 a strange spacecraft landed in Rendlesham Forest and, according to some sources, contact was made between base Commander Gen. Gordon Williams and three aliens.
>
> This apparently preposterous story is given credibility by the publication of a memo written by Lt. Col. Charles Halt to the British Ministry of Defence on January 13 1981. . . . To further reinforce the case a tape was released to [the] authors of *Sky Crash*, which they say records the panic and awe in the voices of Col. Halt and his colleagues on the night of December 29/30. . . .
>
> In October 1984 EADT reporter John Grant spoke to Col. Sam Morgan, a former commander at Woodbridge, who testified to the authenticity of the tape.[26]

5 May 1989

In New York City, Peter Robbins has succeeded nicely in estranging all but the most tenacious of his old friends. Memories of the week in England with Larry are rarely far from his thoughts. That evening, he records another of his phone conversation with Larry:

PR.　I know I was in shock at that point from just what we were seeing in the distance, all of the things off and flying around, and the thing that looked like a car with three tail lights . . . even the cops pulling up and watching. On the tape I say to you, are you sure there's not a town behind there? We knew it was just woods, but it was like several football fields of light coming straight up and, like a big door opened. Part of me says it couldn't have been a big door *really*, but the other part of me says, well, "It's one thing to say you've seen a light in the night sky, it's another thing to say you've seen the forest floor open up and just, a quarter mile of magnesium lights come flying up into the sky!"

LW.　Right! (*Laughing*)

PR.　[I] could have made [you] *prove*, in no uncertain terms, that the NSA connection was real. [I] could have said, "Larry, I *insist* on a meeting with one of these guys." And I said to myself after sleeping on it, "When you cross that barrier and you sit down with one of these hard-faced son of a bitches and he looks at you, it's a different ball game. *You're not in the same league.*" So there's a part of me, I guess, that will always be able to say, I believe Larry, but if I'm ever pushed to it . . . I mean anything can be stage managed.[27]

26 September 1989
From journalist Antonio Huneeus's interview with Jenny Randles:

AH.   What are your current conclusions on what really happened on the Bentwaters case?

JR.   I think that the Bentwaters case involved a real UFO incident. For quite a lot of time, I was delving into the idea that what had probably happened was some kind of catastrophic failure of some system; maybe they'd been testing a Star Wars weapon, which is very feasible in one of the bases around the forest. There, they do lots of top-secret electronic-warfare research, so that was perfectly feasible. This went wrong, and [they] tried to hide it with the story of the crashed UFO. They couldn't keep secret the fact that some event had occurred, so what better than to come out with a crazy story of a crashed UFO and spaceship and leak that out to UFO investigators, whom they hoped would then [give it] to the media, and the whole story would die out very quickly. For a long time, I thought that was the most likely option.

However [I] talked to people directly involved, including one of the key eyewitnesses. We did discuss options, such as possible mind-warp experiments, in the sense that the men had been deliberately put into some kind of situation where they were induced to experience a UFO landing for psychological-warfare testing. It would be a very useful weapon if you had the means[to] make the enemy believe that aliens had landed right in the midst of a battle. Obviously, they would test it first on their own people, and they would have to do it covertly. On the other hand, the witness seemed to be very fairly convinced that he was dealing with a real UFO incident.

The thing [he] found most difficult to comprehend is when he faced this phenomenon, it was so awesome, so out of this world, so different from everything you've ever faced before, that you don't have mental concepts to deal with it. There was a ring of truth about what he said to me, and I think it's perfectly possible that what occurred was a genuine UFO event because of the way [it] was experienced by all these people, because of the diplomatic problems which ensued, the U.S. Air Force had no idea how to handle it. They had no idea how to report it; it occurred on British civil land, not on the base, and therefore they were [in trouble] by being in the area in the first place. There were some degree of problems that occurred between the British and American governments. Although the British civilian police were called, they didn't do anything about it. By the time the incident was followed up by the air force and they'd sent intelligence officers to take the radar tapes away from a British radar base, the British people probably suddenly turned around and said, "What's been going on? We don't know anything about this."

AH.   So you're saying that this diplomatic situation tended to complicate things further?

JR.   Yeah.[28]

9 October 1989

The Tass news agency issues a press release. It begins:

Confirmed UFO Landing in Voronezh, Witnesses Frightened.
9/10 TASS 20
Scientists have confirmed that an unidentified flying object recently landed in a park in the russian city of Voronezh.
They have also identified the landing site. . . .

The incident is made credible by the findings of Russian investigators. International news coverage is massive.

The Pentagon classified ten million new secrets this year.[29]

4. 1990–1992— DEVELOPMENTS

The astonishing thing would be if they did not exist.
Jean Cocteau[30]

Voters view national security as the single most important
quality in a president and they have always been unwilling
to take risks with it.
Robert Teeter, political adviser to President Bush[31]

Speaking at a 1990 State Department security symposium, National Security Council legal adviser Nicholas Rostow bluntly notes:

My experience with the National Security Agency is never, never—we don't exist, we don't collect, we don't know, nobody knows anything—and if there is a bullet coming at the head (of the president) of the United States, then we can tell you precisely what time it is going to arrive.[32]

28 August 1990

Professor Yuri Lozotsev replies to a letter from Peter Robbins. The Russian writes from Voronezh, USSR, where he is an associate professor of engineering. He is also a respected UFO researcher. Lozotsev coauthored *UFOs in Voronezh* and was one of the original investigators of Voronezh's 1989 UFO incident. Robbins had earlier sent the professor a number of UFO-related documents, but only one is singled out in Lozotsev's response: .

> My special gratitude is for the [Halt] document [on the] Bentwaters incident. It is significant that the [Russian] landings that are most known outside the U.S.S.R. . . . also caused heightened radiation. It was less than in England (maximum 0.04 milliroentgens) and recorded in one of the four depressions. . . . This aperture had the diameter of approximately 25 mm and the depth of 370 mm. . . . It is [a] striking fact that the initial shape and dimension of the depressions were perfectly identical to England. . . . The visible form and dimension of Voronezh and Bentwaters vehicles were also alike. . . . [33]

17 May 1991

> The U.S. Air Force yesterday announced the closure of two more bases in Britain, reducing the number of active operating stations in this country to four. . . .
> The neighboring bases of Bentwaters and Woodbridge in Suffolk, home for the 81st Tactical Fighter Wing, with 72 A-10 "tank-buster" aircraft, are to be handed back to the Ministry of Defence by September 1993. The bases . . . employ 3,929 US military personnel, 993 US civilians and 339 British civilians. There are 5,391 American dependants. . . .
> The withdrawal from Bentwaters and Woodbridge had been rumored locally for some time . . . the two bases contributed a total of 45 million to the local economy last year. John Gummer, the Agriculture Minister, whose Suffolk Coastal constituency includes the two bases, said a meeting had been arranged between himself, the Suffolk Coastal District Council and the Defence Ministry to discuss the implications.[34]

Security restrictions on America's classified F-117A Stealth Fighter are lifted high enough for the public to catch a well-staged glimpse of the remarkable aircraft. Even the Stealth's flash—the patch worn by its pilots—is remarkable: a symmetrical, black, highlighted *thing* centered on a burst pattern with F-117A embroidered across the top and TEAM STEALTH across the bottom. Viewed straight on, Stealth looks like nothing so much as a UFO.

Robbins sees a picture of the flash, then compares it to two drawings; they are in the notebook he'd taken to England in 1988. On the afternoon Warren was detained by Bentwaters security, he had seen a pilot wearing an unfamiliar flash on the pocket of his flight suit. Warren had described it as looking like a UFO on a pattern with lettering above and below.

Robbins had then sketched something in his notebook and handed it to Warren. "Was this what it looked like?" he had asked. "No, like this," Warren had replied, making his own depiction.

That sketch had continued to bother the researcher. He had had nothing but Warren's word that such a flash existed. It was not that Robbins hadn't believed his coauthor. The question had simply remained open: what, exactly, *had* that image been? Comparing that drawing to the photo suggested that Warren saw a Team Stealth flash.

24 August 1991
The community room of The Glens Falls National Bank hosts a slide presentation on Bentwaters this Saturday afternoon. The speakers are Warren and Robbins. The *Post-Star* sends a reporter, who writes up the talk later that afternoon, then files it with his editor. He also puts it on the wire service. The article appears in Sunday's newspaper. It also appears in almost seventy other papers around the country.

Several towns away, a husband and wife read the article in the *Post-Star*, then dial information. Does the operator have a listing for a Larry Warren in the area, possibly in Glens Falls? Yes. The husband writes down the number, thanks the operator, then dials.

Larry interrupts a conversation with Peter to answer the phone. Howard, the man on the line, wants to know if this is the Larry Warren in the article. Larry tells him it is. Both Howard and his wife, Grace, are air force veterans who met and married in the service. Both had been sergeants stationed at Bentwaters and very much want to speak with Warren, but not over the phone. They are invited over and arrive within the hour.

The couple were assigned to Bentwaters in 1982 and posted off the following year. For some of that time, Grace had also been billeted at Woodbridge. They had heard about the UFO incidents but wanted to know more. She went on to describe having seen what sounded like a round landing mark near the Woodbridge perimeter line. Additionally, Grace had seen, then asked one of the hangar personnel about, an entranceway inside one of the secured, hardened hangars on Woodbridge. All she was told was that it led down below the structure; to what, she never learned.

Howard tells the writers about the puzzling suicide of a popular captain who'd been found hanging by his young wife. Howard added that, while people take their lives for many reasons, it had been common knowledge on base that Bentwaters had the highest incidence of suicide in NATO. Warren shows the couple what he has of his military record. Howard zeros in on the codes: *they're all wrong.* "Someone screwed you," he says to Larry, "None of these codes apply to anything!"

Later, Robbins sets up the carousel projector in the kitchen, and all view the images projected on the wall. The last slide on the wheel is of a Reich cloudbuster. "Do either of you," asks Larry, "ever remember seeing anything like that on base?"

"Sure," answers the husband without missing a breath, "but it was larger and trailer mounted." Where had he seen it? By the Bentwaters flight line. Larry Warren is no longer a lone witness; someone else remembers seeing a cloudbuster at RAF Bentwaters.

8 September 1991
During a question-and-answer session at a UFO conference in Arizona, Roger L. Scherrer asks Bentwaters witness John Burroughs a question "regarding his freedom to speak out publicly, and how regulations within the UCMJ and JANAP might affect his statements." John Burroughs says he still speaks with the public relations officer of the Department of the Air Force any time he is going to speak out about the Bentwaters-Rendlesham Forest December 1980 incident.[35]

January 1992
A statement from Bentwaters researcher Ray Boeche:

> In early 1992, conversations were held between myself and two researchers, alleging to work for the government of the United States. According to these men, projects were being carried out on teleportation, healing . . . , remote viewing,

and the development of electronic systems able to interpret and record the wave-forms of thoughts, enabling them to be recorded and transmitted. . . .

They detailed their research into so-called psychotronic weapons, and explained that many UFO incidents were a result of psychotronic testing. According to their story, the Bentwaters incident involved the projection of an actual physical, three-dimensional object, which could and did interact with its environment, but was created and controlled by individuals involved in this research.

. . . The presentation seemed very much "scripted," as if they were presenting material memorized from a master script, and was deliberately slow enough to allow me to take notes verbatim, except for portions when I was told to cease writing. The probability of disinformation here seems very high—why shift the emphasis on Bentwaters to psychotronic warfare? It seems like a bizarre cover story to use. . . .

. . . The author has ample reason to suspect that, early on in his research, he was the subject of rather close government scrutiny. Who conducted this investigation remains a mystery, but one government official stated that his office had a file on the author that was "huge." Some of the witnesses still maintain a stony silence regarding what happened to them in the forest, and refuse to engage in any discussion whatsoever.[36]

7 February 1992
Statement by Colonel Donald M. Ware, retired, USAF:

I was working in HQ USAFE/XPP during the Woodbridge/Bentwaters incident. I was not aware of it at the time. However, several years later, after I retired, a friend who worked closely with people in USAFE/DO (Operations) was shown by me LTC Halt's letter of 13 Jan 81 to RAF/CC. He told me that there was considerable excitement concerning that base in a particular office within the DO at that time. That office was the likely one to be concerned with such an incident and he felt the UFO incident must have been the cause.

. . . I think I should not name the particular officer I spoke with or the particular office he mentioned.[37]

23 June 1992
In New York City, Robbins is about to place a call to Virginia. Assorted paperwork is spread in front of him; prominent is an original air force file-bound printout of Warren's USAF U.K. computer whip sheets. They note dates on which Larry did what, was qualified in what, and was posted where. Robbins certainly has no question about their authenticity; Warren had taken them from the air force in 1981. Robbins checks

the wire running between the telephone and recorder, pushes on, and takes a deep breath: he has waited almost five years to make this call. The number is then dialed, and a phone rings in the home of Charles Halt:

CH. Hello.

PR. Mr. Halt?

CH. Yes.

PR. This is Peter Robbins, calling from New York.

CH. Oh, Peter Robbins! How are you? I've looked forward to talking to you.

PR. Same with me. Did I pick a good time to call?

CH. Oh, that's fine, I can talk for about ten minutes or so.

PR. How long have you been retired, sir?

CH. About a year.

PR. Is it all right with you if I record this?

CH. Go ahead.

PR. I know that men who were involved are countering each other's accounts, and you've been very outspoken about what Larry says his participation was in that, and I just wanted . . .

CH. His participation *wasn't.*

PR. Why do you say that?

CH. Because he didn't come on duty until the middle of January, and I can show you documentation to prove that.

PR. Well, obviously, I would like to see it, I'm sitting here with some of his service record in front of me.

CH. Oh, you got his service record, good. Where did you find them? I'm curious.

PR. We're going to publish that, I actually can't say right now, although he did leave the service with some of his records. He actually left . . .

CH. I guess the question I'm asking you, did you get something from Saint Louis?

PR. No.

CH. Ok, that's the question I'm asking you because it has a bearing on other things I might tell you or say.

PR. Fair enough.

CH. I'm not playing a game with you, I'll be very up front.

PR. I appreciate it. One of the things I have here is his assignment to D Flight, 2 December 1980.

CH. That's probably correct. When did he arrive at Bentwaters?

PR. Shortly before that.

CH. Ok, now let me tell you this: there's a six-to eight-week training period where one does not get a radio, a gun, a posting, or anything till one has finished *all* of the training. Would you behlieve that?

PR. Well, I have . . .

CH. And I can produce a hundred witnesses can tell you that, including his supervisor, who I've just talked to, numerous times.

PR. Who was his supervisor?

CH. I'm not going to mention because he requested not to be identified.

PR. What I notice here is the indication at the bottom in Lee Swain's handwriting, "Airman Warren will be posted to duty roster, 'D' Flight, ten December 1980. Intro training will commence 5–12–80." And you're saying that training would have gone on into January?

CH. Six to eight weeks.

PR. Um hum.

CH. And I can assure you, as the deputy base commander, no cop picked up a weapon, picked up a radio, or was given a post until they completed training. I *guarantee* you. NATO came in and evaluated and looked at the records, and they pulled everything from medical records, dental records, the whole works. And we *knew* that up front. That was an ongoing thing.

PR. Well . . .

CH. What I'm trying to tell you is he's a fraud.

PR. *Well* . . .

CH. I don't think he knows he is.

PR. Why do you say that? That's kind of a strange statement to make.

CH. I'm not going to tell you on tape. I'll tell you personally.

PR. I see. Well, let me ask you . . .

CH. You've got a problem, I'm telling you that right up front.

PR. Um hum. Well, I certainly will look forward to seeing some of the stuff.

CH. You should have talked to Larry Fawcett. He figured it all out, or most of it. He didn't get it all, but he figured a lot of it out.

PR. Uh-huh. I've been in touch with Barry Greenwood [Fawcett's coauthor]. He *hasn't* figured it out?

CH. I don't know.

PR.   What you're saying, I can't have any corroboration until I get myself down to your neck of the woods, unless you're willing to send me some of these papers.

CH.   No, I'm not going to send you anything. You'll have to come down here and talk to me.

PR.   Ok. Shortly after the incident, Larry was requested to appear at the medical facility, 2 February '81. The clinic that he is to appear at is the optical retinal clinic, and the reason given here is burn slash EXP, retinal burn exposure.

CH.   In February?

PR.   February second.

CH.   I don't challenge that at all. Why if somebody was exposed to something in December would one wait until February to . . .

PR.   Oh, he didn't wait! He reported it immediately and that was the appointment that he got.

CH.   What do his medical records say? They're available.

PR.   I haven't gotten the records. There's an awful lot of stuff I'm still pulling together. Can I ask you some peripheral stuff on the incident itself?

CH.   Sure.

PR.   In the mid-eighties, Mr. Ray Boeche made contact with you.

CH.   I don't remember him, but go ahead.

PR.   He wrote a paper that anyone familiar with this work knows. It was published in the proceedings of the MUFON symposium.

CH.   But I don't subscribe to that.

PR.   Well, let me read you an excerpt here: "From what began as a very negative response to our request for help, Senator Exon left us with an open-ended opportunity to provide him with further . . ."

CH.   Ok, he *did* call me, I remember the name now, he's the guy that pestered me to death, and he went to Exon, I can tell you that. Exon staffers called me and said we've got this guy driving us half crazy, in so many words, and would you provide us some information? I said, I'll be happy to talk to the senator, have him call me. The senator called me and I talked with the senator, and I was very frank, very open, very honest, on at least two if not three occasions.

PR.   Let me read you what he [Boeche] published here: "I placed a call to Colonel Charles I Halt, on ten April, 1985. I gave the colonel my name and told him that I was a UFO researcher who was attempting to provide Senator Exon with more information on the Bentwaters incident.''

CH.   Actually he was haranguing the senator, I found out later from the staffers.

PR.   Um hum. ''Halt told me he would be quite willing to discuss the matter with Senator Exon. Halt gave me the impression of being quite cordial and open to discussion of the case, and I was led to ask several questions of my own. I asked him about the existence of soil samples and about plaster casts of the landing marks which were alleged to have been made. Halt said that he had one of the soil samples, quote, on my desk in front of me . . . and in regard to the plaster casts, I don't have them here, but I could get my hands on them without much trouble.''

CH.   It is more trouble, but I know where they are.

PR.   [*Laughs.*] Ok.

CH.   I do have the soil samples, yes.

PR.   Ok, that's certainly not a big deal, it's not a concern of mine. ''Halt's most significant statement was when I told him that I had talked with an officer who stated that Colonel Williams was there, and was driven back to Bentwaters with film of the landed UFO. In response to this Halt said, quote, yes, I can verify that for the Senator. I could substantiate that for him.''

CH.   And that's not true. I never told him that. I told him that Williams was never there. The only . . .

PR.   So that's an *absolute* lie.

CH.   Well . . .

PR.   I mean let's . . .

CH.   . . . or misunderstanding.

PR.   Well, this is a quote—with quotation marks.

CH.   I would *never* have said that because Gordon Williams is a very personal friend of mine to this day and was not there. Was *never* there, was never at the site. When he found out about the incident, he was very interested, I mean to the point where he said, ''Hey, you've got to get me into this next time. I want to be involved. Call me the next time you know anything—get me there.'' In fact, some things happened later that I called him. Gordon Williams was *never, never* there, and he will tell you that personally.

PR.   Oh, I'm sure he *will.*

CH.   I've never told anybody that. *Warren's* the only one that's ever said that.

PR.   No, that's not true.

CH.   That's what I know. You may know some other people. I confronted Gordon Williams two days later, on Saturday morning, I believe. It was the tape; he went into shock almost. He said, may I borrow the tape and take it to play at General Basie's, who was then third air force commander. [Williams is] to the point now, he won't talk to anybody.

PR.   I don't blame him. He *never* talked to anybody about this. He . . .

CH.   He talked to me at great length on a number of occasions.

PR.   . . . in the research community is what I mean, not . . .

CH.   Well, you all don't have a good reputation, not you personally, but there's a lot of people in the fringes, should I say.

PR.   Yeah. The question I wanted to ask you: the release of what's become known as the Halt document, are you aware, specifically, of how that found its way out into the . . .

CH.   I sure am. I could explain to you in great detail. In fact, I can remember all the players but one's name.

PR.   Ok, I want to see if there's any similarity to the account that *I* have. If you tell . . .

CH.   You tell me your account, and I'll tell you what, where you err.

PR.   Ok. In late 1982, Larry Warren met Larry Fawcett. By early '83, Larry [Warren] gave him an extended statement—and *only* Larry—Warren that is. It involved the approximate time of the incident.

CH.   Which incident? There are three nights.

PR.   Correct. And he gave as much information as he could including location, names of people who were present. *That* was what Larry Fawcett and CAUS instituted as a Freedom of Information Act action. The result was the release of the document that you had signed. Does that match your understanding, or is there something that I've been, that I have wrong there?

CH.   Mmm.

PR.   I mean that there was *nobody else* involved in making a statement that led to the release of that document, *except* for Larry Warren.

CH.   I don't know. I don't.

PR.   Ok.

CH.   I know how the document came to be . . . not public knowledge, but somewhat *common* knowledge in circles you run in. I gave *one* copy, the original copy that Squadron Leader Don Moreland, who was the RAF liaison officer, after discussing at great length over a period of several weeks. [I asked]. "What does your government want? Do they want anything?" He was very interested, he didn't know, he couldn't get a straight story. I gave him the original letterhead copy, kept a file copy, and it became a non-event so to speak.

PR. Um, yes.

CH. If the British government didn't want to pursue it, I was not going to pursue it. After all, we were guests in their country.

PR. You bet.

CH. We had to respect their sovereignty and their authority.

PR. And it happened off base.

CH. And it happened off the installation. We actually trespassed, with what we did.

PR. Yes, I understand that.

CH. What happened was the copy went to the MOD, but Don Moreland sent a copy, we would call it a boot leg copy, sent it to or *through*, I don't know which, his superior, who was the Third Air Force. Somehow, a copy stayed in Third Air Force, either in his superior's office or in some curiosity seeker's office, and *resurfaced*, several years later, and somebody talked to somebody who talked to somebody. Third Air Force called me and said, what should we do? I said my personal suggestion is *burn* the thing. I don't want all the publicity.

PR. I can't imagine that it was pleasant for you, God knows, to be stuck . . .

CH. Oh, you don't know the *half* of it.

PR. Oh, I don't know the *quarter* of it.

CH. I could write a book on what happened after *that*.

PR. I know that I have no idea of what it's like being you . . .

CH. I said, do me a favor, burn it. And he said, no, we have to release it under the Freedom of Information Act. You have to understand, I was in a primary zone for colonel then, I didn't need all that publicity because, believe me, despite what Dot Street and Jenny Randles and Brenda Butler said, *it did not help me, at all.*

PR. At no point did you feel that this stuff was so *profoundly* important that it *should* be released?

CH. You have to understand where I'm coming from. I have to respect the British government, their sovereignty, and what was happening there, and impact on them.

PR.   What did you think of the *Unsolved Mysteries* treatment of the incident?

CH.   Ah . . . I had some control over it, I'll be very frank with you. They did a pretty fair job. I have learned some things since then that there were a couple of people [who] appeared, one particular person that, uh, may have a, *I can't discuss it on the telephone with you.*

PR.   [*Blunt and straightforward.*] You feel that Larry *totally* fabricated his involvement in this.

CH.   *I* think Larry has been influenced, and I will say no more. By himself, his past experiences, or some agency. I'm going to leave it at that.

PR.   Um hum. Are you aware that there's this phenomena reported of people allegedly being abducted by other intelligences, other beings and that kind of . . .

CH.   I've heard that, I have no firsthand knowledge.

PR.   And you are saying that you have no firsthand knowledge of that happening, in any way involved with this incident, with any of the men on base?

CH.   No.

PR.   Ok.

CH.   However, I suspect some things happened afterward. I have documented all this and left it at a distant location with reliable sources.

PR.   One of the things that happened there I was curious to know your impressions of. Ray Boeche was approached by two men who flashed some credentials that were described to me as CIA, and they took him aside and said, Mr. Boeche—and I'm parahphrasing, of course—you're a researcher in this, you're a guy with a good reputation, we want to set you straight on something so you won't embarrass yourself later. A psychotronic experiment was performed that night. We have technology to create interactive holograms, and what this was was a test of responses and . . .

CH.   The answer to that is BS.

PR.   Yeah, that's what I . . .

CH.   In fact, I had a knock-down-drag-out with Jacques Vallee, you probably know of him.

PR. Oh, yes, he singles Larry Warren out and says this is a man who is believable, who genuinely feels what . . . [38]

CH. I don't dispute what you just said, about "genuinely feels."

PR. Ok. He was involved in another one of our government's experiments?

CH. I will tell you this: Larry Warren was not a player. Larry Warren was in the background, picked up information, and put things together. And I think Larry Warren has been influenced, and I'll leave it at that.

PR. Are you aware, that the morning *after* the incident, he called his mother from a base phone . . .

CH. Yes, I'm aware of that.

PR. . . . and that there is a witness?

CH. Many, many people had phones disconnected there because the telephone system is very antiquated.

PR. That's not the question. If he is fabricating, for whatever reason, he *began* the very next morning. We do have a witness, who was also a security cop.

CH. I don't dispute it. I have no idea, he may *have*, if he says he did, maybe he did.

PR. [Larry] wrote her [his mother]. Shortly after, she wrote him back—in fact, her letter is dated within two days of your memo, so that if, for whatever reason, he was spinning this out of whole cloth, he was doing it within twelve hours of the last incident on the third night. That's curious to me. Literally before lunch, the next morning, he was on the phone to the States telling his mom that he had been involved in this.

CH. It's very simple to explain: the cop dormitories were going *crazy* with talk. I mean, they were literally running up and down the halls.

PR. You've got paperwork there that supposedly will set me straight on this.

CH. I've got witnesses, too.

PR. Um hum, we have witnesses, too. Adrian Bustinza for one.

CH. Ah, not very credible. Be careful.

PR. Oh? Adrian's also fabricating that he was with Larry that night?

CH. Adrian's over his head. Adrian doesn't want to do too much.

PR. Of *course* not, but he was right there next to Larry and that machine of undetermined origin and beings. So Adrian has also, apparently, been influenced, as you say?

CH. I can't comment.

PR. Uh-huh. Ok.

CH. But some *very* funny things have happened, that's all I'm going to say.

PR. Well, I guess this leaves us at a dead heat.

CH. It's called disinformation. I think you understand it.

PR. But again, it's also called lying, if the disinformation . . .

CH. Not if one doesn't believe they're lying.

PR. I see. You think Larry has been, shall we say, brainwashed, as far as this goes.

CH. You said that, I didn't.

PR. OK, but . . .

CH. I don't know. I've never met Larry.

PR. I do want to ask you though, do you feel that there is any chance that *you* have been misled as to Larry's involvement.

CH. No, I don't think so. I will tell you this, if you publish the book with disinformation, I'm going to go back to the publisher and I will make some noise about it 'cause there's . . . I think you're being used. Honestly I do, and I'm just going to tell you that right now. For what it's worth.

PR. Um hum. Well, it's certainly not the first time I've heard it.

CH. No. I have talked to enough of the other players that are far enough removed on the peripheral, but knew who was involved and knew enough about it to know there's some funny things afoot.

PR. Would you be willing to sit down with Larry *and* me, in Washington if we can get down there . . .

CH. Sure, come on down.

PR. . . . and run this stuff through, and present it to *us*, as opposed to just me?

CH. Sure.

PR. Fair enough.

CH. Now, I don't have all the documents right here at my house, and I'm waiting for some to come.

PR. OK. I think we should plan to take you up on that, and it certainly won't be . . .

CH. I'd recommend it before you publish the book. It will save some embarrassment in professional circles for you. I mean that's just a recommendation.

PR. No, I hear you.

CH.   Larry Warren is just a name. I have no strong feelings any way toward him. I think he went way out on a limb, but I don't know why. I've suspicions. I intentionally was involved in keeping him out of the NBC program [*Unsolved Mysteries*] because it [Larry's account on CNN] was too radical and too far off.

PR.   Yeah, that's what got back to me.

CH.   Well, that's true, and I told them, "Tell him!" when he kept calling in and trying to get involved.

PR.   That was at the end, when we *finally* found out about it. If they'd told us, of course, at the beginning . . .

CH.   I told them if they were going to go off like CNN did, I wasn't going to be involved. They couldn't quote me, I wouldn't appear, and so on, so . . . well, I've unloaded on you a bit I know.

PR.   That's OK, I expected it.

CH.   I'm not hostile, I'm just telling you . . .

PR.   I know that. Hey, look, you got burned on this, too, no question about it.

CH.   Continuously.

PR.   Yes, [but] you're saying here, quote unquote. "Yes, I can verify that for the senator," namely that Gordon Williams was not only there, but that he . . .

CH.   Call Exon and talk to him. I talked to him at least two or three times.

PR.   I don't know what went on between you and Exon, and this is specifically relative to your conversation with . . .

CH.   I refused to talk to his staffers. I talked directly to him because too many people were running me around the tree.

PR.   Again, if you want to be cryptic that's OK; is it fair to say that you feel there's still stuff about this that's not come out?

CH.   There's a *lot* that's not come out, but it's after the fact: you understand?

PR.   I think so.

CH.   Good. I think you're picking up on what I'm trying to tell you.

PR.   I'm not sure if I am.

CH.   I think you've missed the mark on the book, I guess is what I'm telling you.

PR.   Oh, obviously . . .

CH.   There's a book there, but you're missing it.

PR.   Obviously you feel that because you feel that Larry is a bit Manchurian candidated or something here.

CH.   Larry's not alone. I've got some pieces of the puzzle that, uh—there's something funny, that's all I'll tell you.

PR.   Well, I'll tell you, the best thing to come out of this [call] is I finally get a chance to speak to you, and you are somebody who I do have a lot of respect for, and I have to say that. I also have a lot of respect for Larry. I am somebody who is very much in the middle of this. But you're saying *in no way* he had completed his training.

CH.   *No way.*

PR.   Ok.

CH.   Now, if he's gonna tell you someone gave him a gun and gave him a radio, my answer to that is BS. Nobody—I don't care whether you're Larry Warren or you were a *colonel.*

PR.   The contradiction here is whether or not he had *finished* that training. You're saying he hadn't.

CH.   And I know the individual that has the records that show when he was actually *assigned* to Flight, but he wasn't *posted* to Flight until he finished the training. They were posted to Flight early on.

PR.   You say, *no way* had he finished his training by the end of December.

CH.   No way.

PR.   Ok.

CH.   It was mid-January, I think the eighteenth or the twentieth.

PR.   Are you familiar with a debriefing, supposedly that happened *after* the third night of incidents. A debriefing in . . .

CH.   Probably within the squadron maybe, and if he said he knew something, he was probably dragged in and debriefed. We can discuss that later, I've got to run.

PR.   Ok, sir. Thank you for your time.

CH.   Ok, take care, bye.

PR.   Bye-bye.[39]

Robbins makes a copy of the tape and mails it to Charles Halt. Larry Warren arrives back in New York City two days later and that evening listens to the recording. Robbins places a second call to the retired colonel soon after.

PR.   I hope I'm not getting you at a busy time.

CH.   Oh, sort of, but what's your question?

PR.   Larry's down here this weekend, we're working on the book, and I wonder if we might both call you back at a time that's more convenient.

CH.   I suppose so, what are the particulars you're talking about?

PR.   I had asked you several times if you felt there was *any* chance that Larry had gotten his PRP by 15 December or so, and you said absolutely not. But if we could establish for you, on your own terms, with official air force documentation, that he had been assigned to Flight by mid-December and was on Flight that night. If we could establish that for you, would you feel that, perhaps, there are other problems with . . .

CH.   You show me the documents and then . . .

PR.   Can Larry actually speak to you about the documents that we have here?

CH.   I'd rather see them, because I've seen other documents that say he was assigned later. Something's wrong.

PR.   Well, what I'm asking you is, will you speak to Larry on this point right now?

CH.   Sure.

PR.   And again, I'd like to tape this. Whatever any of us say is right on the record, and I'll be delighted to forward you a copy if you'd like.

CH.   Certainly.

PR.   Ok. Here he is.

LW.   Mr. Halt?

CH.   Yes, how are you doing?

LW.   Ok, how are you? Thanks for talking to us, sorry to bother you on a Sunday. Peter played back the conversation you had with him last week. I don't know what you have, in fact, I was quite intrigued by what you *did* have to say. I share your point of view on a *lion's* share of this stuff. I don't know what perceptions you have of me. The UFO field is irritating at best.

CH.   I'm only a player by chance.

LW.   Absolutely. The same applies to me.

CH.   Well, I have not chased after it, it has seemed to follow me.

LW.   I know that. Unfortunately, your name was associated with the document.

CH.   That document was never intended to be released, as you probably are well aware.

LW.   Yeah. I know you've been told an awful lot of things about me,

I don't know *officially* what you know, but I'd like to know some things. The reason I asked Peter Robbins to work on this book is to try to get some answers. The book is not an attack on the air force at all. Or the security police or any of the divisions. It's critical of certain other elements of the government.

CH. I have to assume you're talking about the NSA.

LW. Yeah. There's an account of what happened to me over there.

CH. I guess the first question is, when?

LW. December of '80. When I went through tech school, we had air-based ground defense, or if you didn't get assigned to that, you took it over at your first base. I had ABGD all set in Texas. A lion's share of my class were all assigned to Bentwaters. I was assigned to RAF Alconbury, and I swapped assignments. That's how I got to Bentwaters. There was [an unrelated, non-UFO incident] at the time and manning in security police was at a rather low point. I have documentation . . .

CH. Yeah, we . . . , I remember.

LW. You do remember though, Ok.

CH. Oh, yeah. I worked with the OSI, they worked for me, in so many words.

LW. I want this book to serve some good purpose. It is not about aliens and flying saucers, commanders shaking hands and fixing flying saucers, which I've *never said—it's completely ridiculous.*

CH. Well, you've made a lot of statements that don't make sense or that don't add up or are definitely false. Now, whether you've done them intentionally or you were misunderstood or got the players wrong, I don't know. That's something you have to resolve.

LW. I understand that, but . . .

CH. You have people in places impossible for them to be. You have people involved doing things that I know didn't do things, and I'm quoting some of the tapes that John Burroughs sent me and somebody else sent me a tape and I have to assume it's an accurate tape. Larry Fawcett sent me some stuff, and you've obviously heard the tape I sent back to him?

LW. Yes, I did.

CH. I was very frank with him, I just . . .

LW. Oh, you were! Absolutely. You're more direct than most people you encounter in this field. Burroughs is a whole other enigma in himself. I knew him over there.

CH.   Oh, I knew John very well, probably better then you did.

LW.   I'm sure you did.

CH.   You haven't answered my question.

LW.   I'm sorry.

CH.   When were you supposedly out in Tangham [Rendlesham] Forest?

LW.   It was sometime after Christmas but before New Year's Eve 1980. I never knew the exact date. I was in Germany for two days, leading up to [the] three nights of events. I was unaware of the two previous.

CH.   So, you were there and claimed Gordon Williams was there.

LW.   I saw a person out there that . . . I'm not the only one who has said these things, in fact, I wasn't even the first. I was certainly on duty though in December and had a radio and a weapon.

CH.   Do you have your Flight-assignment document?

LW.   I do, indeed.

CH.   Because somebody else has documents that indicates you were assigned to Flight in mid-January.

LW.   On the eighteenth or twentieth [of January]—you said in that vicinity of 1981 I was posted. I was TDY. A number of us—and I have documentation for this—were over at Wiesbaden when the hostages came back. I'd already worked on Flight. By late January, I was moved into office and support areas, typing . . . with [Major] Drury and people like that. Major Zickler, I used to play darts with him at the Rod & Gun Club, knew him very well, but I certainly did work on Flight. The second day I was there, we started classes on Woodbridge.

CH.   If what you say is true, he had to get fifty people and all he wanted was bodies.

LW.   In fact, I made an arrest, or assisted in an arrest, that is documented, in the officer housing area at a party with a lot of kids. One kid threw a big flowerpot through a window. I had an M16 at the time.

CH.   At Bentwaters or Woodbridge?

LW.   On Bentwaters . . . and absolutely went through guard mount. We were issued the weapons, I have my serial numbers, the date, everything. *Why* I have that I will explain to you when we get together. You're aware apparently that I have had other experiences in my life.

CH.   I've heard that [from] second sources.

LW.   I was approached, at least three times throughout [the] eighties, by certain people. They explained certain things, they said things that *couldn't* have been true, and it was very confusing. They said certain things happened to us over there. This is why you're intriguing me about certain things you spoke about recently. I think only in person we should explore that. My records aren't in Saint Louis, you may know that. I had an honorable discharge, I have an RE code that is on *no* books, and yet the reason for separation was breach of contract. I'll bring my DD-214 to you to see: breach of contract on the air force's part. I wasn't performing the jobs my AFSC stated I was gonna do. I went to Egypt, I was with Gordon Williams at the change-of-command ceremony, I was his bodyguard, I have the documentation for that.

CH.   I suppose you were picked by Zickler or the first sergeant.

LW.   Yeah, yeah. I was a good cop. I didn't do the drugs. When I was young with this, I was very cocky. I felt burned by the military—I wanted to go in and stay for twenty years. I wish I had. I wasn't snapped out, I stayed away from those people. I knew some people that messed up. I know there's ill health effects that came from this, I've had them. Now, if I didn't go through something, what . . .

CH.   Be a little more specific, I don't understand.

LW.   There were health effects, and I believe from exposure to *something*. John Burroughs said he's had heart problems, eye problems, I have documented eye problems. I was sent to Lakenheath, to the hospital there, for extensive eye situations; I got glasses out of it. It does state burns to the retina. It's crazy. I didn't light a match and burn my eyes. I had problems *after* this thing that I saw happen.

CH.   Have you ever obtained your records?

LW.   I tried. My family was very disappointed I got out that quick, they didn't understand. I got very depressed that I left, God, I wanted to go *back*. So I went down to the same guys that put me into the service, and I said can I go back in?

CH.   You didn't realize what you were getting into when you became a security cop.

LW.   No, no, I didn't.

CH.   Most people don't.

LW.   As far as aliens and all that, I have to tell you that there was *something* there that was brightly lit with depth to it. Burroughs said they were just lights, they weren't beings.

CH.   Were you there with Burroughs?

LW.   I saw Burroughs out there.

CH.   Was he in uniform?

LW.   No. No, he wasn't. If it was *mind,* if there were psychotronics and things like that going on, I'm very angry at that. I'm not against the air force, because they weren't the players in this. I've talked to certain people that have identified themselves as working for certain, a certain agency, and I was very unfamiliar with what that agency was, and they said *numerous* things. We've had phone problems.

CH.   By the way, this is all being monitored I'm sure.

LW.   Absolutely. That's why I don't expect you to, you know, whatever, that's fine.

CH.   That's why I don't say much.

LW.   No, and that's why I'd like to meet. I don't want to jeopardize you. I'm either a player or the Manchurian candidate, from whatever—and I didn't like when my partner said that, but I think you'd find him a very levelheaded . . .

CH.   By levelheaded, you're talking about Peter Robbins?

LW.   Absolutely. He basically put this in perspective for me. We've been back to England, we've been working on this thing for five years, and Mr. Halt, I've got to tell you, it is an open-ended thing.

CH.   I think you sincerely believe what you're saying, and you may be right, and I can't say you're lying, but I find flaws here and there that I have to have resolved for myself.

LW.   I admit there are . . .

CH.   My suspicions are one of three things: number one, somebody has *played* with you.

LW.   I know.

CH.   Number two, you have gotten, you know, some facts, distorted through the years or been fed some disinformation, or you're just an outright fraud, and I don't think the latter. I, I honestly think somebody's meddled with you.

LW.   And that's what I hate about the whole thing.

CH.   I hate to tell you that, but that's my personal opinion. I've buried some things some places, and I don't mean in the ground. But if anything ever happens to me, they will surface, and key people will be notified. I think you have some company.

LW. I know that. I have *had* interaction with something very strange through the years that is mind-blowing. I hate feeling I'm manipulated by them *or* us, or who or what. But I don't believe the air force did us.

CH. I think the air force is a bystander.

LW. Absolutely. I agree with you.

CH. I know that from the reaction of certain key people when this occurred, and I don't think they were *ever* brought in the loop, ever.

LW. No, not at all. I hate feeling like somebody's science project, but, you know, we all may be to a degree.

CH. Who knows? I'll tell you what you do. I'm going to have to go. Tell Peter to bundle up a copy of the tape he just made, send it off to me. Let's talk a little later, and we'll talk about getting together some time and discuss it. Fair enough?

LW. Absolutely. We'll take you to dinner, how's that?

CH. Oh, why not.

LW. I appreciate your time, and for saying what you can say publicly. I don't care if I end up in the worst light in the world as long as *something* comes out about this because I want to know.

CH. Ok, well, I have an open mind.

LW. I know you do. How could we not, right? [*laughter.*] But let me let you get back to your day, and I do appreciate your time.

CH. You're quite welcome.

LW. Have a good day. Bye.

CH. Okay, take care, bye.[40]

In 1992, 6.3 million new documents were classified.[41]

5. | 10–16 FEBRUARY 1993

Whistle-Blowers are defined as being part of the heroic tradition of the country, though they are never treated that way by their organizations. Think of the movie *High Noon*, in which a lawman stands against a town that is not living up to its responsibility. That was Frank Serpico's favorite.
Dr. Myron Glazer[42]

The year began with an invitation to go south. Our editor Linda now lived in South Carolina, but continued to keep up with our seemingly endless draft revisions. Hers was an invaluable service, but some manuscript problems needed to be worked out in person. Our plan was for me to come down for a week, and as long as I had to return through the Washington area, Larry would meet me there. So would Charles Halt, we hoped.

From the beginning, Linda had been one of the few people I'd been able to stay open with about Bentwaters. She took the matter seriously from the start and volunteered her services to us unconditionally, which was all the more remarkable because some of the implications of being involved with Larry and me genuinely frightened her.

The sleepy little town of Kingstree, South Carolina, was a long ride from Linda's, but still the nearest rail connection. That's where she picked me up Wednesday night, 3 February 1993. Linda had also been typesetting a French translation of Dr. Elsworth F. Baker's Man in the Trap *for our friends the Cammarellas. By good chance, they were also visiting, and they and I took turns with our editor. Our time flew by in work, conversation, laughter, and some great meals; I was just happy we were all together.*

The following Wednesday, Linda drove me back to the Amtrak station at Kingstree. We arrived early and got two coffees from the little cafe in the depot. Since they weren't really open yet, we took our cups back to the car and drank them there; it was another cold morning in South Carolina. Good-byes followed coffee, and we waved to each other as the car pulled away. No writer ever had a better editor, I thought, or a better friend.

I lit a cigarette by the tracks and looked around. Across the way a sign proclaimed, "Take Jesus as your savior now or burn in hell forever!" God, how depressing, I thought; love mutated into fear so easily. The train pulled in on schedule, and I climbed aboard.

Larry and Gus Russo greeted me at Baltimore's Pennsylvania Station that night. Larry had arrived several days earlier and was staying with Gus. The three of us talked until about 1:30 A.M., then hit the hay. Our friend was now working as a reporter for an upcoming Frontline *special on Lee Harvey Oswald and had to fly to Boston in the morning. The meeting at WGBH-TV would keep him there overnight. Gus had already documented a number of new bomb-shells for the November broadcast and was now in the process of developing some leads that gave me the chills.*

The next morning, Dan Smith drove us to Rosemary Ellen Guiley's, a writer who had also opened her home to us. Rosemary and Dan had visited East Anglia the preceding summer and also found the area somewhat unnerving.

After establishing our new beachhead, I left phone messages for investigative reporter Chuck DeCaro and several members of the Fund for UFO Research. I had contacted them in January 1993 about meeting with us and hoped we could confirm it for this weekend. Larry called Dr. Bruce Maccabee and researcher Bob Oechsler.

Several times over the preceding months, Larry had spoken to members of Congressman Gerald Solomon's New York staff. It had been almost a dozen years since Solomon's inquiry had yielded that ridiculous letter from the office of the secretary of the air force citing medical reasons for Larry's permanent disquali-fication. Now the congressman headed the House Committee on Veterans' Affairs. Several months earlier, Larry had reapproached Solomon's Saratoga office and requested a meeting on his service-related health problems. Larry also told a staffer named Mary Ellen that I would be calling Mr. Solomon's Washington office when we arrived. Mary Ellen said she would fax our request to Solomon's Washington aide Skip Cook. It was Ms. Cook I was about to call.

Ms. Cook had no idea of who I was or what I was talking about. She'd never heard of Larry Warren, RAF Bentwaters, or me, and she had certainly never received any such fax from the Saratoga office. In any case, the congressman was out of town, but she would reach Mary Ellen and I should call her back on Monday.

Don Berliner called later from the Fund for UFO Research. Could we meet with some of their members on Saturday afternoon? No problem, I told him; Gus or Rosemary would be able to get us there. Then DeCaro phoned—he'd try to meet with us tomorrow, but would have to confirm in the morning. I called Halt last. He would see us if he could, but unfortunately would be out of town for the weekend. Maybe sometime next week.

Friday the twelfth was a rainy Lincoln's Birthday, but Chuck brightened it up when he called at eleven. He could meet with us that afternoon, and we set the time for three at a nearby restaurant. Rosemary drove us and stayed for the duration. We were on our first cups of coffee when Chuck's Jeep pulled into the lot; it was good to see him again.

After shaking hands and introducing Rosemary, the first thing he asked Larry was whether he'd spoken with Adrian Bustinza recently. Chuck wanted to know if Adrian was still having "those nightmares." They had apparently been pretty bad for a while. Larry said he didn't know. Was Larry still having nightmares? "Sometimes," he answered. With tape recorder now running, I asked the reporter what, in hindsight, were his thoughts on the possible alien factor at Bentwaters. I should have known better.

CD. I'm an investigative reporter. There's a great deal of difference from being a ufologist and pursuing this story and being an investigative reporter. My involvement in this is standard, investigative, journalistic methodology, and the methodology deals with a paper trail. The reason why I first got into this story in the first place was the paper trail.

Now you've got to understand, I'm an investigative reporter specializing in defense. Whenever something comes up that's nonstandard in defense, I want to know why. And the Bentwaters incident is of much greater import in the real-world, journalistic ability to garner a story when it is juxtaposed with the security of nuclear weapons. Granted that if you could prove that there are extraterrestrial beings, that would be the story of the millenium since the Second Coming. Fine, it ain't gonna happen. What *is* going to happen—the paper trail, that you can force, that you can lever—is the security of nuclear weapons.

The question that I finished my report at CNN was, If those guys were lunatics, were on drugs, were hallucinating, why were they on duty the next day?[43] OK? If they weren't hallucinating, what is it that they *did* see, that can fly over an air force base with impunity? Those are the stories you can question the air force about in the real world, and if UFOs happen to fall out of it by the air force's admission, fine. So, the Bentwaters story to me is a nuclear-weapons story. When I asked, was there a Broken Arrow, was there a Faded Giant, they said, no.

Nineteen eighty was the height of the cold war. The morale of the U.S. forces in 1980, early 1981, was very low. We were at the verge of a war with Iran, there was global terrorism, and you were sitting at this base where nuclear weapons were stored. There were still F-4s at the time, right?

LW. We had [A-]10s. They had just transitioned, in '79.

CD. OK. So the weapons-storage sector's still there and active. So what needs to be looked at is, during the time of high international terrorism, dealing with terrorists *at the gate*, a foreign power that could make fifteen, twenty heavily armed security police patrolmen run away—I'd want to know what it was, so I can prevent that the next time. *Why wasn't anything done?* Why did these guys run away?

   . . . so alien beings, whether they were imagery or the real thing, you have to travel this story in plateaus. One plateau at a time: *why wasn't there the nuclear incident?* Why wasn't there retraining? Why wasn't there commanders called? Why why why why—OK? And the only way you can do this is to go back and remember incidents that did occur. Why did Greg Battram swear that he went across the fence with a clip loaded? Absolutely against training—why? Why?

PR. Scared.

CD. No, no, not when you're armed, you're scared when you're unarmed! Now you're armed, and you go click, you know, with your right thumb, OK? It's on semiautomatic and you're pointing at the target, and your hair is standing on end and the quote was, we got too scared, we turned around and ran. Now that's an ideal terrorist weapon, or that's an ideal reaction to a weapon you want to use *against* terrorists.

   The air force is a big machine. It reacts like a machine. It's called standard operating procedure. Why did the deputy base commander decide to go out the night before Christmas? If the base commander, sub-commander saw this thing shooting lights down to the ground, why? What happened? Who did these guys talk to? Nothing was said? And you leave the security of nuclear weapons to 'em? Over and over and over again is *who was guarding the dump?* What precautions were taken the next night? In the Freedom of Information Act, let's go back and look at, uh, what do you call those teams that SAT had, with the UH1F [helicopter]?

LW. SAT?

CD. Yeah, the special action teams. You had all these nuclear weapons, on birds sitting in holes in the ground, and a deer would bump against the fence [*laughter*] and the alarm . . . Now what happens is you go over and it's a goddamned deer. So you take out air force from 65–1, you know: deer hits. All right. OK? Where's the reports? So that's the story. Not anything further away. That's achievable because the air force has a mechanism for doing all those things, and if you say, well nothing happened, then nobody did a Faded Giant, nobody did a Broken Arrow? How come? What are the procedures? So you FOIA the procedures for Broken Arrow, FOIA the procedures for Faded Giant, possible nuclear-weapons incident. Why wasn't Faded Giant declared? Why was it covered?

LW. Covered Wagon and Security Option Three was . . .

CD. Covered Wagon, possible C Alert? It used to be Aces High, then it became Covered Wagon, then there was one more . . .

PR. Helping Hand?

CD. Helping Hand—possible terrorist, possible intrusion. How many times were two squads of police out there—loaded. Where were the reports for the light-alls the next day? That's what you have to research.

PR. I'm most interested in hearing you as a specialist in what you do . . . who got into this.

CD. Look at the methodology. Somebody FOIAed those questions that we had with John Kirkwood [a major assigned to the Pentagon's Office of Public Affairs, media relations division]. Now Kirkwood is my professional counterpart: he got stuck with the CNN account, and we had to do business with each other, not just on this story but on many other stories. Personal friends, professional enemies, OK? And we almost lost our friendship over Bentwaters. But you know he's at the end of a string, too, and so we clashed. It just didn't make a lot of sense. The air force couldn't come down on fifteen of its own people, and by the way, Halt got promoted after he got done with that, kind of a backwater job. He went into AWACS, Halt was no dummy.

PR. You know what rank he retired at?

CD. Colonel. Full colonel.

LW. Chuck's an officer. Are you still in the military?

CD. No.

LW. I had a great interaction with Halt, I thought. We've been pitted at each other—he was very nice.

CD. You tell him I said hi.

PR. We will. Probably we'll see him Monday or Tuesday.

LW. [*To Rosemary Guiley*] Tell him what went down . . . this thing about . . . why he's pissed at me and all.

RG. Well, it was the gossip that Halt had not made general because of Bentwaters, because of what came out of Bentwaters, and he was very bitter about that and blamed Larry primarily for it and was hell-bent to disparage Larry and was going to sue him up one side and down the other side . . .

CD. No, I don't think so.

RG. . . . that he was a liar and that he was going to prove it.

LW. And yet on the phone with me . . .

CD. You're getting far away from the point. The problem that I find with dealing with ufologists is tremendous ego bashing. It's off the point. Who cares? There are so many vagaries in the air force officer's selection system, getting promoted to colonel in the air force and not being a rated pilot is not an easy thing to do. A lot of people get washed out before O-6. That's perfectly respectable and making general officer, a lot of that has to do with a crapshoot, patrons, and a lot of that kind of stuff. So I discount anything about it.

LW. OK.

CD. I found him to be very straightforward [and] just as curious as you or Bustinza or Burroughs. Whatever happened was a gut-level reaction. He even says, I went out to debunk the thing, then all of a sudden . . . Extraordinary circumstances *whatever* it was. [But] it's a defense story, not a UFO story, until such time as you get beyond a whole bunch of things. That also means that I don't disbelieve you. One, I wasn't there. Two, I still don't get the whole context of the story 'cause few people want to talk. But as a defense reporter, you start putting things together that make sense.

I'm not saying . . . It is possible a UFO . . . [but] the air force, the military is a gigantic organization that, you know, bumps into extraterrestrials on a regular basis. You can think about it, it's possible, but can you prove it: that's something else. But you can prove other things that happen on the way, and the answer is definitely, yes. You can find the machinations of why information was destroyed or shunted off.

LW. Halt said, how did you get your records? I said I'll tell you when I see you. I stole them. I thought there would be a time. I have medical records that are definitely from eye damage, and I'm not the only one. Burroughs went through it, too.

CD. Did you use a starlight scope?

LW. No. I didn't even have a weapon. I had a Motorola on me and a flashlight.

CD. Did anybody get hit by one of those beams?

LW. Yes.

CD. Who was illuminated?

LW. Well, Burroughs. You remember when you interviewed me in '84, before the show aired, I gave you a lot of names of the guys that were there that I knew I could trust?

CD. Yeah, I asked you, you told me the names.

LW. I've met with Burroughs a couple of times now; he's telling me he's had heart trouble from this, his eyes were all flashed out.

CD. Who were the three guys who went out first? Burroughs, Bustinza, . . .

LW. Penniston.

CD. Penniston. OK. They went out, uh, who tried to tackle it? Burroughs tried to chase it.

LW. Burroughs grabbed it—and it moved ten meters with him on it. He told me exactly what happened out in California.

CD. Is that when he got his burns? Didn't it burn his flesh?

LW. Not really. It was all internal. My records were at NSA, they were taken out of Saint Louis. I couldn't get them unless I came here with a . . .

CD. You just mentioned a class-action suit. Flash burns on active duty. The probability of denial doesn't work up against it, if there are more than two or three people who have flash burns at the same time. Nothing to do with UFOs—nothing. It has to do with the multiplicity of flash burns on active duty, OK? Then the air force has to come back and say, you did or you didn't. You shouldn't be disappointed if you find out that this isn't a UFO though, if it was something else, OK?

LW. I'm not! I have suspicions, because of other things in my life, that this was very different. The surgeon general of the air force rendered me disqualified for reenlistment five months after I got out because I couldn't extend my right arm, and yet my reenlistment code is not on the books, it's a 4-M. It's not medical. No one knows what the hell that is, but it means do not process. This stuff goes on so deep.

CD. These stories are similar to the atomic-soldier stories, the Agent Orange stories, the MK-ULTRA stories. It wasn't like they didn't know what to do—there was a plan. They may not know what to do with it instantly, but there was a plan there, plan B already in place. There has to be. And if there's a reason, there must be a database. And if there's a database, there's something behind it. The reason I didn't pursue Bentwaters any further: my boss said, you already broke the story. Let somebody else finish it. Seven years later, *Unsolved Mysteries* did the same story, except that now Burroughs and Halt were out of the military and talked to 'em. I kind of chastised the producer about that. I spent CNN's money. That's probably why I got as far as I did. I could travel, and I was a network correspondent with a contact network in place and the ability to pursue. I flew to Europe, your place, flew to Texas, went down to [name of state]. I had to walk around [name of town] until I found Bustinza's house! He didn't have a phone.

LW. He was a good guy, but really angry.

CD. Well, maybe angry. I think he was kind of, concerned with the mystery. I think I see the same thing in Halt, almost identical. Different cultural backgrounds, but same—what the hell happened to me and I want to know. Like the guy who got in a car crash and can't remember those last four seconds before he hit.

LW. He [Halt] goes, I know you've had dealings with the NSA, and I go, well . . . And then I'm like the Antichrist to other people the way he paints me, but I want to meet him. I want to sit down with the guy.

CD. You're a lousy Antichrist. [*Laughter.*]

LW.   Thanks.

PR.   We're gonna quote you on that. Have you ever been able to restore some of the contacts you had had with the Pentagon that seem to have been disrupted after doing the story? Do you have the access to sources that you used to? [*Silence*] No comment? Fair enough. [*Laughter.*]

CD.   The ultimate irony of this is that the air force, the National Defense University, and others have hired me as a consultant to *them* on new kinds of warfare.

LW.   Sounds like a book for you to do on Bentwaters.

CD.   I've got other things I've got to do. The kind of book that I'm talking about, the money that goes in, could easily eat your advance. I'm talking big. I'm talking six-, seven-figure advances. You could easily blow, five hundred thousand or a million bucks digging this out. But for a million bucks you could dig a lot out. You have to know where to look. Besides, you're too close to the project.

There are some things in the paranormal arena that I simply see as science, undefined. It's just that there are some areas in astral travel and telepathy and psychokinesis where there is apparent methodology available to replicate at least minimal amounts of certain paranormal phenomena, on a replicable basis. The CIA had an operation going called Grillflame. It was pretty interesting. It was like a psychic reconnaisance squadron. I think what we touch as telepathy and other paranormal phenomena are just science that hasn't been explored. I wouldn't go leaping forward into way-far-out stuff; at the nar edge is a lot of stuff. And sometimes I think I see those two stories crossing over at Bentwaters. I still think the best thing that you can do is to look into those flashburns. That's hot stuff.[44]

Chuck's insights, knowledge, and machine-gun stream of consciousness left me feeling more than a little amateurish. The man was in another league entirely. Oh, for a background in journalism, the right contacts, a million dollars, and a small staff!

Rosemary drove us back to Gus's on Saturday. After unloading our bags and switching cars, Gus drove us to Virginia. His WGBH meeting had gone great, and as we headed out of Baltimore, Gus began a riveting update on a man whose life he had gotten to know intimately over the years: Lee Harvey Oswald.

About a quarter mile from the Pentagon, we pulled up in front of Rob

Swiatek's apartment building. Not all of the Fund for UFO Research members had been able to join us, but those present gave us a warm welcome: they included Rob, Richard Hall, Don Berliner, Larry Bryant, and Susan Mitchell; soon to be Susan Swiatek. I spoke first, but only to introduce the papers we'd brought. It was Warren's show, and he carried it well. Three hours and twenty minutes later, members were still asking questions.

It was dark when we left, but the Lincoln and Jefferson Memorials were bathed in light, easily visible from the Beltway; the Capitol dome glowed in the distance. They really were beautiful buildings, I thought, but tonight they only made me feel sad and angry. As we headed into Maryland, the conversation returned to UFOs, the Kennedy assassination, Lee Oswald, Jack Ruby, LBJ, J. Edgar Hoover, and the crop-circle phenomenon.

I spent most of Sunday afternoon transcribing the conversation we'd had with DeCaro. Because Gus was flying to Los Angeles in the morning, he drove us back to Rosemary's. That night, I called Charles Halt again.

Things didn't sound promising. Tomorrow was no good, and he had a dinner engagement for Tuesday. I felt my hopes sinking. It was back to New York on Wednesday, so Tuesday would be our last chance. But hold on—he was now asking if Tuesday afternoon worked for us. Could we meet him about 1:30? Yes, wherever he wished. Did we have a car or a ride? No, but we would by tomorrow. I'd call back in the morning to confirm, but unless things screwed up, we'd be meeting with Halt on Tuesday.

We confirmed the next morning. When I asked if he wanted us to come to his office, he said he preferred a public place. The Pentagon was near where he worked. We would meet at the central food court on the ground floor of Pentagon City Mall at 1:30. Now I had another call to make.

Skip Cook answered at Congressman Solomon's office. She remembered me immediately and couldn't have been more courteous. Unfortunately, today would be out of the question, and the congressman's schedule was pretty well locked in for the rest of the week. I thanked her and hung up the phone. Yeah, right, I thought. So much for any help from Congressman Solomon.

Because Gus was now in Los Angeles and Rosemary had another commitment, Larry called Bob Oechsler to ask for a ride to Washington. Bob had the afternoon free and would be glad to drive us; we were on the road by 11:45.

I don't think it occurred to either Larry or me until we were actually in the food court that neither of us had a clear picture of what Halt looked like. We hadn't thought to review the Unsolved Mysteries *episode he appeared on, and Larry hadn't seen him in the flesh since 1981. But I knew we would find him or he would find us. As I scanned the faces, a voice came from behind me: "Peter Robbins?"*

I turned to find a dark-haired man in a business suit. "Mr. Halt?" I asked. "Yes," he answered, and we shook hands. After introducing him to Larry and Bob, we headed for an empty table.

Halt took the inside chair, and I sat across from him. With Larry on my right, Bob settled into the remaining seat. If there was any small talk, I don't remember it. I do remember making an almost immediate mental note that I would not like to play poker with this man. With the rarest exceptions, Halt's expression remained fixed over the next hour and twenty minutes. He made very little eye contact and was unrelentingly serious.

It was agreed that I would record what was said here and send him a copy; Bob would record a backup.

Charles Halt looked at me for a moment, then asked why we had written the book. "To give Larry's experience, as he remember it," I said. "The main thing I wanted you to know to start with is that we don't have an angle, we're not trying to prove this is aliens, we just don't know."

CH.   What's the purpose of the book then?

LW.   I might be able to pick that up.

PR.   Yeah, it's your experience.

LW.   When I fell into this, as time went on, I started to see so many distortions on what I had said.

     As Larry began, I realized that I was famished. No one else was hungry, but I would bring back some drinks for them; the recorder would tape what I'd miss.

LW.   A writer in general will take liberties with things, re-create things. I had a few people around me say "write a book," so I thought about it. I said I need a researcher to come in on the thing, I'm not a researcher. There's a lot of distortion about me out there, and anyone that goes public in this stuff, in one way or another, gets it up the kazoo, eventually.

CH.   I'm aware of that.

LW.   The main thing is that the book has outgrown what we are. I don't think it was the first time something like this has happened involving the military and probably won't be the last.

BO.   Can I interrupt just for one second? Are you aware of what Larry alleges is his experience, in relation to the Bentwaters.

CH.   All I know is what I've gained from two or three tapes that Larry Fawcett and somebody, I don't even remember who now, shared with me. In fact, one time I agreed to cooperate with Larry Fawcett; you were working with him to try and provide information so the story could be told.

LW. Right.

CH. And I provided him a lot of information, and he sent me a tape and I sent a tape back. He may have played the tape for you.

LW. I got a copy of the tape through Barry [Greenwood]. Larry and I split for a number of personal reasons.

CH. Oh, I have no personal affection for Larry, other than he appeared to be a recognized author, and was hopefully telling the story.

LW. I'm being a cop, too, and I want to try my best to put you at ease with some things. I have had events in my life, that are ongoing. But years ago, they said, you can't have more than one experience in your life. Well, unfortunately, I and many others do. When Bentwaters happened, I wasn't the first one to say what I said, I was just the loudest. What I experienced over there is very different than other things I had experienced in my life. I, without a doubt, experienced *something* over there. That I know. It doesn't have to be alien.

I don't really trust my memory—or the *imagery* that's in my mind because of some things that maybe we can or cannot go into now, which sound more logical to me. Also, having spoken to other witnesses that haven't been public—I was *with* these guys, things went *on*—all I want to know is, what the hell happened to me? I told you on the phone I don't blame the air force particularly, but there were elements to this thing that continued after I got out of the service.

CH. You're aware that the story you've told or the stories you've told over the years don't fit in with what I recollect and other witnesses recollect.

LW. And yet I have statements from other guys that were right next to me at certain elements of this thing . . . my military records . . . how I got them? I didn't tell you on the phone, but, I took 'em. I had to hand carry them from one place to another and after all this had happened, I said, I'm gonna take 'em, because they're not going to be there eventually, and I was right. I don't have them all, but I have enough of them. I have records.

CH. Have you taken a polygraph exam relative to what you recall, as the events occurred related to you?

LW. You mean a lie-detector test?

CH.   Yeah.

LW.   Not a lie-detector test. I took a VSA, voice-stress analysis, through Fawcett, three times, through the Connecticut State Police actually.

BO.   Apparently he believes the events that he is relating are as he recalled them.

CH.   Oh, I've conceded that to him. I said you obviously believe very strongly in what he [Larry] thinks has happened. His perceptions are pretty well embedded, there's no doubt about that.

BO.   I have a question that's really for both of you. Admiral Inman related to me that these issues, not specifically the events that happened over in England, but these issues themselves are covered under national secrecy laws. Are you aware of that? Are you aware of any specific statutes?

[I returned to the table.]

CH.   No. Let's put it this way, any particular statutes are publicly in a black program. I don't think you'll find them anywhere in the clear.

BO.   OK.

CH.   If you want to turn off your recorder for a minute.

[Tape *off/tape on*]

LW.   It does deal with that agency. Do you think they took advantage of a situation over there and did some things with some impressionable young people?

CH.   I don't know for a fact. I have suspicions that you have been meddled with, and I told you that, and several other people that I'd rather not mention their names . . .

LW.   What do you mean by meddled with? Could you clarify that?

CH.   Well, I can't because I don't know whether it was drugs or hypnosis or some things we aren't aware of. There's an awful lot of strange things that have been under study for a long time, there are people who can do things that you would not believe.

BO.   When you say people, are you referring to essentially military people?

CH.   Everything from remote viewing to you name it. There's some stuff that's way, that's so far out, that if you published it, people would laugh. And there are people that actually practice some of these things with great success.

LW. But if I was played with, and others had things done to us—and I was trying to serve my country . . . I wanted to go into the air force and signed up for six years. I wanted to be in there, and it went to shit right after certain things happened. It just collapsed. I wasn't a troublemaker, I wasn't a drug ad . . .

CH. Do you have a coded discharge?

LW. Yes.

CH. Do you know what the code is?

LW. Yes.

CH. What does it say?

LW. 4-M. Like Michael.

CH. I'd have to go . . .

LW. If you can find out . . . I want to show you something here, this is where I . . .

CH. I'm going to have to make a phone call on this.

LW. If you could, I would be grateful. I want to show you something.

CH. Now, I don't know the codes, but I think I can maybe find out.

LW. No one can find that code as far as recruiter levels. I'd be curious what you do find.

CH. Well, I'm not sure my contacts are still active, if you know what I mean. I could have done it very easily . . .

LW. I know. Some people say, "For No Reentry—Medical." It's not the case. M does not represent medical. I know that much.

CH. It may not be a published code.

Halt's beeper went off. He needed to call his office and went off to find a phone. A few minutes later he returned.

  [*Tape off/tape on*]

CH. The real story, I think, is what happened afterward, not what happened there. And I've told that to several people.

LW. Why did all the paper trail happen to me this way? I don't say, "Colonel Halt actually shook an alien's hand and fixed the craft with a . . ."—that is nonsense! This was all created and blown out of proportion.

CH. Where did the story come from that, number one, Gordon Williams was there? Gordon Williams was at another social function that night, I *know* he was.

LW. Well, I know, but I . . .

CH. Where did the little green men come from?

LW. They weren't green [*laughs*].

CH. Or whatever.

LW. They weren't green. And there was something there that was *alive*. There wasn't this . . .

CH. There are two nights that are intertwined now, you're aware of that?

LW. No.

CH. You have events from the first night and the third night intertwined together, which is very puzzling.

PR. What are the events that are intertwined?

CH. The actual confrontation with a craft or whatever you want to call it . . .

PR. You don't feel there were several . . .

CH. No, no.

PR. Oh, you don't.

CH. None of the witnesses that I've talked to from the third night say there was anything physical they could catch other than lights.

PR. It sounds like a lot of minds were jerked around with then. I have a question for you. Let's say there were certain *real*, unexplainable events that happened, and they were taken advantage of, to do some testing, or whatever. Certain of the men—Larry, Adrian, to name two—remember certain things that were a mixture of what happened and what was programmed for them to remember. Larry *remembers* Colonel Williams being there. Could that have been part, for some reason to keep this . . .

CH. [*Indicates no.*] When I took the tape on the following Saturday morning, I ran into Gordon Williams, so I stopped in the corridor, and we talked, and I told him about it, and I told him about the tape. He said, "Do you have the tape?" and I said, "Yes, it's in the office," I went in and got it. He said, "I want to take it down and play it for General Cragie at the staff meeting." I said, "Oh Lord, don't do that." He said, "No, I want to do that." And he was totally surprised by the whole thing. He listened with very keen interest: put the tape on, played it, and brought the tape back.

   I said, "Well, what happened?" He said nobody knew what to do. "I played it at the staff meeting, and Cragie asked one question," he says, "Is Halt credible? Is this true?" [Williams] said,

"There's no doubt in my mind." So the staff mulled it over for a long time, and they left, with indecision. Gordon Williams brought the tape back and gave it back to me and said, "Call me the next time. I want to be there, too." Several weeks later, one of the law-enforcement types thought he saw something. I'd told all the law-enforcement and several of the security supervisors, if they see any, call me.

LW.   That was a friend of mine, Steve LaPlume.

CH.   No, it was Staff Sergeant Wendel Palmer. Palmer called me directly, on the radio—he called law enforcement and they called me. I had the little orange Triumph at the time, and I went right out the back gate at Bentwaters. I had the top down and it was right under the gate onto the flight line, down the flight line, across, called the tower, got permission to cross, went right over to Woodbridge. Williams was right behind me, but he had to go around because he had the staff car. By the time I got there, there was nothing. He came about five minutes . . .

LW.   Did you guys have family members with you on that . . . no.

CH.   Just jumped in the car and went over, was there in six or seven minutes. But it was only a light they thought they saw, and I'm not even sure they saw anything. But Gordon Williams did not, I'm positive, know anything about it. Whenever the press came around after [fall] 1983, I was fast enough to go to public affairs and pull my picture out of the file—his appeared in the paper. I never thought they'd take his picture. When they couldn't find mine, they took his!

PR.   I'm sure that was a real happy day for him.

CH.   It landed in the *News of the World* and he went crazy! In fact, today he doesn't even want to talk about it, because he's the vice president for a large company and it would not sit well with the company.

LW.   I have never wanted to embarrass or hurt anybody.

CH.   I don't accuse anybody of that, other than some of the press and a few loonies in England. Do you remember two separate distinct nights or were you involved in one night? [*Larry indicates one.*] Do you have the 2095 assigning you to Flight?

LW.   Yes.

CH.   Why don't you show me what you have.

They reviewed his 2095, December 1980 letter from Major Zickler, D Flight in-processing sheet, separation approval, honorable discharge, and U.K. whip sheets:

That's a copy, we have the original of that file. I had PRP instantly when I was there. I was posted on the eleventh or the fifteenth. Of course, OJT continues throughout your career, so there's a lot of courses I never even got to take. [*Indicating document.*] I was certified on 15 December.

Larry explained the terms under which he'd left the service and about going to see the base advocate attorney:

LW.   And he said, you can get out, honorable discharge, and then go back in in the States.

CH.   Did you actually initiate the request?

LW.   Oh, yes, absolutely. I wasn't doing my job, and I was worried about a few things going on. I do want you to notice here, "Non-fulfillment of guaranteed enlistee training." When I got out, I went to my old recruiter, and all of a sudden up on the computer it said, "Do not process. Nothing follows." I got in touch with my congressman at that time, he got in touch with the Department of the Air Force trying to find something on it. This is what they sent back.

Halt read the medical discharge letter:

CH.   What?

LW.   Months after I even got out.

CH.   Do you have a problem with your right arm?

       [*Larry indicates no.*] This sounds like somebody that didn't know what they were writing put this together.

PR.   Or they knew what they were writing and figured nobody was going to follow up on it.

CH.   I don't think a doctor would . . .

PR.   It's from the surgeon general's office.

CH.   I can't explain that, but that doesn't necessarily mean somebody's out to get you or smear you or anything else. As an officer, you can always . . .

LW.   But I just think they didn't want me back in. I flapped my lips the next day and got in trouble from that.

CH. Nobody has ever approached me, I mean officially, about any of this, suggested I say, or not say, participate or not participate, nothing. Never. Does that make sense to you? I was in a very, very sensitive position in my last job, where I had access to things that we can't even think about. Never had a problem, I've had to update my clearance at least twice since then, never had a problem.

LW. It confuses me even more.

CH. My name was in the CNN special several years ago, even though they didn't film me.

LW. . . . reminds us instantly that we met with Chuck DeCaro the other night.

CH. Oh, you finally found that rascal! I had a question for him.

PR. He's looking forward to seeing you. We got his business card for you.

CH. Yeah, I'd like to talk to him. I ran into a lot of people who bumped into him through the years. Apparently he's got an airplane and gets around the country. We were watching the Desert Storm briefings, and there he popped up asking questions on the screen! [*Laughter.*] He was standing in the back row pointing and hollering!

PR. He was very complimentary to you in the interview we had done with him.

CH. I was reasonably cooperative, although he was rather intrusive.

PR. Well, that's his job.

CH. He showed up at my door in Oklahoma City one Friday night as this cute little redhead and I were just about to have a bottle of champagne in front of the fire, and then there he is out there banging on the door with his camera crew.

PR. Get lost!

CH. And that's what I told him. He ruined the whole evening 'cause then she had to know the whole story and . . .

PR. That really puts a damper on things; that's helped us a lot in relationships, too.

LW. He [DeCaro] said, "Don't be disappointed if it isn't a UFO." What do you think this was?

CH. I don't know. It's more than one thing. It's more than one thing.

LW. Do you remember, I mean, obviously, we never forget these things, but you were out there, you know what it was like looking up, you're squinting, you're looking, the lights are shining down, things are scooting over your head, you know you're just, your mind . . .

CH. They weren't scooting. No, the interesting thing was, what we initially saw was very similar to what they put on the NBC thing, because I worked with the guy from Apogee Productions. They do all the, they did *Superman, Star Wars.* I sat down with a guy and described a lot of things to him. And then he did it in sketches, and I said, no, it was this way or that way. His rendition of the craft or whatever it was was not very accurate. The lights were not in proper placement and things. But whatever this first object was, the red glowing object, was actually moving in the trees around, you know, maneuvering back and forth and then went out into the field, before it broke into five objects.

LW. I saw that thing. When you discount one thing, something else jumps in you've got to look at. It's just a constant big bag of worms. I should have been easy to blow out of the water, but there's too many problems. One thing I wanted to cut to the chase on: soon after this, I started to have eye problems. Whether I saw a thing explode or I didn't see a bright source of light . . .

CH. You couldn't have been too close—you were not in front of us— there were no people in front of us. There were only five people past that point, except when Burroughs, I think, came forward. You had to have been well behind us, at least a hundred, two hundred yards, when you saw the object. That doesn't mean you didn't . . .

LW. I had eye problems anyway, within days. I went to the Bentwaters clinic, my eyes *hurt.* Burroughs has eye problems due to this sort of thing. He grabbed the thing, and it moved. He can best handle that himself, but this is when I started.

CH. He was out there on two occasions, I can talk to you about that. He was one of the three cops that actually approached or claimed to have approached something and initially started the whole thing.

LW. I had nothing to do with that.

CH. I came on duty that morning, just as they say on the NBC thing, real early in the morning. McCabe was on the [LE] desk, about five o'clock I walked in. He was tidying up the blotters, getting ready to close 'em out at six. He said, "What do I put in there?" I said, "Penniston and Burroughs, and, uh, I've forgotten who now, were out chasing a UFO all night!'' You know I kind of laughed, I thought he was joking and said, "I don't know what to put in the blotter." He said, "Skip the entry, don't put anything in it." I said, "Oh, you got to put an entry in the blotter, you don't have to put a UFO. They saw lights, they thought it was a plane, they saw this . . ." I said, "They saw some lights here, whatever, put the times in there because, who knows? Something could happen, be important, have that in the log." By the way, those logs all disappeared. But I think I know where they went.

LW. Do you think they exist? [*Halt nods.*]

CH. I think a former member of the security police squadron has them. He retrieved them before somebody got them. Maybe even the security blotters too, which would be more interesting to see than the law-enforcement blotters because the law-enforcement blotters are a very innocuous thing. It just said "lights." I'm saying the security blotter may have a lot more information in it. I tried to retrieve them later on—they were gone.

LW. If they weren't gone, would they be disposed of?

CH. I looked while I was still at Bentwaters, about a year or so later— '83 I went looking for them. That day, both of them were gone. But I think one of the participants took them.

LW. [*Going on to the next document.*] This is the thing where they sent me up because they suspected I had burns to my retinas.

CH. Did Lester Sharpton look at you? He was the eye doctor at the time.

LW. I can't re[member]. But I went up to Lakenheath, and I had an appointment.

CH. We only had one eye doctor.

LW. I was put under anesthetic when they did this thing, I was there overnight. I don't have those records, but my stuff, I can't even touch it. I mean I know outright, I had guys come to me and try to play around with this thing—NSA, all the way. I didn't even know who NSA was years ago.

CH. Why would they approach you, and why wouldn't they approach me? Because you're talking publicly?

PR. This guy was a loose cannon, he identified himself as a problem, he has a big mouth, he's pushy—I know that real well—and that's not comfortable.

LW. You know, I'm not a crazy person. I would rather this had not been the case.

CH. Meaning obsessed?

PR. . . . and so have I become over the past five and three-quarter years on this.

CH. You know, I don't live and breathe and whatever for *this*.

PR. I look forward to putting it in the background, too. I mean, life's got to go on.

CH. Sometimes it gets to become a big nuisance.

PR. More than that. I don't know. As a close party here that wasn't involved that night, *I* felt that you two have more in common than you have separating you. This couldn't have been fun, it's humiliating. All of a sudden you're an officer who is associated with UFOs. There's all this idiocy in the media. Was there *any* positive benefit for you over the years of this? Of course not.

CH. No.

We gave Halt copies of the report on the 1956 Bentwaters incident and some of the responses to our FOIA actions and inquiries.

PR. If you can't get the truth, it's nice to get every variation of evasion possible.

LW. After these events happened and some of us talked, there were things that they had had happen to them before, Bustinza being one of them. There seems to be a kind of fine line here, that certain guys were identified because of their previous experiences and maybe used in some way.

CH. I went out to debunk the thing, quite frankly, that's how I got involved. Lieutenant Englund came in to the covered-dish dinner and said, "It's back." I laughed and said, "What are you talking about?" but he was obviously shaken. The whole cop squadron was going crazy on us here now, everybody's seeing things. So [Base Commander] Conrad had to stay and make the awards, and I said, "Well, I'll go home and put my fatigues on and go out and get rid of this, once and for all."

PR. And the rest is history.

CH. Yeah, and that's how I got involved. I just happened to pick up my little recorder and just happened to think, well, I better take [Airman Greg] Nevels. He was on standby for disaster preparedness, so he came along so that we can take a Geiger counter and *say* that there's no radiation because someone will say . . .

PR. Absolutely. Did you check?

CH. [*Indicates yes.*] I intend someday to have my day in court in England, publicly, if I have the opportunity. I'd like to state for the record what I saw, and they'll be some people that are very embarrassed.

LW. A lot of people get hurt by this phenomenon. They just do—I'm one of them. What I'd like to do is give you an opportunity, in our book, to state what your feelings are. Write whatever—if you say "Larry Warren is a liar," whatever—no editing, no censoring, nothing.

CH. I'll certainly entertain that.

PR. The other thing is, on this tape, where it's been on the record, do you feel there's anything that we've recorded here that you might not want me to quote from?

CH. No. If I think I was going to say something, I've already asked you to turn the tape off once, and I'll tell you a couple of other things if you turn the tape off.

[*Tape off/Tape on*]

CH. There was no revelation that I know of. There was a lot of excitement, static electricity in the air, if you know what I mean, but I was very very curious, yes. I certainly would like to have answers to some things, and I suspect I may never have.

PR. When I started on this, when I met Larry and he asked me to work on the book—of course, I had no idea of what I was getting into—I had this little idealistic thought that wouldn't it be good if we do a book that's so powerful and impacting that other men would come forward and support his story. You know what? I'm going to encourage everyone that hasn't come forward to not come forward. Why bother? It's not going to prove anything. Another witness is another target. Another person coming forward just becomes another curiosity to be picked at and hurt. Until this breaks big time, I've become quite a cynic on that, and I really don't feel that twenty more guys coming forward and backing him up is going to do anything but give fuel for twenty more tabloid TV shows. I'm sorry to say that, but I really feel that.

CH. You're probably right. But it won't add any impact to your book, because your book will probably be bought by a select audience that already has their *own* perceptions and is convinced that there *is* something out there, or something here or whatever.

PR. We can understand why you say that, but . . .

CH. A disbeliever is not necessarily going to pick up your book and become a believer.

PR. We understand that.

LW. In the book, all avenues point [to] the NSA's office. I'm so low-level on this stuff. If you talk to these guys, you know better than I do, you know because you've dealt with some people out there that are in that stuff, it's a joke! They just sit back and laugh, but they're doing something. They did something to me when I was twenty.

PR. The question he [Halt] asked was why has the story changed.

LW. Number one, I wasn't going to say I saw a life-form or anything like that. There was no Halt document out, there was just . . . I read a thing in *Omni* magazine two weeks after I spoke to Fawcett. The timing was amazing!

CH. They tricked Conrad into saying that, and he was livid when he read that! The guy called him long distance on the phone and asked him a couple of questions to finish that article. He had no idea what was going on or anything else.

LW. Those witnesses weren't even me. In fact, I was on record with Fawcett two weeks before that *Omni* came out. By the time we did an interview on the BBC, he said, "You saw 'em. There's more to this story and you're not saying it." I said, "Well, there was something that was alive there." It progressed from there. [*Clear Intent*] had me blacking out. The easy way to deal with what I could deal with . . .

CH. . . . referring to the two tapes I have.

LW. I'd have to hear what the differences are, they might be just subtle. But the story has been rather consistent for twelve years. I didn't add anything on to make it more marketable. So if it is psychotronics and drugs and all this, why? To what advantage were these guys, or some of us, dealt with in that way? Did they move in and take advantage of a situation that was already going on? I dragged my wife there [to Bentwaters] on my honeymoon.

PR. Good move, huh?

LW. I said, "You've got to see this place." The marriage lasted three years. I took Peter back. I said "To *do* this, you really have to go to this base. It's a *strange* area. It feels funny over there."

CH. Are you aware there's a lot of strange things about the area, in addition to RAF Bodzy. Are you familiar with Bodzy?

LW. I remember the name of the place, but . . .

CH. RAF Bodzy's where all the original radar research was done during World War II, and there were a lot of strange experiments done there that may have, you know, sent out a lot of different frequencies and done some strange things that attracted some attention, who knows. In fact, the little village outside Butley Village—outside the back gate?—I'm told, is where witchcraft started in England.

LW. That's right.

CH. There's a lot of strange things in that area. The whole area is fraught with East End Charlie stories. I can't tell you how many young cops would tell me out at the back gate, "I need help," or "I need relief," or something, and I'd send somebody out or just stay out there with them for a little while.

LW. East End Charlie. Remember that, druid ceremonies?

CH. Guys over at Woodbridge saw stuff, too.

LW. The lady without a face.

CH. Pilots dragging World War II leather helmets behind them.

LW. Oh, yeah! Over to the Air Rescue.

CH. I don't know how much of it was imagination, staying out there for eight hours a night, you know you could see all *kinds* of things.

LW. I bring Peter back to England, and we stay right in Eyke, at this inn there. The first night we're out there . . .

CH. You told me, you saw something.

LW. Oh, it was like a Busby Berkley production on Broadway—it was unbelievable. . . . [*On the soil changes:*] we walked up, stand on the rise, and in this field, it was right there, a dark discoloration in one central spot, and we looked at it.

PR. My first thought was, this is an anomaly, it's a play of light; certainly it's not . . . Even if that thing landed, or was right where Larry said it was, it wouldn't leave a mark after eight years.

CH. I still have an original soil sample taken that night.

PR. Good souvenir.

LW. Have you ever had it analyzed?

CH. No, I started to a couple of times. [   ] was going to analyze it for me, he never got back with me so . . .

PR. What would you want to analyze?

CH.   Well, I don't know. At the time I was taking samples, I just took a 35 millimeter film cassette which I had and just scooped up a . . .

PR.   That's what I did.

CH.   . . . full soil sample, out of curiosity—this might come in handy some day—put it in my pocket and forgot about it, dropped it in my desk drawer, then found it a few years later. I just put it aside.

BO.   Without a control sample, there's not . . . you can't really do much.

CH.   I realize that now. My intent was if it were necessary at *that* time, I'd use it, which I never did.

LW.   You know, talking with a lot of other guys over the years with this, even if they state things on the public record, it's amazing what they tell you when you're sitting with them in an isolated . . . and then after that it was, *hell, no, I didn't* . . .

CH.   Well, something happened. What happened, I don't know. It wasn't an experiment, definitely wasn't. There was no lost time. We were on three different radio frequencies at the same time, and there was enough interplay between all the different nets that we weren't off any of them for more than thirty seconds at the most. My recollections fit very closely in with all the people, the four or five people that were with me that night, and I've had an opportunity through the years to talk with them. In fact, Bobby Ball, you remember him?

LW.   Absolutely.

CH.   I talked with him when we did the NBC thing, I talked with Verrano at great length, and everything all fits together. There were no discrepancies other than somebody remembers this detail a little better or that detail a little better.

LW.   Which is common.

CH.   Oh, yeah. For instance, Bobby Ball pointed out when he saw the things in the sky, he thought it was a grid pattern and they were searching. I'm not sure I remember it that way, I remember the pattern, but I'm not sure if it was a *grid*. There were sharp angular movements, and I'm not—I wouldn't argue with him.

LW.   I didn't see anything flying except a red light, except when we went back.

CH.   One of the most interesting things . . . You want to turn the tapes off?

[Tape off/tape on]

CH.   My intent isn't to destroy anyone.

LW.   Oh, not you, no, I understand.

CH.   My intent is to—if anybody asks—to keep it as factual as possible. There's enough distortions and enough people looking for things out there that take a scrap here and a scrap there, and build something . . .

LW.   I agree.

CH.   Good luck. That's all I can say.

LW.   Thank you.

Halt had to go back to his office. The three of us stood and shook hands with him, then he walked away. Bob said something, but I wasn't listening. I wasn't anything for a moment and could only wonder how Larry was doing. We sat there briefly, then began walking, but not far. Larry needed to sit for a minute, you could see he was shaken—I knew I was.

BO.   I can't wait to see what you actually come out with. There was one really interesting comment he made, essentially indicating he wasn't all that concerned about the book, because he considers it will be focused at a very special-interest group, and nobody's going to read it.

PR.   Yep. It's another flying-saucer book.

LW.   Everything connects.

PR.   When you're obsessed . . .

LW.   Yeah. I am glad that Bob was there and heard, I really am.[45]

I was glad that I had recorded the conversation and looked forward to reviewing the tape later. But I couldn't stop thinking about some of what Halt had just told us. The SP log and Blotter for the nights in question had disappeared. More than one "thing" had happened, and "the real story" was "what happened afterward." He'd tried to be nice about it, but the man was adamant. Larry had been "meddled" with, yet it hadn't been "an experiment." Then there were his off-the-record comments! Jesus Christ, how deep did this go?

Whatever the answer to that question, we all agreed it had been a solid, respectable contact. The colonel had not questioned any of Larry's paperwork, which reminded me: he never produced, or even mentioned, the documents he'd repeatedly referred to in our phone conversations. Had he forgotten to bring them? I didn't think so. Had they been a bluff? I doubted that, too. Maybe they just weren't that convincing, especially after seeing the papers in Larry's possession.

It was now past three, and both Larry and Bob longed for lunch, but somewhere away from Pentagon City. As Bob started walking toward the escalator, Larry turned to me and said, "You know, Peter, for the first time in years, I really feel scared." You should, *I thought; so should I.*

As we drove back past the Pentagon, I strained to remember something I'd copied into one of my notebooks months before, something Bill Moyers had written:

We were taught to look at government as a blessing and to respect authority for its own sake. The splendid monuments with their noble inscriptions merely confirmed the altruism we had been taught to believe was the essence of the American experience. But for forty years a secret government has been growing behind these stately tributes to American ideals, growing like a cancer on the Constitution.[46]

What a coincidence, I thought; so much for Mr. Smith Goes to Washington. *"National security" meant whatever its definers wanted it to mean. Our precious republic was quietly becoming a national security state: a place where keeping secrets had proven to be more important than safeguarding the most decent aspects of our American democracy. Screwing over the lives of a bunch of young airmen hadn't been personal, just necessary: it was a matter of national security.*

I left Baltimore Wednesday morning feeling pretty beat. So much so that as I sat down next to a sleepy girl, I felt as if I was going to cry. The dozing teenager in the window seat hadn't noticed, but the moment left me feeling shaken.

As the car shuddered to a start, I put a cassette in my Walkman, put on my headphones, and tried listening to some music. But I wasn't keeping it together very well. In fact, my mind was racing through the hows and whys that had elevated this great unspoken postwar "thing" into the mother of all secrets. About Truman, and the men who had first pulled the wagons into a circle, and about the men who had turned that circle into an institution. And Bentwaters! Memories of people, places, details, and particulars of a hundred parts of the story came flooding back as we rolled through Maryland. All the miles, letters, research, and interviews. All the questioning and re-questioning, the friends lost over the years. What had I done with my life? For all our efforts, for everything Larry had been through, what had we really gained? We were being worn down, and I knew it. We were fighting a tank with a spiderweb.

Looking around me, I began to notice the faces in our car. They were of almost every type and color: black, white, Asian, Latin, Middle Eastern. I didn't know any of these people, but found myself wondering about their lives.

About the nurse and her daughter I'd ridden down to South Carolina next to, and the grandmother I'd been laughing with as we entered Baltimore. Would all of them really go to pieces if they knew what I thought I knew? It might not be easy, but I expected they would all make it through the revelation.

It was about then that I began to wonder if I would. I knew I was tired, exhausted really, but this feeling had a different source, and for the next few minutes, all optimism fled from me.

There was no longer any question in my mind: we had what we needed to produce a book that American and British readers could take seriously. A number might even begin to demand their own answers. Some satisfaction attached to that possibility, but so did a sense of regret. Larry was already on record about his contacts with the NSA, but without the supporting research, his account would be left to swing in the wind, and the agency's involvement might come off as little more than another endnote. The research and organization for our book had been all mine, and the fact was, I was beginning to regret it. There was really no denying that drawing attention to the NSA could prove to be the most reckless thing I had ever done. The thought frightened me.

The term "paranoid" expressed my feelings nicely. I can only say that I now faced a very uncomfortable fact: my actions might have put my life at risk. For all I knew, everything on my computer could be in Fort Meade Maryland right now.

"You're overreacting," I said to myself, but myself would have none of it. How would they react if they knew how tightly I'd woven them into the book? No one else knew where all the disks were, or our original tapes, notes, documents, and backup copies. Take me out, and Linda would drop the book real quick; whether Larry would complete it on his own I couldn't say; I only knew that I'd get the message if Larry had an "accident"—probably even if it was an accident.

The interior of the passenger car felt small and claustrophobic, and I eased myself out of the seat. A cigarette, I thought; nothing like some smoke in the lungs to deaden sensation temporarily. Lighting up between cars, I told myself there was nothing to worry about. The wind coming through felt good. I was alone and should calm down. They, whoever "they" were, probably weren't losing any sleep over me, or Larry.

Relax, I told myself, but it wasn't happening. I had to be careful. Wasn't it just possible that someone had been told to board this train because I had boarded it and, knowing I was a smoker, sat reading his paper until the voice in his earpiece told him that I was now alone between the cars. And wasn't it just as possible that he was now walking calmly toward this compartment, would enter, nod, then suddenly turn, and try to throw me . . .

No! But for a moment, I truly expected to see some half-crazed version of Joseph Cotten come crashing through the door and try to throw me off the train,

as he had tried to throw Teresa Wright off one at the climax of Hitchcock's
Shadow of a Doubt.

*I cannot tell you exactly how I recovered my life in that moment, but it did
have something to do with the sudden, mental guest appearance of this charming
and luminous actress—especially as a point of identification! The absurdity just
seemed to slam head-on into my concerns of NSA extermination, and I just let
go behind it. I started to laugh so hard that I could not stop. I laughed until
I was all laughed out. I don't know if the sound of my outburst carried back
into the car, but no one intruded on me during the scene, and I returned to my
seat unnoticed.*

*The girl to my right was just waking up. We started to talk, stopped to
introduce ourselves, then began a real conversation. The next thing I knew we
were pulling into Penn Station and saying good-bye like old friends. "Keep
writing," she called after me, never having asked what it was I wrote about.*

*I exited onto Eighth Avenue and walked over to wait for a bus. I lit another
cigarette with the Zippo I had had out in the field with us that first, fateful
night in England, then looked around; it was great to be back in the city. I'd
really have to give up smoking, but not today, 16 February 1993. Five years
and a day earlier, Larry and I were just arriving in England.*

6. 1993 TO THE PRESENT

March 1993

*The MoD has announced that it has no future long-term
defence requirement for Bentwaters, or its sister base at
Woodbridge.*

The last of Bentwaters' A-10s are assigned to the 510th Fighter Squadron and depart for Spangdahlem, Germany. The Eighty-first's remaining F-4s become part of the 561st Fighter Squadron at Nellis AFB in Nevada.[47]

22 March 1993

The damage that "absurd" and disturbing cold-war security clearances have done to American ideals is the subject of a *U.S. News and World Report* business story:

> A guide for National Security Agency contractors (marked "for official use only")
> forbids employees to have "close and continuing associations, which are char-
> acterized by ties of kinship, affection or obligation," with any non-U.S. citizens.
> . . . [They] may even refuse to release information to cleared personnel from an-
> other agency.

LARRY WARREN & PETER ROBBINS | 371

... Intelligence information is especially tightly controlled; a special clearance to receive "sensitive compartmentalized information" (SCI) is needed, and even then the originating agency will often stamp documents "ORCON"—originator controlled—meaning that the data cannot be incorporated into any other documents . . . in many incorporated into any other documents . . . in many cases this means vital information must be left out of a report.

... "Declassification" is a painfully slow process, however. "It takes a scandal to compel government action," says Steven Aftergood, who edits the *Secrecy & Government Bulletin* for the Federation of American Scientists. . . . "If we're going to fight this issue by issue, it's never going to end."[48]

19 September 1993

Secrecy is not just a way of life at spy agencies; it is a state religion. The National Archives is steward to 325 million classified documents, including still-secret files dating to World War I. When documents are declassified, key passages are often blacked out, on the pretext of protecting sources and methods. But keepers of these secrets are equally protective of evidence of gross misjudgments and abuse of power.[49]

30 November 1993

Numerous individuals observe UFOs over the Glens Falls, New York, area in sightings that continue through 9 December 1993. All witnesses agree the lights are silent and do not behave like conventional aircraft:

Dan Ripley, manager of the Glens Falls Flight Center at the Warren County Airport, said . . . "The only explanation I would have is that a lot of military helicopter training has been going on at the airport." . . . However, he noted that military helicopters make a loud noise.[50]

24 January 1994

The National Security Agency is trying to establish a standard for electronically scrambling computer communications, a move that would go far beyond the agency's usual military and intelligence domain to include civilian activities like electronic tax returns and computerized medical payments.

The plan by the N.S.A., which may be announced as early as today, worries business executives and privacy advocates, who fear government encroachment. And some officials in the Clinton administration believe that the N.S.A. is overstepping its bounds.[51]

4 February 1994

Turning aside vehement objections from computer makers, communications companies and civil rights groups concerned about privacy, the Clinton administration adopted a technology today that would enable law enforcement agencies to intercept coded telephone and computer communications. . . .

   The Clipper Chip . . . was designed in cooperation with the National Security Agency. . . . The technology contains a secret "back door" that enables law enforcement officials to unscramble the coded phone calls or computer data that flow through networks.[52]

9 March 1994

This morning Earl Howe, Forestry Minister, will plant a little oak in Suffolk. This will mark the 75th anniversary of the Forestry Commission, and will also complete the replanting of Rendlesham Forest. The forest took a terrible battering in the 1987 hurricane. The commission says one million trees were blown down, and Earl Howe's oak will be the two millionth planted in replacement.[53]

15 March 1994

BBC News reports that a request from the Suffolk business community to develop land on now-closed RAF Bentwaters has been turned down by the Ministry of Defence. Business representatives say they cannot understand why.[54]

June 1994

The London firm of Central Productions Ltd. has made documentary films for decades. Recently completed is a new documentary on UFOs for ITV. Producer Lawrence Moore's project has taken seven years to realize and months in filming and postproduction. The finished product conforms to Central's usual high standards and has taken their crew as far as Russia and as near as East Anglia. Their visit in March 1994 marked the first time a professional film crew had visited the sites of the Bentwaters incidents with one of the original air force witnesses: Larry Warren.

29 June 1994

Central Productions consultant Timothy Good writes to Peter Robbins:

The Central documentary is now complete, and will be transmitted throughout the ITV Network on 18th October at 10:40 p.m. I'm a little disappointed since so much has had to be cut in order to squeeze it into one hour . . . but on the whole it's good, and we have some *excellent* interviews with Russian military personnel. And Larry's interview is absolutely first-rate![55]

25 July 1994

Col. Charles Halt, a former American Air Force base commander, will be in Britain to deliver lectures on UFOs and will recount his own experience of an unearthly encounter.

Col. Halt, who retired in 1992 after 28 years service will be . . . in Manchester on Saturday to speak about what happened at RAF Woodbridge in Suffolk in December 1980.

. . . In a taped interview with Mr. (Harry) Harris, Col. Halt said, "I became involved in UFOs as a non-believer but I am now convinced we saw something beyond anything we can understand and was not built by any government on earth."[56]

1 August 1994

Documentary producers Moore and Livia Russell write to Warren and Robbins from London: the Learning Channel in America will begin broadcasting Central's UFO documentary in September or October 1994, and ITV's airdate is holding at 18 October. Reassured of the airdate, Warren and Robbins begin plans for a coincident visit. At the least, they can meet with a publisher at an optimum time. Warren's current passport is near expiration, and he applies for a renewal. The standard application asks an optional question: does the holder already have a destination planned? Warren writes "England" in the box. Form, fee, and passport are then sent to the National Passport Center.

Within the week, Livia Russell updates Larry by phone; the U.K. airdate has been pushed back a few days.[57]

4 September 1994

Timothy Good writes to Peter Robbins:

The Central Productions documentary—in which Larry features prominently—has been postponed to "sometime next year." This is very frustrating for all of us. . . . This may or may not affect your plans for coming over this fall. . . . [58]

Robbins and Warren cancel their travel plans.

16 September 1994

The Department of State notifies Larry Warren by form letter that his passport cannot be returned to him; it "has been altered or mutilated." He will now have to appear before a passport agent or designated court employee with acceptable proof of his U.S. citizenship, fill out his form in their presence, and "submit a signed written statement explaining the reason for the condition of your altered/mutilated passport."[59]

5 October 1994

Larry Warren calls the State Department's Portsmouth Consular Center in New Hampshire. He is connected with a woman at the National Passport Center (NPC) who quickly brings his records up on her computer screen. Warren briefly explains his predicament and asks if she can help to clarify it. Yes, the NPC employee confirms, the State Department did send him the "altered/mutilated" form letter on 16 September, but only at the behest of the Department of Defense (DOD). Larry's passport dilemma is the result of his speaking out on "sensitive defense issues in a public forum on foreign soil." He should be aware that the DOD currently considers him to be in violation of the National Security Act of 1947. A forthcoming letter would confirm this and cite the particulars, but no letter of this description ever arrives.[60]

13 October 1994

Warren again telephones the State Department's regional office and again explains his situation to the woman taking his call. She attempts to access his file, but finds there is no file to access. At some point the preceding week, all records pertaining to Larry Warren had disappeared off the department's computers. Somewhat shaken, Warren ends the call and makes one to his coauthor. Both agree it is now imperative they consult with a lawyer. Robbins phones their literary agent to apprise him of the development.[61]

17 October 1994

Excerpts from a letter from Peter Robbins to Ramsey Clark, attorney at law:

Dear Mr. Clark,

First, thank you again for taking the time to speak with me on Thursday morning. . . .

This letter, and the selection of attached letters, documents and articles will serve to introduce you to my co-author, Larry Warren, and our current circumstances. I have also asked our editor to send you some excerpts from *Left At East Gate*. . . . It should arrive at your office Friday. . . . We felt you should have some idea of its scope. . . . The chain of events which have led me to write you defy a brief summation, but I will attempt to sketch out the basics.

. . . The Request For Separation was initiated by him, and began with a December 1980 incident in which he and other Air Force personnel were involved in, and later briefed on, what I can only describe as a UFO incident real enough to burn the retinas of his eyes (see Air Force Medical Report attached). Larry identified himself as a problem for the Air Force almost immediately. . . .

Within twenty-four hours of the event itself, Larry and a number of other military witnesses were made the subjects of a National Security Agency operation in which their legitimate memories of the incident were "meddled with." This [quote] is what we were told by Col. (ret.) Charles I. Halt, Bentwaters Deputy Base Commander in December 1980, and witness to another part of the incident. Halt is convinced that he and the men he was with "saw something beyond anything we can understand and was not built by any government on earth."

Larry attempted to re-enlist in the Air Force . . . [but] his service record . . . was, and continues to be, held at the Ft. Meade Maryland Headquarters of the National Security Agency.

. . . This past March, we returned to England to assist in the filming of Central Productions' UFO documentary (video and producers' letter enclosed), and to speak at the invitation of a Nottingham research group. . . .

Looking to take advantage of the 18 October broadcast date for the documentary, we had planned a corresponding visit to London . . . [but] the trip was canceled. . . . By this time though, Larry had applied for a new passport. As stated in the National Passport Center's form letter of September 16 (attached), Larry's passport had arrived "altered or mutilated," and as such would not be returned to him.

Last week, Larry was informed by phone that the Department of State had revoked his passport at the behest of the DOD . . . because he spoke out on "sensitive defense issues" in public. The truly sensitive issues here concern Air Force involvement in a legitimate UFO incident, and an NSA operation with the moral character of the CIA's LSD experiments of the 1960s. . . .

. . . But what we need now is someone to help Larry get his passport reinstated. . . .

. . . I still remember how the press gave it to you when you visited Hanoi. If you should choose to associate yourself with our fight, you can certainly expect the same again, and then some. I can only say that the Bentwaters incident in

specific, and the UFO cover-up in general, are as real as the crisis in Bosnia. . . .
Like these other trouble spots, it will not go away if ignored.
    . . . Thank you again for considering our "case." . . . [62]

Larry Warren begins to assemble the items he will need to reapply for his passport. It will be his third, but he must file as though it were his first. Ramsey Clark is able to meet with Robbins on a Monday afternoon in December. The two talk for more than an hour. Clark, a former attorney general, takes the matter seriously and says he will be glad to assist as he is able. Larry's application for a passport is turned down in late spring 1995.

The authors meet with Clark on 15 June 1995 to discuss their possible courses of action. In re-reapplying, as per Clark's instruction, Larry is careful to inform the passport agency's local representatives—in this case, the postal employees who have been attempting to assist him—of the former attorney general's interest in the successful disposition of this application. The State Department issues Warren a new passport in July.

January 1995
Paul Pittock and his wife, Marty, live in a house on what used to be the RAF Bentwaters residential area. While driving from Woodbridge through Melton, they see a bright light above the base. It is too low and too close to be a star. Pulling off the road, they watch the light all but stop then begin to move slowly from side to side. The couple get back in their car and head for home, and their binoculars. Paul knocks on his neighbor Richie Warnock's door first and tells him what they've seen. Richie goes for his camera.

Paul cannot find the binoculars, but knows where his telescopic sight is: a standard rifle-type with a sixteen-power magnification. He pockets the scope and goes back to the car. Richie climbs into the backseat, and the three head back to the area. It is now about a quarter after six; the weather is clear, the sky, dark.

As they are approaching Bentwaters, the light goes down toward the flight line and disappears. By the time they stop the car, the glowing has virtually stopped. Disappointed, the trio decides to pull off on the shoulder of the road and watch the sky for a while. They are standing there talking when the first vehicle rumbles into view, then the second, then the third, then the fourth. They just keep going. Paul, Richie, and Marty count something like thirty military vehicles: military and civilian cars, lorries, two military ambulances, and assorted vans, including a big, white one covered with aerials. The convoy is heading toward the main gate of RAF Bentwaters, closed by the Americans sixteen months earlier. All enter the closed base through the main gate.

Their eyes now drawn to the base, all three see the vehicles that are already active there. Some of them are moving fast, but others are driving in a positively frantic manner—you can hear their tires screaming. Behind the trees, flashlights and searchlights are visible, including a very powerful searchlight that projects an intense beam up into the night: it is not the Orford lighthouse. Several helicopters come in over the area Then they see the cause of all the activity.

About 150 yards to the right of the main gate—the place where the light went down—there is an orangy red glow coming from something on the flight line. It is a triangular, glowing shape with a distinct outline. First Paul, then Marty and Richie observe it through the scope. All can see the thing quite clearly, but cannot determine what it is.

Although quite amazed by what they are seeing, at no time do any of the three friends choose to venture in closer for a better look. They stay for a while longer, then leave.[63]

15 July 1995

What follows is the transcript of a hypnotic regression with Larry Warren. It concerns the one thing he has not wanted to confront about his Bentwaters experience and, in fact, never has. The regression is conducted by Budd Hopkins at his home in New York City.

BH.   I want you to see yourself as if you could look into a mirror, a huge, huge full-length mirror, that you're standing in front of. I want you to look at yourself in the mirror, as you were as a young man, a much younger man, air force, civilian clothes this time, the kind of clothes you used to wear when you weren't on duty; be casual. I want you to look at your face, at your eyes, and see in your eyes, first of all, that you're really much younger; in a certain sense, more innocent, and in another sense, there's something in your eyes, that you can see. It has to do with the experiences that you've been through in the past couple of days before this—the past day or so. Very very upsetting and confusing experiences.

   I want you to bring your friend [inaudible] Adrian, also, so he can stand next to you and look in the mirror with you. His face, with the same look that you do, having been through something very confusing, very strange, more difficult to assimilate or to understand.

Look at yourself in the mirror. Then as we move the mirror away, we fade the scene. We want us to go to that particular night, when you were in the dormitory, and you were going to get a call. Somebody's going to call you to the phone. When I count to three is the time they're going to call. Somebody wants you to meet a car outside. When I count to three, you'll take that call; you can tell me what they say. So one, the phone is about to ring and you're about to get called. Two, right on the edge now. Three. Speak whenever you like, I want you to tell me what you hear when you're called to the phone.

LW. "Airman Warren, leave your dormitory right now and meet the black car in the parking lot. You'll recognize it."

BH. Uh-huh. You do anything first? You change your clothes or anything or you just go right out?

LW. No, I'm dressed, all afternoon.

BH. I see. For outside?

LW. Um, no. I have a radio playing in my room upstairs, and I have to turn it off, and I got cigarettes, over by the refrigerator . . .

BH. Um hum.

LW. . . . and I'm having trouble finding a jacket that's appropriate,'cause I'm not in uniform. Have a Yukon Jack sweatshirt . . . has red arms, and says "Heublein, Hartford, Connecticut" on it. "One hundred proof."

BH. Um hum. What are your feelings about this call, while you're getting yourself ready?

LW. I'm in trouble.

BH. What do you think you're in trouble about?

LW. The, uh . . . I feel danger [inaudible]. The situation I'm in is horrifically bad. I want anyth . . . I just don't want to be there.

BH. Um hum. But you know you have to go.

LW. Yeah, I feel sick, confused. I want to . . . get out of there. Um.

BH. So you got your cigarettes and you go downstairs now?

LW. Yeah, uh, I leave actually, second floor, end of the building, down the stairs. Ronnie Hendrickson I see, uh . . . "See you later."

BH. Um hum.

LW. [With slight laugh.] I don't care for him anyway.

BH. So you go outside?

LW. I do.

BH. What do you see when you go outside?

LW. Ah, streetlights are just going on, car pulling up near the stairway, staff sergeant who goes in the building, downstairs. I, I'm looking in the parking lot. I'm looking *at* the parking lot. New housing. Over the fence, there's a car, there . . .

BH. And you said . . .

LW. . . . near a dumpster.

BH. You said there's a black car that you're supposed to meet. Is that the one you see over there?

LW. Yeah.

BH. Um hum. By the dumpster?

LW. Right.

BH. Let's get a look at that car.

LW. [*Pause.*] A black . . . silver—chrome trim, whitewalls, spoked hubcaps.

BH. What kind of car is it you think?

LW. I think an '80 Caddy.

BH. Um hum.

LW. They're cut different, they're different, they're smaller now. Ah, two people, near the driver's side, and I see Bustinza leave his building across the way, and I'm going to go down the stairs. I'm going there, so . . . He's heading in the same direction, uh, streetlights buzz on; everything's yellow. "Airman Warren," yeah. [*Pause.*] I'm talking with Bustinza.

BH. Um hum.

LW. [*Pause, then as if in conversation.*] "No, I w . . . Don't say anything if you don't have to. I'm not gonna, and we're, uh, absolutely, so we're gonna . . . get in the car then." [*Long pause.*] These are not friendly people.

BH. Did they identify themselves by name and rank or anything?

LW. No, but they're asking *me* if I am who I am. Bustinza's in his, uh, working greens, so he's dressed. I'm feeling self-conscious, um, "Yes, I am," and, uh . . . [*Change in pitch and tone; now speaking slightly higher and faster.*] One of them has gone around the front of the car to the other side, and he is opening the front door and kinda looking at us, basically. The back door of my side, on the left side, and, uh, the New York plate, I see, I can see the plate very clearly, I'm right on the corner.

BH. Can you read it?

LW. It is a New York State, '81 is the . . .

BH. Is the year?

LW. No, '81 is the tag, the registration tag on the back. There is, uh, God, 6J9-2B. New York, and '81 is their, February '81 is their expiration. [*Two or three words to self, inaudible.*]

BH. Want to give me that again so I make sure I got it?

LW. 2J1-6B, it's 2J1-6B, there's someth . . . [*Pause.*] January '81 . . . '81 January is how it's . . .

BH. Yeah, OK. Do you look at that for any particular reason, or just casually notice that?

LW. Because it's New York.

BH. I see. OK. So let's see how you get in the car. Does somebody tell you to get in?

LW. Ah, he opens the door, and, uh, I'm rather hesitant, and I'm not s . . . sure about Bustinza. I call him Busty.

BH. When you get in the car, I mean he opens the door . . .

LW. There's a, a folder, on the seat, paper.

BH. Like a file folder, or . . .

LW. Black leather-bound folder, with paper. Ah, [car] interior is dark material, and as I . . . the light is very bright inside, the *right* front dash . . . it's not right. [*Pause.*] As I, uh . . . there's like a deodorant can.

BH. Um hum.

LW. . . . uh, I'm *hit*, with that.

BH. What do you mean?

LW. *I'm sprayed.*

BH. Who sprays you?

LW. [*Pause.*] The cat that opened the door.

BH. He spray it just in general?

LW. There's an aerosol rush of, uh, something at my face.

BH. Yeah.

LW. It's obnoxious, it's horrible. My breathing is, uh, my chest is tight, and, uh, tears . . . and I'm *pushed.*

BH. Did you cough?

LW. No. No, I'm trying to hold my breath, 'cause there's this lingering . . . um, I'm half, I'm half in the car!

BH. Yeah.

LW. And I think I'm getting hit again! But it burns; it burns the eyes, it's burning my mouth and nose, and breathing is hard, it's difficult, and I'm *pushed* [*pause*], and I'm furious.

BH. You, try to get back at him?

LW. I expect it. I expect this. I, I'm trying to hang on to the roof of the car—the lip of the roof—and *pushed*. I keep getting pushed in the chest, in the ribs . . . and I'm on my, on the *floor* of the car, and I, I literally am trying to breathe, and I'm, uh, scared to hell.

BH. Now, when you say you're pushed and you're on—are you actually *lying* on the floor of the car or standing on it or what?

LW. I'm laying on the floor, my head's on the, uh, the axle.

BH. Um hum.

LW. Uh, and I can't get up, I can't get out of this confined, uh, and I'm being like squashed, my legs are being squished in, under the *seat*, and, uh, I'm furious, and I can't breathe.

BH. How do your legs get up on the seat, if you're lying . . .

LW. I'm being *pushed*. I can't even see anything I'm being pushed . . .

BH. Yeah.

LW. . . . but it's these cats doing it, and that's, uh—it's bullshit.

BH. You say anything to them?

LW. Every time I open my mouth, I'm getting hit with this stuff.

BH. Yeah.

LW. I'm not . . . I can't breathe, uh, I feel a heavy . . . I feel, uh, sweat, uh, *hot*, being pushed, *moved*, um, *nauseous* . . .

BH. Um hum.

LW. . . . and, my *head* pushed. I'm sitting upright, my head's pushed back, against the backseat.

BH. So, somehow you were lifted up on this seat, or . . .

LW. I'm being slapped around without even being allowed to fight back, these fuckers. . . . Uh, and I'm, um . . . I can't open my eyes. I can't breathe, at all, and I can't move. A bright light, like a flashlight in my eye, and its horrific—horrible to look at it; my left eye: a white, bright light, and there's . . . I can't really move, and I feel, tired.

BH. Do either of these men say anything more to you, other than . . .

LW. They're saying, they're yelling, and I think it's at Busty, but it's not, clear. It's, *slow*, like a slow record.

BH. Now, at this point, do you feel that the car's moving, or is it still still?

LW.   St . . . moving, now, but there's a long, uh, I *really* have cau . . . given a problem, and I think Busty is as well, to these people. There's black . . .

BH.   Um hum. Now let's just see what you're experiencing as you drive along, with this problem of being nauseous and not being able to breathe well, not being able to see.

LW.   Just, uh, I *can't*; the eyes, I can't open, they burn, it's a burning feeling in my eyes, and my throat burns—the back of my throat burns, and my breathing burns—and it's, the . . . I don't have mobility. I hear traffic. I feel, uh, to my left, the ashtray, in the door; the handle—I can't even move it. My fingers are on the handle—nothing.

BH.   Have you ever felt anything like this before?

LW.   No.

BH.   This is unique, so far . . .

LW.   Uh, never. Never.

BH.   Ever been around tear gas in any training?

LW.   Once.

BH.   Was it like that?

LW.   No. Tear gas is, uh, it doesn't inca . . . it won't put you *down*. It won't, it doesn't make, your limbs stop. In fact, you want to *run*, when you're around it; you do.

BH.   Right. So, you feel the traffic? You hear the traffic? You feel the ashtray? Door handle to your left . . .

LW.   I, I haven't . . . I see a bright pin spot of, white light in my left eye. It's the only imagery, and it's all I have, is to see, is this white . . .

BH.   Um hum.

LW.   . . . and, um, cigarette, smell.

BH.   Are either of these men touching you?

LW.   No.

BH.   Now let's go through the first time you sense a change in this, in your situation. Maybe for instance, suddenly you're, or gradually you're able to move? Perhaps you're able to see. Perhaps you hear something. Perhaps the car stops—it could be any number of things. Let's move this on to the next thing that you notice as a change.

LW.   Um, the doors open, on both sides of the car, uh, it's cold—it's cold *out*, and it's, uh, uh, someone behind my *head*, is pulling me out, of this car, grabbing my head.

I feel like I'm—part of me . . . I'm laying on the ground, and I'm, uh, my cheek is on ice, uh, pavement and ice. And I'm picked up, by it has to be more than two people, but I can breathe better, and, uh, I'm afraid that I'm going to be dropped on my face. Uh, I'm outside, I know it. This is on the flight line, and you can hear the A-10s, you could . . . very close, very close. Uh, door opens, uh, I feel like I have a bloody nose.

BH. How can you tell the door opens?

LW. I hear it. I hear it, and they're maneuvering, me, in through a door, this is . . .

BH. Um hum.

LW. There's a . . .

BH. You have a nosebleed . . .

LW. I feel like, my nose is running, and I'm embarrassed, I . . .

BH. Yeah.

LW. . . . I'm not sh . . . , but I, I can't tell. [*Pause.*] This, uh . . . it's bright, it's a, somewhat like a, an elevator, and I can *see* this.

BH. So your eyes can open and close.

LW. I can see the back corner of an elevator, a small room, and, and it's very *rapid*; it's, there's descent . . . I see people standing [inaudible]. I'm facing, I'm facing down.

BH. Um hum. Now, let's see the positions you would feel the parts of your body, what is pinching where you're being held.

LW. [*Exhales.*] The, uh, rib cage, pelvis, and my ankles, and prob . . . uh, my forehead, but there's something, uh . . . the *sides* of my head . . . it's, uh, near the top.

BH. So this is rapid descent; still, is there any conversation you pick up, from the people you're with?

LW. I hear, a conversation, I can't, uh, it's all like a record, a slow record. There's a [*pause*], a, that fades . . . that's . . . that's not becoming clear, anymore. [*Pause.*] That room is not clear anymore.

BH. [inaudible] about the room?

LW. This, uh, this *elevator* is not clear, it's a—the *imagery*, it's not there . . . it's not a . . . [*pause*] at all.

BH. Um hum. Do you feel at all you've been hit again by this stuff, or do you . . .

LW. No. I feel a void.

BH. Um hum. OK, so when, do you feel the elevator *stopped* at some point? You said you felt a descent.

LW. I just feel, going down, like the Empire State Building. Uh, that was, that was it.

BH. Now, what's the next thing that becomes clear, next change; all this is very chronological. Is this elevator feeling, the rapid descent, that your nose is running and so forth . . . Let's see, what happens next that's a memorable kind of change.

LW. [*Pause.*] I'm sitting upright, and there's a [*pause*] doctor . . .

BH. Um hum.

LW. . . . eyewash? You know, eyewash—Visine, a, and a cup, and a— my eyes, burn. And my—he wipes my face off, with a cloth. And, uh, sitting in a chair.

BH. Um hum. Can you, now that you see a little better, could you see anything about this doctor? Does he have a laminated name tag or anything like that?

LW. No. Uh, receding hairline, dark, short, military, haircut. Ah . . . six foot, and, um, it's hard to say, brown eyes, nose kind of like mine, and, um, thirty-nine, forty.

BH. Um hum. What does he say to you?

LW. Nothing. Nothing at all . . . nothing.

BH. And is this doctor someone you may have seen before somewhere on the base, or is he some . . .

LW. No. No, but my impression is, of a doctor. The white coat, and the room is, very medically oriented [*pause*], like an emergency room. There are some other areas with curtains, and there's a door to this room and glass windows with, in the door and in the office, the room, and you can see other areas like an emergency room.

BH. Um hum.

LW. [*Long pause.*] I have no clue what a . . . really, no clue, at all, with . . . uh . . .

BH. Were you able to speak? Ask?

LW. I, I'm just not asking; I'm just sitting, and looking [*slight laugh*]. . . . I've *been* in a clinic on Bentwaters—this isn't it. We only have one, on the base, it's not it.

BH. Um hum.

LW. [*Pause.*] And then another person comes in . . . air force, um . . . full colonel! "Airman Warren," uh, "come with me and sit in this other room." There's another room across the hallway from this. We go past these curtains, these partitions . . . to a hallway, *cross* the hallway is a, room . . . uh, Bustinza's sitting there: "How you doing?'' We both . . . "How are you? What's . . ." just, numb. And, there's [Larry names four individuals] . . . a lot of people I know.

BH.   Um hum. How many would you say in all?

LW.   Seven.

BH.   Um hum. And everybody's sitting down?

LW.   Yeah [*pause*], and . . . there's something wrong with this. [*Long pause.*] There, there is, a meeting ! Uh . . .

BH.   Um hum.

LW.   . . . but this is not the same, situation here [as the debriefing earlier in the day], um . . . [*Long pause.*] This a . . . I'd like to jump out of this mode, I think. I think I really would like to! This is, um, this isn't right.

BH.   Larry, would you like to end this right now?

LW.   Yeah, I think so, oh, I would . . .

BH.   OK, we'll come back another time.

LW.   I would. I really would.

BH.   OK. [Budd begins to bring Larry out. End of this regression.][64]

21 August 1995

The annual British UFO Research Association conference is held in Sheffield and well-covered by a variety of media. The *Times* of London carries this piece at the top of page four of Monday's edition:

The ufologist everyone wanted to meet at the Sheffield UFO conference was Larry Warren, a bearded, bespectacled American. He is the co-author with Peter Robbins of *Left At East Gate*, to be published next year, about an incident at a US airbase in Woodbridge, Suffolk, in 1980 which seems to be a classic case of unearthly beings and terrestrial cover-ups.

On the night of December 28–29, Mr Warren, then 19, was minding nuclear material when he was asked to join an expedition through an East Anglian forest. "We came to a clearing," he said. "The first thing I noticed was a luminous fog covering the ground. There were a lot of security police and senior officers and two cameras and a lot of stills being taken. A red light approached very fast from the direction of the North Sea. When it came over us it was basketball size.

"There was a burst of intense, bright light. After that, a massive structured object could be seen on the ground where the fog had been. There were no windows, but a band of colbalt-blue light around the bottom and a rainbow effect all over. It was rounded, 20 or 30 feet high, concave at the front with pyramid-like appendages, but, no landing gear that I could see.

"Three entities, life forms—I don't use the word alien—appeared, suspended in bright light, bluish gold, almost ghost-like. They had faces and what could have been arms. Very small, only about 3 ½ feet."

Back at the base, men spoke of entities passing through windscreens and flying objects shooting down beams of light. Witnesses were warned to keep their mouths shut and that "bullets are cheap."

Larry Warren is self-deprecatingly humorous about the experience. "I can't say it was alien for sure. But it was certainly alien to me."[65]

2 September 1995

Brussels. The European parliament has decided to investigate a UFO sighting over the English Channel. They will also consider a proposal to fund a permanent European observation station for the sighting of unidentified flying objects. This news is not well received in London. Sir Teddy Taylor, a Tory M.P., attacks the proposal and the French, who, he claims, are supporting it only to get another EU-funded facility on their territory. The Ministry of Defence declines to comment on the sighting and makes no public comment on the proposed tracking center.[66]

29 March 1996

A senior Ministry of Defence official has confirmed the existence of UFO's, it was claimed today.

Believed to be a member of the RAF, he was coaxed into appearing on a TV documentary. . . . In a programme to be shown on BBC2 next month, the official reveals how some case reports of UFOs over Britain consistently to defy rational explanation.

. . . The programme also features a former head of a Government UFO monitoring unit confirming reports of a craft moving at huge speeds. "We had radar reports of objects traveling at 4,000 mph across the North Sea into British airspace—objects as big as battleships," he reveals.

. . . However, a Military spokesman poured scorn on the claims, adding: "We have one person in the RAF secretariat answering inquiries about UFOs—that's it."[67]

23 April 1996

Defence chiefs have broken decades of silence with an unprecedented statement dismissing the possible existence of UFOs. Whitehall has finally decreed that flying saucers and visitors from distant worlds are simply a product of the imagination.

The announcement has astonished defence analysts, who point out that the Ministry of Defence has never before responded despite thousands of reports of mysterious sightings.

The official statement—published in RAF News—comes just a fortnight after a television documentary claimed that the highest levels of government had not discounted the possibility of life on other planets. . . .

. . . It [RAF News] was said to have been ordered to print the article in a bid to quell public interest which had escalated since the broadcast.[68]

27 April 1996

Its OFFICIAL—There are aliens out there and they have been visiting Earth for years, breaching air defences and endangering national security. At least this is the belief of a Ministry of Defence official who has investigated more than 600 alleged UFO sightings and had access to all the top-secret departmental files over 40 years. Nick Pope, a 30-year-old civil servant, was in charge of the MoD's X-Files section—prosaically titled Secretariat (Air Staff) 2a—which handles inquiries into unexplained air phenomena. He arrived in 1991 as a sceptic and left three years later convinced.

Mr Pope still works for the Ministry, which stresses that his opinions are his own and are not shared in Whitehall. . . .

. . . Mr Pope said he had dealt with more than 200 sightings a year and, during his spell at the department, found about 80 that could not be explained. He believes Britain's most famous alleged sighting, on a December night in 1980, in Rendlesham Forest, Suffolk, was compelling evidence of visitors from outer space. . . .

[An MoD spokesman] stressed Mr Pope's job had been purely administrative: "It was not his job to investigate. I am not aware that our air defence has ever been penetrated."[69]

27 May 1996

Nottingham. Monday's edition of the *Evening Post* publishes an extract from Nick Pope's new book, *Open Skies, Closed Minds*. It is on the Bentwaters incident:

At three in the morning on December 27, 1980, two security patrolmen on a routine tour of the perimeter of the RAF/USAF airbase at Woodbridge in Suffolk saw bright lights among the trees of the adjacent Rendlesham Forest. Their first assumption was that an aircraft might have overshot or misjudged the runway and had been forced into the trees, although they had heard no noise. They asked permission to investigate beyond the camp gates, which was duly granted.

In the forest it soon became clear that the object was no aeroplane. They saw a triangular craft unlike anything they had seen before and chased it through the trees. And that was not the end of it.

Two nights later, there was a similar sighting and a larger team led by the deputy base commander, U.S. Air Force Lieutenant-Colonel Charles Halt, went out to investigate.

Halt and his men advanced into the forest, leaving others in the vicinity of the powerful lights, known by the military as light-alls, that had been brought up to illuminate the scene. Their equipment behaved strangely. Although the tape recorder, Geiger counter, and night-vision scope were in perfect working order, all three machines experienced interference. The light-alls refused to work.

It is eerie to hear the 18-minute recording of Halt and his team as they edged their way through the undergrowth to within 150 yards of the light source. . . .

. . . Halt remembered the light vividly in later years: "It pulsated as though it were an eye blinking at you and around the edges it appeared to have molten metal dripping off it. Here I am, a senior official who routinely denies this sort of thing and works to debunk them, and I'm involved in the middle of something I can't explain."

. . . Halt's report mentions that the following day checks were made in the woodland. . . . The ground readings on the Geiger counter were 25 times the background level. . . .

. . . U.S. airman Larry Warren was with another team. He is still able to pinpoint the exact spot where he saw the light, in a strange circle of mist, in a field. The whole field was lit by a bright light. A glowing red ball approached from across the field and at first Warren thought it was an A-10 aircraft coming in to land. But it stopped over the circle of mist and exploded without a sound, without heat, into a galaxy of coloured lights.

. . . The mist and colored lights transformed into a structured object. He estimated it to be 30 ft across the base and 20 ft high. There was a bank of blue lights on the underside and the whole thing shown with a rainbow or mother-of-pearl effect.[70] Larry Warren, who returned to Suffolk in 1994 to give an interview to *Network First*, is co-writing a book on his experience, LEFT AT EAST GATE. His co-author is Peter Robbins, who works with abduction expert Budd Hopkins.

. . . "Take me out of the story," Larry Warren challenges, "And you still have a story. This one will not go away."[71]

June 15, 1996

Saturday night June 15 found me glued to my computer screen. The sign-off draft of Left At East Gate *was due at our publisher's on Monday morning and I was fully enmeshed in the revision. It was not a moment I'd have chosen for the phone to ring, but ring it did.*

"Hello, Is this Peter Robbins?" "Yes, who is this?" "David Dickinson, returning your call." David Dickinson—now this was someone I was interested in speaking with.

I began with a few of personal questions. David lives in California. He has a job, a wife and children, friends, and a range of interests and responsibilities. His answers seemed free of any guile, weirdness, or agenda, and the impression I got was that I was talking to someone who was both bright and grounded. In short, Mr. Dickinson is a decent man living what I would term a fairly normal life. He wanted nothing out of our conversation except the opportunity to tell me about some things that had happened to him while he was in the service, and maybe get an answer or two. The relevant stats? Between November 1981 and November 1983, he had been an Air Force Security Policeman stationed at RAF Bentwaters. I was free to use his name in our book and might publish his comments as I saw fit.

David had recently heard Larry Warren interviewed on "UFOs Tonight," a national radio show originating in Los Angeles and hosted by Don Ecker, Research Director for UFO Magazine, *During the call-in portion of the show, David had spoken with Larry, then given a production assistant his home number to pass along to me. Although the call was easily the most significant of the night, there were several things he had been unwilling to discuss, or even mention on the air. I phoned him shortly after, but the family was out and I left a message on the answering machine. Now I reached for a pencil and paper and settled in to listen to what he had to say. I was not disappointed.*

Airman David Dickinson arrived at RAF Bentwaters eleven months after the incident had transpired. He was assigned to A Flight and worked the day shift. After two years, he was rotated back to the states and Nellis AFB in Nevada. He left the service in 1991 as a staff sergeant.

David knew Greg Battram and liked him a lot. Greg had a great sense of humour and David "thought he was a crack-up." He also knew Sergeant Gulias, who had helped to investigate one of the landing sites. Like Larry and Greg, Gulias had been interviewed by Chuck DeCaro for CNN's Special Investigation.

Airman Dickinson also knew Colonel Halt. They'd first met when David was standing guard during a military exercise and the Deputy Base Commander ran right by him. "Halt!," yelled the airman after the officer, "Halt, sir!" Charles Halt did halt, then walked back to the young guard and introduced himself by

name. They'd had a laugh about it, and from then on, the officer always ac-
knowledged the airman when he saw him. But there was another reason Halt
stood out in his memory. At mealtime's, the colonel always sat with the Security
Police instead of the officers. David remembered Halt as quiet and down-to-earth,
someone who shared a real bond with his men, as though they had been "in-
volved in something together."

During that first year on base, Airman Dickinson never heard a word about
the events of December 1980. By his second year though, "people seemed freer to
talk about it," and a number of them hinted that strange things had happened
there. In late 1982, he learned what they were.

It was his flight chief, a master sergeant, who'd told him about it, and it was
the third night's incident. The two men were driving back to the base at the
time. The chief had been stationed on Bentwaters in December 1980 and took
the matter very seriously. He'd almost been involved that night himself—almost,
because he'd been ordered to guard the site—and refused! It was the only time
he refused to follow an order in the Air Force, and interestingly, had not been
punished for it. The chief knew many of the particulars of the incident, and
mentioned the names of some of the men who'd been involved. They included
Colonel Halt and an airman named Larry Warren.

Dickinson also recalled a memorable shift change during the winter of 1983.
A Flight was relieving C Flight at the Bentwaters Weapons Storage Area, and
at the changeover, the men of A Flight were informed that somebody—or some-
thing—had been seen in the enclosure. The intruder was described as a tall,
shadowy, upright figure, and C Flight had searched everywhere for him without
success. As a result, A Flight spent the entire shift re-sweeping the WSA, but the
intruder had somehow managed to disappear without a trace. Strange as it was,
the experience didn't hold a candle to what was waiting in the wings.

It took place during a three day break, early in the summer of 1983. David
and his fiance had had a fight and the airman decided to clear his head with
a drive from Snipe, where he had been staying, to the Orford Keep, an outstand-
ing tenth century fortification I knew well. He was driving through the forest
when the bright orange light appeared in his rear view mirror—the thing was
above and to the rear of his car, and it was following him.

David Dickinson felt like he was in a dream state. While not scared, he knew
he was driving fast, and continued to, until he saw a person up ahead, standing
by the road. The orange light was still behind him, but had now dropped down
to tree-top level. "Don't you see that!?," he yelled twice to the figure. But the
man didn't move. He just stood there like he was frozen. That was enough for
David. He hit the accelerator and didn't stop until he was in the Orford Keep
parking lot.

A little shaken, the airman stepped from the car, paid his admission, and climbed the tower stairs to the battlement. From here, the orange light was visible over the North Sea, but not for long. Something had been launched from RAF Bawdsey and a missile trail was now moving toward the light.

As the missile closed, the light went out like a light bulb. David recalled standing there, looking out over the North Sea and thinking something that just didn't make sense to him—"it must have been a test of something." That was his last thought for a while. The next thing he remembered was being back in his house.

The following day, David was able to confirm that no known aircraft were responsible for what he'd seen. Also, a local paper ran an article about a nearby UFO sighting. The day before, several teachers, and several hundred children, had observed a large, bright orange light moving through the sky above their school.

That was what he had wanted to tell me. I thanked David for calling back, for his account, and for his courage in coming forward. We wished each other well and ended the call. Whew. I turned back to the word screen and sighed. I'd have to write this up of course, but there was no chance it would appear in this *draft. As I shifted back into the revision, I could not help wondering how many other David Dickinsons' there were out there. After a sip of cold coffee, I returned to the keyboard. It was going to be another long night.*[72]

7. CLOSURE

All Truth passes through three stages. First it is ridiculed. Second it is violently opposed. Third it is accepted as being self-evident.

Schopenhauer

"**A**nybody who works is a fool. I don't work, I merely inflict myself on the public!" The satirist Robert Morley said that. His quote was given to me by my friend Julie, who thinks the part about inflicting oneself on the public pretty much sums me up, and I agree.

The part about not working does not apply. *Left at East Gate* has been more work than Peter or I ever could have imagined back in the summer of 1987, when we set out to document my experience at RAF Bentwaters. I'm amazed we've done it.

I'm thirty-five now, and in the years since those recounted in my last chapter, I've been blessed with some more hard times and so many good times. I've learned lessons and changed, or, better yet, grown up and faced many of the personal demons that have challenged me over the years since December 1980. Some of those demons were unquestionably my fault, others were not. Sixteen years after the Bentwaters-Woodbridge UFO incidents, I know that, because of my fear and confusion, I burned a lot of bridges with folks who didn't understand what I'd been through; I resented them for it. In reality, I didn't understand either, and only in the last years have I begun to.

My friend Stevie Ray Vaughan sang a line in his and Doyle Bramhall's song "Tightrope": "My heart goes out to others who fail to make amends." Thanks, Stevie. I think I have!

The American flag was lowered for the last time at the twin bases in September 1993. Peter and I returned a month later to do some further research on this book and to see our friends in the area again. I was also looking for personal closure and felt that the recently closed air bases would in some way afford me that.

UFOs were still being seen by people who live in the communities surrounding Bentwaters and Woodbridge. It was refreshing to find that they now spoke openly about the events of December 1980.

For a closed air base, Bentwaters was locked down pretty tight by the MOD security police. RAF Woodbridge now housed units of the Royal Army. Standing at the gates of either base, it appeared that all American influence was now definitely gone. Or was it?

On a foggy night in October 1993, two friends and I saw a jeep on Bentwaters containing three U.S. Army Special Forces personnel. They were sitting back in the shadows of the main gate, back beyond the MOD security, back where the secrets were kept. I wondered at the time if some of those secrets remained, long after the last American had gone home. We now know they did.

Unknown to many, RAF Bentwaters and Woodbridge secretly housed the largest stockpile of tactical battlefield nuclear weapons in the whole of the NATO infrastructure. That fact had been true since the 1960s. Officially, the United States did not bring nuclear weapons to Britain until 1982, when the MX missile arrived. I knew, during my first week stationed at Bentwaters, that RAF Greenham Common, the site of many antinuclear demonstrations, was in fact only a diversion and deception, played upon the British people by its government and my government, to keep the protesters away from our front door at the twin bases. For a time, this deception worked.

Peter and I had the pleasure of addressing an English audience for the first time during a March 1994 visit to Nottingham, England. I finally had a chance to speak directly to the people who I feel will be on the front lines in bringing down the house of cards known as the Bentwaters UFO incidents.

The talk, presented by the East Midlands UFO Research Association, was a success in that those in attendance heard about our work without the distortions of the press. In that public forum, I felt free enough to discuss the nuclear aspect of the Bentwaters incidents for the first time anywhere.

The information really made some people mad! A man in the audience asked me if I worried about government reprisal because of what I was saying. My response to him: "What can they do, maybe take away my passport so that I can't come to England and rile people up? But I doubt it will ever happen." As you've read, it did happen, in the first reprisal for any UFO witness in the modern era of UFO research.

Over the years, I'd heard tales of government harassment, but never was anyone able to prove it. Peter and I had tons of evidence of government-sponsored "silly fucking games" (that's Intel slang for "messing with people's heads"). We experienced everything from officially opened and resealed mail, to phone taps, to the theft of items we mailed overseas, to a Sikorsky Bell Ranger helicopter, with illegal mirrored windows obscuring any view inside, nearly touching down in my backyard so photos could be taken of the house. In Intel circles, harassment, a word overused in UFO circles, is known as "destabilization." If you know any former Black Ops guys, ask them!

The suspension of my civil and constitutional right to leave the country was the most brazen abridgment of my rights in civilian life. After ten frustrating months of battle, with everyone from the U.S. Postal Service (they wanted to know if I was American!), to the State Department (they wanted me to reestablish citizenship, as my birth certificate wasn't enough!), to every other bureaucratic bird's nest I was referred to, I almost gave up. Luckily, Ramsey Clark took interest in my plight, advised me of my rights, and openly expressed interest in my situation. Peter, Clark, and I discussed my position, and I felt very comfortable telling the former U.S. attorney general my UFO story.

Clark compared my situation with that of Philip Agee, a former CIA operative and author of the fascinating book, *CIA Diary*. The only difference was that the agency sent hit squads after Agee, on top of suspending his passport. Clark felt that my suspension arose from the UFO element at Bentwaters, rather than my talking about nuclear weapons. Either way, he knew that someone with power was turning the screws on me.

A week after our eye-opening meeting, my passport was suddenly returned, with apologies from the State Department. They had made a mistake, they said, but never told me what that mistake was.

Strangely, the news of my passport suspension was only reported in the UFO trades in England. The American UFO publications ignored it. We certainly told many of the players, and, of course, many responded with support. My detractors in UFOland wrote off the significance of my passport situation as nothing more than a "low-level action." That one was almost as good as the lighthouse theory.

I don't want to waste my last chapter complaining about the cheap shots taken at me through the years by a small minority, both inside and outside the UFO field, because I'm not the only one who has experienced it. Nor have I experienced some of the gutter attacks directed at other blameless, high-profile witnesses. People who follow in our footsteps, who want to bring their UFO experiences to public light, may decide against it. Please check the water before you dive in.

By 1993, Peter had developed a rapport with now-retired Colonel Charles I. Halt. I also had a chance to speak with Halt by telephone, and I found that we could be civil to one another. A meeting was planned between the three of us in Washington, D.C. I was financially strapped at the time, but was not about to miss an opportunity to speak to Halt in person and get some insight from a man who, one would hope, had more knowledge than I about the Bentwaters incident. I sold my prize record collection, including Elvis Presley's first RCA release, just to cover expenses for the trip. Ouch! But I could live with that if our meeting was productive.

Once in the D.C. area, many things Peter and I had planned seemed destined not to happen. Congressman Gerald Solomon's staff misled us, and Solomon blew us off altogether. Looking back, I doubt he would have helped us anyway, just as he didn't help me in 1981. What do we elect these people for? Other congressmen and senators have quietly been brought into the loop and have held secret meetings concerning the Bentwaters incidents. We the people have the right to be brought into that loop as well.

The meeting with Halt was set. We all, including researcher Bob Oechsler (he had the wheels), sat down at a table in Pentagon City, a shopping mall near the Pentagon itself. We had what I thought was a very productive conversation with Halt. So productive that I asked him if he would like to write the foreword to this book. I was half joking, but Halt surprised me when he said that he would entertain my request.

Halt also warned me that those pursuing the truth about Bentwaters could very likely be in danger. He had hidden away some evidence in the event that something should happen to him. I truly felt for the man and the position he must have been in, and still do. Bentwaters is bigger than all of us.

Sadly, in the last few years, Halt has, on occasion, taken to disparaging my character in public. I've had to take protective action of my own because his charges were baseless. I suspect he may have been manipulated into making statements bidding. It wouldn't surprise me.

With the conclusion of this work at hand, I know that Halt is still not free to discuss whether we had any nuclear weapons at the air bases, so how can he be free to discuss the UFO incidents in any great depth? He has a lot to lose. His oath is still in effect as he surely held a top-secret (or higher) clearance. His hard-earned pension would be at risk as well. That is the simple difference between us: I have less to lose; he could lose everything. I hope someday he and a few other witnesses will be free to tell all they know, and when they do, I hope UFO researchers treat them with the dignity they felt I did not deserve.

The media, in relation to Bentwaters, can only be compared to a trash can. Don't get me wrong: in recent years, we've had some excellent media experiences, including a favorable article in the *Times* of London, a wonderful BBC World Service radio production, and participation in the Network First television program *UFO*. However, this is not always the rule, and most UFO witnesses will agree. When will the media learn that this subject can not be presented in the form of sound bites and lurid re-creations?

We were kept out of the loop during preproduction of some tabloid TV programs in the early 1990s that attempted to re-create the Bentwaters incidents. The programs lumped the three-night incident into one and totally misrepresented fact. The witnesses who did participate did not seem to mind the glaring distortions, which was strange to us. It was frustrating because we had offered information that would have helped complete an accurate picture of the Bentwaters incidents. In the end, when the programs aired on network television, so embarrassing were they that I was grateful we had not taken part in them.

I've never, in fourteen years of public life concerning my experience, brought my story to the media. Ever. Some writers have put that spin on my account. In reality, the media came to me and still do. But I've learned over the years whom to speak with and whom to avoid. I remember one writer under contract to *Omni* magazine who was so obnoxious and seemingly lacking in ethics that, if licenses were issued to practice journalism, she'd have lost hers long ago. Bless the unbiased reporter who treats UFO witnesses as human beings.

The Bentwaters UFO incidents happened over three nights. On the first night, one of the witnesses ended up missing after the encounter. Not only did the air force have a UFO incident to investigate and cover up, they had an airman missing on foreign soil, whose disappearance might be connected to the UFO incident. I don't know if the airman was ever found. The evidence of the first UFO landing was discovered in the course of that search.

Here was a huge public-relations problem for the air force. How can you cover up both a UFO encounter and missing personnel? How can you keep the local police, media, and other attention away from the largest stockpile of nuclear weapons in Europe? A huge problem indeed!

The next night, while command personnel drafted plans for the cover-up, the UFOs returned. For the course of that night, they remained airborne, conducting what appeared to be grid searches of the area. By the end of the second night, NATO and USAFE command had readied itself for another possible return of the unknown crafts.

Night number three, 28–29 December 1980, the "big night" as it's come to be known, brought that return. Photographs and film were shot, and later classified. Witnesses were debriefed; later, some were meddled with by members of the intelligence community, who played an opportunistic, or parasitic role, after the fact. Purpose unknown.

On the morning of 29 December, tactical teams flew in from Germany in an unmarked C130 aircraft, complete with its own security personnel. They were at Woodbridge base to check damage to the nuclear arsenal, as the UFOs had fired pencil-thin beams into the bunkers that housed them.

People later committed suicide or died in other ways. Lives were changed forever, and our governments couldn't have cared less! The deception intact, power brokers continue this cover-up unhindered.

I believe the U.S. government sets policy for our allies concerning the cover-up of UFO reality and has done so since July 1947. I believe the craft and life forms we saw in Rendlesham Forest were from another reality altogether. This stuff doesn't have to be from planet X, does it? The phenomena may originate closer than we think. Yes, folks, UFOs are real, and as my favorite TV cop, Baretta, would say, "You can take that to the bank!"

As for my experience in the alledged underground facility at RAF Bentwaters, I definitely can say that some of what I remember is accurate, but after my partial regression with Budd Hopkins last year, I've had to reevaluate other, more bizarre recollections from that experience. It took me fifteen years to have the nerve to explore any of it. The flashbacks and nightmares persist to this day, but, with help, I've learned to live with them. Aliens may or may not be underneath Bentwaters, but I do know that someone wanted us to believe they were. As Colonel Halt told me, the air force was on the sidelines during that aspect of the events. Another witness told me that elements of the CIA's M.K. Ultra program, including the infliction of narcotic-induced "memories," were carried out on some of the witnesses, myself included. I agree

Under hypnosis, my recall is somewhat different from my conscious recollection. Those guys beat us up, drugged us, and took us away against our will. I hold the National Security Agency responsible. Does the American government really believe in civil rights any more?

Sooner or later, I'm sure the lid on this part of the story will blow, but someone else will have to light the fuse. As for the UFO incidents at Bentwaters, they are the best-documented multiple-witness UFO events. And it was a UFO event, not a bomb, not a plane crash, not a lighthouse, police car, drug party, Elvis, or government troop-response experiment, as one hero of the militia movement arrogantly suggests. It involved a number of vehicles and living beings, alien in every sense, that do not reside in our concept of reality.

Writing this book has surely been an adventure, and thanks to Peter Robbins's help I've accomplished an important personal goal. Thanks, Peter, for sticking with this thing for so long. Very few people could have. I'm sure Peter and I will have more intrigue waiting for us down the road, after publication, it just won't be East Gate Road! I hope this book has made you think a little more about our governments' role in the fifty year UFO cover-up. If so, I've done what I set out to do.

"Of no defense significance:" this is what the U.S. and British governments want you to believe about the Bentwaters UFO incidents. Know this: a breach of the Bentwaters-Woodbridge weapons-storage area by a misguided airplane alone would be of major defense significance. Unidentified flying objects firing beams of light at the nuclear arsenal could have been the end of us all.

I hope a few decent people are still in Congress and can see the value in open hearings concerning Bentwaters. Watergate is nothing compared to this! Over the years since the bases closed, RAF Bentwaters has steadfastly been kept from public use. A false report circulated that Maharishi Mahesh Yogi was going to buy the air base, so that followers of transcendental mediation could bounce on their assess to attain enlightenment. The sale has never happened, and people who live in the area know it never will.

A secret is still at being kept Bentwaters. Our governments do not want us to know what that secret is. By now, you might venture a guess. The destruction of Rendlesham Forest fits in well with an accident or miscalculation involving a possible weather weapon. People who reside in the area feel that the windstorm of 1987 that destroyed the forest was not a windstorm at all. Many of them feel that the reason for the disaster centers on the U.S. Air Force and exotic-weapons testing that took place on Bentwaters at that time. So do I.

I'm happy to say that the beautiful forest is slowly returning; however, it is sad that so much was lost that will never return. If you ever visit this part of East Anglia, respect the wonderful people who live there, and you, in turn, will be respected, and maybe hear a UFO story, or better yet, see them; many have. These people are my friends; in one way or another, they have supported this book from the start.

So much changes in sixteen years. Some people in the UFO community, whom I once perceived as enemies, are now friends. I may have seemed rather harsh about certain experiences I have had in the UFO field, but I've felt obligated to discuss some of the negative things that happen to people in my position, and for that I do not apologize. As for the positive change in attitude toward me over the last few years, I believe tenacity must have had something to do with it.

At Capel Green, you can see the dark circle in the farmer's field to this day. Evidence of a great happening, and for some, a memorial of loss. I love that black circle of earth. When I stand there, the sight of it brings all the memories back. Everything is as it was. To the land-lord's wife, who might have preferred to run me over with her horse for trespassing and for making her field a tourist attraction: I never meant to. So please remember, if you visit the site, it is on private property and can best be viewed from the Forestry Commission land that borders it.

I shouldn't make light of the UFO incidents at Bentwaters, but in a strange way, I will always be grateful to those little translucent fellows for having a lousy exhaust system! Because, in a farmer's field that borders a large forest on the eastern coast of England, I will always be able to pick up a handful of my deepest fears, hold it a moment, then let it go. In this place, I will always be nineteen years old.

PART IV
Notes

1. Michael Bowyer, *Action Stations—East Anglia*, pp. 59–60. Credit: D. Walsh, MOD, Air Historical Branch.
2. Ibid., p. 60.
3. Ibid.
4. D. Campbell, *The Unsinkable Aircraft Carrier: American Military Power in Britain* (London: Michael Joseph Ltd., 1984), p. 31.
5. Bowyer, *Action Stations*, p. 60.
6. J. Bamford, *The Puzzle Palace* (Boston: Houghton, Mifflin, 1982), preface and p. 1.
7. Ibid.
8. P. Brookesmith, ed., *The UFO Casebook* (London: Orbis Publishing Ltd., 1982), pp. 25–26; J. Randles, "Impact—and After," *The Unexplained* (March 1983); app. 3, incident report.
9. Campbell, *Unsinkable Aircraft Carrier*, p. 154.
10. Bowyer, *Action Stations*, pp. 59–60.
11. Bamford, *Puzzle Palace*, p. 282.
12. Ibid., pp. 88–89.
13. David Wise and Thomas B. Ross, *Invisible Government* (New York: Random House, 1964), p. 207.
14. Ibid
15. Ibid., pp. 204, 206, 208.
16. Campbell, *Unsinkable Aircraft Carrier*, pp. 161–162.
17. Ibid., p. 166.
18. Document on file. The exerpted paper appears in appendix 1. Credit: ICUFON Archive, New York.
19. P. Brookesmith, ed., *The UFO Casebook* (London: Orbis Publishing Ltd., 1982), p. 26.
20. Bowyer, *Action Stations*, p. 60.
21. Petition for a writ of certiorari to the United States Court of Appeals for the District of Columbia Circuit; notes and review of the case. Citizens Against UFO Secrecy, petitioner, versus National Security Agency, respondent. U.S. Supreme Court, October 1981. Rothblatt, Rothblatt, and Seijas, Bronx, N.Y., January 1982. Credit: P. Gersten.
22. Campbell, *Unsinkable Aircraft Carrier*, p. 160.
23. Tape on file.
24. Sandia National Laboratories is a Department of Energy coordinator in New Mexico.
25. Original tape on file.
26. *East Anglian Daily Times*, 25 April 1989, pp. 18–19.
27. Tape on file.
28. Interview on file, 26 September 1989. Credit: Antonio Huneeus.
29. "America's Secret Military Budget," *America's Defense Monitor*, Public Broadcasting System, 18 January 1992.
30. George Kocher, "UFOs: What to Do?" (Rand Corporation, November 1968), p. 8.
31. "Did Someone Say Domestic Policy?" *New York Times*, 3 March 1990, sec. 2, p. 1.

32. "Little-Known Agency Is Government's Ears on the World," *Sunday Times Union*, 25 March 1990.

33. Letter on file.

34. Michael Evans, "Americans to Shut Down Two More British Air Bases: Bentwaters and Woodbridge in Suffolk," *The Times*, 18 May 1991. Credit: M. Glover.

35. Unsolicited statement of Roger L. Scherrer, 8 September 1991; on file.

36. Ray Boeche, "Bentwaters, Part II: A Decade of Research," *Fate* 46, no. 9 (September 1993), pp. 68–69.

37. Letter on file from Donald Ware to author, 7 February 1991.

38. Jacques Vallee discusses Larry Warren and the Bentwaters incidents in *Revelations* (New York: Ballantine, 1991), pp. 153–160.

39. Tape on file.

40. Tape on file.

41. Stephen Budiansky, "Keeping Research Under Wraps," *U.S. News and World Report*, 22 March 1993, pp. 48–50.

42. Philip J. Hilts, "Why Whistle-Blowers Can Seem a Little Crazy," *New York Times*, 13 June 1993, sec. 4, p. 6.

43. Warren, Bustinza, and a number of other D Flight personnel were not on duty the following day, or the day after.

44. Tape on file.

45. Tape on file.

46. Bill Moyers, *The Secret Government*, Seven Locks Press, Carson, Calif, 1990 p. 18.

47. "Last A-10s Leave," *Air Forces Monthly* 63 (June 1993), p. 7; "Spangdahlem Moments," ibid., p. 19.

48. Budiansky, "Keeping Research Under Wraps," pp. 49–50.

49. "The Secret War over Secrecy," *New York Times*, 19 September 1993, p. 16.

50. "Talk of the North Country: UFO Reports in Bay Road Area," *Glens Falls Chronicle*, 16–21 December 1993.

51. John Markoff, "U.S. Code Agency Is Jostling for Civilian Turf," *New York Times*, 24 January 1994, p. D1.

52. Edmund L. Andrews, "U.S. Plans to Push Giving F.B.I. Access in Computer Codes: 'Clipper Chip' to Be Used," *New York Times*, 5 February 1994, p. 1.

53. Maev Kennedy, *The Guardian*, 9 March 1994, p. 22.

54. BBC-TV News, 15 March 1994.

55. Letter on file.

56. *Evening News*, Bolton, U.K. ; Dave Toomer, "Man in UFO Probe Talks," 25 July 1994.

57. Letter on file.

58. Letter on file.

59. Letter on file.

60. Warren and Robbins, phone conversation, 5 October 1994.

61. Warren and Robbins, phone conversation, 13 October 1994.

62. Letter on file.

63. Tape on file.

64. Tape on file.

65. Andy Martin, "The Night They Landed in Suffolk," *London Times*, 21 August 1995, p. 4.

66. Jasper Gerard, "Brussels Investigates Admiral's UFO Claim," *The Sunday Telegraph*, 3 September 1995, and Steve Doughty, "Eurocrats' Close Encounter of the Expensive Kind," *Daily Mail*, 2 September 1995.

67. Sean Rayment, "The MoD Man and Some Close Encounters," *Daily Mail*, 30 March 1996, p. 12. Credit: C. Fowler.

68. Sean Rayment, "UFOs a Flight of Fancy Says MoD," *Daily Mail*, 24 April 1996, p. 17. Credit: C. Fowler.

69. Ron MacKay, "ET Was Here, Says MoD Man," *The Observer*, 28 April 1996. Credit: C. Fowler.

70. ". . . It Did Not Originate on Earth," *Nottingham Evening Post*, 26 May 1996. Credit: C. James.

71. *Open Skies, Closed Minds* by Nick Pope, Simon & Schuster, London, 1996, p. 151

72. David Dickinson's interview with Peter Robbins; notes on file.

AFTERWORD
Peter Robbins

There is no proof. There are no authorities whatever. No president, no academy, no court of law, congress or senate on this earth has the knowledge or power to decide what will be the knowledge of tomorrow. There is no use in trying to prove something that is unknown to somebody who is ignorant of the unknown, or fearful of its threatening power. Only the good, old rules of learning will eventually bring about understanding of what has invaded our earthly existence.[1]

On the night of 26–27 December, through the night of 28–29 December 1980, *a series of events occurred with which the reader now possesses an intimate familiarity. When those first four law-enforcement police walked into the forest near RAF Woodbridge to investigate a strange glow, they also walked into history. Over the next two nights, a goodly number of their comrades would follow. This was not the history we were taught as students or that we celebrate in holidays; it is history hidden, history classified.*

The episodes that make up the Bentwaters-Woodbridge incident constitute the single most important military-UFO event on record. Paralleling this is a nuclear security breach, a Black Ops mission, a military crisis in Europe, and a near diplomatic crisis between the governments of the United States and the United Kingdom.

In Left at East Gate, *we have tried to present the human side of the story, as well as the case file, because in the end, it all comes down to people, individuals just like, and different from, you and me: human beings whose lives were changed forever, then classified. The evidence that has been presented here is as real as any that might be introduced to jurors in an English or American court of law. It is direct, supporting, circumstantial, corroborating, physical, photographic, conflicting, and historic. After reading through the appendixes, this case will be yours to deliberate.*

Larry and I returned to England six times in the preparation of this book. After nine years of investigation, I have come to my own conclusions about Bentwaters. Some conclusions have taken me considerable time to arrive at; others were self-evident. For me, these findings break down into four categories: what I know, what I think I know, what I believe, and what I suspect.

As this manuscript developed, it seemed increasingly logical that readers should have access to as much of the material as I had, or at least as much as was practical in book form. How else could they come to their own best-informed conclusions? In a subject that literally defies understanding through brief treatments, that was the only course to follow. That is why you have had to wade through so much information, rough edges and all.

What constitutes proof for you? For me, it varies, given the situation. I approached this research in the same spirit I've approached jury service: by weighing all the evidence presented in as impartial a manner as I was able, then considering every aspect of reasonable doubt, then coming to a decision. Ultimately, that is all we can ask of you.

Larry Warren's Credibility

How should we rate Larry Warren's credibility as a witness? He admits that when he first came forward, he gave an incomplete account of what he remembered. Given the circumstances, what would you have done in his place? Although none of us can say with certainty how we would behave in a given high-stress situation, I cannot imagine handling this situation any differently than Larry did. The same would apply to his saying, "a guy I know," when he was really referring to himself or himself and another witness.

Yes, he initially withheld certain information from me. And, yes, he introduced material in the second person until he was ready to talk about it in the first. What should matter here is that in nine years of working together, I never once caught him in a case-related distortion or lie.

Of all the personnel involved in these events, how did Warren come to be the first to blow the whistle? The law of probability is certainly against it. I have no idea why it wasn't any of the other men, except the obvious: it was a damned stupid thing to do. But I do hold a strong opinion as to why it was Larry. Upbringing, temperament, DNA—whatever combination of factors make us the unique individuals we are, combined to make Lawrence Patrick Warren incapable of acting otherwise. He was, and is, by definition and inclination, a textbook example of a whistle-blower. I've no point to argue here, only a question to ask: Does the following description remind you of anyone?

Why do whistle-blowers persist? Is it something in their psyches that makes them willing to face up to overwhelming odds and keep complaining, keep pushing, when many others would have written off government fraud or incompetence as just another part of life? . . .

Both psychologists and the congressional investigators and reporters who work with whistle-blowers say they carry on because they are different.

"When they are ignored, told to back off, threatened in some way, they just say to themselves that those threats are inappropriate behavior, and they push ahead," said Dr. [Myron] Glazer. "Rather than being intimidated, these people get their backs up."

"One crucial characteristic is that they believe . . . that organizations should live up to their principles. . . . They suffer from the delusion that the system works. After being punished, they continue on, absolutely convinced at each level that justice will prevail."

Most of the 64 whistle-blowers . . . studied "went through absolute hell," . . . but most eventually found new careers that satisfy them. And most say they would do it again.[2]

Contact with Other Intelligences

We all cherish certain illusions, and there are things many of us would simply rather not know. High on most people's list is the possibility of interaction with an intelligent, nonhuman life-form. Although it goes against much of what we officially know or personally believe, it does happen. The pre-and post-Bentwaters visitations and contacts that thread their way through my coauthor's life are examples of this phenomenon in action. Why him? Damned if I know. Why anybody? I cannot tell you who or what these life-forms are or how many species of them exist. I do not know if they come from another galaxy, another dimension, or another time. I am, however, convinced beyond any reasonable doubt, that they are real, have their own agendas, and come and go with impunity.

Some of the best material published on them is listed in the bibliography, which includes titles by Budd Hopkins, Dr. David Jacobs, Thomas Bullard, Raymond Fowler, John Fuller, C. D. B. Bryan, and David and Andrea Pritchard.

What About the Underground?

Is there a classified underground facility below the twin bases, or is Warren's recollection of it the result of a carefully controlled and guided hallucination, so effective that he retains the "body memory" of his ears popping during the elevator descent, and so unnerving that he put off facing his memories of it for fifteen years?

That is one hell of a hallucination—or it would have been, if nobody else had shared it.

Only two possibilities make sense to me. Either the base exists, and Warren and others involved were put through some kind of experience there, or someone went to a great deal of trouble to convince them they had been taken to such a place. For the record, there is no question in my mind that the facility is real or that Larry and others were brought there against their will on the evening following the Capel Green incident.

Naive? A "secret underground base" sounds more like Buck Rogers than Bentwaters, but not to all of us:

Art Wallace offered us precise directions regarding the exact location of the complex. He remembered one of the entrances because he knew where he was after emerging and regaining conscious awareness. We checked it out, and it all fitted in perfectly. . . . Officially there is nothing there, but our engineering contacts, who claim to have built the complex, gave coinciding information which, if nothing else, supports the Wallace claims. By maintaining a watch on this area we have seen sufficient activity to give us grounds for believing the Wallace story.[3]

Classified underground installations are not science fiction. They are realized examples of strategic fact. Modern governments and their militaries have constructed many belowground facilities, and some of them are well belowground. If such a base had been contemplated for England, East Anglia would certainly have rated consideration as a site: it is one of the most strategic locations on the postwar map. And, lest anyone doubt it, twentieth-century technology is more than up to the task. Modern mining operations routinely involve dropping shafts five miles or more. The secret rocket factories at Nordhausen, Germany, were huge affairs, connected by a series of tunnels. They were four miles underground and in place more than fifty years ago. West Virginia's congressional bunker was built in secret in the 1950s. It was designed to accommodate eight hundred people and required the hauling away of millions of tons of earth and rock, which, in turn, necessitated a landfill where it could be discreetly disposed of. This was all accomplished over a course of years without arousing local suspicion.

While East Anglia has more people than rural West Virginia, most of it is still sparsely populated countryside. Had such an undertaking been attempted there, the North Sea could have sufficed as a landfill; the bases are less than six miles from the coast.

Allegations of huge tunnels connecting the complex to other locations, including the sea, are also well within the bounds of current technology. Any doubters need only take a ride through the Channel tunnel or learn something about Rudloe Manor.[4] The complex below Bentwaters-Woodbridge could even be based in a natural series of caverns and passages, or, at the paranoid extreme, be the product of nonterrestrial engineering. I heavily discount the latter possibility; but if such a facility had been considered necessary, it certainly could have been built—and in secret.

Any reader interested in the more technical aspects of such an undertaking should read Dr. Richard Sauder's work on the subject or the U.S. Army Corps of Engineers' "Literature Survey of Underground Construction Methods for Application to Hardened Facilities." Whether the sum total of what we are dealing with in this installation is nonhuman as well as human, I do not know, but there is a "presence" in parts of East Anglia, and its history goes back considerably farther than the bases it is home to.

There is one more thing the reader should be aware of. In the spring of 1996, a reliable source conveyed some significant new information to Larry and me. Some months earlier, another of the original Bentwaters witnesses had the courage quietly and professionally to face some very troubling service-related memories. They dated from late December 1980. The witness's sessions with a therapist were recorded and are now being painstakingly transcribed. Our source has not heard the tapes, but is in contact with someone who has. From what we understand, some of the information contained on them very closely matches the transcript of Warren's 15 July 1995 hypnotic regression with Budd Hopkins. By the way, our source is unaware of the contents of that session. We hope whatever this witness has learned through these regressions will bring him closer to resolving these memories. We will also look forward to the eventual publication of the transcript.[5]

There is a strong case for a classified underground facility. Not to take Larry's account seriously is naive.

The Air Force Role and the Nuclear Issue

The means used to guard military secrets may be more elaborate, extensive and ingenious than most, but they do not differ in kind from those used for other shared secrets. The aims are identical: to limit the number of individuals sharing the secret information; to act upon their loyalty or their fears and thus lessen the chances of betrayal; to store the information safely; to disguise it or transform it by means of special forms of language; to limit it by censorship; to leak false secrets; to provide an overload of information as additional camouflage; and to evade or lie about the secret information if pressed.[6]

Either, large numbers of people, including the commanding general at Bentwaters were hallucinating—and for an American Air Force nuclear base, this is extremely dangerous—or, what they say happened, did happen. In either of those circumstances, there can only be one answer, and that is, that it was of extreme defence interest to the United Kingdom, and I have never had a satisfactory rebuttal of that view.[7]

The role the U.S. Air Force played in the Bentwaters incidents was assigned. The air force does not set its own mission any more than the other service branches do. That is up to the Pentagon, which has kept its air wing running interference in UFO matters since the air force was created in 1947. The air force is a central player, but not by its request.

Certain elements of Warren's account imply that Bentwaters, December 1980, was not the first time something similar had happened in ranks. Early in our interviews, Larry related to me that twice during his security-specialist training, he and others destined for RAF Bentwaters were taken from Lackland AFB to a location in Harlingen, Texas. There, they were put through a series of tests and procedures that seemed to have nothing to do with the duties of a security specialist; or did they? Certain security actions, such as Helping Hand, were put into effect during the third night's incident, but the behavior of key personnel suggested to Larry that other procedures were also in place. Were they all related to a possible nuclear incident, or were some designed with another situation in mind?

Chuck DeCaro said the air force is a huge machine. Like a computer, it is programmed to do a variety of tasks, and, like a computer, keeps a record of them all. There is no question that the machine left a paper trail that could answer a lot of questions, if the trail had not been "rightly and properly classified."

Were Bentwaters base commanders and the Pentagon justified in slamming down the security lid as hard and fast as they did? Unquestionably. For those three nights at least, things were very much out of the air force's control. With the most sophisticated weaponry and security systems in place, unidentified flying objects were violating the airspace over Bentwaters' most restricted location—the weapons-storage area. The objects were firing laserlike beams of light into the compound's hardened bunkers. The bunkers were full of nuclear bombs that were being held on base without the official knowledge or consent of Her Majesty's government. Other confirmed unidentified lights and machines were moving in, through, and above the surrounding woods, several also shooting down beams. Someone had issued an order that was in full violation of the treaty with Great Britain; namely, security police and other personnel were taking loaded weapons onto English soil. A machine of unknown origin and its occupants had appeared in a field near RAF Woodbridge, and an airman had disappeared without a trace. Amid all this, the base had gone to code red over the situation in Poland: NATO was now one step away from war with the Soviet Union. What orders would you have given? The air force and the Pentagon had no choice. The cover-up began immediately. Once begun, it escalated and continues to this day.

No agency or office of the U.S. Air Force has ever admitted to filing any report on or conducting any investigation into the events in question.

The British Role

What was the British military's role in this affair? Bloody minimal at best. I do not believe they played a role at all, which is a bit awkward, considering where the incidents took place. Beyond this, I can only speculate and wonder.

The Cloudbuster

Over the course of our visits to Suffolk, Larry and I had the chance to ask a wide range of area residents about their impressions of the so-called freak storm of October 1987. The consensus among those who were willing to speak with us was best summed up by a woman who had lived in Suffolk for over fifty years. She had weathered every storm to hit that part of the country, but this one was different from any she remembered: "It just wasn't natural," she said. I am inclined to agree with her. I do not believe it was a storm at all. The destruction, which ranged well beyond Suffolk, was more likely caused by an experimental weather-weapon test gone horribly wrong, or, worse, the result of a deliberate action.

Larry and I would have greatly preferred to keep this matter out of our book. We certainly had no need for the added dramatic content. But it is a subject that deserves in-depth investigation. This book was not the forum for it. We hope someone else's will be. If you are interested in learning something about this remarkable technology, its history, and environmentally positive applications, consult the last section of the bibliography and appendix 8. If you think the claim some sort of joke, pseudoscience, or exaggeration, you owe it to yourself to do some of the same reading.

Witnesses, Researchers, and Confidence Keepers

There is a sequence in Central Production's documentary Network First: UFO *where we see Larry back at Capel Green. After walking viewers through the event, he pauses and says, "Take me out of the story, and you still have a story."*

Nothing, of course, could be truer. Many of the other witnesses involved in the Bentwaters incident have appeared in these pages, a few in some depth, but most in passing. Many more remain anonymous. If you are a researcher, do not seek them out. They have more than earned the right to continue living their lives without us in their faces. The same basic courtesy applies to the named witnesses. If they want to speak with us, they will let us know.

If you are an air force veteran who served at one of the twin bases during the period in question and had some involvement or awareness of the events set down in Left at East Gate *(or any other UFO incident for that matter), you may have considered, or may be considering, coming forward with your account. As a researcher, I say, welcome; your courage in doing so is respected, and the contribution you make will hopefully be appreciated.*

As a witness, consider carefully what you may be bringing on yourself, as well as those around you. Consult first with the people who love you, then with those whose opinions you respect, then use your common sense. Never deal with anyone whose intentions seem less than straightforward, or who simply makes you feel uncomfortable.

The people I've met who do the research and investigation are an over-whelmingly decent lot, who, like you, me, Larry, and Richard Dreyfuss's character in Close Encounters of the Third Kind, *"just want to know what's going on." But I have also met a few with minimal to no scruples. They tend to view witnesses as case files first and human beings second. Not that a certain amount of formality is bad. Remaining dispassionate in the heat of an investigation is crucial to any type of good detective work. But unless investigators are professionally as well as ethically responsible enough to put the well-being of their subject before any self-serving research goal, they might want to direct their energies into another specialty. You may encounter* anything *in a witness case, and that is more than a lot of us are prepared for.*

Witnesses—if nothing we have said has dissuaded you from coming forward, God bless and good luck. I hope the public, the media, and the research community show you a bit more tolerance and goodwill than some of them showed Larry.

For the record, the reader should be aware that I have excluded certain accounts, statements, and evidence from these pages: either because the individuals supplying the information changed their mind about having it included or shared what they knew purely as an off-the-record courtesy.

In a few of those instances, I have found myself wishing I could throw my ethics out the window: the information I'd been presented with was that compelling. Two of the people involved stay very much in my thoughts. Each approached me in a different part of the country, on occasions separated by several years. One was a former NSA employee who had an outstanding account of an incident he'd witnessed at a remote agency listening post. The other was a family member of a Bentwaters veteran who had taken his life after leaving the service. She not only gave me a poignant account of her loved one's decline into self-destruction, she supplied me with his official service record and some fully authentic supporting paperwork that made my jaw drop. Several polite phone calls and written requests did not sway either of them into participation, and that was where the matters ended. But despite these and a few similar disappointments, Larry and I have still been able to produce a book we're proud of.

Privileged information should stay that way. Unfortunately, we are imperfect people living in an imperfect world. I keep confidences well: it's just the way I was brought up. But during the nine years I pursued this story, there were a few occasions, very few, when I shared particulars of a Bentwaters confidence with someone else. Two of these people were Budd Hopkins and David Jacobs, both trusted colleagues and longtime friends. Another was our editor. But once, I confided in the wrong person.

He introduced himself as a writer, was polite, well-spoken, intelligent, and made a good first impression. He was working on what he described as an objective book about the UFO abduction phenomenon; because I worked as Budd Hopkins's assistant, any contribution I might make would be valuable. He did an excellent job gaining my trust and asked if we could conduct the interview over lunch—day and restaurant my choice.

Lunch was very good, his questions intelligent. It was over dessert, as I recall, that he asked, "strictly off the record," if I would be willing to share any truly confidential material with him. My answers had really piqued his curiosity.

I was quite surprised that he would ask such a question, but his calm, good-humored argument won me over before the check arrived: he was really very good at what he did. I told him three things—each no more than a sentence.

I never saw him after that. He published all three facts several months later, and in bastardized versions at that. He even threw in a few lies for good measure. It stung, but I got off easy in comparison to some I know. No morality tale intended here; I'm just saying that any of us can be misled, especially if someone is really working to mislead us.

With these exceptions aside, to the best of my knowledge I have broken confidence with no one in what you have read here. I take no pride in the fact that I am about to.

Colonel Halt

In December 1980, Deputy Base Commander Lieutenant Colonel Charles I. Halt was an air force career officer serving his country with distinction. Being identified as the highest ranking officer to witness any of the events, as well as the author of what is still the only authentic document to surface on them, was undoubtedly the worst thing that ever happened to his military career. By 1991, when he retired as a full colonel, Halt had taken more Bentwaters heat than any other officer in the air force. It is my belief that during the incidents themselves, in their aftermath, and ever since, he has continued to serve the air force with more distinction than any of us will ever be able to appreciate. I respect Halt, admire his sense of loyalty, and only wish him the best in life; however, I cannot and will not condone certain things he has said about my coauthor: they're just not correct. Let me backtrack.

As I understood it, the air force documents Halt had referred to in our phone conversations came to him via a Pentagon contact. It is clear in the transcripts that he had no doubts about their validity, and if Larry and I could get down to meet him, he would show us them to us.

We had been looking forward to seeing those papers, but never did. I think the reason was that at some point during our talk, perhaps after reading through some of Larry's service record, Halt realized there could have been a problem with his own papers. My feeling is that they were Pentagon-generated disinformation, designed without Halt's knowledge to make him believe that Warren could not have been posted to D Flight, or any other flight on the night in question, thus reinforcing his belief that Warren was not telling the truth. I'm not sure what Larry or Bob Oechsler made of it at the time, but the impression was real enough for me that I chose not to press the issue.

I am convinced that the lion's share of information that Halt did share with us was the truth as he knew it or suspected it to be. Some key points of what he told us are worth reviewing. More than one thing happened. The real story was what happened afterward, "not what happened there." Larry had been "meddled with," but it was not an experiment. The Bentwaters security-police logs and blotter for the nights in question had disappeared. Larry and I had no clear idea of what we had gotten ourselves into, or how deep in it we were. We should assume our phone lines were dirty and be as concerned about our health and well-being as he was about his.

He told us several other things, but not before asking me to turn off the recorder. I complied with each request. Although he did not say, "I am telling you this in confidence," that was what I understood him to mean.

In July 1994, Halt returned to England and addressed a UFO conference in Manchester. Sometime during that weekend, he was speaking informally with a group of audience members when one of them asked a question about Larry Warren. Larry had not been there, came the answer; his account was untrue. If anything was not true here, it was the colonel's answer.

A year and a half earlier, Halt said to Warren: "I think you sincerely believe what you're saying and you may be right, and I can't say you're lying, but I find flaws here and there that I have to have them resolved for myself."

Yes, it is true; maybe Larry only believed what he was saying, and that was the extent of it. And yes, I have felt the same compulsion Halt did: to find the flaws and resolve them. But the fact is that Halt knows that what Larry is saying may be correct.

I never served in the military, but have grown to appreciate the code that many who have served live by. I think that Halt, like many retired career officers, continues to adhere to the standards of that code in civilian life. I can only commend him for it. But I live by a code, too, and Halt broke it when he answered that question in Manchester. We know he made the remarks because a researcher friend of ours asked the question. No, we hadn't asked him to. There were also two other people in the group who'd heard Larry and me several months earlier in Nottingham. The pair never spoke with our researcher friend, but all contacted us with the same news shortly afterward.

For me, Halt's response was the equivalent of breaking a confidence. That is why I have decided to break the confidence that was implied when Halt asked me to turn off my tape recorder. He told us three things: He was very much aware of the NSA's interest in Larry. He had personally attempted to gain access to Larry's military record, without success. Light beams had penetrated the hardened bunkers of Bentwaters' weapons-security area. That was it, and that is plenty.

I hope Halt understands why I have taken this action. Larry wanted to do it himself, but his doing so might have appeared personally based. This is not a personal matter.

I agree with Larry's conclusions as to why a retired officer would not be free to speak as openly as, in this case, a former airman. As such, I do not expect Halt will ever be able to comment publicly about the nuclear weapons at Bentwaters.

As to concerns for our safety: I am convinced that publishing the facts herein will only lessen the chances of harm to the colonel, myself, and Larry. Unless I'm mistaken, quite a few of our readers will be taking an inordinate interest in the health and well-being of all three of us. I think that disclosure will be our best insurance.

Wing Commander Gordon Williams

Colonel Gordon Williams is either the officer most central to the third night's action, or a wrongly identified innocent. Of all the contentions Halt and I *sparred over, none of my questions drew more vehement or emotional responses than those about Williams. That's only natural. The two were, and still are, close personal friends. In October 1983's premier Bentwaters article, it was Williams's photograph that appeared on the front page of the* News of the World. *But unlike his friend Colonel Halt, from then on Williams was shielded from the press, the television media, and the likes of me. He left the air force a two-star general and, from what Colonel Al Brown told us in 1988, took an executive position out west.*

Williams himself maintains he was not there. Halt told us that Williams was very interested in what had happened (who wouldn't be?), and even wished he had been there. He wanted to be notified if it ever happened again, and even borrowed Halt's audio tape to play for Third Air Force Commander General Basie. Now, that's enthused, *but proves nothing.*

However, the officer interviewed by Ray Boeche not only remembered seeing Williams there, he remembered the colonel being driven from the scene in a jeep with a canister of the film that had just been shot. I never met that officer, but know who he is. More important, my confidence in the investigator is rock solid. Ray Boeche is a highly principled and fully professional researcher.

Warren is certain that it was Williams who stepped through the circle of airmen and faced off with the life-forms. Halt is certain Williams was no-where near the site. Halt and Warren are equally adamant, and both seem equally sincere. It is possible that Colonel Williams was involved, but not al-lowed to share that information with his friend. From what I understand, Halt's vantage point would not have allowed him to make out the details and faces at the site.

Why is Larry so certain it was Williams? It was dark, it was confusing, and, God knows, it must have been frightening. Fear breeds shock, and shock breeds distortion. For that reason alone, we should be at least as wary of Larry's rec-ollection as we would be with that of a witness to a car crash. Except for one big, solid physical detail: Williams is what most of us would consider a very tall man. I have been told that he is six feet five inches, but cannot confirm that. He is however, well over six feet tall, and would stand out in almost any crowd. That was what set him off from the other officers there, and this is why Warren is sure it was Williams. Corroboration? I think so.

In April 1984, Coventry, Connecticut, police lieutenant Larry Fawcett con-ducted a wide-ranging telephone interview with Adrian Bustinza. During the Covered Wagon maneuver, Sergeant Bustinza stood next to Airman Warren. As such, Adrian would likely have seen what Larry saw that night. Fawcett is a professional investigator, and his interview style is very effective. He managed to elicit an amazing amount of information from Bustinza—at least to the degree that Adrian remembered it or was willing to answer.

At the point in the interview that covers the officer entering the ring and standing facing the beings, Fawcett says to Bustinza:

LF.   [Larry Warren] gave me the officer's name, I can't remember who it was now. It was a big guy, whoever it was.

AB.   Lieutenant Colonel Halt.

LF.   Halt, OK.

Then he continues on.

What happened here was crucial. Adrian saw Williams too, but in that moment on the phone, confused him with Halt, then continued answering the questions with that misunderstanding in place. Inconsequential? Not to me. I believe that Williams was right there, and that Larry Warren never forgot it.

The National Security Agency

The National Security Agency is the most secretive, official organisation ever created by the United States' government. The NSA is accountable to none of us. Its stated purpose and mission were deeply classified at the agency's birth and have never been released to the public. The contents of its charter are similarly unavailable. So is the NSA's annual budget, and budget disbursement. We are not allowed to know anything about its worldwide operations, high-tech breakthroughs, or involvement in the events which comprise the Bentwaters incident. They are all classified as matters of national security, as are the documents which comprise Larry Warren's service record.

The National Security Agency first captured my serious attention in the spring of 1988; this was as a result of my learning that I had captured theirs. The relevant NSA information I was able to piece together has led me to a series of conclusions about this agency. They are all based on circumstantial evidence, but in the court rooms of the United States and the United Kingdom, countless guilty individuals have been properly convicted of their crimes on considerably less.

Putting the actual and perceived post-war Soviet threat aside for the moment, the National Security Agency was created at the height of the Cold War, but our genuine interest in the Russians cloaked the heart of its charter: to oversee and address official concerns about UFOs and their implications. The organisation would need to be secure at every level as it would be dealing with particulars of our biggest secret: we had neighbors, and they were visiting us. Shortly after its inception, the organization began to establish a presence in Great Britain.

In late December of 1980, The NSA ran a disinformation operation at RAF Bentwaters in Suffolk, East Anglia. As a result, an undetermined number of the Air Force personnel involved in a legitimate UFO incident, were drugged, then taken to a highly classified facility below the twin base complex. There, the already traumatised young airmen were subjected to a series of staged and/or chemically induced scenarios, the memories of which, it was hoped, would so entangle with their actual UFO-related memories, that separating the two would prove to be an impossibility. This, it was felt, would destroy their credibility as witnesses, and define the success of the mission. Not a bad plan, considering the situation they found themselves in.

Power has no moral qualities. To a great degree, the operation accomplished what it set out to do, but in the dark tradition of the CIA's LSD mind control experiments of the sixties, effects on the subjects varied. Whatever personal suffering had attached to the experience, most kept quiet and did their best to get on with their lives. A percentage experienced the effects of nightmares, clinical depression, substance abuse, failed marriages, episodes of violent behaviour, breakdowns, suicidal tendencies, and a few suicides. Then, of course, there were the long-term effects on the friends and families of the witnesses. Many, many lives were affected, and none for the better.

Very early on, one airman in particular identified himself as a problem. This man's movements were monitored for the remainder of his time in the Air Force, and the surveillance continued after his honorable discharge. But he was not approached—until he began to express an interest in going public with what he knew, and possibly write a book about it. At this time, agency employees did contact and meet with him; other meetings followed. The individual was kept enticed with actual information or disinformation; in particular, photographs of the craft he had seen in December 1980. During these meetings, the witness was told that he could carry on with his plans if he wished, then reminded of the inevitable folly such acts always end in. He was also cautioned that should he continue to speak out publicly, or write a book, he should not refer to the nuclear ordnance stored at the twin bases in 1980–1981. When the agency learned he had secured a collaborator on the book, a standard background check was run on the writer. The witness was informed of this at his final meeting with agency personnel.

The irregular monitoring continued, but the former airman was never seen as a threat to the security of the National Security Agency, nor was the book which he and his co-author were alleged to be working on. As a result, the surveillance on both remained irregular. Their occasional public appearances raised little, if any concern at headquarters; neither of the men had ever once mentioned the agency in their talks.

This is what I believe to be the truth; a part of it anyway. The supporting evidence is not reiterated here. With the exception of Appendix 1, You have already read it. I am convinced these allegations are factual beyond any reasonable doubt. As for the centerpiece of the third night's event—the craft and the beings—if they were NSA special effects, and not the real thing, I can only congratulate the agency on a spectacularly successful operation. How did you guys do that?

What is the National Security Agency's post-cold-war mandate? What is at the core of its mania for security? To what degree is it involved in monitoring UFO movements and locations? Aside from their (only) admitted function— signals intelligence and communications intelligence—does any congressional representative or committee have a full understanding of what this agency really does? I seriously doubt it. How much the President is cleared to know, or allowed to know, is purely a matter of speculation; even for him.

Another matter presses for attention here; no matter who you are, the NSA represents a threat your privacy. We know the agency intercepts the diplomatic and military communications of both friendly and unfriendly nations, but we have no way of ascertaining how far their eavesdropping has penetrated into our places of business, government and civil offices, organisations, computer systems, telephone networks, and homes. I am as certain as I can be, that since 1988, the NSA has monitored my telephone conversations. I cannot tell you how regularly; there is no way to know, and no way to find out how to know.

Without the justification or cover of a Soviet threat, we really have to ask ourselves: what is the National Security Agency still doing in the United Kingdom? What keeps their remote, restricted, multi-billion dollar listening stations busy these days? Nothing you and I are allowed to know about. The NSA definition of national security is classified, and does not allow for anything approaching democratic due process. On the contrary, it has been used as a cover for illegal activities—though that's a misnomer—the NSA is above the law— in two countries at least.

Who does the National Security Agency work for? Is it us, the people of the United States of America? It should be, but it isn't. And if it isn't us, who do they work for? The President? To a degree. They were certainly not working for Larry Warren, or the other traumatized young airmen they snatched, drugged, and tried to program. The NSA works for the Department of Defense, which is headed by the Secretary of Defense. But first and foremost, the NSA works for the NSA, and its first loyalty is to itself. There is something terribly wrong here, and if we wait very much longer, it is something we may never be able to set right again.

At the very least, isn't it time for the Senate Intelligence Oversight Committee to call for a hearing, or hearings, on the NSA and UFOs? Maybe it is time for the citizens of the United States and the United Kingdom to take a stand on this: bad things happen when good people do nothing.

If you wish to write to the National Security Agency, their address is, National Security Agency, Fort George G. Meade, Maryland, 20755-6000.

National Security and the truth about UFOs

At some future time, the UFO cover-up will be appreciated for what it is—an important key to understanding the history of the second half of the twentieth century. Too bad it is not so appreciated now.

It is a sad fact, but secrecy has become more important than democracy in America. The citizens of the United Kingdom face an almost identical dilemma. The Ministry of Defence need only put a D (Defence) notice on anything the government feels is, or may be, a national security risk, and that item disappears into the files.

National security has become our state religion. Big Brother is watching us, and the situation in both countries is urgent. There is a pathology at work here; it will not stop itself.

The American-English cover-up of the Bentwaters incident is part of a broad, historic program of UFO disinformation and fact suppression. The secrecy continues to be justified on the basis of national-security concerns, but the concerns seem to be held by fewer and fewer of the people whose security is supposedly being protected. The rationale is unwinding.

If and when the leaders of our two countries take to the airwaves and solemnly inform us that we are not alone, will the national security of these two nations be shattered? Will the Western world fold up in resignation or fly into chaos? I don't think so. Enough of us are made of stronger stuff than that. But that's of no concern to our secret keepers.

With the rarest exceptions, even concerned politicians know enough to keep their public distance from this subject. Who can blame them? The potential for ridicule is too high. Those who have taken the plunge can tell you it's a no-win situation: just ask Senator Exon of Nebraska or Congressman Schiff of New Mexico.

Is there a case for a parliamentary inquiry into the Bentwaters incident and its cover-up? We certainly feel there is. Is there a case for a congressional investigation of the matter? Without question. *The implications of East Gate far surpass those of Watergate. I know that there are decent, even courageous men and women in the Senate, the House of Representatives, the House of Commons, and the House of Lords—individuals who do not think UFOs are a joke, and have, albeit quietly, been pressing the matter on their own. I do not know what degree of networking has been going on among them, but I understand they are not just sitting in their offices talking to themselves.*

That does not change the fact that in cold, hard political terms, the UFO cover-up is the postwar era's most supremely uncomfortable issue. Until constituents make their own interests in this problem known to the people they send to Washington and London, Washington and London will continue to do one of the things they do best: sit on it.

Nothing less than our right to the truth is at stake. We are not now, nor have we ever been entitled to the knowledge our intelligence agencies collect about UFOs, because UFOs are seen as a matter of national security, and we average citizens are seen as security risks by our governments. Will somebody tell me what is going on here?

There is only one way we can even begin to straighten this situation out and it has nothing to do with UFOs: it is called participating in democracy. Whatever your politics, a truer nonpartisan issue has never been before us. If you genuinely want to see a change in these policies, do something about it. Write to your representatives, senators, or members of Parliament, and tell them how you feel about this issue. If they know you actually take this matter seriously enough to even consider letting it influence your vote, then we all may be in for some interesting developments.

It is up to you to make this a political issue. Until then, there will be no parliamentary inquiry, no congressional investigation, and the denials will continue to flow.

*   *   *

When history's locomotive turns a corner, all the thinkers fall off the caboose.[8]
Karl Marx

H. G. Wells said he thought civilization was a race between education and catastrophe. This canny observation has never been truer than it is now. I can't say how the UFO controversy should be rated against other pressing social, political, and environmental issues facing the human race, just that this is one of them, and it very much needs addressing.

Whatever their intention—whatever threat or benefit these other intelligences may manifest or represent—we are still left with an inherently human problem: some people do not want to know the truth, others do, and the agencies that do know something, refuse to tell us. The truth here is simple: we are not alone many of us and will do almost anything not to face that fact.

Cartoonist Walt Kelly's thoughtful little possum, Pogo, expressed the dilemma best after a memorable cartoon battle: "We has met the enemy, and they is us."

They is, and will continue to be, until we grow up a bit more. For many people, that will mean having to modify or even let go of some cherished beliefs and notions, and there is little that is more difficult than that. Fear of the truth is a powerful motivator, but so is the love of it. Having more tolerance for each other and each other's beliefs wouldn't be a bad place to start.

We are, all of us, in this thing over our heads, but we are in over our heads together. The things that separate us from each other seem almost inconsequential when viewed in relation to our differences with "the neighbors."

There is an old Chinese saying: "May you live in interesting times." Oh. do we ever. This story is far from over. In fact, its just beginning to get interesting. Believe it, my friend.

AFTERWORD
Notes

1. Wilhelm Reich, *Contact with Space* (New York: Core Pilot Press, 1957), p. xxiii.
2. Philip J. Hilts, "Why Whistle-Blowers Can Seem a Little Crazy," *New York Times*, 13 June 1993, sec. 4, p. 6.
3. Brenda Butler, Dot Street and Jenny Randles, *Sky Crash*, p. 244.
4. See Timothy Good, *Beyond Top Secret* (London: Sidgwick & Jackson, 1996), and the articles of Matthew Williams, editor, *Truth Seekers Review*
5. Warren, Robbins, and source, phone conversations, 24 and 25 April 1996.
6. Sissela Bok, *Secrets: On the Ethics of Concealment and Revelation* (New York: Pantheon, 1982), p. 197.
7. Larry Warren, interview, *Network First: UFO*, ITV/Central Productions, 1994. Credit: L. Moore.
8. Credit: John Leonard, *CBS Sunday Morning*, 14 April 1996.

ACKNOWLEDGMENTS

There is no way we can adequately thank the many individuals who have helped in the writing of this book. Over the years, they have been there to assist us at every turn in the road, no matter how dark things may have seemed at times. They are friends, family, colleagues, and strangers. They are writers, retirees, students, shopkeepers, parents, programmers, researchers, Ph.D.s, attorneys, artists, airline employees, educators, researchers, doctors, cops, musicians, customs officials, filmmakers, railway workers, innkeepers, nurses, firemen, British and American military personnel, and more. All have contributed their time, efforts, leads, statements and accounts, research, and support. A number encouraged us at times we needed it most or put us up for the night, drove us from one place to another, bought us dinner, made us laugh, or just stood by us. To them and the many unnamed individuals, both here and abroad, who have always been there for us, we can only say, thank you: with your help, *we did it.*

England unless otherwise indicated
Colin Andrews; Matthew Appleton; Linda, Stan, Rose, and Steve Audsley; BBC World Service; Laurie Bell (Australia); Graham W. Birdsall; Mark Ian Birdsall; Kay Borgine (France); Richard Branson; Al Brown;

Sally Brown; Jeanette Brown; Brenda Butler; Ami and Joseph Cammarella (France); Duncan Campbell; Central Productions Ltd., London; the proprietors and staff of the Cherry Tree (Bromswell, Suffolk); Peter Barry Cliffe; Ingrid Connell; Gordon Creighton; Gloria Heather Dixon; Ian Dorothy (South Wales); East Midlands UFO Research Association; Chris Fowler (South Wales); Omar Fowler; Moussia Gamaleia (France); Jane Goldman; Timothy Good; Anthony Grey; Harry Harris; M. L. Hatch; Angela Hind; Graham Hobson (South Wales); S. Holmes; Mohsen Iravani; ITV-London; Anthony James; Carole James; Derek Kersey; Morley Legg (Australia); Gordon Levitt; Yuri E. Lozotsev (Russia); Philip Mantle; Lawrence Moore; Carl Nagaitis; Lord Peter Hill Norton; Leslie and Michael O'Mara; Nick Pope; Jenny Randles; Nicholas Redfern; Jean-Luc Rivera (France); C. T. Ruffin; Livia Russell; David Smith; Graham W. Stewart (Scotland); Dorothy Street; the students of Summerhill (Leiston, Suffolk); Gladys Sweetland; Virgin Atlantic Airways; Jan, Tony, Richard, Peter, Alexander, and Granny Warnock; Jim Waterman; D. Watson; Matthew Williams (South Wales); and Junishi Yaoi (Japan)

United States
Andy Abercrombie; Alan Abrams; Joy Abrams; Janice Adelman; Mariah Aguiar; Sal Amandola; Walter Andrus; Ben Ark; Laurine Ark; John Ashbaugh; Elsworth F. Baker; Robert Baker; Melody Baker; Gregory Battram; Timothy Green Beckley; Christine Belfor; John Bell; USAF Sergeant José Benabe. Don Berliner; Lex and Donna Bernstein; Peter Bertine, Jr.; Osiris Bey; Raymond W. Boeche; Lyn Bohon; William Bohon; Albert Bouchard; Mark Brinkerhoff; C. D. B. Bryan; Larry Bryant; John Burroughs; Adrian Bustinza; Joe Cantcz; Susan Caraban; John Carpenter; Center for Air Force History, Historical Reference Branch; Melinda Chance; Sarah Chisolm; Pamela Christian; Pat Cifone; Ramsey Clark; Richard Cohen; Scott Colborn; Linda Cortile; Marc Davenport; Marc Davis; Mary DeBarth; Chuck DeCaro; James DeMeo; Maurice DesJardins; Stan and Robin Dezjot; David Dickinson; Brian Downing; Don Ecker; Vicki Cooper Ecker; Diane Edgerly; Russ Estes; Robert F. Eure; Larry Fawcett; Manuel Fernandez; George A. Filer; Stanton T. Friedman; Patricia Frost; Marie R. Galbraith; Dixie L. Gaspard; Phylis Giarinese; Robert Girard; Monica Girard; Lisa Glover; Ray Gomez; Tony Gonzales; Nancy Gordon; George M. Greenfield; Barry Greenwood; Alan Grossbardt; Richard Hall; Charles I. Halt; Joseph Hammer; Linda Hammer; William P. Heizerling; Sue Hickerson; Richard

Hoagland; Budd Hopkins; Craig Hopkins; Dean Hoskins; Julie Hoyenski; Antonio Huneeus; ICUFON archives; Richard B. Isaacs; Steve Isaacson; David M. Jacobs; Temple University; Ray Jett; Pete Jones; Debbie Jordan; Larry Ketron; Linda Ketron; Bruce Kilmartin; Kalie Kimball; Perry Knowlton; Bill Koopman; Mike LaPoint; Steve LaPoint; John Lear; David Levine; Lorrie Levine; Liggett family; Jeff Lindsay; Ted Loman; Betty Andreasson Luca; Robert Luca; Bruce Maccabee; James C. Macmillan; Steve Madden; Tim Magraw; Pat Marcatillio; Linda Mashnig; Bill Mashnig; Paul Matthews; Meier-Levi family; Airman Mike; Jim Moorehead; Matthew Moniz; Brian Moorehead; Scott, Pat, and Mark Morrissey; Joyce L. Murphy; Mystery Science Theatre 3000; Linda Napolitano; New York Public Library; Robert Oechsler; Bill Paquin; Andrew Pope; Cindy Potocki; Dennis Preato; Jim and June Pritchard; Emily Putterman; Allan Robbins; Marci Robbins; Anne Robbins; Dick Robichaud; Mike Rogers; Alan Ross; Gus Russo; the volunteers of the New York City branch of The Samaritans International; Roger L. Scherrer; Cathy and John Schleining; Stanley Schnier; Springborn Environmental Laboratory; Brad Steiger; Marion Stokes; Clifford Stone; Whitley Strieber; Leonard H. Stringfield; John Strough; Robert and Susan Swiatek; Al Terzi; The Learning Channel; Alice Thompson; W. Reid Thompson; Alice Thompson; John P. Timmerman; Robert Todd; Gary Treibert; Owen Tucker; Carla Turner; Elton Turner; Matt Valerio, Stevie Ray Vaughan; Colman VonKeviczky; Travis Walton; Randy Warden; Donald M. Ware; Bill Warren; Joann Warren; Lawrence Warren, Sr.; Sandra Warren; Scott Warren; John Weber; Helen Wheels; Grace Wherry; John White; Barbara White; Fred Whiting; Joey Wildey; Joseph Wildey, Sr.; Nancy "Sam" Wildey; Katie Wildey; and the X-Files.

APPENDIX 1
Excerpts from "UFO Hypothesis and Survival Questions"

In 1968, an NSA employee wrote and filed a draft for a paper titled "UFO Hypothesis and Survival Questions" "to consider some of the human survival implications suggested by the various principal hypotheses concerning the nature of the phenomena loosely categorized as UFO."

Though hallucinations, hoaxes, natural phenomena, and secret earth projects were considered explanations for some UFOs, the paper focuses on the implications of a fifth possibility:

5. Some UFOs are related to extra-terrestrial intelligences: hypothesis has a number of far-reaching human survival implications:

   a. If "they" discover you, it is an old but hardly invalid rule of thumb, "they" are your technological superiors. Human history has shown us time and again the tragic results of a confrontation between a technologically superior civilization and a technologically inferior people. The "inferior" is usually subject to physical conquest.

   b. Often in the past, a technologically superior people are also possessors of a more virile or aggressive culture. In a confrontation between two peoples of significantly different cultural levels, those having the inferior or less virile culture, most often suffer a tragic loss of identity and are usually absorbed by the other people.

c. Some peoples who were technologically and/or culturally inferior to other nations have survived—have maintained their identity—have equaled the differences between them and their adversaries. The Japanese people have given us an excellent example of the methods required to achieve such a survival:

(1) full and honest acceptance of the nature of the inferiorities separating you from the advantages of the other peoples,

(2) complete national solidarity in all positions taken in dealing with the other culture,

(3) highly controlled and limited intercourse with the other side—doing only those actions advantageous to the foreigner which you are absolutely forced to do by circumstances,

(4) a correct but friendly attitude toward the other people,

(5) a national eagerness to learn everything possible about the other culture—its technological and cultural strengths and weaknesses. This often involves sending selected groups and individuals to the other's country to become one of his kind, or even to help him in his wars against other adversaries.

(6) Adopting as many of the advantages of the opposing people as you can, and doing it as fast as possible—while still protecting your own identity by molding each new knowledge increment into your own cultural cast. . . .

The final answer to this mystery will probably include more than one of the above hypotheses. Up until this time, the leisurely scientific approach has often taken precedence in dealing with UFO questions. If you are walking along a forest path and someone yells, "rattler" your reaction would be immediate and defensive. You would not take time to speculate before you act. You would have to treat the alarm as if it were a real and immediate threat to your survival. Investigation would become an intensive emergency action to isolate the threat and determine its precise nature—it would be geared to developing adequate defensive measures in a minimum amount of time. It would seem a little more of this survival attitude is called for in dealing with the UFO problem.[1]

1. Document on file. A complete photocopy of this paper may be purchased from the Fund For UFO Research. Their Address can be found in our bibliography.

APPENDIX 2
Freedom of Information Actions and Query Responses

In November 1992, I sent the first of a series of inquiry letters and FOIA requests. Most, but not all, were directed toward various departments of the air force. My objective was twofold: to find out whether that department, branch, office, division, agency, or unit had conducted (or would admit to having conducted) an investigation of the Bentwaters incidents; and to inquire whether they had (or would admit to having) in their possession any incident-related report, memorandum, or document issued by any other agency or office. All correspondence went out with a copy of Lieutenant Colonel Halt's 13 January 1981 memo attached. These were some of the responses:

Assistant Secretary of State for Intelligence and Research
November 23, 1992

Dear Mr. Robbins,

The Bureau of Intelligence and Research has no record of any of the materials referred to in your letter of November 7, 1992.

Sincerely,
Douglas P. Mulholland

*   *   *

Department of the Air Force
Office of the Inspector General
December 3, 1992

Dear Mr. Robbins,

This is in response to your November 6, 1992 letter to the Air Force Inspector
General concerning investigations regarding incidents that took place in England
almost twelve years ago. We are sorry to inform you that our records do not go
back that far. Therefore, we can offer no comments on your questions.
     Thank you for your correspondence.

Sincerely,
Chiquita Y. N. English, Major, USAF
Staff Officer, Inquiries Support Office
Office of the Inspector General

*   *   *

Office of the Undersecretary of Defense (Acquisition)
Defense Technical Information Center
Alexandria, Virginia
November 19, 1992

Dear Mr. Robbins,

This is in reply to your request for information from the Defense Technical Information Center (DTIC).
     The DTIC does not have the type of information you are requesting . . . Since
we do not have any information related to the described phenomena, we are
unable to refer you to another source for answers to your inquiries.

Sincerely,
Maureen J. Malone
for Chief, Reference Service Branch

*   *   *

Department of the Air Force
Air Force Office of Special Investigation
Bolling Air Force Base
Washington, D.C.
December 22, 1992

Dear Mr. Robbins,

This is in response to your 6 November 1992 request for information. We received your request on 2 December 1992.

We have conducted a search of our files and we have determined that the Air Force Office of Special Investigations is not maintaining any information responsive to your request.

If you interpret this "no records" response as an adverse action, you may appeal it to the Secretary of the Air Force within 60 days from the date of this letter. . . .

Sincerely,
Cecil W. Fry, SA
Director, Information Release
Investigative Operations Center

*   *   *

Headquarter United States Air Force
November 23, 1992

Dear Mr. Robbins,

Thank you for your inquiry regarding the incident at RAF Woodbridge, referred to in the 81st Combat Support Group letter of 13 January 1981. We have no record of any investigation in HQ/USAF Security Police files here in Washington or in our Air Force Security Police Agency's files at Kirkland AFB New Mexico. Additionally, we contacted the Air Force Office of Special Investigation at Bolling AFB and they report no record of an investigation of this incident.

Sincerely,
John E. Tucker, Colonel, USAF
Chief, Policy Division
Chief of Security Police

*   *   *

Department of the Air Force
Office of the Secretary
December 4, 1992

Dear Mr. Robbins,

We received your November 5, 1992, Freedom of Information Act request addressed to the Office of Public Affairs on November 19, 1992.

To process your request properly, we find a time extension is necessary because we need to search for, collect, and examine a substantial number of records you requested.

We will respond not later than December 18, 1992.

Sincerely,
Carolyn W. Price
Freedom of Information Manager

*   *   *

Department of the Air Force
Office of the Secretary
December 11, 1992

Dear Mr. Robbins,

This is in response to your November 5, 1992, Freedom of Information Act (FOIA) request to the Office of Public Affairs.

We are not the originating office of the records requested. Therefore, your request has been forwarded to USAFE/IM. . . . They will reply directly to you.

Sincerely,
Carolyn W. Price
Freedom of Information Manager

*   *   *

Headquarters
United States Air Force in Europe
December 21, 1992

Dear Mr. Robbins,

This is in response to your response to your 5 November 1992 Freedom of Information Act request addressed to the office of Public Affairs FOI and Security Review Director of Washington DC 20301.

Your request was forwarded to this headquarters for processing. We received your request on 21 December 92 and forwarded it to 100 MSSQ/MSID (FOIA) UNIT 4925 BOX 285 APO AE 09459.

Sincerely,
Latricia D. Grace
Command Freedom of Information Act Mgr
Directorate of Information Management

* * *

Department of the Air Force
United States Air Forces in Europe
January 11, 1993

Dear Mr. Robbins,

Reference your 5 November 92 Freedom of Information Act request for any records concerning an incident that occurred in late December 1980 involving unexplained lights at RAF Bentwaters in East Anglia, Suffolk, England. A search for the requested records has indicated that no records exist. Please note that this does not constitute a denial of your request. . . .

Sincerely
Robert L. Brotzman, Colonel, USAF
Vice Commander

* * *

Department of the Air Force
81st Tactical Fighter Wing (USAFE)
RAF Bentwaters, nr Woodbridge, Suffolk, IP12 2RQ

Dear Mr. Robbins.

Thank you for your enquiry concerning Unidentified Flying Objects. Project Blue Book, the Air Force study of UFOs ended in 1969, after 22 years of scientific investigation.

More than 12,500 reported sightings were investigated; the vast majority—about 95%—were explainable. They were caused by such natural phenomena as meteors, satellites, aircraft, lightning, balloons, weather conditions, reflections of other planets, or just plain hoaxes. Of the very few that remained unexplained, there was no indication of a technology beyond our own scientific knowledge, or that any sighting could be considered an extraterrestrial vehicle.

Most importantly, throughout Project Blue Book, there was never a shred of evidence to indicate a threat to our national security. Project Blue Book was ended based on these findings, as verified by a scientific study prepared by the University of Colorado, and further verified by the National Academy of Sciences.

All of the Project Blue Book materials were turned over to the Modern Military Branch, National Archives and Records Administration, 8th Street and Pennsylvania, Washington DC 20408, and are available for public review and analysis.

I hope you find this informative and that it address helpful in your research. This is all the information we have regarding UFOs at the Twin Bases. . . .

Sincerely,
Lewonnie E. Belcher, Capt, USAF
Chief, Public Affairs

*   *   *

Air Historical Branch 3 (RAF)
Ministry of Defence Room 308
3-5 Great Scotland Yard, London SW1A 2HW

Dear Mr. Robbins

Thank you for your letter of 15 December 1992 concerning US presence at Bentwaters and Woodbridge. . . . As far as the sighting of the UFO is concerned you should direct your enquiries to Mr. N Pope Sec (AS), Room 8245, MOD Main Building, Whitehall, London SW1A 2HB. . . .

Yours Sincerely,
M L Hatch

APPENDIX 3
Report on the 1956 Bentwaters Incident[1]

Our source is a former National Security Agency employee. While he would not confirm that the report had originated with that agency, he did not deny it either. The document's most likely origin is the NSA or the air force.

---

1. Report on file. Credit: R. Estes.

I. RADAR SIGHTINGS, BENTWATERS

    A. First Sighting
        1. Target picked up 25-30 miles ESE moving on 295 degree heading; lost 15-20 miles NW of Bentwaters.
            a. Object had strong radar echo comparable to typical aircraft, weakening at end of scope path.
            b. 4,000 mph (or more) estimated speed.
            c. Duration of sighting was 30 seconds.

    B. Second Sighting
        1. Multiple targets sighted 8 miles SW of Bentwaters moving in northeasterly direction.
            a. Larger group (scattered) preceded by small group (3) in triangular formation.
            b. Radar echo weakening as moving to NE.
            c. Estimated speeds of 80-125 mph.
        2. Maneuvering of objects.
            a. Objects combined to form one very strong echo.
            b. Stopped and remained stationary 10-15 min.
            c. Continued NE for 5-6 miles.
            d. Stopped for 3-5 min.
            e. Moved northward off of scope.
        3. Duration of sighting was 25 minutes.

    C. Third Sighting
        1. Object sighted moving rapidly from 30 miles E to point 25 miles W of Bentwaters.
            a. Disappeared by rapid motion out of radiation pattern.
            b. Speed estimated at 4,000 mph or more.
            c. Duration of sighting was 16 seconds.

    D. Fourth Sighting

        1. Object picked up 30 miles E traveling almost due west.
            a. Estimated speed was 2,000-4,000 mph.
            b. There were concurrent visual ground and air sightings.
            c. No sonic booms were emitted by the high speed object.

II. VISUAL GROUND SIGHTING

    A. First Sighting
        1. Nocturnal light 10 degrees elevation to SSE of Bentwaters.
            a. Intermittently appearing, disappearing.
            b. Duration of sighting was approximately one hour.
            c. This sighting was possibly a planet.

The Lakenheath Sightings (continued)

B. Second Sighting
   1. Lakenheath RAF Station sighted luminous object moving on SW heading.
      a. Object stops then moves out of sight to the east.

C. Third Sighting
   1. Two moving white lights sighted.
      a. Lights join and disappear in formation.
      b. No discernable features.
      c. Reportedly traveling at terrific speeds, stopping, changing course immediately.

III. RADAR SIGHTINGS, LAKENHEATH

A. First Sighting.
   1. Object seen traveling from 6 miles W to 20 miles SW.
      a. Object stopped, remained stationary for 5 min.
      b. Object then traveled to 2 miles NW of Station and stopped.
      c. There were supporting ground visual and radar sightings made.

B. Second Sighting
   1. Object maneuvering in rectangular pattern 17 miles E of Station.
      a. Object stopped and started rapidly.
      b. Estimated speed was 600-800 mph.
      c. Moving Target Indication and Plan-Position Indicator used in attempt to identify object.

IV. AIRBORNE RADAR AND VISUAL SIGHTINGS

A. First Sighting
   1. Venom aircraft scrambled to identify object.
      a. Pilot picked up target on radar.
      b. Visual sighting of bright white light made by pilot.
      c. Pilot lost both visual and radar targets.

B. Second Sighting
   1. Venom aircraft vectored to new target.
      a. Concurrent ground radar sighting.
      b. Venom craft suddenly lost target.
   2. Target began tail chase of Venom craft.
      a. Aircraft maneuvered to evade target.
      b. Maneuvers failed and pilot asked for assistance.
   3. Second craft was scrambled but returned to base because of mechanical problems. Original craft returned when fuel supply ran out. The target was not identified.

"Lakenheath" Case

1. First Radar Sighting:

   A. When:

   2130 Z (9:30 P.M., Greenwich Zone Z Time)

   B. Where:

   Bentwaters RAF Station located six miles east of Ipswich, England

   C. Who:

   Ground Controlled Approach operator

   D. What:

   Target 25-30 miles ESE which moved at a very high speed on constant 295° heading across his scope until he lost it 15-20 miles northwest of Bentwaters. Described as a strong radar echo, comparable to that of a typical aircraft, until it weakened near the end of its path across his scope. He estimated speed at 4,000 mph; however, a transit time of 30 seconds is given. That, combined with the reported range of distance traversed, 40-50 miles, a speed of about 5,000 to 6,000 mph results. Finally, GCA operator stated it covered 5-6 miles per sweep of the radar he was using. The sweep period for that set is given as 2 seconds (30 rpm) so this yields an even higher speed estimate of about 9,000 mph.

2. Second Radar Sighting:

   A. When:

   2130Z to 2155Z

   B. Where:

   Bentwaters RAF Station

   C. Who:

   Ground Controlled Approach operator (T/Sgt)

   D. What:

   On the same radar set, a group of 12 to 15 objects about 8 miles southwest of Bentwaters. T/Sgt. pointed out that these objects appeared as normal targets on the GCA scope and normal checks made to determine possible malfunctions of the GCA radar failed to

indicate anything was technically wrong. The dozen
or so objects were moving northeast together at speeds
ranging between 80 and 125 mph and the 12 to 15 unidentified objects were preceded by 3 objects which were in
a triangular formation with an estimated 1,000 feet
separating each object in this formation. The dozen
or so objects to the rear were scattered behind the
lead formation of 3 at irregular intervals with the
whole group simultaneously covering a 6 to 7 mile
area. Consistent radar returns came from this group
during their 25 minute movement from the point at which
they were first picked up, 8 miles southwest, to a
point 40 miles northeast of Bentwaters, their echos
decreasing in intensity as they moved off to the northeast, they all appeared to converge to form a single
radar echo whose intensity is described as several
times larger than a B-36 return under comparable conditions. It then resumed motion to the northeast
for 5 to 6 miles, stopped again for 3 to 5 minutes
and then moved northward and off the scope.

3. Third Radar Sighting:

   A. When:

   2200Z

   B. Where:

   Bentwaters RAF Station

   C. Who:

   Ground Controlled Approach operator (T/Sgt)

   D. What:

   Five minutes after the second sighting moved off scope,
   T/Sgt detected an unidentified target about 30 miles
   east of Bentwaters GCA station and tracked it in rapid
   westward motion to a point 25 miles west of the station
   where the object suddenly disappeared off the radar
   screen by rapidly moving out of the GCA radiation
   pattern. Here again discordant speed information
   appears. T/Sgt gave the speed only as being in excess
   of 4,000 mph, whereas the time-duration of the tracking,
   given as 16 seconds, implies a speed of 12,000 mph
   for the roughly 55 mile track length reported.

4. Fourth Radar Sighting:

   A. When:

   2255Z

   B. Where:

   Bentwaters RAF Station

C. Who:

Ground Controlled Approach operator

D. What:

Fast moving target was picked up 30 miles east of
Bentwater, heading almost due west at a speed given
as 2,000 to 4,000 mph. Target passed almost directly
over Bentwaters disappearing from their GCA scope for
the usual beam-angle reasons when it came within 2 to
3 miles moving on until it disappeared from the scope
30 miles west of Bentwaters.

The radar tracking was matched by concurrent visual
obserations by personnel on the ground looking up and
also from an overhead aircraft looking down. Both
visual reports involved only a light described as
blurred out by high speed, but since the aircraft
was flying at only 4,000 ft., the altitude of the
unknown object is bracketed within rather narrow
bounds.

Apparently, immediately after the 2255Z events,
Bentwaters GCA alerted GCA Lakenheath to the WNW.
It is implied in the Condon report that Lakenheath
ground observers were alerted in time to see a luminous object come in at an estimated altitude of 2,000
to 2,500 feet and on a SW heading. At or subsequent
to the Bentwaters alert message, Lakenheath ground
observers saw a luminous object come in out of the
northeast at low altitude, then stop, and take up
an easterly heading and resume motion eastward out
of sight.

The precise sequence of the subsequent observations
is not clear, but is is clear from the Lakenheath TWX
which was sent in compliance with AFR200-2, that many
interesting and scientifically baffling events soon
took place.

No follow-up from Bluebook or other USAF sources was
undertaken.

5. Lakenheath Sightings:

A. Following the 2255Z alert by GCA Bentwaters, USAF
ground observers at the Lakenheath RAF Station observed
a luminous object come in on a southwesterly heading,
stop and then move out of sight to the east. Subsequently, at an unspecified time, 2 moving lights were seen
and ground observers stated one white light joined up
with another and both disappeared in formation together.
No discernable features of these luminous sources were

Page 4

noted by ground observers but both the observers and
radar operators concurred in their description that
the objects traveled at terrific speeds and then
stopping and changing course immediately.

In summary of the ground visual observations, it
appears that three ground observers at Lakenheath saw
the following:

1. At least two luminous objects over an extended,
    although uncertain, time period
2. Saw them execute sharp course changes
3. Saw them remain motionless at least once
4. Saw two objects merge into one and
5. Reported motions in general accord with concurrent
    radar observations.

B. Radar unknowns were observed at Lakenheath until about
    0330Z, the total duration of this entire episode being
    about six hours.

A Venom jet interceptor was scrambled. The exact time
of this scramble is unknown but believed to be around
midnight. The pilot reported white light in sight.
He then reported loss of target and white light. The
UFO the Venom tried to intercept was recorded by ground
radar, airborne radar and visually.

Lakenheath Case

1. **First Radar Sighting**
A. When:
2130 Z (9:30 P.M., Greenwich Zone Z Time)
B. Where:
Bentwaters RAF Station located six miles east of Ipswich, England
C. Who:
Ground Controlled Approach operator
D. What:
Target 25–30 miles ESE which moved at a very high speed on constant 295 degree heading across his scope until he lost it 15–20 miles northwest of Bentwaters. Described as a strong radar echo, comparable to that of a typical aircraft, until it weakened near the end of its path across his scope. He estimated speed at 4,000 mph, however, a transit time of 30 seconds is given. That, compared with the reported range of distance traversed, 40–50 miles, a speed of about 5,000 to 6,000 mph results. Finally, GCA operator stated it covered 5–6 miles per sweep of the radar he was using. The sweep period for that set is given as 2 seconds (30 rpm) so this yields an even higher speed estimate of about 9,000 mph.

2. **Second Radar Sighting**
A. When:
2130Z to 2155Z
B. Where:
Bentwaters RAF Station
C. Who:
Ground Controlled Approach operator (T/Sgt)
D. What:
On the same radar set, a group of 12 to 15 objects about 8 miles southwest of Bentwaters. T/Sgt pointed out that these objects appeared as normal targets on the GCA scope and normal checks made to determine malfunctions of the GCA radar failed to indicate anything was wrong. The dozen or so objects were moving northeast together at speeds ranging between 80 and 125 mph and the 12 to 15 unidentified objects were preceded by 3 objects which were in a triangular formation with an estimated 1,000 feet separating each object in this formation. The dozen or so objects to the rear were scattered behind the lead formation of 3 at irregular intervals with the whole group covering a 6

to 7 mile area. Consistent radar returns came from this group during their 25 minute movement from the point at which they were first picked up, 8 miles southwest, to a point 40 miles northeast of Bentwaters, their echos decreasing in intensity as they moved off to the northeast, they all appeared to converge to form a single radar echo whose intensity is described as several times larger than a B-36 return under comparable conditions. It then resumed motion to the northeast for 5 to 6 miles, stopped again for 3 to 5 minutes and then moved northeast and off the scope.

3. Third Radar Sighting
A. When:
2200Z
B. Where:
Bentwaters RAF Station
C. Who:
Ground Controlled Approach operator (T/Sgt)
D. What:
Five minutes after the second sighting moved off the scope, T/Sgt detected an unidentified target about 30 miles east of Bentwaters GCA station and tracked it in rapid westward motion to a point 25 miles west of the station where the object suddenly disappeared off the radar screen by rapidly moving out of the GCA radiation pattern. Here again discordant speed information appears. T/Sgt gave the speed only as being in excess of 4,000 mph, whereas the time-duration of the tracking, given as 16 seconds, implies a speed of 12,000 mph for the roughly 55 mile track length recorded.

4. Fourth Radar Sighting
A. When:
2255Z
B. Where:
Bentwaters RAF Station
C. Who:
Ground Controlled Approach operator
D. What:
Fast moving target was picked up 30 miles east of Bentwater, heading almost due west at a speed given as 2,000 to 4,000 mph. Target passed almost directly over Bentwaters disappearing from their GCA scope for

the usual beam-angle reasons when it came within 2 to 3 miles west of Bentwaters.

The radar tracking was matched by concurrent visual observations by personnel on the ground looking up and also from an overhead air-craft looking down. Both visual reports involved only a light described as blurred out by high speed, and since the aircraft was flying at only 4,000 ft., the altitude of the unknown object is bracketed within rather narrow bounds.

Apparently, immediately after the 2255Z events, Bentwaters GCA alerted GCA Lakenheath to the WNW. It is implied in the Condon report that Lakenheath ground observers were alerted in time to see a luminous object come in at an estimated altitude of 2,000 to 2,500 feet and on a SW heading. At or subsequent to the Bentwaters alert mes-sage, Lakenheath ground observers saw a luminous object come in and out of the northeast at low altitude, then stop, and take up an easterly heading and resume motion eastward out of sight.

The precise sequence of the subsequent observations is not clear, but it is clear from the Lakenheath TWX which was sent in compliance with AFR200-2, that many interesting and scientifically baffling events soon took place.

No follow-up from Bluebook or other USAF sources was undertaken.

5. Lakenheath Sightings

A. Following the 2255Z alert by GCA Bentwaters, USAF ground ob-servers at Lakenheath RAF Station observed a luminous object come in on a southwesterly heading, stop and then move out of sight to the east. Subsequently, at an unspecified time, 2 moving lights were seen and ground observers stated one white light joined up with another and both disappeared in formation together. No discernable features of these luminous sources were noted by ground observers but both the observers and radar operators concurred in their description that the objects traveled at terrific speeds and then stopping and changing course immediately.

In summary of the ground visual observations, it appears that 3 ground observers at Lakenheath saw the following:

1. At least two luminous objects over an extended, although uncertain, time pe-riod.
2. Saw them execute sharp course changes
3. Saw them remain motionless at least once

4. Saw two objects merge into one and

5. Reported motions in general accord with concurrent radar observations.

B. Radar unknowns were observed at Lakenheath until about 0330Z, the total duration of this entire episode being about six hours.

A Venom jet interceptor was scrambled. The exact time of this scramble is unknown but believed to be around midnight. The pilot reported white light in sight. He then reported loss of target and white light. The UFO he tried to intercept was recorded by ground radar, airborne radar and visually.

APPENDIX 4
Selections from Larry Warren's USAF Service Record

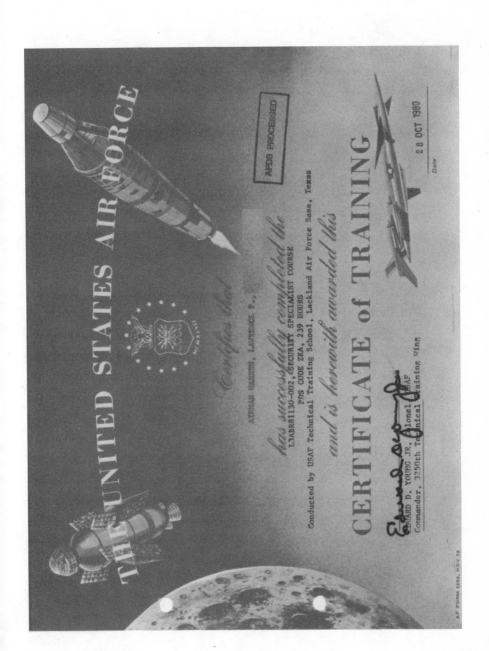

Bus takes Parkway lot at 4:35 PM. Have All Alert gear! Every night.

81ST SECURITY POLICE SQUADRON
INPROCESSING INSTRUCTION SHEET

at work at 750 F C

WELCOME: YOU ARE ASSIGNED TO _D_ FLIGHT. YOUR SHIFT COMMANDER IS _Maj. Zicklin_ AND YOUR FLIGHT CHIEF IS _SMSgt Farias_. THEIR PHONE NUMBERS ARE 2175 OR 2176.

WE WOULD LIKE FOR THIS PERIOD OF PROCESSING TO GO AS SMOOTHLY AS POSSIBLE. IN ORDER TO ACCOMPLISH THIS YOU WILL BE REQUIRED TO REPORT TO THE FIRST SERGEANT EACH DUTY DAY AT 0730 HOURS. THE ONLY EXCEPTION WILL BE DRIVERS TRAINING. THIS CLASS STARTS AT 0730 SO YOU WILL BE REQUIRED TO REPORT TO THE ORDERLY ROOM DURING YOUR LUNCH BREAK.

IF YOU HAVE ANY PROBLEMS DURING YOUR INPROCESSING PLEASE CONTACT ONE OF THE FOLLOWING INDIVIDUALS:

SGT HUDSON	SQUADRON INTRO MONITOR	2260/2750
SMSGT SWAIN	SQUADRON FIRST SERGEANT	2260/2750

OTHER POINTS OF CONTACT:

SMSGT FARIAS	SECURITY	2153
SMSGT THORNTON +	LAW ENFORCEMENT	2880
MSGT HARRELL +	LAW ENFORCEMENT	2880

AFTER DUTY HOURS CONTACT THE LE DESK: 2240

Lee Swain
LEE SWAIN, SMSGT, USAF
FIRST SERGEANT

1ST IND

I UNDERSTAND THAT I AM TO REPORT TO THE FIRST SERGEANT AS STATED ABOVE.

Lawrence P. Johnson
SIGNATURE

2-Dec-80
DATE

Badge # W08.

AIC Johnson-Warren will be Posted To Duty Roster - D-Flight 10/December/80 - Intro Training will commence. 5-12-80

Lee Swain

ASSIGNMENT/PERSONN ACTION	DATE 5 DEC 80	PERS NEL ACTION NO. A—	7149

TO: (Organization) 81 CSG /DPME FROM: (Organization and Office Symbol) 81 CSG/DPMUM

SECTION I INDIVIDUAL IDENTIFICATION

NAME (Last, First, Middle Initial) WARREN, LAWRENCE P	GRADE A1C	SSAN	UNIT 81 SPS

SECTION II PERSONNEL DATA CHANGES

ASSIGNMENT INFORMATION

CAFSC FROM _____ TO _____ EFF _____
DATE DEPARTED LAST DUTY STN 26OCT80
DATE ARRIVED STATION 1DEC80/1530
NUMBER DAYS ENROUTE TDY _____
ASSIGNMENT AVAILABILITY CODES
1ST _____ DOA _____
2ND _____ DOA _____
ASSIGNMENT LIMITATION CODES
1ST _____ DOA _____
2ND _____ DOA _____
DIRECTED DUTY AFSC _____ REASON _____
DDA-TVL-RESTRICT-EXP DATE _____
FUNCTIONAL CATEGORY _____
OVERSEAS INFORMATION
STRD 23JUL80 ODSD 23JUL80 DEROS 30NOV82
AAC STATUS _____ REASON UNACC _____
TOUR STATUS 1 TOUR LENGTH 24/UK
TOUR START DT 30NOV80 TOUR STOP DT _____
DATE ARRIVED/DEPARTED CONUS 30NOV80
DUTY ASSIGNMENT INFORMATION
DAFSC 81130 EFF DATE 1DEC80
OFFICE SYM SP SPOS-D DUTY PH 2275
POSITION NR 0103463 OSC MPCGDC
CMD LVL BASE/WING/BASE DUTY TITLE

OJT INFORMATION

EFFECTIVE 1 DEC 80
ENTER/CONTINUE AFSC 81150 TS CODE B
WITHDRAW AFSC _____ TS CODE _____
SPECIAL EXPERIENCE IDENTIFIER(S)
AIRMEN
CAFSC SEI _____ GENERAL SEI _____
DESIGNATE SEI _____ WITH ( ) AFSC _____
DESIGNATE SEI _____ WITH ( ) AFSC _____
WITHDRAW SEI _____ FROM ( ) AFSC _____
EFFECTIVE _____ REASON _____
MISCELLANEOUS INFORMATION
ADSCD 30NOV82 REASON M
OFFICER-PROJ CLASN UPGRADE DT _____
DLA ENT _____ IMM AREA B
CLINICAL EXAM CODE M 8012 PRP YES
REASON FOR ESTB. EXT. CURTAILMENT OF OFFICER
DOS _____
RESERVE INFORMATION
MSL OVERAGE CODE _____
MSL OVERAGE CODE EXP DATE _____
AIR RESERVE FORCE SECTION ID _____
TECHNICIAN-ART ID _____
ART POSITION NUMBER _____
SECURITY SPECIALIST

MEMBER'S REPORTING OFFICIAL IS (Grade, Last Name, SSAN, Date supervision begins) 1 DEC 80 SRA SLIWOWSKI,	MEMBER RATES (Grade, Last Name, SSAN, Date supervision begins) NONE

DATE	TYPED NAME, GRADE, TITLE, DUTY PHONE SUPERVISOR/REQUESTING OFFICIAL	SIGNATURE

SECTION III CONCURRENCE OF MEMBER

DATE	I ☐ DO ☐ DO NOT CONCUR ☐ SELF INITIATED	SIGNATURE

SECTION IV INTRA-BASE ASSIGNMENT ACTIONS

RNLTD/EFF DT	ASGN ACTION NO.	ASGN FROM	ASGN TO

SECTION V REMARKS

SECTION VI ACTION BY COMMANDER OR AUTHORIZED REPRESENTATIVE   DATE

☐ APPROVED ☐ DISAPPROVED ☐ RECOMMEND APPROVAL/DISAPPROVAL

FOR THE COMMANDER	TYPED NAME, GRADE AND TITLE	SIGNATURE

SECTION VII ACTION BY PERSONNEL OFFICIAL   DATE 11 Dec 80

☑ APPROVED ☐ DISAPPROVED ☐ INDORSED   HEADQUARTERS

FOR THE COMMANDER	TYPED NAME, GRADE, AND TITLE P.N. MARTINEZ, S GT, USAF NCOIC DEROS MANAGEMENT	81CSC/DPMUM APO NY 09755 SIGNATURE

SECTION VIII UNIT/CBPO COORDINATION RECORD

DPME	1. DPM	2. DPM	3. DPM	4. DPM	5. DPM	6. DPM	7. DPM	UNIT

AF FORM 2095 DEC 78 PREVIOUS EDITION WILL BE USED.

RATING OFFICIAL/TRAINING

LABEL #00190 AVKH02OOO1A11126O1A1127OOO0OOOOOOOOONVKROO OOOOOUOO BEGIN LABEL PRINTED OOOOOO OF OOOO53 LINES 2-PART

PERSONAL DATA - PRIVACY ACT OF 1974

PREPARED 81-MAY-06 16:09 REPORT ON INDIVIDUAL PERSONNEL (PA) AS OF 81-MAY-06 PCN N130070-BF 8P-00F-064

SEPARATION APPROVAL NOTIFICATION

AIC: WARREN LAWRENCE D OFFICE SYMBOL: SPOSD

UNIT: RI SECURITY POLICE SQ
BENTWATERS RAF UNKIN 09755 DUTY PHONE: 2175

THIS IS AN IN-SYSTEM NOTIFICATION OR CONFIRMATION OF SEPARATION
APPROVAL TO BE EFFECTIVE 810518. SEPARATION PROGRAM DESIGNATOR
KDQ APPLIES, CHARACTERIZATION OF SERVICE CODE 1 APPLIES. AN
EXPLANATION OF THE SEPARATION PROGRAM DESIGNATOR CODE AND
CHARACTERIZATION OF SERVICE CODE WILL BE PROVIDED BY YOUR CBPO
REPRESENTATIVE AT THE TIME YOU ACKNOWLEDGE THIS NOTIFICATION.

SIGNATURE OF MEMBER: *Lawrence D Warren*
(OR REPRESENTATIVE IF MEMBER NOT AVAILABLE)

DATE NOTIFICATION ACKNOWLEDGED: *15 may 81*

FOR CBPO USE: THE FOLLOWING SEPARATION DATA APPLIES:

RET-SEP-EFF-DATE-PROJ: 810518   RET-SEP-SON-PROJ: KDQ

SEP-CHAR-DISCH: 1   RET-SEP-IO-PROJ: Q

SEP-LVL-APPR-DISAPPR: 3   DOS: 860722

FAS-SEP-ACC: AFR-SECT-IO-SEP-ACC:

APPL-RET-SEP-NAR-RMKS:

REMARKS:

CBPO NOTE: AUTOMATIC ACTION HAS BEEN SET FOR GENERATION OF DD
992 (CONFIRMATION) ON THE SEPARATION EFFECTIVE DATE.

*NOTE: TERMINATION OCCUPATIONAL PHYSICAL REQUIRED/CONTACT
ENVIRONMENTAL MEDICINE.

END PAGE   1

PCN N130070-BF   SEP-NOT
LABEL #00190 AVKH02OOO1A11126O1A1127OOO0OOOOOOOOOOOOONVKROO OOOOOUOO FINAL LABEL PRINTED OOOO53 OF OOOO53 LINES 2-PART

PERSONAL DATA - PRIVACY ACT OF 1974

REPORT ON INDIVIDUAL PERSONNEL (PA)   AS OF 80 DEC 11 PCN N130070 BF BFODFBST

PREPARED 80 DEC 11 21:16

REPLY TO
ATTN OF: CBPO/DPMPC

SUBJECT: DESIGNATION OF CAFSC-SEI AND UPDATE
         OF SEI-RQMT-DT

TO: 61 SECURITY POLICE   SQ   /CC
    BENTWATERS   RAF UNKIN

1. AIC WARREN LAWRENCE P , HAS
HAD HIS CAFSC-SEI UPDATED TO 327 (AB GRND DEFENSE).
MEMBER IS CURRENTLY FILLING POSITION NUMBER 0103463
AND SEI 327 WAS DESIGNATED TO THAT POSITION. MEMBER'S
SPEC-EXP-RQMT-DT IS 01DEC80.

2. THE FOLLOWING ADDITIONAL DATA IS PROVIDED FOR
YOUR INFORMATION:

   A. DAFSC IS 81130 .

   B. CAFSC IS 81130 .

   C. DUTY TITLE IS: SECURITY SPECIALIST

   D. DY-EFF-DATE IS: 01DEC80

3. MEMBER'S MASTER PERSONNEL FILE HAS ALREADY BEEN
UPDATED. IF YOU DO NOT CONCUR NOTIFY CBPO/DPMPC
OF ACTION YOU WANT TAKEN NO LATER THAN 30DEC80.

THOMAS A. MOSELEY, TSGT, USAF
NCOIC, CLASSIFICATION & TRAINING

SEIDES   END PAGE 12
PCN N130070 BF
LABEL #00473 AVKRO2000180346601803470000000000000000000000NVKROO 0000000 FINAL LABEL PRINTED 000588 OF 000588 LINES 2-PART

PRINTED IN U.S.A.

SPECIAL TASK CERTIFICATION AND RECURRING TRAINING

TASK OR RECURRING TRAINING AND STUDY REFERENCES	EVALUATION OR TRAINING				EVALUATOR OR INSTRUCTOR	TRAINEE INITIAL	SUPERVISOR OR CERTIFYING OFFICIAL
	TYPE	DATE COMPLETED	SCORE OR HOURS	DUE DATE			
A	B	C	D	E	F	G	H
Use of Force ESBI B1	POW	11 Dec 80	SAT	Dec 81	Slack	LPW	
Practices Weapons Safety ESBI B2	POW	11 Dec 80	SAT	Dec 81	Huntzinger	LPW	
Performs Communications Procedures ESBI A1	POW	15 Dec 80	SAT	Dec 81	Huntzinger	LPW	
Challenge, Identifies Persons ESBI A4	POW	10 Dec 80	SAT	Dec 81	Slack	LPW	
Detects Alleged Breeches in in Security/Sound Alarms ESBI E5	POW	11 Dec 80	SAT	Dec 81	Huntzinger	LPW	
Controls Entry into Restricted Areas ESBI B3	POW	10 Dec 80	SAT	Dec 81	Slack	LPW	
Conducts Person, Equipment Searches ESBI D10	POW	12 Dec 80	SAT	Dec 81	Huntzinger	LPW	
Identifies credentials ESBI A3	POW	10 Dec 80	SAT	Dec 80	Slack	LPW	
Uses Identification Support Tech. ESBI A3	POW	10 Dec 80	SAT	Dec 80	Slack	LPW	
Secures Accident, Incident, Disaster Scenes ESBI D6	OJ	12 Dec 80	SAT	Dec 81	Huntzinger	LPW	
Security Priority/Areas ESBI A1	OJ	11 Dec 80	SAT	Dec 81	Huntzinger	LPW	
Apprehends & Detains Intruders ESBI A4	POW	12 Dec 80	SAT	Dec 81	Huntzinger	LPW	
Participates in Guardmount ESBI D2	OJ	11 Dec 80	SAT	Dec 81	Huntzinger	LPW	

CERTIFICATION DATE 15 DEC 80

TRAINEE	SUPERVISOR	QUALITY CONTROL	SCHEDULING
Laurence S Warren	Monte E. Weef		

NAME OF TRAINEE (Last, First, Middle Initial)	SSAN	GRADE	AFSC
WARREN, LAURENCE P.		AIC	81130

AF FORM 1098
NOV 73

☆U.S. G.P.O. 1979-629-885

MEDICAL/DENTAL APPOINTMENT

(THIS FORM IS SUBJECT TO THE PRIVACY ACT OF 1974 - USE BLANKET PAS - DD FORM 2005.)

INSTRUCTIONS

1. Please meet the appointment(s) made for you promptly.
2. Bring this slip with you and give it to the appointment clerk.
3. If you are unable to keep this appointment, cancel it at least 24 hours in advance.

I. IDENTIFICATION DATA

TYPED NAME OF PATIENT (Last - First - Middle Initial)   GRADE
Warren Lawrence   A/C

ORGANIZATION OR HOME ADDRESS (Include Zip Code)   DUTY PHONE
81 SPS   2.

SSAN

II. APPOINTMENT DATA

HOUR	DATE	CLINIC	DOCTOR	TELEPHONE NUMBER	DATE ISSUED	VERIFIED
1300	2 Feb. 81	OPTI / Ret Buid. / Exp	Echols	3967	10 Jan 81	J.B.

REMARKS *Bring All records & X Rays*
Full Exam @ 11/4 Lakenheath Eye/Ear Clinic - Med Rec
c/o USAFH Lak   APO ... Sat ...
2/3 Feb 81

AF FORM 490   PREVIOUS EDITION WILL BE USED.
FEB 79

OFFICE COPY

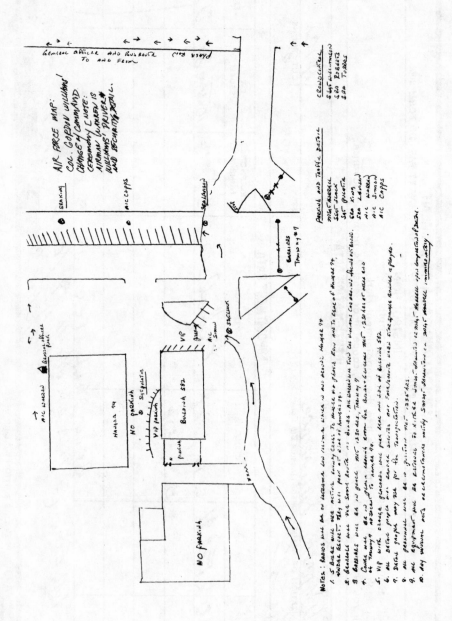

CC

Request for Separation -- A1C Lawrence P. Warren,

51 CSG/DPMS

1. I approve the Honorable discharge of A1C Lawrence P. Warren from the United States Air Force to be effective on or about 15 May 1981.

2. I carefully reviewed his application and conclude that the intent of AFR 39-10, Chapter 3, Section B, Para 3-8n -- (Nonfulfillment of Guaranteed Training Enlistee Program Agreement) -- has been met. Approval of A1C Warren's request to separate from the service is in the best interests of himself and the United States Air Force.

SIGNED

GORDON L. WILLIAMS, Colonel, USAF
Commander

1 Atch
Request for Separation

Honorable Discharge

DEPARTMENT OF THE AIR FORCE · UNITED STATES OF AMERICA

from the Armed Forces of the United States of America

This is to certify that

LAWRENCE PATRICK WARREN   AIRMAN FIRST CLASS REGULAR AIR FORCE

was Honorably Discharged from the

United States Air Force

on the ___18TH___ day of ___MAY 1981___   *This certificate is awarded*

as a testimonial of Honest and Faithful Service

PRESTON S. BEARD, LT COL, USAF
MCGUIRE AFB, NEW JERSEY 08641

THIS IS AN IMPORTANT RECORD — SAFEGUARD IT!

DD FORM 256 AF
1 NOV 51

DEPARTMENT OF THE AIR FORCE
WASHINGTON, D.C. 20330

OFFICE OF THE SECRETARY

Honorable Gerald B. Solomon
United States Representative
285 Broadway
Saratoga Springs, NY 12866

4 DEC 1981

Dear Mr. Solomon:

This is in reply to your letter in behalf of Mr. Lawrence P. Warren concerning

his interest in enlisting in the Air Force.

Authorities in the Office of the Surgeon General, USAF, advise that Mr. Warren

was permanently disqualified by the USAF Air Training Command Surgeon on September 17,

1981, by reason of congenital partial ankylosis radioulnar joint, proximal, bilateral (cannot

fully extend his right arm).

Thank you for your interest in Mr. Warren. Please be assured his disqualification

for medical reasons is no reflection on his character or record of prior service.

Sincerely,

Thomas M. Alison

THOMAS M. ALISON, LtCol, USAF
Congressional Inquiry Division
Office of Legislative Liaison

M: DEPARTMENT OF THE AIRFORCE
      81st Combat Support Group (USAFE)
      APO New York 09755   (28 April 1983)

JECT: Request for Records of Unknown Aircraft Activity

: Lawrence Fawcett
   Asst Director (CAUS)
   471 Gooselane
   Coventry, CT 06238

Reference your letter dated April 8, 1983 requesting information about
known aircraft activity near RAF Bentwaters. There was allegedly some
range activity near RAF Bentwaters at the approximate time in question,
: not on land under United States Air Force jurisdiction and therefore
official investigation was conducted by the 81st Tactical Fighter Wing.
us, the records you requested do not exist.

Regarding the other statements in your letter; no photos of the alleged
aft were taken by the Air Force. Also, there is no requirement under the
edom of Information Act to create a record for the purpose of fulfilling
request. I can assure you that if there were such records we would provide
em to you.

Henry J. Cochran

RY J. COCHRAN, Colonel, USAF
   Commander

55

Lawrence Fawcett
Asst Director (CAUS)
471 Gooselane
Coventry, CT 06238

DEPARTMENT OF THE AIR FORCE
HEADQUARTERS AIR FORCE ACCOUNTING AND FINANCE CENTER
DENVER CO 80279-5000

WARREN LAWRENCE P   BALANCE DUE $95.42
574 STANLEY ST 2ND FLOOR   DATE DUE   01/26/82

NEW BRITAIN CT   06051   LETTER DATE   10/08/86

WE ATTEMPTED TO CONTACT YOU ABOUT YOUR DEBT WITH US BUT WERE UN-
SUCCESSFUL. WE REPORTED YOUR NAME AND ACCOUNT INFORMATION TO A CREDIT
BUREAU. SUCH A REPORT COULD ADVERSELY AFFECT YOUR CREDIT RATING.
ADDITIONALLY, WE MUST TAKE ACTION TO OFFSET THE AMOUNT OF YOUR DEBT
AND ADMINISTRATIVE COSTS AGAINST YOUR FEDERAL INCOME TAX REFUND FOR THE
CURRENT YEAR. YOU ARE LEGALLY RESPONSIBLE FOR PAYMENT OF ANY BALANCE
IF YOUR TAX REFUND DOES NOT SATISFY YOUR DEBT.

IN ORDER TO STOP THE OFFSET TO YOUR TAX REFUND, MAKE YOUR CHECK OR
MONEY ORDER INCLUDING YOUR ACCOUNT NUMBER PAYABLE TO AFO/AFAFC.
MAIL YOUR PAYMENT TO AFAFC/ACF. P. O. BOX 20030,DENVER CO 80220-0030.
FUTHERMORE, TO STOP OUR REFERRAL OF YOUR DEBT TO THE INTERNAL REVENUE
SERVICE IRS , YOU HAVE 60 DAYS FROM THE DATE OF THIS LETTER TO SEND
US WRITTEN EVIDENCE PROVING THIS DEBT IS NOT VALID. ANY FALSE STATE-
MENTS OR REPRESENTATIONS YOU MAKE MAY SUBJECT YOU TO CIVIL OR
CRIMINAL PENALTIES UNDER THE APPLICABLE STATUTORY AUTHORITY.

THE IRS WILL NOTIFY TAXPAYERS, WHO FILE JOINT RETURNS, HOW TO PROTECT
THE SHARE OF THE REFUND WHICH MAY BE PAYABLE TO THE SPOUSE WHO DOES
NOT OWE THE DEBT.

THESE ACTIONS ARE BEING TAKEN PURSUANT TO THE DEBT COLLECTION ACT OF
1982 AND THE DEFICIT REDUCTION ACT OF 1984, WHICH CONGRESS PASSED IN
ORDER TO RECOVER MONIES OWED THE U. S. GOVERNMENT BY THE PUBLIC. WE
URGE YOU TO CONTACT THIS OFFICE IMMEDIATELY TO SETTLE YOUR DEBT.

SINCERELY

ROBERT J. GRANDINETTI
CHIEF, ACCOUNTS RECEIVABLE BRANCH
DIRECTORATE OF SETTLEMENT
   AND ADJUDICATION

United States Department of State

Washington, D.C. 20520

Department of State, U.S.A.
Passport Agency
IN REPLY REFER TO: Thomas P. O'Neill Building
10 Causeway Street
Boston, Massachusetts 02222

JUN 2 7 1995

Lawrence Warren

☐ 1. It is assumed that you have abandoned your plans to travel abroad since a reply to our correspondence has not been received. Therefore, your request for passport services is being filed without further action.

☐ 2. Since your appearance in this office, we have had no word from you regarding the completion of your application. Therefore, your request for passport services is being filed without further action.

☐ 3. Your request for passport services has been canceled as requested.

☒ 4. The United States Treasury will be requested to refund directly to your any passport fee submitted. According to law, the fee for the execution of the application cannot be refunded. (Please allow from six to eight weeks for the processing of your refund.)

☒ 5. *Your original application has been sent in for a refund. Your mutilated passport has been returned with your file.*

Enclosure(s):
☐ Birth Certificate
☐ Baptismal Certificate
☐ Naturalization Certificate
☐ Photographs
☐ Other

LETTER
DSL-710A
7-82

APPENDIX 5
Bentwaters Soil Analysis

March 17, 1993

Peter Robbins
315 West 57th Street, 20D
New York City, NY 10019

Matthew Moniz
Springborn Laboratories, Inc.
790 Main Street
Wareham, MA 02571

In 1991, I had an opportunity to meet with Mr. Peter Robbins in Connecticut. He expressed a wish to have some soil samples analyzed of an alleged UFO landing site. Mr. Robbins then introduced me to his associate, Larry Warren. Mr. Warren then proceeded to tell me more about the event that he had witnessed outside of Woodbridge R.A.F.B., U.K. Mr. Robbins had made arrangements to send to me some of the soil that they had collected on their last visit to England. Upon receiving the samples, I conducted some cursory examination of the three soil samples (being LS, 50", 100") and noted the following anomolies:

1. There was visible color and texture differences between the three samples. (NOTE-This itself is not uncommon in a field, given the distance of approximately fifty feet between each sample site, but it is notable given the other anomolies involved.)

2. Percent Moisture Factors of the three soil samples were taken. The two control samples were close in their percentages, whereas the noted landing site soil dessicated very rapidly and had a lower field moisture capacity than the controls.

3. Following Percent Moisture, rehydration was attempted. The two control samples rehydrated quite easily, whereas the landing site sample required a great deal of manipulation to achieve homogenity. The water tended to bead up and roll off of the sample.

4. Close examination under a microscope revealed no noticable differences between the two control samples, whereas the landing site sample was visibly different.

5. The landing site sample had a higher content of silica that is indicative of exposure to high temperatures or energy.

CONCLUSION: The conditions that the samples were stored under and the time that elapsed after the event took place is unfortunate. Yet, it is my professional opinion that these anomolies observed do warrant further investigation.

PROJECT FIND
RESEARCH FACILITY

September 21, 1996

To Whom it may concern:

In 1992, I conducted cursory tests on a small amount of sample material provided by Peter Robbins and Larry Warren. The samples sent were obtained from an area called Chapel Green in East Anglia, Suffolk, UK. This area was alleged to have been affected by a UFO encounter. After examining the samples, I found the following anomalous results.

1. The soil from the affected area had a lower field moisture content than the control sample. This was determined by using Sartorius Moisture Analyzer.

2. This affected soil was also resistant to re-moisturization/rehydration. Water, when applied to the soil, would "roll" off the soil sample.

3. Under the microscope, the affected soil had higher degrees of silicate or glass globules, indicating that the sand had been fused to form these tiny glass beads.

In 1995, I was given new soil samples from the same site to examine. After receiving the samples, I archived them in appropriate storage until I was able to study them. When the samples were removed from storage, They were allowed to achieve room temperature. I then performed a visual examination of the soil and noted that the affected soil was visibly different from the control. The landing site soil was lighter in color (rust-colored) than the control (deep brown), indicating more decayed organic matter. This prompted me to conduct a microbial survey. The results of the survey proved to be startling and are as follows:

1. The control soil showed normal microbial growth, including various colonies of different types of microbes.

2. The landing site soil showed no microbial growth of any type.

This second finding concerned me since all the soil samples were carefully prepared and treated in identical manners. I can only think of two things which could account for this sort of discrepancy: a sterilizing agent such as gamma radiation or intensely applied heat. However, I was informed that various sorts of plants still grow there, indicating the soil was not entirely sterile, but that the microbial counts were significantly low enough to evade the detection methods I employed. Based on the descriptions of the types, color and growth of the local flora in that specific area, I was able to determine that the latter part was true. , Since microbes and plants have an entirely symbiotic relationship. The absence or depreciation of either one, would have a marked effect on the other. Since both the flora and the microbes were drastically limited in number compared to the control sample, I was forced to look at the soil construct. The appearance of glass globules in a rust-colored soil, indicated that somehow the soil had been oxidized to such an extent that the pH levels were altered. This would affect microbial growth, as microbes in general are sensitive to changes in pH levels. I have since sent portions of the sample material for electron microscope analysis. However, as of this date the results have not been received.

I have found these preliminary results to be most intriguing. A larger, more comprehensive study would be required to determine the overall range of effects this bizzare encounter has produced.

Sincerely,
Matthew Moniz

APPENDIX 6
New Britain General Hospital Emergency Treatment Record for Larry Warren, 18 July 1984

VALUABLES LIST

CASH	
JEWELRY	
OTHER:	

DISPOSITION OF: VALUABLES ☐ Family ☐ Patient ☐ Hospital Safe

CLOTHING ☐ Family ☐ Patient ☐ Security

NEW BRITAIN GENERAL HOSPITAL
NEW BRITAIN, CONNECTICUT 06050

EMERGENCY TREATMENT RECORD

MEDICAL RECORD NO.	TIME IN	DATE IN	CLERK	BILLING NO.	
		7/18/84		3700155	AGE
LAST NAME	FIRST NAME	MIDDLE/MAIDEN/OTHER		8/24/61	22
WARREN	LAWRENCE				
STREET	CITY-STATE	ZIP	PHONE	SEX	RACE
73 CHRISTINE DRIVE	SOUTHINGTON CT	06489	621-2701	M	W
MAR. STAT. PRIOR PATIENT DATE	NAME		PLACE OF BIRTH		
S ☐ Yes ☐ No 7/18/84			NEW YORK		
EMPLOYER				SSN	

EMERGENCY NOTIFY				RELATION	
WARREN, LAWRENCE				FATHER	
STREET		CITY-STATE		PHONE NO.	
73 CHRISTINE DRIVE		SOUTHINGTON CT		621-2701	
FATHER'S NAME	OCCUPATION	STREET		CITY-STATE	
MOTHER'S NAME	OCCUPATION	STREET		CITY-STATE	

GUARANTOR NAME				RELATION	
WARREN, LAWRENCE				SELF	
STREET		CITY-STATE		ZIP PHONE NO.	
73 CHRISTINE DRIVE		SOUTHINGTON CT		06489 621-2701	
EMPLOYER				EMPLOYER PHONE NO. LGTH. OF EMPL.	

PATIENT COMPLAINT/INJURY				DATE OF INJURY	TIME OF INJURY
BLEEDING BACK OF NECK				0/00/00	0000
PLACE OF INJURY			IF AT WORK-COMPANY		

AUTO ACCIDENT	YES NO NO	AUTO INSURANCE INFORMATION			
		COMPANY		AGENT	

CODE	INS. CO. NAME		CARRIER		
200	OTHER COMMER. I				
PRIORITY 1	PLAN MEMB. NO.		SUBSCRIBER WARREN		RELATION TO PATIENT SELF
CODE	INS. CO. NAME		CARRIER		
PRIORITY	PLAN MEMB. NO.		SUBSCRIBER		RELATION TO PATIENT
CODE	INS. CO. NAME		CARRIER		
PRIORITY	PLAN MEMB. NO.		SUBSCRIBER		RELATION TO PATIENT

BLUE SHIELD NO.	VET	PUB. AMT. NUMBER	MODE OF ARRIVAL ☐ AMBULANCE ☐ PRIV. CAR
			☐ POLICE ☐ OTHER

NBGH FORM NO. 472 REV. 3-83

MEDICAL RECORDS

EMERGENCY TREATMENT RECORD

NEW BRITAIN GENERAL HOSPITAL

PLACE TOP OF REPORT #4 HERE

PLACE TOP OF REPORT #3 HERE

PLACE TOP OF REPORT #2 HERE

742249 3 790195
WARREN, LAWRENCE
73 CHRISTINE DR
SOUTHINGTON CT

7/18/84   12 16 AM '84

	DATE ORDERED	TIME RECEIVED
ROOM NO.		☐ ROUTINE ☐ PRE-OP ☐ EMERG.
REMARKS	ORDERED BY DR.	

HEMATOLOGY

☐ CBC   ☐ Hgb   ☐ Hct
☐ DIFF. ☐ WBC   ☐ PLATELET
☐ VENOUS ☐ CAPILLARY

LABORATORY REPORTS

APPENDIX 7
UFO Organizations, Publications, and Information Sources

United States

Arcturus Books Inc., 1443 S. E. Port St. Lucie Boulevard, Port St. Lucie, FL 34952; monthly and special catalog. Robert and Monica Girard run Arcturus, the best UFO-related book and information service we know of. If you can't find what you're looking for, write them.

Cleveland Ufology Project, 7653 Normandie Boulevard, Apt. C-33, Cleveland, [ZIP] OH. Contact: Mary Ann Hawk. The oldest UFO organization in the United States

Computer UFO Networks, P.O. Box 832, Mercer Island, WA 98040.

Citizens Against UFO Secrecy publishes *Just Cause*, Barry Greenwood, editor, P.O. Box 176, Stoneham, MA 02180.

Fortean Research Center, P.O. Box 94627, Lincoln, NE 68509; books publications, newsletter, and conferences.

Stanton T. Friedman, 79 Pembroke Crescent, Fredericton, NB, E3B 2V1 Canada.

The Fund for UFO Research P.O. Box 277, Mt. Rainer, MD 20712; publishes papers, reports, and document reprints.

Global Communications, P.O. Box 753, New Brunswick, NJ 08903; UFO books.

ICUFON Research Archive, 35–40 75 Street, Suite 4-G, Jackson Heights,

APPENDIX 7 | 467

NY 11372; Colonel Colman VonKeviczsky, retired, director. ICU-FON publishes reports, memorandums, and documents.

Intruders Foundation, P.O. Box 30233, New York, NY 10011; Budd Hopkins, director; publishes the *IF Bulletin*, papers, and reports on the UFO abduction phenomenon.

J. Allen Hynek Center for UFO Studies, 2457 Peterson Avenue Chicago, IL 60659, publishes the *Journal of UFO Studies*, America's most scholarly journal on the subject. Dr. Michael Swords, editor.

The Enterprise Mission, 122 Dodd Street, Weehawken, NJ 07087; publishes the journal *The Enterprise Mission* Susan Karaban, editor.

The Mutual UFO Network (MUFON), 103 Oldtowne Road, Seguin, TX 78155–4099; the world's largest UFO organization; holds annual conference and publishes the *MUFON UFO Journal*, research papers, and symposium proceedings; local and international chapters.

Omega Communications, P.O. Box 2051, Cheshire, CT 06410; John White, director; holds annual UFO conference; books and audio and videotapes.

Paranet Information Service, P.O. Box 928, Wheatridge, CO 80034.

Puget Sound Aerial Phenomena Research, 4109 Lake Seattle Boulevard, Seattle, WA 98118.

Dr. Richard Sauder, 1109 S. Plaza Way, Ste. 173, Flagstaff, AZ 86001.

UFO magazine, P.O. Box 1053, Sunland, CA 91041.

UFO Encounters, Aztec Publishing, P.O. Box 1142, Norcross, GA 30091–1142.

UFO Newsclipping Service, Rte. 1, P.O. Box 220, Plumerville, AK 72127.

England

ASSAP, Saint Aldheim, 20 Paul Street, Frome, Somerset BA11 1DX.

The British UFO Newsclipping Service, Ceti Publications, 247 High Street, Beckenham, Kent, BR3 1AB.

The British UFO Research Association (BUFORA), 1 Woodhall Drive, Batley, West Yorkshire, WF17 7S; the largest UFO research organization in the U.K.; holds annual conference and publishes *The BUFORA Journal, BUFORA UFO Newsfile*, conference proceedings, reports, and papers.

Contact UK, 11 Ouseley House, New Marston, Oxford OX3 OJS.

Devon UFO Research Organization, "Coplestons," 21 Cotfield Close, Honiton, Devon EX14 8QX.

East Midlands UFO Research Association (EMUFORA), 8 Roosa Close, Bulwell, Nottingham NG6 7BL.

The Flying Saucer Review Gordon Creighton, editor, FSR Publications Ltd., Snodland, Kent, ME6 5HJ; the U.K.'s most venerable UFO journal.

Gloucestershire Earth Mysteries, P.O. Box 258, Cheltenham GL53 OHR.

Hereford UFO Research Group, 6 Whitehouse Drive, Kingstone, Hereford HR2 9ER.

Lancashire Aerial Phenomena Investigation Society, 22 Brooklyn Avenue, Layton, Blackpool, Lancashire, FYD 7RP.

The New Ufologist, 71 Knight Avenue, Canterbury, Kent CT2 8PY.

NLUFOIG, 89 Bare Lane, Morecambre, Lancashire LA4 6RN.

Norfolk UFO Society (NUFOS), Thanet, 33 Cromer Road, Mevingham, Norwich, Norfolk NR10 5QX.

Northamptonshire UFO Research Group, 30 Stonebridge Court, Lings, Northampton NN3 8LY.

Northern Anomalies Research Association, 6 Silsden Avenue, Lowton, Warrington WA3 1EN.

Northern UFO Network, 37 Heathbank Road, Cheadle Heath, Stockport, Cheshire SK3 0PU.

Northern UFO Research and Investigation, 14 Longhirst Drive, Woodlands Park, Wideopen, Newcastle upon Tyne NE13 6JW.

Para-Search, 145 Tudor Way, Dines Green, Worcester WR2 5QX.

Phenomena Research Association, 12 Tilton Grove, Kirk Hallam, Ilkeston, Derbys DE7 4GR.

Quest International, P.O. Box 2, Grassington, Skipton, North Yorkshire BD223 5UY.

Skylink magazine, 10A Tudor Road, Barking, Essex IG11 9RX.

Skylon International, 25 Amersham Grove, Burnley, Lancashire BB10 2RP.

Somerset UFO Research and Investigation Network, 50 Polkes Field, Stoke Saint Gregory, Taunton, Somerset TA3 6EX.

Southampton UFO Group, 25 Weston Grove Road, Woolston, Southampton, Hants SO2 9EF.

Southern Paranormal Investigations, 249 Purbrook Way, Bedhampton, Havant, Hants PO9 2RX.

Surrey Investigation Group on Aerial Phenomena, 126 Grange Road, Guilford, Surrey GU2 6QP.

UFO Investigation Bureau, 33 Crest Court, Bobblestock, Hereford HR4 9QD.

UFO Magazine, 15 Picard Court, Temple Newsam District, Leeds LS15 9AY.

UFOMEK, 53 Cowper Rock, River, Dover, Kent CT17 0PL.

The UFO Network Nationwide UK, 88 Wincover Drive, Old Farnley, Leeds West Yorkshire, LS12 5JT, UFO research and investigations, twenty-four hour hotline: 0133 279 7378.

UFO WATCH, 176 Coal Clough Lane, Burnley, Lancashire BB11 4NJ.

Other U.K. Groups and Information Sources

Irish UFO Research Association (IUFORA), P.O. Box 3070, Whitehall, Dublin, Ireland.

Strange Phenomena Investigations, 41 The Braes, Tullibody, Clackmannanshire, FK10 2TT, Scotland.

Scottish Society for Physical Research, 131 Stirling Drive, Bishopbriggs, Glasgow, G64 3AX, Scotland.

Truth Seekers Review, Matthew Williams, editor; 25 Upper Canning Street, Ton-Pentre, Mid Glam, CF41 7HG, South Wales.

International

Archives for UFO Research, P.O. Box 11027, 60011, Norrkoping 11, Sweden.

Australian Center for UFO Studies, P.O. Box 728, Lane Cove, NSW 2066, Australia. Arcturus publishes a selection of their reports and papers.

The Australian Society for Physical Research, P.O. Box 395, Cloverdale WA 6105, Australia.

Australian UFO Bulletin, P.O. Box 43, Moorabbin, Victoria 3189, Australia.

Bulletin of Anomalous Experience, 2 St. Clair Avenue West, Suite 607, Toronto, Ontario, M4V 1L5, Canada; a newsletter for mental-health professionals and interested scientists. Dr. David Gottlib, Editor

Cambridge UFO Research Group, 170 Strathcona Street, Cambridge, Ontario, NC3 1R4, Canada.

Canadian UFO Research Network, P.O. Box 15, Station A, Willowdale, Ontario, M2N 5S7, Canada.

Canadian UFO Research Organization, 4534 Queen Street, Unit 3, Niagara Falls, Ontario L2E 2L5, Canada.

CERPA, B.P. 114, 13363, Marseille Cedex 10, France; investigates, publishes journal, and holds an annual international conference.

CEPEX, Rua Visconde de Maua, 67-Jd., Joao Paulo II, Sumare, SP Brazil.

CHNAP, Eisenacher Weg 16, 6800 Mannheim 31, Germany.

DEGUFO, P.O. Box 2831, D-55516 Bad Kreuznach, Germany; German-speaking association for UFO research.

Japan UFO Political Party, Norito Yasuda 41, Babashito Shinjuku, Tokyo 162, Japan; Tokuo Moriwaki, president.

Japan UFO Science Society, C.P.O. Box 1437, Osaka, 530-91 Japan.

Lumieres dans la nuit, B.P. 3-77123 le Vaudoue, France; produces an outstanding UFO journal.

Magazin 2000, M. Hesemann, editor, Worringer Strausse 1, D-4000 Dusseldorf 1, Germany.

Ovni Presence magazine, Yves Bosson, editor.

Perspectives Ufologicas, H. Escobar, editor; Apartado Postal 73-394, Del. Benito Juarez, D. F. Mexico.

Phenomena is a French organization and magazine. Perry Petrakis, director.

Puerto Rican Research Group, W. D. Urbana, director, Palestina St. No. 184, Hato Rey, Puerto Rico 00917.

Russian Ufology Research Center, 5700 Etiwanda Avenue, Suite 215, Tarzana, CA, 91356;, Paul Stonehill, coordinator.

SOBEPS, Avenue Paul Janson 74, B-1070, Brussels; Belgium's (and Europe's) largest UFO research organization. They maintain offices and an extensive archive; Michelle Bougard, director.

UFO Afrinews, Cynthia Hind, editor, available from Arcturus Books. Her other writings are recommended as well.

UFO Research Australia, P.O. Box 2044 GPO, Adelaide, South Australia 5001.

UFOs on the Internet

There already hundreds, if not thousands of UFO-related web sites on the World Wide Web. Here are a few of them:

Mutual UFO Network http://www.rutgers.edu/~mcgrew/muFON/

British UFO Research Association http://www.citadel.co.uk/citadel/eclipse/futura/bufora; shbufora.htm

Intruders Foundation on Line http://www.spacelab.net/~jrif/bhhp.html

Alberta UFO Research Association http://ume.med.ucalgary.ca/au-fora/nwt/index/html

The World's Biggest UFO Archive http:/www.iinet.com. aush~bertino/index.html

The Internet Guide to UFOs http://users.aol.com/iufog/

UFOs in the '90s http://www.execpc.com/vjentpr/vjufos/html

Flying Saucer Review http://www.cee.hw.ac.uk:80/~ceewb/fsrhome.htm

The UFO Project http://www.serve.com/tufop/

Institute for the Study of Contact with Non-Human Intelligence http:/www.iscni.com/index.html

The Ultimate UFO Page http:/www.serve.com/tufop

WWW UFO Library http:/ernie.bgsu.edu/~jzawodn/ufo/

Internet UFO Group http://users.aol.com/iufog/

UFO Folklore http:/www.qtm.net/~geibdan/

Library: Unidentified Flying Objects http://ernie.bgsu.edu/~jzawodn/ufo/

Dragonbanes UFO Page http://ccwl.cc.utexas.edu/~drgnbane/ufos-pecific/ufopage.html#websites

UFO Update Dailies ebknapp@yesic.com

National UFO Reporting Center http://nwlink.com/~ufocntr/

UFO Directory and Forum http://galaxy.einet.net/galaxy/Commu-nity/Parascience/Unidentified-Flying-Objects/mark-hines/ufo-forum.html

UFO's: A Closer Look http://www.tcet.unt.edu/~chrisl/ufos.htm

Search Engines:

Yahoo http://www.yahoo.com

WebCrawler http://www.webcrawler.com

Excite http://excite.com

Alta Vista http://altavista.digital.com

APPENDIX 8
Information on Cloudbusting

Over the past twenty-seven years, *The Journal of Orgonomy* has published numerous papers on the results of cloudbusting operations and other functional research. Reprints and some back issues available. P.O. Box 490, Princeton, NJ 09542.

The Eden Press publishes the books and papers of Jerome Eden, pioneer UFO researcher and cloudbuster operator. They also offer the work of other select authors. P.O. Box 399, Careywood, ID 83809.

Orgone Biophysical Research Laboratory conducts cloudbusting operations, holds seminars, and publishes *Pulse of the Planet*, an outstanding journal of current cloudbursting operations and other functional research. P.O. Box 1148, Ashland, OR 97520.

The Wilhelm Reich Museum is Reich's former home and laboratory; cloudbusting operations were first conducted here. Bookstore on premises. P.O. Box 687, Rangeley, ME, 04970.

Bioenergy, 3-27-5 Kodatsuno, Kanazawa, 920 Japan.
Emotion, Karlsbergallee 25-E, D-1000 Berlin 22, Germany.
Lebensenergie, Memelstrasse 3, 6930 Eberbach, Germany.

Revista de Ciencias Orgonomicas, Fundacion Wilhelm Reich, c/Paris, 147 3 2a08036 Barcelona, Spain.

Sciences Orgonomiques, published by SEDIFOR, "La Rose des Sables," Allée du Chene Vert, Parc Liserb, 06000 Nice, France; France's outstanding orgonomic journal.

GLOSSARY

Acronyms and Abbreviations

ABGD	air base ground defense
Aces High	serious security violation; Preceded use of the term, Covered Wagon.
AFB	Air Force Base
AFFRES	Air Force Reserve Center
AFOSI	Air Force Office of Special Investigation
AFSA	Armed Forces Security Agency
AFSS	Armed Forces Security Service; a field arm of the NSA.
AFSC	Armed Forces Specialty Code
ALC	Airman first class
AP	Associated Press
AWACS	airborne warning and control system
BMTS	basic military training school
Broken Arrow	nuclear security violation
BUFORA	British UFO Research Association
Capt.	Captain
CAUS	Citizens Against UFO Secrecy
CIA	Central Intelligence Agency

CNN	Cable News Network
CO	Commanding Officer
Col.	Colonel
COMINT	Communications Intelligence (NSA)
COMSEC	Communications Security (NSA)
Covered Wagon	A procedure initiated in response to a serious security violation; upgraded from Helping Hand
CSC	commander, security control; also, central security control
DFP	defense post
DOD	Department of Defense
DODJOC	DOD Joint Operations Center
EMUFORA	East Midlands UFO Research Association
FAA	Federal Aviation Authority
Faded Giant	A procedure initiated in response to a nuclear weapons security violation
FBI	Federal Bureau of Investigation
FOIA	Freedom of Information Act
GCA	ground-controlled approach violation
ICUFON	Intercontinental UFO Research and Analytic Network.
JANAP	Joint Army Navy Air (Force) Publication
LE	law enforcement
Lt.	Lieutenant
Lt. Col.	Lieutenant Colonel
Maj.	Major
MoD	Ministry of Defence
MOD	Ministry of Defence
M.P.	Member of Parliament
MUFON	Mutual UFO Network
NASA	National Aeronautics and Space Administration
NATO	North American Treaty Organization
NCO	non-commissioned officer
NCOIC	non-commissioned officer in charge
NPC	National Passport Center
NSA	National Security Agency
NSC	National Security Council
NSCID	National Security Council Intelligence Directive
NSDD	National Security Decision Directive
OJT	on-job training

ONI	Office of Naval Intelligence
ORCON	originator controlled (Information)
OSI	Office of Special Investigation
PACAF	Pacific Air Command Air Force
PRP	personal reliability pledge
RAF	Royal Air Force
R/D	Research and Development
RE	reenlistment
SAT	Special Action Team
SEC	Office of Security (NSA)
SEC	Secretary
SECDEF	Secretary of Defense
SECSTATE	Secretary of State
Security Option II	preset response to serious security breach, involving the recall of all off-duty security personnel and additional manning of all missile sites
Sgt.	Sergeant
SIGINT	Signals Intelligence (NSA)
S.M.Sgt.	Senior Master Sergeant
SP	security police (AF)
SUSLO	Special United States Liaison Office
SWAT	Strategic Weapons Assault Tactics
TAC	tactical
TASS	Soviet news agency
TDY	Temporary Duty Assignment
TI	training instructor
T.Sgt.	Tech Sergeant
UH1F	secured radio frequency
UKUSA	United Kingdom/United States of America; a highly classified security agreement made in 1947
UPI	United Press International
USAF	United States Air Force
USAFE	United States Air Force Supreme Headquarters, Europe
VA	Veteran's Administration
WSA	weapons-storage area
WSC	wing security control
10–13	radio code signal for "security policeman needs distress assistance"

BIBLIOGRAPHY

Ideas can get suppressed, ideas can get stomped on, books can get burned. The beauty of the truth is that any reasonable mind, on reflection, can arrive at it all over again. . . . The dream of democracy is an informed citizen.[1]

Left at East Gate was built on a great deal of research. Some of the sources we have drawn from are now out of print or difficult to locate, but a good deal of the material is accessible and well worth reading in full. Related titles and information sources follow.

General
Alien Encounters. Alexandria, Va.: Time-Life Books, 1992.
Clark, Jerome. *The UFO Encyclopedia*, vols. 1–3. Detroit, Mich.: Apogee, 1990–96; see also other books and articles by this author.
Fowler, Raymond E. *Casebook of a UFO Investigator*. Englewood Cliffs, N.J.: Prentice-Hall, 1981.
Good, Timothy. *Above Top Secret: The Worldwide UFO Cover-up*. London: Sidgwick & Jackson, 1987.
Hall, Richard. *Uninvited Guests*. Santa Fe, N.M.: Aurora, 1988.
Hynek, J. Allen. *The UFO Experience: A Scientific Inquiry*. Chicago: Henry Regnery Co., 1972.
Knapp, George, prod. *UFOs: The Best Evidence*. P.O. Box 2249, Livonia, Mich. 48151; videotape.

1. Timothy S. Healy; "The People's Palace: Secrets of the New York Public Library," *The American Experience*, Public Broadcasting System, 1991. Tape on File.

Lindemann, Michael, ed. *UFOs and the Alien Presence: Six Viewpoints.* Santa Barbara, Calif.: The 2020 Group, 1991.

Randles, Jenny. *UFO Study.* London: Robert Hale, 1987.

Bentwaters

James, Carole. "Visitors at Rendlesham Forest." *UFO Magazine* 13, no. 1 (1994).

Randles, Jenny. *Out of the Blue.* New Brunswick, N.J.:Global Communications, 1991.

Butler, Brenda; Street, Dot; Randles, Jenny. *Sky Crash.* Sudbury, U.K.: Neville Spearman, 1984.

"Rendlesham!" *UFO Magazine* 13, no. 5 (1995).

Return to Bentwaters. U.K.: EMUFORA, 1994; an on-location video documentary featuring Larry Warren, available in PAL format.

Intelligence and Military Awareness of or Involvement in UFOs

Clark, Jerome. *The Emergence of a Phenomenon: UFOs from the Beginning Through 1959.* Detroit, Mich.: Omnigraphics, 1992.

Davidson, Leon. *Flying Saucers: An Analysis of the Air Force Project Bluebooks Special Report No. 14.* White Plains, N.Y.: privately published, 1956.

Eden, Jerome, ed. *UFO Witness Testimony of Dr. James McDonald.* Careywood, Idaho: Eden Press, 1987; McDonald's other papers are available through Eden Press, Arcturus Books, and the Fund for UFO Research.

Fawcett, Larry, and Barry Greenwood. *Clear Intent.* Englewood Cliffs, N.J.: Prentice-Hall, 1984; retitled *The UFO Cover-up.* New York: Fireside/Simon and Schuster, 1992.

Flammonde, Paris. *The Age of Flying Saucers.* New York: Hawthorn, [1971].

Friedman, Stanton T. *Top Secret MAJIC.* New York: Marlowe & Co., 1996.

Fuller, John G., ed. and intro. *Aliens in the Skies: The New UFO Battle of the Scientists.* New York: Putnam, 1969; testimony of six leading scientists before the House Committee on Science and Astronautics, July 1968.

Good, Timothy. *Alien Liaison* London: Century, 1991.

———. *Beyond Top Secret* London: Sidgwick & Jackson, 1996.

Jacobs, David. *The UFO Controversy in America.* Bloomington: Indiana University Press, 1975.

Maccabee, Bruce. *UFO Landings near Kirkland AFB: Or, Welcome to the Cosmic Watergate.* William Moore Publications, 1985.

Pope, Nick. *Open Skies, Closed Minds.* New York: Simon and Schuster, 1996.

Randles, Jenny. *The UFO Conspiracy.* New York: Barnes & Noble Books, 1987.

Stone, Clifford E. *UFOs: Let the Evidence Speak for Itself.* Published by the author, 1991.

Trench, Brinsley LePoer. *The House of Lords UFO Debate.* London: Open Head Press, 1979.

VonKeviczsky, Colman. *The Blue Memorandum.* New York: ICUFON Archives, 1979.

UFOs and the Press
Girard, Robert *An Early UFO Scrapbook.* Port St. Lucie, Fla.: Arcturus, 1989.

Gross, Loren E. *UFOs: A History,* 8 vols. Port St. Lucie, Fla.: Arcturus.

Strentz, Herbert J. *A Survey of Press Coverage of Unidentified Flying Objects.* Port St. Lucie, Fla.: Arcturus, 1982.

Corporate Awareness
Oechsler, Robert, Debby Regimenti, and the Annapolis Research and Study Group. *The Chesapeake Connection.* 1989.

Roswell and Other Crash Recoveries
Friedman, Stanton T., and Don Berliner. *Crash at Corona.* New York: Marlowe, 1992.

Maccabee, Bruce. *Documents and Supporting Information Related to Crashed Flying Saucers and Operation MJ Twelve.* Mt. Rainer, Md.: Fund for UFO Research, 1987.

Whiting, Fred. *Recollections of Roswell.* Mt. Rainer, Md.: Fund for UFO Research; video with printed summary.

UFO Abduction
Bullard, Thomas E. *UFO Abductions: The Measure of a Mystery.* Mt. Rainer, Md.: Fund for UFO Research, 1987.

Fowler, Raymond E. *The Allagash Abductions.* Tigard, Oreg.: Wildflower, 1993.

———. *The Andreasson Affair.* Englewood Cliffs, N.J.: Prentice-Hall, 1979.

Fuller, John G. *Incident at Exeter: Unidentified Flying Objects over America Now.* New York: Putnam, 1966.

————. *The Interrupted Journey*. New York: Dial, 1967.

Hopkins, Budd. *Intruders: The Incredible Visitations at Copley Woods*. New York: Random House, 1987.

————. *Missing Time: A Documented Study of the UFO Abductions*. New York: Marek, 1981; New York: Berkley, 1983; New York: Ballantine, 1988.

————. *Selected Articles on the UFO Abduction Phenomenon*. New York: Intruders Foundation, 1991.

————. *Witnessed: The True Story of the Brooklyn Bridge UFO Abductions*. New York: Pocket Books, 1996.

Jacobs, David. *Secret Life*. New York: Simon & Schuster, 1992.

Nagaitis, Carl, and Philip Mantle. *Without Consent*. Cheshire, U.K.: Ringpull, 1994. Pritchard, David, and Andrea Pritchard, eds. *Alien Discussions*... Proceedings of the Massachusetts Institute of Technology Abduction Study Conference, Cambridge, Mass., 13–17 June 1992; includes more than one hundred papers on the subject.

Walton, Travis. *Fire in the Sky*. New York: Marlowe & Co., 1996.

UFOs in History and Prehistory

The Airship Chronicle. Mt. Rainer, Md.: Fund for UFO Research, n.d.

Blumrich, Joseph. *The Spaceship of Ezekiel*. New York: Bantam, 1974.

Cohane, Philip. *Paradox: The Case for the Extraterrestrial Origin of Man*. New York: Crown, 1977.

Downing, Barry H. *The Bible and Flying Saucers*. Philadelphia: Lippincott, 1968.

Greenwood, Barry. *The New England Airship Wave of 1909*. Port St. Lucie, Fla.: Arcturus, 1993.

Hoagland, Richard C. *The Monuments of Mars*. Berkeley, Calif.: North Atlantic Books, 1987.

Jessup, M.K. *UFO and the Bible*. New York: Citadel, 1956.

Michell, John. *The View over Atlantis*. London: Garnstone; see also other books by this author.

Naud, Yves. *UFOs and Extraterrestrials in History*, 4 vols. Geneva: Editions Ferni, 1978.

Sitchin, Zecharia. *The 12th Planet*. New York: Stein and Day, 1976; see also other books by this author.

Trench, Brinsley Le Poer. *The Sky People*. London: Neville Spearman, 1960.

Winkler. *Catalogue of UFO-like Data Before 1947.* Mt Rainer, Md.: Fund for UFO Research.

Other Titles of Interest

Amandola, Sal. *UFOS: A Sociopolitical View.* New York: S.R. V + 1,1990.

Brian, William L., II. *Moongate: Suppressed Findings of the U.S. Space Program.* Portland, Oreg.: Future Science Research Publishing Co., 1982.

Howe, Linda Moulton. *Alien Harvest.* Littleton, Colo.: LMH Productions, 1989.

———. *Glimpses of Other Realities.* Littleton, Colo.: LMH Productions, 1993.

Rodeghier, Mark. *UFO Reports Involving Vehicle Interference.* Evanston, Ill.: Center for UFO Studies, 1981.

Sauder, Richard. *Underground Bases and Tunnels: What Is the Government Trying to Hide?* Abingdon, Va.: Dracon, 1995.

Vallee, Jacques. *Forbidden Science.* New York: Marlowe & Co., 1996.

———. *UFO Chronicles of the Soviet Union.* New York: Ballantine, 1992.

Information on Cloud Busting

Eden, Jerome. *Planet in Trouble: The UFO Assault on Earth.* New York: Exposition, 1973.

———. *Sincerely, Elsworth F. Baker: The Correspondence of Elsworth F. Baker and Jerome Eden.* Careywood, Idaho: Eden Press, 1988.

Reich, Peter. *A Book of Dreams.* New York: Harper & Row, 1973.

Robbins, Peter. "Wilhelm Reich and UFOs." *Journal of Orgonomy.* 24, no. 2 (1990); 25, no. 1 (1991).

INDEX